Reports of the Research Committee
of the
Society of Antiquaries of London
No. XXXVII

Mount Pleasant, Dorset: Excavations 1970-1971

Incorporating an account of excavations undertaken at
Woodhenge in 1970

By

G. J. Wainwright

with major contributions by
D. Britton, R. Burleigh, J. G. Evans, R. A. Harcourt and I. H. Longworth

Published by
The Society of Antiquaries of London
Distributed by
Thames and Hudson Ltd
1979

ISBN 0 500 990298

PRINTED IN ENGLAND BY
ADLARD AND SON LTD
BARTHOLOMEW PRESS, DORKING

CONTENTS

LIST OF FIGURES

LIST OF PLATES

PREFACE

THE low hill called Mount Pleasant lies across a ridge on the eastern edge of Dorchester in West Stafford parish. Distinguished by a copse of trees crowning a barrow on the western bank of the enclosure which surrounds its summit, the original earthworks have for the most part been spread and flattened by centuries of ploughing. Sufficient of the bank remains, however, for the site to have been classified as a possible henge enclosure on the basis of a barely surviving segment of the earthwork, which indicated that the ditch was sited within the bank. The enclosure was scheduled as an ancient monument in 1960 and in the Inventory of Historical Monuments in the County of Dorset was recommended for preservation 'both because of the increasing rarity of such monuments and because the extent and impressiveness of the surface remains are not alone indicative of archaeological importance. This last can be revealed only by excavation'.[1] This recommendation had been reinforced by rescue excavations between 1967 and 1970 at comparable sites in Wessex. In 1967 a new road route through the Durrington Walls enclosure near Amesbury in Wiltshire had necessitated rescue excavations which revealed the post-holes of two circular buildings. The larger of these had its roof supported on concentric rings of posts, both were associated with pottery of the Grooved Ware ceramic tradition and were dated by radiocarbon to the century around 2000 bc.[2] Similar ceramic associations and radiocarbon dates were obtained for the surrounding earthwork, which is distinguished by its large size (480 × 470 m.). The foundations of similar buildings had previously been recorded at Woodhenge Wilts.,[3] and the Sanctuary on Overton Hill,[4] but were not related to the large earthworks of the Durrington type. Following the 1967 excavations, a survey was made of enclosures similar to that at Durrington. They were not numerous and occurred at Marden in the Vale of Pewsey, Avebury—a site famous on account of its stone circles and avenue—and Mount Pleasant near Dorchester. A fifth enclosure at Waulud's Bank near Leagrave in Bedfordshire can probably be placed in the same category. Both the Marden and Mount Pleasant enclosures were in arable cultivation and it was considered that if post-holes of similar structures occurred within them, such remains were in danger of destruction by plough erosion. Excavations were therefore carried out at Marden in 1969.[5] The north entrance into the enclosure was investigated and a small timber structure recorded within that entrance in the same relative position as the large building at Durrington Walls. The earthwork was associated with pottery of the Grooved Ware ceramic tradition and produced a radiocarbon date approximating to 2000 bc. As a result of this excavation the entire enclosure has now been put down to grass. In order to complete the excavation programme, work was begun at Mount Pleasant in 1970 and carried to a conclusion in 1971. As at Durrington Walls and Marden the earthwork was associated with Grooved Ware and radiocarbon dates around 2000 bc. Within the enclosure were the post-holes of a large building, comparable to those

[1] RCHM Dorset, 1970, Vol. 2, pt 1, xxxiii.
[2] Wainwright and Longworth, 1971.
[3] Cunnington, 1929.

[4] Cunnington, 1931.
[5] Wainwright, 1971.

at Durrington Walls and Woodhenge, and which was also associated with Grooved Ware and radiocarbon dates of around 2000 bc. An unexpected development was the recognition of a massive foundation trench for a timber palisade which was built to surround the hill-top in 1700 bc, at the same time as the timber building was replaced by a stone setting. The hill-top had been under plough for centuries and the post-holes of the building were much eroded. Had the process continued without excavation much evidence would have been lost and unrecorded.

To supplement work at these sites Dr. John Evans and the author undertook a small excavation at Woodhenge in the summer of 1970 in order to obtain environmental and dating evidence. The results of the excavation have been included in this volume for the sake of completeness.

Throughout the project, which covered a period of some five years from its inception at Durrington Walls to its conclusion at the end of the 1971 season at Mount Pleasant, one was aware that broader issues were involved, separate from those surrounding the general subject of 'henge monuments'. The enclosures in question occurred at focal centres, represented at an earlier date by causewayed camps and their related long-barrow distributions. A case can be made for the enclosures of Durrington type succeeding the causewayed camps and in the Maiden Castle/Mount Pleasant area continuous settlement can be adduced from causewayed camp to Iron Age hill-fort and into later periods. Clearly the development of these foci is of considerable significance from the viewpoint of socio-economic development in southern England from 3000 bc and the role played by the enclosures of Durrington type urgently required elucidation. The project was therefore concerned with problems relating to the organization of society and with settlement rather than with ceremonial themes represented by 'henge monuments'.

It gives the author great pleasure to acknowledge assistance received in the field and in the preparation of publications by colleagues whose cooperation was retained throughout the whole programme. The effectiveness of the field team was greatly enhanced by the presence of my Assistant Director, Mr. Peter Donaldson, whose practical insight has been invaluable, not only through this project but also on numerous excavations in England and Wales during the last decade. Acknowledgement should also be made to Mr. Dave Buckley who has shouldered considerable responsibility in the field and made a major contribution towards the preparation of this volume. Throughout this project the author has derived great benefit from his association with Dr. Ian Longworth, not only on account of his invaluable ceramic studies, but also on the wider issues of interpretation and presentation. Other colleagues who have given freely of their expertise and time are Dr. John Evans and Mr. Richard Burleigh who have respectively reported on the environment and the radiocarbon chronology. Mr. Ralph Harcourt and Mr. Graham Morgan have also reported on the animal bones and charcoals respectively for the entire project. Such consistent collaboration in the field, laboratory and study has, it is hoped, resulted in some continuity of thought and treatment. Certainly the author has not only derived considerable personal pleasure from this association but is also aware that the present volume is in essence a collaborative exercise which he has been responsible for organizing and nursing to published form.

The logistics for the field operations were in the capable hands of Mrs. Susan Wainwright who in the final season at Mount Pleasant also undertook responsibility for the photography.

In respect of the Mount Pleasant excavations our gratitude must go first to the owner of the land, Lt.-Col. S. N. Floyer-Acland, and his tenant, Mr. F. Kellaway of Frome Farm, who permitted the excavations and facilitated them in every way. In the pre-excavation period a contour survey of the hill was undertaken by Mr. R. S. Dawson of the Land Survey Branch and was completed by Mr. R. Stewart in 1971. The geophysical surveys carried out by Messrs. A. J. Clark and D. Haddon-Reece of the Ancient Monuments Laboratory not only enabled a plan of the enclosure to be prepared but was also the means by which the trench plan was laid out in 1971 when the palisade trench was investigated. The field staff in 1970 in addition to those already mentioned were Miss L. Glashan and Messrs. J. P. Y. Clarke, J. Coppen, P. Sandiford (photography) and G. Smith. In 1971 the staff were augmented by Miss F. Parry and Mr. J. S. Jefferies.

Specific assistance received whilst this report was in preparation has been acknowledged in the text. In particular the author wishes to thank Dr. D. Britton for his report on the bronze axe, Mr. J. Schweiso for his account of the Saxon graves, Mr. P. Curnow for his note on the coins, Messrs. P. Sandiford and C. Stringer for their report on the human remains, and Mr. A. J. Clark for his account of the geophysical work. The illustrations of the plans, sections and pottery have been prepared for the report by Mrs. C. Boddington who also illustrated the reports for Durrington Walls and Marden. Mr. F. Gardiner prepared the illustrations of the other finds. All the material has now been deposited in the County Museum, Dorchester, and the report completed for publication in August 1975.

SUMMARY

EXCAVATIONS between 1970 and 1971 within the earthwork surrounding the top of Mount Pleasant hill near Dorchester recorded the post-holes of a circular timber structure similar to those recorded at Durrington Walls, Woodhenge and the Sanctuary on Overton Hill. The earliest evidence for occupation on the site pre-dates the enclosure and has been assigned by radiocarbon determinations to the latter part of the third millennium bc. The bank and internal ditch surrounding some 11 acres were constructed around 2000 bc and were entered by four causeways as at Avebury. At the same time a large circular timber structure inside its own ditch was constructed within the enclosure. Grooved Ware sherds together with associated flint and bone artifacts and animal bones were recorded from the enclosure and the timber structure. Sometime before 1800 bc the enclosure ditch was enlarged at the west entrance and the enclosure bank was crowned by the Conquer Barrow in its west sector. Around 1700 bc the timber structure was replaced by a stone 'cove' with outlying monoliths at the same time as the hill-top was surrounded by a strong timber palisade. The latter enclosed some ten acres of the hill-top with two entrances in the north and west and may have stood at least 6.00 m. high above ground level. The structure and the stone cove were associated with numerous beaker sherds. Occupation on the hill-top down to 1000 bc is attested by radiocarbon dates and stratified pottery from the enclosure ditch. Sporadic occupation occurred during the first millennium bc when the stone cove was destroyed and the hill given over to arable cultivation. Two pagan Saxon graves provide the final evidence for settlement.

INTRODUCTION

SITE DESCRIPTION

THE Winterbourne Valley is dominated by the earthworks of Mount Pleasant to the north and Maiden Castle to the west (fig. 2). Both sites are on low hills dominating spurs of upland which project into the valley. The region south of Maiden Castle forming the southern edge of the valley is dominated by the Ridgeway with its irregular linear barrow cemetery. Only isolated barrows occur in the valley but settlement in the latter is indicated by the single entrance henge at Maumbury Rings, one mile west of Mount Pleasant, while one mile north of Maumbury is the Grooved Ware occupation site at Poundbury.

The Mount Pleasant earthwork (SY 710899) encloses an irregular oval or egg-shaped area on a low ridge running east–west between the valley of the Frome to the north and the South Winterbourne to the south. Rather more than one mile east of Mount Pleasant the two waterways join to form the river Frome, which flows in an easterly direction to join the river Piddle, both entering Poole harbour half a mile east of Wareham. South of Mount Pleasant, the South Winterbourne is barely more than a stream flowing through a broad fertile valley from its source south-west of Maiden Castle, which itself lies two and a half miles south-west of Mount Pleasant. The gradient from the valley north to Mount Pleasant hill is gentle, but the latter is still a prominent feature when seen from the bank of the stream. North of the hill, the ground slopes steeply to the river Frome, which lies in its broad valley some 250 m. distant. To the south the hill is bounded by the Dorchester–Wareham road (A352) and the minor road which leads to West Stafford village; whilst at the foot of the steep slope to the north is the railway track and cutting which serves those same towns. The western edge of the enclosure is bounded by the Came View housing estate, the gardens of which have encroached on the western slopes of the Conquer Barrow. Only in its eastern approaches is the hill not built upon (pl. *Ib*) and from its summit one can identify the low ridge which must have provided the easiest access route and on whose axis were sited two successive entrances into the prehistoric enclosures.

The site lies on Upper Chalk, which in this area is soft and flintless. The author is indebted to Dr. F. W. Anderson of the Institute of Geological Sciences for visiting the site whilst the excavation was in progress, commenting on the geology and providing the following report:

'The site lies on Upper Chalk, here a soft flintless chalk. The Geological Survey map records the area of the camp as "bare chalk". Frome Hill, a third of a mile ESE has a capping of Pebble Gravel, one of the relict patches of Eocene sediments found scattered over this area and probably of Bagshot age. There is a patch of Bagshot (sandy clay) south of Winterbourne Came and of both Bagshot and Reading Beds (brown sand with quartz pebbles and white sand) at Whitcombe. There is a strong presumption that at one time Mount Pleasant also had a capping of Eocene sediments. Evidence for this lies in the material filling solution pits in the chalk. These are numerous and contain either a coarse limonitic quartz sand, sometimes cemented into a hard rock, or a fine white marly quartz

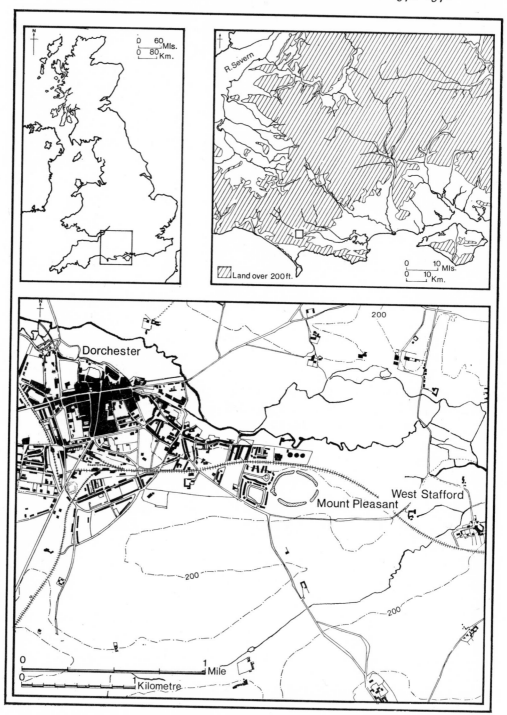

Fig. 1.   Location map

sand rather like a brickearth. The solution pits were therefore almost certainly formed when the chalk had a covering of Tertiary sands. The filling material is not Plateau Gravel, a sub-angular flint gravel as seen a little over a mile to the north at Stinsford and Kingston and at about the same level at the site. Nor is it likely to be an alluvial deposit (River Alluvium or Terrace Gravel) such as that surrounding Mount Pleasant on three sides but

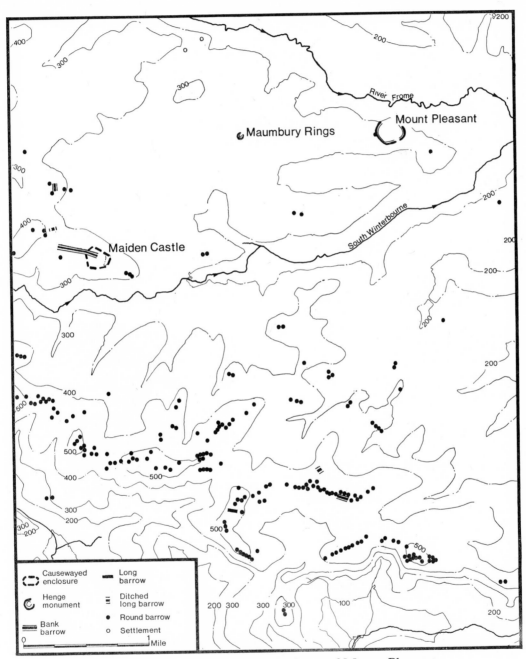

FIG. 2.   The archaeological environs of Mount Pleasant

at a much lower level. There are fragments of Sarsens on the site. These are relics of the Bagshot Beds, but could have been brought to the site from nearby.'

Dr. Anderson's comments on the sarsen stones will assume more significance when a stone setting on top of the hill is discussed.

The enclosure is sited between the 63.00 and 68.00 m. contours and is crossed by a hedge-bank from west to east, rather to the north of its central axis. The area enclosed is an egg-shape aligned along the ridge with the narrow end to the east. The over-all maximum dimensions are now difficult to determine on account of plough erosion but appear to have been in the order of 370 m. from west to east and 320 m. from north to south. The earthworks have been under plough for millennia and are now so spread and eroded as to be invisible for the most part. They are best preserved in their southern sector where it can be seen that the bank is external and broken by an entrance in the south-east 32.00 m. wide.[1] The exception to this general destruction lies under the coppice on the Conquer Barrow, which is a large though somewhat disturbed mound, built on top of the enclosure bank in its west sector. It is some 32.00 m. in diameter and still stands 3.00–4.00 m. high above a lower mound 8.00 m. wide and 4.00 m. high which presumably represents the original height of the neolithic bank when the barrow was built. Two smaller barrows, one of them extremely doubtful, are sited one quarter of a mile south-east of the enclosure.

The preservation of the bank height under the Conquer Barrow serves to emphasize its destruction elsewhere. When under plough in its only visible segment it can be seen as 16.00–18.00 m. wide, composed of chalk rubble and standing to a height of about 1.50 m. where it is best preserved. Within the bank is the ditch which is generally some 17.00 m. wide. To the east of the south-east entrance the bank can be traced on the ground around the eastern perimeter of the enclosure where a second entrance gap 32.00 m. wide occurs on the axis of the ridge. To the north of the hedge-line, all traces of the bank soon vanish. On account of this erosion, assistance was requested from the Geophysics Section of the Ancient Monuments Laboratory. The two surveys undertaken by this section have been described in detail by Mr. A. J. Clark (Appendix IV), and only the outcome is discussed here. In brief, they confirmed original entrances in the south-east and east and also recorded unsuspected entrances in the west and north (fig. 3). By means of traverses the line of the ditch was established where it had been completely obscured by erosion. In addition, the survey established the precise location of the ring ditch, previously recorded only on oblique aerial photographs. Finally, the surveys located and planned a previously unsuspected feature — a palisade trench 1.00–2.00 m. wide and 3.00 m. deep which surrounded the whole hill-top.

The palisade trench was not visible on the ground nor had it appeared on any air photographs of the site. The only internal structure which had occurred on the latter was a ring ditch which had been interpreted as a barrow (*vide* RAF VAP CPE/UK 1934: 5081–3; 58/271; 5128–30 and St Joseph No GF 13, which has been reproduced as pl. Ia of this report). It was this ring ditch that was located in the 1969 geophysical survey and which was investigated in 1970.

Visual inspection, geophysical aids and aerial photographs therefore established that the 12-acre enclosure was surrounded by a bank and internal ditch which was breached by four

[1] Cf. fig. 3 and RCHM Dorset, pt 3, 504–5.

entrances. Within the ditch and also surrounding the hill-top was a linear feature — either ditch or palisade trench—whilst south-west of the centre of the enclosure air photographs had indicated a large ring ditch. Clearly the hill-top was undergoing erosion by ploughing and rescue excavation was imperative.

THE EXCAVATIONS OF 1970 AND 1971

The excavation in 1970 had as its general objective the clarification of the presumed relationship between Mount Pleasant and the Durrington Walls and Marden enclosures, both of which had been investigated in previous years. To achieve this it was necessary to determine the ceramic and lithic associations of the enclosure, supported if possible by radiocarbon dates, and also to ascertain whether the enclosure surrounded a timber structure similar to those already recorded at Durrington Walls, Marden, Woodhenge and the Sanctuary. The area available for excavation was governed by the farmer's cropping programme and was confined to the west half of the southern field. The detailed objectives were therefore:

i. To investigate the west entrance into the earthwork enclosure (fig. 3, Cuttings I and II).
ii. To investigate the internal ring ditch which had been revealed on air photographs (fig. 3, Cutting IV).
iii. To investigate the character of the narrow linear feature revealed in the geophysical survey (fig. 3, Cuttings III, V–VIII).
iv. To obtain evidence relating to the environment of the time.

In addition, a single trench (X) was excavated across an anomaly recorded in the geophysical survey which proved to be a natural feature. A small cutting (fig. 3, IX) was also excavated to confirm the line of the main enclosure ditch south of the hedge.

As a result of these investigations it was necessary to return in 1971 with three objects:

i. To obtain more information regarding the plan and date of the palisade enclosure recorded in Cuttings III and V–VIII. This was an unsuspected development in 1970 and was clearly of the greatest importance. The line of the palisade trench was therefore determined by geophysical methods and small trenches were excavated along its length at regular intervals (fig. 3, XII–XXV, XXXIV–XLV) so that its entire plan was confirmed. Two entrances in the north and east were recorded in these excavations.
ii. The numbers of pot-sherds in the terminals of the enclosure ditch at its west entrance had been disappointingly few and it was decided to investigate the north entrance at the point where the enclosure was most nearly approached by the river Frome (fig. 3, Cuttings XXVII–XXX).
iii. During the excavation of the west entrance in 1970 the terminal of a ditch was recorded in the west edge of Cutting II. Trenches were also excavated in 1971 to establish the character and plan of this ditch (XLVI–LI) which it is thought may have been related to the Conquer Barrow.

In addition, cuttings were excavated across the enclosure bank in its west and east sectors to supplement the information obtained in 1970 (XXXI–XXXIII), a single slit trench was excavated into the enclosure ditch to confirm its course (XI) and an anomaly revealed by the geophysical survey was investigated (XXVI).

PREVIOUS ARCHAEOLOGICAL HISTORY

Previous accounts of the site are few and have been summarized by the Royal Commission Inventory for Dorset.[1] This account also contains a description of the visible remains and a plan. Warne in his *Ancient Dorset* called it 'Vespasian's camp' and recorded the finding of 'a sword and a few ancient relics'.[2] A plan and description was also included in a survey o stone and earthen circles in Dorset[3] and in Professor Atkinson's survey of henge monuments in Britain where it was recorded as a doubtful site.[4] No excavations had been carried out within the enclosure prior to 1970 and no chance finds recorded. However, immediately to the east of the enclosure, five inhumations have been recorded since 1951 in the course of building the Came View estate. These may be related to a group of inhumations recorded in the garden of Wareham House, a few hundred yards to the west in 1846 and 1884.[5]

[1] RCHM, 1970, pts 1 and 3, xxxii–iii, 504–5.
[2] Warne, 1872, 150–1, 242.
[3] Piggott, S. and C. M., 1939, 158, fig. 11.

[4] Atkinson *et al.*, 1951, 104–5.
[5] RCHM, 1970, 575, 578.

PART I. THE STRUCTURES AS REVEALED BY EXCAVATION

I. THE PRE-ENCLOSURE SETTLEMENT

THE poorly preserved bank provided few opportunities for investigating the character of the fossil soil preserved beneath it. With one exception (under the Conquer Barrow) the bank is best preserved in its southern sector where it is spread over a width of 16.00–20.00 m. and stands 1.50 m. high — although a proportion of this mound must be preserved natural subsoil. Beneath the Conquer Barrow the bank is preserved to a height of 4.00 m., which probably approximates closely to its original height. Such accidents of preservation provided an insight into the destruction of earthworks resulting from ploughing over centuries and millennia and which has caused such a substantial earthwork to be quite destroyed.

Four cuttings were sited to investigate the bank and its underlying fossil soil (fig. 3).

Cutting I, excavated in 1970, was intended to investigate the bank and ditch at the west entrance (fig. 22; pls. II*a* and *b*). It was 52.00 m. long and 4.00 m. wide, expanded to 12.00 m. wide for a 13.00 m. length over the terminal of the bank. In addition, a *sondage* 1.40 m. wide was dug into the natural subsoil to a depth of 80 cm. The bank was preserved only as a single or double layer of chalk lumps, 7.40 m. wide and at most 8 cm. thick. It covered a ridge of preserved subsoil, 18.00 m. wide and 50 cm. high at maximum, which may provide an indication of the former width of the bank and agrees well with the dimensions of the latter in its south sector. The fossil soil consisted of a dark, brown, humic loam between 2–5 cm. thick, overlain by 10–15 cm. of paler but still humic material. The subsoil was a fine buff-coloured material including chalk lumps 60–80 cm. thick, overlying an uneven chalk surface. A single lump of sarsen 50 × 40 cm. protruded from this matrix and proved to be a natural feature. Below the surface of the fossil soil occurred a spread of charcoal associated with sherds of plain Neolithic bowls. A sample of this material produced a radio-carbon determination of 2122 ± 73 bc (BM-644).

Cutting XXXI was a trench 14.00 m. long and 2.00 m. wide sited to examine the bank where it appeared as a low mound to the north of the hedge in its east sector. Throughout the cutting the chalk bed-rock occurred immediately beneath the turf-line. The bank and fossil soil beneath it had been entirely removed by ploughing, the original position of the earthwork being indicated by a ridge in the bed-rock.

Cutting XXXII (fig. 4) was a rectangular cutting 10.00 × 6.00 m. to examine the bank and fossil soil in its west sector. The area selected lay at the edge of the field under a hedge where the plough would have turned and therefore not bitten so deeply into the bank. The latter was indeed well preserved at this point to a height of 42 cm. and overlay a fossil turf-line of dark-brown humic loam between 2–5 cm. thick which was underlain by 10–15 cm. of humic stony material. As in Cutting I, the subsoil consisted of fine buff-coloured material with coarser chalky debris. Three samples from the buried soil were examined for mollusca by Dr Evans whose analyses reveal that the assemblages are dominated by species which favour a dry grassland environment. It can be assumed that Mount Pleasant hill was under grass at this time, possibly maintained by grazing.

MOUNT PLEASANT : ENCLOSURE BANK

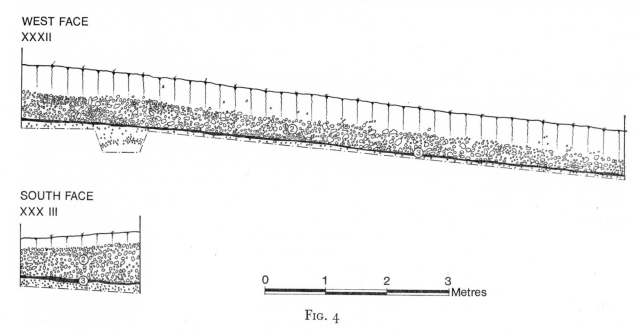

WEST FACE
XXXII

SOUTH FACE
XXX III

0 1 2 3 Metres

Fig. 4

Cutting XXXIII (fig. 4) was a trench 8.00 m. long and 2.00 m. wide, sited 17.00 m. south of XXXII. The bank was well-preserved in this cutting to a height of 62 cm. and overlay a fossil soil of the same character as that recorded in XXXII.

The finds are described in detail in Part II of this report. The pottery from the old land surface comprised, with the exception of two sherds of Grooved Ware, sherds of plain Neolithic bowls, and the 1084 flint artifacts from the same context include cores, scrapers, serrated flakes, blades with edge retouch, a flake from a polished axe and two transverse arrowheads. A plano-convex knife was recorded from the plough-soil in Cutting XXXII. Small fragments of animal bone include *bos* (2) and sheep (1). Fragments of hazel-nut shells were recorded from the old land surface in Cutting XXXIII.

II. THE TIMBER STRUCTURE: SITE IV

(figs. 5–19; pls. IIIa, b–XVIIIb)

Introduction

PRIOR to the excavations of 1970 the only structure identified on the hill within the earthwork enclosure was a ring-ditch, visible on air photographs (e.g. pl. Ia), which had been interpreted as a barrow ditch. In 1969 this ditch was located precisely by means of a proton magnetometer area survey across the interior of the main enclosure. As a major objective of the excavation was to locate timber structures comparable to those previously discovered at Woodhenge, the Sanctuary, Durrington Walls and Marden, this ring-ditch and the area it enclosed was clearly an area to be investigated.

The ring-ditch was sited to the south of the highest part of the hill on gently sloping ground between the 77.00 and 79.00 m. contours. In the initial phase of its excavation the plough-soil was removed by machine to within a few centimetres of the chalk bed-rock over an area which covered the whole structure with the exception of a sliver of ditch in its east sector. This area excavation was named Site IV. The remaining plough-soil was then removed by hand (pls. IIIa, b–IVb). The chalk bed-rock was of a soft consistency containing patches of large flint modules and occasional solution holes. In its east sector the enclosure ditch had been dug through one such large patch of clay. When the surface of the chalk had been trowelled and after a subsequent thunderstorm it was noted that the surface was scored by a lattice pattern of plough-marks, presumably of modern derivation, which were clearly destroying the structural evidence and had in fact removed some post-holes. There was no sign of the bank which had stood outside the ditch, nor was there a rise in the level of the chalk to denote its former presence. Clearly, the structure in this exposed position just to the south of the hill-crest had been subjected to ploughing for millennia and the post-hole settings within the ditch, although still fairly complete, bore little relation in terms of post-hole size to the originals. It is impossible to establish how much of the natural surface might have been removed by ploughing and other agencies of erosion. It will be recalled, however, that a ridge of natural chalk some 50 cm. high was preserved under the main enclosure bank near the west entrance under circumstances which were more favourable for preservation than those prevailing on the exposed hill-top. One may speculate, therefore, whether the erosion on Site IV has been in excess of this figure — an important factor when considering the interpretation of the post-hole settings.

The remains, which for the sake of brevity have been given the over-all designation of Site IV, produced a structural sequence of considerable interest which it is convenient to summarize at this juncture before embarking on the detailed descriptions.

Phase I. A ditch 3.00–4.00 m. wide and with a maximum depth of 2.00 m. was excavated to surround a circular area 43.00 m. in diameter. The bank appears to have been external and a single causeway 7.50 m. wide was provided in the north. Within this ditch was a structure which comprised five rings of post-holes with a maximum diameter of 38.00 m. and with the innermost ring surrounding an area 12.50 m. in diameter. The lay-out of the structure is very regular and was designed around four corridors which divided the rings into quadrants. Radiocarbon determinations assign this structure to the period around 2000 bc and the ceramic associations are principally with the Grooved Ware tradition.

Phase II. When the ditch was approximately one-third full of silt and a weathered horizon had formed, the timber structure was replaced by a central setting of pits and sarsen monoliths representing a 'cove'. Outlying pits and monoliths were recorded to the west, north and east. This rebuilding was associated in the ditch with sherds of beaker pottery and a radiocarbon determination of 1680 ± 60 bc (BM-668).

Phase III. Iron Age settlement on the site is represented by a gully partially defining a hut 11.00 m. in diameter and associated pits. It seems likely that at this time the sarsen structure was demolished. A rectangular enclosure, probably of Romano-British date, was built over the enclosure in its north-west part and ultimately a Saxon grave inserted into the ditch in its west sector.

The detailed description of the remains is prefaced by that of the ditch in which these phases are represented as stratified deposits.

The Ditch
(figs. 5–13; pls. VI*b*–X*b*)

The ditched structure (Site IV) is sited some 50.00 m. east of the palisade trench recorded in the 1970 excavations and 60.00 m. from the main enclosure ditch at the west entrance (fig. 5; pl. III*a*). The inner edge of the ditch, although representing the upper limit of the weathering cone, describes an almost perfect circle with a radius of 21.50 m. The centre of this circle coincides with that for the north-west arc of Ring C in the post-hole setting (fig. 6). It is crossed by a single causeway in the north, some 7.50 m. wide between the ditch terminals, facing in the direction of the contemporary north entrance into the main enclosure and the River Frome. The latter would, however, have been invisible to anyone standing on the causeway on account of the intervening hill-top. No pits or post-holes were recorded on the causeway but the west terminal was particularly rich in artifacts and refuse. The profile of the ditch was extremely variable (figs. 8–13; pls. VI*b*–X*b*), varying from a classic wedge-shaped profile with straight converging sides and a flat base to a relatively shallow bowl profile. There were some irregularities in the ditch bottom and sides but these were not numerous and presumably resulted from a failure to finish the ditch in a consistent fashion. Seventeen sections across the ditch indicated that its average width is 3.48 m. with extremes of from 2.60 to 4.60 m. The average depth from the modern ground surface is 1.65 m., with extremes of from 1.36 to 2.00 m. It should be remembered, however, that the width of the ditch as measured in 1970 from lip to lip represents a product of weathering. Attempts have therefore been made to establish the original dimensions of the ditch by projecting the angle of its lower unweathered walls up to the modern ground surface. This produced an estimated original width for the ditch of 2.47 m. with extremes of from 1.75 to 3.30 m.

The original position of the bank is assumed to have been outside the ditch because of the presence of the outer ring of post-holes at a short distance within the latter. This is confirmed by the later ditch silts in parts of its circuit which contain spills of chalk rubble. These are assumed to have come from the bank and were invariably derived from outside the ditch (e.g. Sections IB, IIB, VA, VB and XI alpha A; figs. 8, 9 and 12).

MOUNT PLEASANT
GENERAL PLAN OF SITE IV

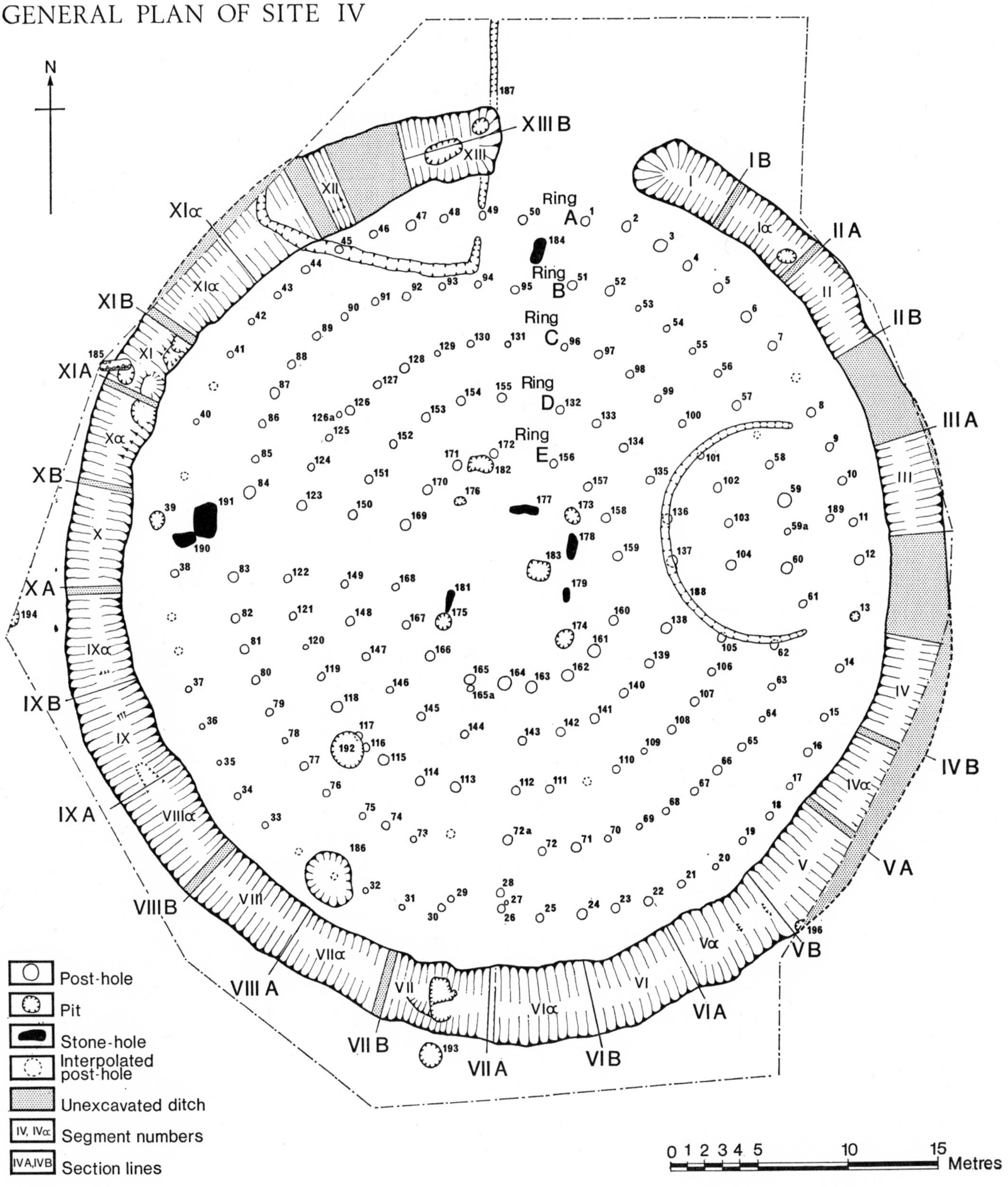

N

XIII B
XIII
XII
XI α
XI α
XI B
XI
XI A
X α
X B
X
X A
IX α
IX B
IX
IX A
VIII α
VIII
VIII B
VIII A
VII α
VII
VII B
VII A

Ring A
Ring B
Ring C
Ring D
Ring E

I B
I
I α
II A
II
II B
III A
III
IV
IV α
IV B
V A
V
V α
V B
VI A
VI
VI α
VI B

Legend:

- ○ Post-hole
- ⊙ Pit
- ◼ Stone-hole
- (dashed) Interpolated post-hole
- (shaded) Unexcavated ditch
- IV, IVα Segment numbers
- IVA,IVB Section lines

0 1 2 3 4 5   10   15 Metres

Fig. 6

For purposes of recording the ditch was divided into segments (fig. 6, I–XIII), after a trial trench 1.00 m. wide (XII) had been excavated to obtain a preview of the deposits. Twenty-two such segments were excavated, representing slightly more than 80% of the total ditch deposits. Those segments that were not excavated (between II and III, III and IV and XII and XIII) had been disturbed by burrowing animals and were so deficient in finds as to make their excavation not worthwhile. As far as was possible the layer numbers were standardized throughout the ditch. The individual segments have been described in detail below but the stratigraphical sequence in the ditch was standard. This sequence therefore precedes the detailed segment descriptions and incorporates the results of analyses of a series of samples obtained by Dr. Evans from Segment VIII. The layer numbers used throughout the general description refer to Segment VIII and a layer concordance can be obtained from the subsequent description of the individual ditch segments.

Primary Fill. Coarse chalk rubble becoming finer towards the top with some admixture of flint nodules (layer (7)). Samples for radiocarbon dating this early stage in the silting of the ditch were obtained from Segment VII, layer (10) (fig. 10) and produced determinations of 1961 $\pm$ 89 bc from charcoal (BM-663), 1991 $\pm$ 72 bc from antler (BM-666) and 2038 $\pm$ 84 bc from animal bone (BM-667). The associated pottery is principally of the Grooved Ware ceramic tradition.

Buried Soil. A dark-brown stony loam with numerous bands of chalky rubble (layer (6)). A woodland molluscan fauna prevailed in this buried soil.

Pale Loam. A friable pale loam which in some areas of the ditch contained a thick deposit of ash and charcoal (layer (5)). A hearth from the base of this deposit (Segment X, layer (5)) produced oak charcoal for a determination of 1680 $\pm$ 60 bc (BM-668). A hearth from the surface of this deposit (Segment VIII alpha, layer (5)) provided charcoal for a determination of 1324 $\pm$ 51 bc (BM–669) and was associated with sherds of Collared Vessels and Food Vessels. The molluscan fauna in this deposit indicates that the woodland conditions were generally maintained although there is some slight disturbance. A large quantity of sarsen flakes (300 lb. or 1452 fragments) was found in the thick deposit of ash and charcoal related to BM-668. Many flakes were large and fresh, retaining the original cortex of the sarsen block and possessing clear percussion bulbs. Three mauls or hammerstones were also recorded. The sarsen flakes were recorded in Segments IV, IX, X, X alpha and XIII, and provide clear evidence for the preparation of stone monoliths on the site at a period related to BM-668 and associated with beaker sherds. This debris can be related to quantities of fresh sarsen flakes from the pits and stone-holes which form a central setting or 'cove' within the confines of the ditch and by implication provide a date for the latter. The distribution of sarsens within the ditch segments is also of interest, for the great quantity of flakes from Segments IX, X and X alpha are presumably related to the erection of stones in holes 190 and 191; and those from Segment XIII to the erection of a monolith in hole 184. The concentration of flakes in Segment IV on the other hand is not related to any surviving evidence for an adjacent monolith, unless that evidence had been destroyed by erosion.

Buried Soil. A dark-brown loam with a pronounced stone-line (layers (3) and (4)). The molluscan evidence is for a sudden and total clearance phase at the base of this deposit and the appearance of an environment of short-turfed grassland. Dr. Evans suggests an

MOUNT PLEASANT
SITE IV : PHASE I

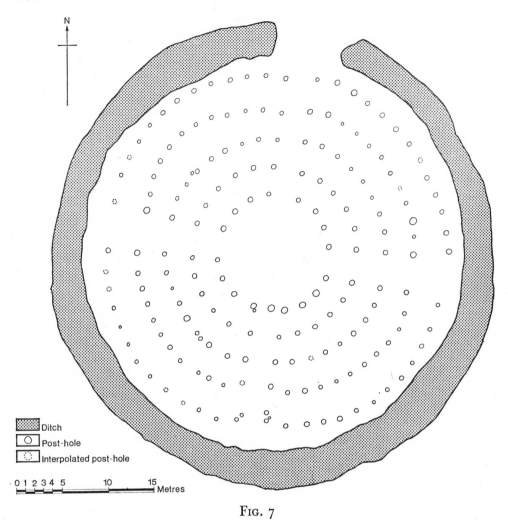

FIG. 7

equivalence with the aeolian deposit and buried soil in the north terminals of the main enclosure ditch. Iron Age pottery was recorded from the equivalent of layer (3), but not from
below the stone-line which normally appears between layers (3) and (4).

Plough-wash. A plough-soil normally producing Romano-British pottery and occasional
sherds of glazed seventeenth-century fabric.

There follows a description of the individual ditch segments which showed some variation
in profile and stratification.

Segment I (fig. 8). The ditch in this segment is 2.95 m. wide and 1.65 m. deep from the modern ground
surface. The estimated original width of the ditch at a level equivalent to the modern surface is 2.10 m.
The excavated area covers the east terminal of the ditch, which at this point was dug into a patch of

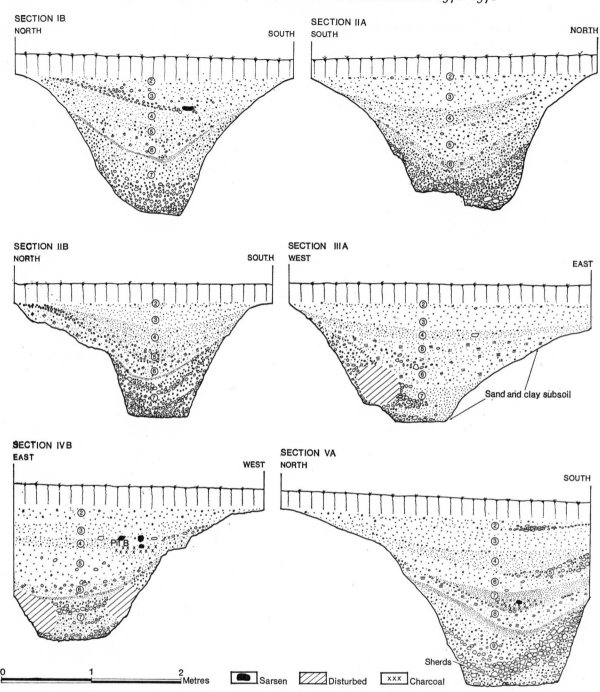

Fig. 8.   Site IV: ditch sections

sandy clay. The terminal is irregular in profile, with sides sloping steeply to a rounded base. The deposits range from a primary rubble fill at its base (layer (7)) through a buried soil (layer (6)) and pale loam (layer (5)) to an upper buried soil (layers (4) and (3)) and plough-wash (layer (2)).

Segment I alpha (fig. 8). The ditch in this segment is 3.00 m. wide and 1.60 m. deep with an estimated original width of 2.10 m. The steeply sloping sides converge towards an irregular flat base 1.10 m. wide. The sequence of deposits is similar to that in Segment I.

Segment II (fig. 8). The ditch in this segment is 3.00 m. wide and 1.60 m. deep with an estimated original width of 1.75 m. It has a straight-sided profile with a narrow flat base 65 cm. wide, but its symmetry is disturbed by an irregular ledge on its north face. The sequence of deposits is the same as that already described for Segment I.

Segment III (fig. 8). The ditch in this segment is in excess of 3.30 m. wide and is 1.46 m. deep with an estimated original width of 2.60 m. It has sloping sides and a flat but irregular base 1.00 m. wide. The profile and silting is probably conditioned by the cutting of the ditch through a pocket of clay and sand on its east side. The deposits have also been disturbed by burrowing animals but their sequence resembles that described from Segment I, with the proviso that a lens of finer silt in the primary chalk rubble (not showing in section) was designated layer (8).

Segment IV (fig. 8). The ditch in this segment is in excess of 2.40 m. wide and 1.64 m. deep with an estimated original width of 2.90 m. The steeply sloping sides of the ditch converge to a flat base 70 cm. wide. The sequence of deposits is the same as that for Segment III but was much disturbed by burrowing animals. A small pit (B) was cut through the base of layer (2).

Segment IV alpha (fig. 8). The ditch in this segment is in excess of 3.20 m. wide and is 2.00 m. deep with an estimated original width of 2.60 m. The steeply sloping sides converge to a flat base 1.00 m. wide. The sequence of deposits is essentially the same as that previously described, being chalk rubble at the base (layer (9)), overlain by a buried soil and friable loam containing burnt material and sarsen fragments (layers (7) and (8)), which in turn is overlain by an upper buried soil (layers (4) and (6)) with a layer of intervening chalk lumps (layer (5)). Overlying this sequence is a plough-wash deposit (layers (2) and (3)).

Segment V (fig. 9). The width of the ditch in this segment is 3.80 m. and depth 1.88 m. with an estimated original width of 2.80 m. The steeply sloping sides converge to a flat base 75 cm. wide. The stratification is essentially the same as that described for Segment IV alpha with the same numbered sequence of layers.

Segment V alpha (fig. 9). The width of the ditch in this segment is 3.50 m. and depth 1.72 m. with an estimated original width of 1.90 m. The steeply sloping sides converge to a flat base 80 cm. wide. The sequence of deposits is essentially the same as that described for Segment I, with primary rubble (layer (7)) overlain by the lower buried soil (layer (6)) and pale loam (layer (5)), with no trace of burning in the latter. Over this deposit occurs the upper buried soil (layers (4) and (3)) and the plough-wash (layers (2) and (3)).

Segment VI (fig. 9). The ditch in this segment is 4.00 m. wide and 1.85 m. deep with a presumed original width of ?3.10 m. The profile is very irregular with an uneven rounded base. The stratification is the same as that for Segment V alpha with the same numbered sequence.

Segment VI alpha (fig. 10). The ditch in this segment is 3.40 m. wide and 1.65 m. deep but it is difficult to estimate the original width. The profile is that of an extremely irregular scoop and has the appearance of being unfinished. The layer sequence comprises a chalk rubble at the base (layer (8)), succeeded by a buried soil (layer (7)), immediately on top of which occurs a lens of charcoal and sarsen fragments (layer (6)). The normal pale loam (layer (5)) overlies this deposit, with a lens of burning near its surface, and is overlain in turn by layers (2)–(4).

Segment VII (fig. 10; pl. VIII*b*). The ditch in this segment is 4.30 m. wide and 1.36 m. deep, with a profile which resembles a broad shallow scoop. In the floor of the ditch (*vide* fig. 6) was an irregular

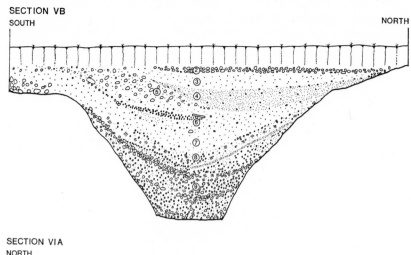

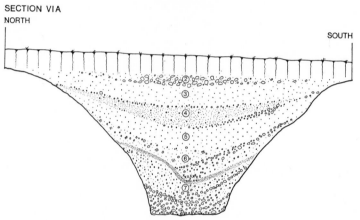

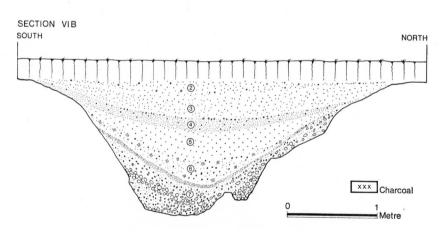

FIG. 9.   Site IV: ditch sections

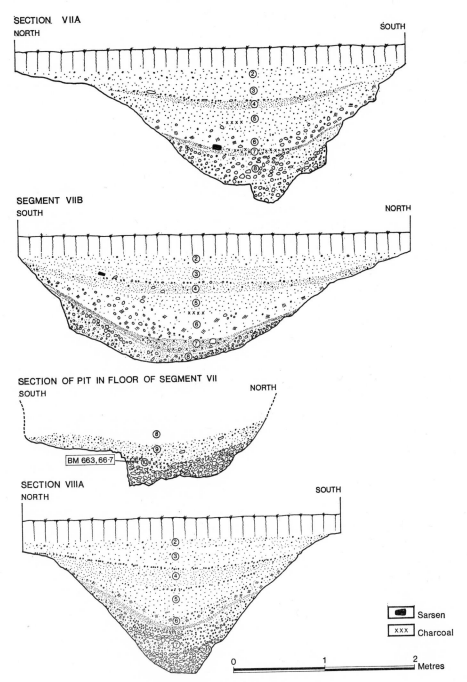

FIG. 10.   Site IV: ditch sections

pit 35 cm. deep. The sequence of deposits resembles that from Segment VI alpha. The base of the pit was filled with a primary chalk rubble (layer (11)), overlain by a thick lens of ash and charcoal (layer 10) which produced animal bones, antler picks, a few flints and sherds. Three samples of different materials were taken from this pit (layer (10)) for radiocarbon determinations. The results were: from oak charcoal, 1961 ± 89 bc (BM–663), from antler, 1991 ± 72 bc (BM–666), and from animal bone, 2038 ± 84 bc (BM–667). These determinations must relate to a very early phase in the silting of the ditch. The pit was sealed with a deposit of earth and chalk rubble which in the ditch proper can be equated with layer (8) — the chalk rubble lying on the ditch floor. Overlying this rubble is the lower buried soil and pale loam (layers (6) and (7)), with a deposit of ash and sarsen at the base of (6). Overlying this loam is the same sequence of deposits as recorded in Segment VI alpha with a similar hearth within layer (5).

Segment VII alpha (fig. 10). The ditch in this segment is 3.20 m. wide and 1.65 m. deep with an estimated original width of 2.70 m. The steeply sloping sides converge towards a narrow, slightly rounded base, some 35 cm. wide. The stratification within the ditch consists of chalk rubble at the base (layer (7)), overlain by the lower buried soil (layer (6)) and pale loam (layer (5)). Sealing the pale loam is a thin scatter of chalk lumps above which is the upper buried soil and plough-wash.

Segment VIII (fig. 11). The ditch in this segment is 4.60 m. wide and 1.70 m. deep with an estimated original width of 2.80 m. The sides converge from an unusually broad weathering cone to a narrow flat base 55 cm. wide. The sequence of deposits is essentially the same as that in Segment VII alpha with chalk rubble at the base (layer (7)), overlain by a buried soil and a pale loam which in its lower half contains many spills of chalk rubble (layer (6)). A finer loam overlying this deposit included a hearth which extended into the adjacent Segment VIII alpha but which is not represented in the published section. Charcoal from this hearth, collected in Segment VIII alpha, produced a radiocarbon determination of 1324 ± 51 bc (BM–669). Overlying this hearth is the upper buried soil and plough-wash.

Segment VIII alpha (fig. 11). The ditch in this segment is 3.70 m. wide, 1.80 m. deep and with an estimated original width of 2.50 m. The sides slope steeply to an irregular flat base and the sequence of deposits is the same as for Segment VIII except that the upper hearth does not show in section.

Segment IX (fig. 11; pls. X*a* and *b*). The ditch in this segment is 3.90 m. wide and 1.50 m. deep with an estimated original width of 2.10 m. The irregular sides converge at an angle, which is more gentle than usual, to a flat base 1.10 m. wide. The sequence of deposits is a standard one with chalk rubble at the base (layer (7)) overlaid by a buried soil and pale loam (layers (5) and (6)) which in turn are sealed by the upper burien soil (layers (3) and (4)) and plough-soil (layer (2)). An extensive area of burning and sarsen flakes was recorded from near the base of layer (5).

Segment IX alpha (fig. 12). The ditch in this segment is 3.25 m. wide and 1.84 m. deep. The original width is uncertain as the profile is unusual, with a very narrow base some 35 cm. wide and irregular but steeply converging sides. The sequence of deposits is the same as for Segment IX and the area of burning is particularly pronounced.

Segment X (fig. 12; pls. IX*a* and *b*). The ditch in this segment is 3.15 m. wide and 1.73 m. deep with an estimated original width of 2.25 m. The profile is irregular, with uneven walls descending steeply to a narrow rounded base. The sequence of deposits is the same as for Segment IX. The area of burning and sarsen flakes at the base of layer (5) was especially pronounced and charcoal from it provided a radiocarbon determination of 1680 ± 60 bc (BM–668).

Segment X alpha (fig. 12). The ditch in this segment is 3.20 m. wide and 1.47 m. deep with an irregular shallow bowl profile. The sequence of deposits is the same as for Segment X — large quantities of sarsen flakes being found in the area of burning within layer (5).

Segment XI (fig. 12). The ditch in this segment is 2.95 m. wide and 1.42 m. deep with an estimated original width of 2.65 m. The profile is that of a shallow bowl, with a rounded base 80 cm. wide, which

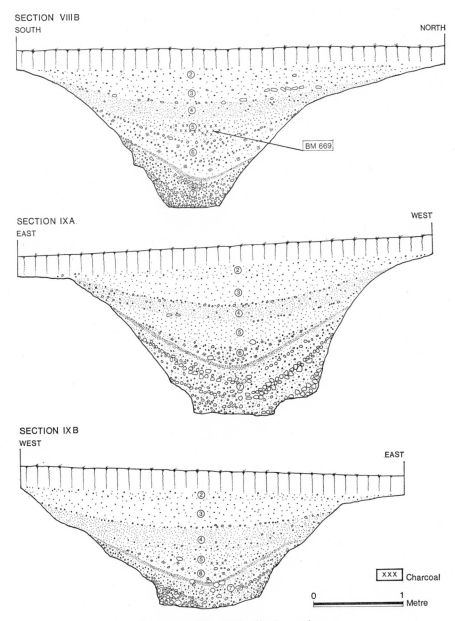

FIG. 11. Site IV: ditch sections

is related to what could either be an earlier pit or more probably a particularly irregular part of the ditch. Similar pits were recorded in the vicinity (*vide* fig. 6) and can be regarded as part of the irregular ditch profile. The sequence of deposits is the same as for Segment X. A grave of Saxon date partially overlay the ditch in this segment.

Segment XI alpha (fig. 12). The ditch in this segment is in excess of 3.60 m. wide and is 1.70 m. deep with an estimated original width of 3.30 m. The walls slope to a flat base 1.10 m. wide. The silting sequence comprises a primary rubble (layer (10)), overlain by a buried soil and pale loam with much

2

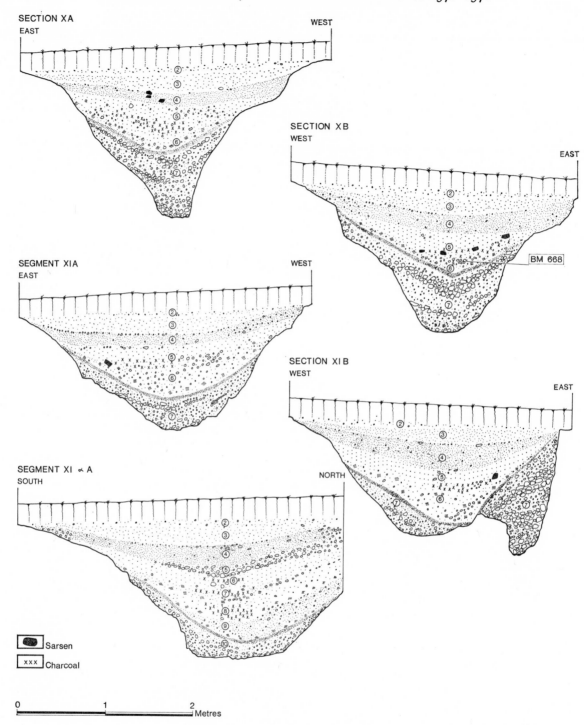

FIG. 12.   Site IV: ditch sections

burning (layers (7) to (9)). At the top of the pale loam is an upper hearth (layer (6)) which is directly sealed by a subsequent spill of chalk blocks (layer (5)). The upper buried soil and plough-wash deposits complete the sequence. The ditch of a rectangular enclosure of possible Romano-British date partially overlay the ditch in this segment.

Segment XII. This was a trial trench 1.00 m. wide designed to test the deposits and profile of the ditch before fuller excavation took place. The sequence of deposits comprised chalk rubble at the base (layers (7) and (8)), overlain by a buried soil and pale loam (layers (5) and (6)) with an area of burning at the base of layer (5). The upper buried soil and plough-wash deposits overlay the pale loam. The deposits, however, had been disturbed by burrowing animals.

Segment XIII (fig. 13; pl. VI*b*). The ditch in this segment is 3.70 m. wide and between 1.65 and 2.00 m. deep. The segment incorporates the west ditch terminal and the latter slopes in an irregular fashion from the causeway to a pit in the floor of the ditch. Quantities of debris had been thrown into the ditch terminal from the causeway, particularly in the secondary stages of its filling. Unfortunately, the deposits had been disturbed by burrowing animals and the stratification is in some respects slightly suspect. The sequence of deposits comprises a primary chalk rubble (layer (7)), overlain by a buried soil and a burnt deposit containing quantities of sarsen (layers (5) and (6)). This in turn is overlain by a brown soil with scattered chalk lumps and an upper hearth (layer (4)) which produced sherds of a Food Vessel. Over this occurred the upper buried soil (layers (3) and (3a)) and plough-soil (layer (2)).

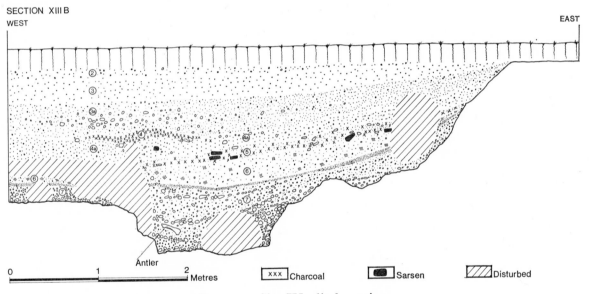

FIG. 13.   Site IV: ditch sections

For descriptive purposes the finds from the ditch have been divided into three broad categories, related to the silting sequence which is fairly standard in each segment.

Primary. The chalk rubble in the base of the ditch produced Grooved Ware and no securely stratified Beaker sherds. Very few flint artifacts were recovered, the only recognizable implements being seven scrapers. Only ten fragments of sarsen were recovered — a significantly small quantity in relation to the concentration of such flakes in the secondary ditch silts. Chalk artifacts include a single chalk ball and 11 antler picks were recorded. The only bone artifact was the tip of a pin or awl whilst the faunal remains were of pig, *bos*, sheep, dog, red deer, fox and bird (common crane).

Secondary. Those artifacts from the lower buried soil and pale loam related to the intermittent deposit of ash and sarsen flakes which it is suggested was the debris from the construction of the stone cove. The bulk of the identifiable pottery is Beaker although Grooved Ware is also well represented. The Beaker displays a great variety of styles. In deposits immediately overlying the ash and sarsen layer only four sherds of Grooved Ware were recorded, Beaker pottery remains well represented and sherds of Food Vessel, Collared Vessel and other Bronze Age wares were recorded. Sherds of a ridged Food Vessel were recorded in direct association with a radiocarbon date of 1324 ± 51 bc (BM-669).

More than 3000 flint artifacts were recorded of which over 100 were recognizable implements. Scrapers are the most numerous type; other implements include transverse arrowheads, barbed and tanged arrowheads, serrated flakes and blades with edge retouch. Comment has already been made on the quantities (300 lb.) of fresh sarsen flakes found in an intermittent deposit of ash and charcoal at this level in the ditch. Together with the associated stone mauls this debris has been related to the construction of the stone cove and its outliers. Antler artifacts include two picks and three spatulae but no bone implements were found. The animal bones include *bos*, pig, sheep, dog, red deer and birds (greylag and pintail).

The Later Silts. These deposits comprise those overlying the pale loam and including the upper buried soil and plough-wash. The upper part of the buried soil (layer (3)) produced a quantity of Iron Age pottery which is presumably related to the hut and pits found elsewhere on Site IV.

Romano-British pottery and bowls and pans of seventeenth- or eighteenth-century date were obtained from the plough-wash. Because of conflation, it is not possible to be certain regarding the cultural attribution of any artifacts from these deposits. These comprise large numbers of flint implements, including transverse arrowheads, barbed and tanged arrowheads and a plano-convex knife. Other artifacts include fragments of burnt clay, a bronze brooch and a glass bead. Some $45\frac{1}{2}$ lb. of sarsen fragments were obtained from these late silts and provide evidence for the view that the stone settings were demolished in the late first century B.C.

Phase I: The Post-hole Rings
(figs. 6, 7, 14, 15; pls. IIIb–Va, XIa–XIVa)

The post-hole settings within the ditch consist essentially of five rings, the outermost having a maximum diameter of 38.00 m. This outermost ring is at a distance from the present inner lip of the ditch which varies from 2.00 to 3.00 m. The design of the structure is very regular and is based around four corridors aligned on the cardinal points which divide the rings into four quadrants. The five arcs of post-holes within each quadrant are struck from centres which occasionally coincide within each quadrant but are only rarely common between different quadrants. The plan of the structure is not therefore based on five concentric rings of post-holes struck from adjacent or common centres, but each ring is composed of four arcs, each of which normally has a different centre. Despite this disparity the four arcs comprising each ring invariably possess the same number of post-holes.

TABLE I

Site IV: Details of the post-hole rings

Ring	Mean diameter		No. of posts in each ring			Average spacing	Average post-hole diam. (cm.)	Average post-hole depth (cm.)	Average post diam. (cm.)
	North to South	West to East	Excavated	Presumed	Replacements etc.				
A	37·30	38·00	45	52	3	2·10	43	26	28
B	29·50	30·80	46	48	—	1·93	45	30	—
C	24·00	24·60	35	36	2	1·98	44	29	—
D	18·30	18·20	24	24	—	2·21	48	34	—
E	12·20	12·50	16	16	2	2·11	53	36	—

TABLE II

Site IV: Details of the arcs

Ring	Arc	Mean radius	No. of posts (minus replacements)
A	NE	21·80	13
	SE	16·30	13
	SW	15·70	13
	NW	16·50	13
B	NE	15·20	12
	SE	12·50	12
	SW	15·20	12
	NW	11·30	12
C	NE	12·80	9
	SE	10·40	9
	SW	12·10	9
	NW	10·20	9
D	NE	8·70	6
	SE	7·60	6
	SW	8·70	6
	NW	8·20	6
E	NE	5·80	4
	SE	5·10	4
	SW	6·20	4
	NW	6·80	4

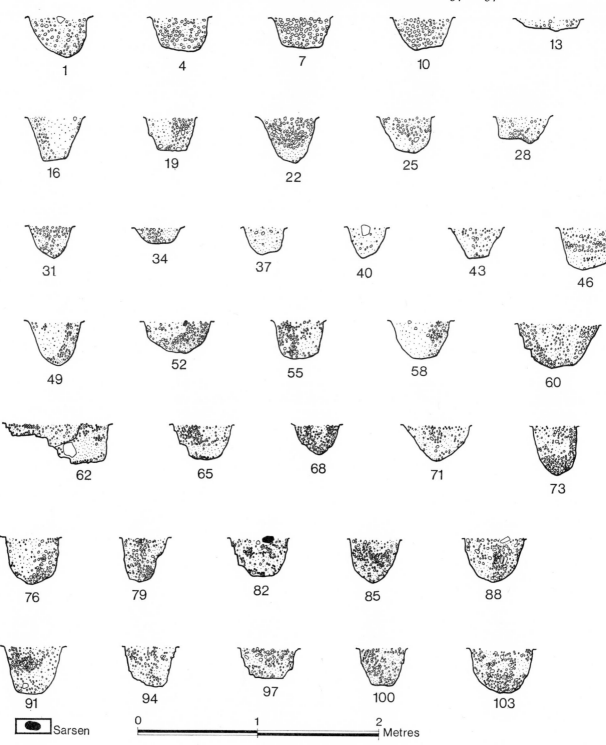

Fig. 14. Site IV: post-hole sections

The essential data for the arcs and rings have been summarized in Tables I and II, and the rings have been described in detail below. From these tables it will be clear that there is no consistency in the striking of the arcs but that nevertheless each ring contains the same number of posts, some of which had been replaced during the life of the structure. Because of the way in which they were laid out, the rings were not true circles but were greater in diameter from west to east than they were from north to south.

In addition to the regular post-hole lay-out, the four corridors are the dominant feature of the structure. The north and south corridors have virtually parallel sides whilst those in the

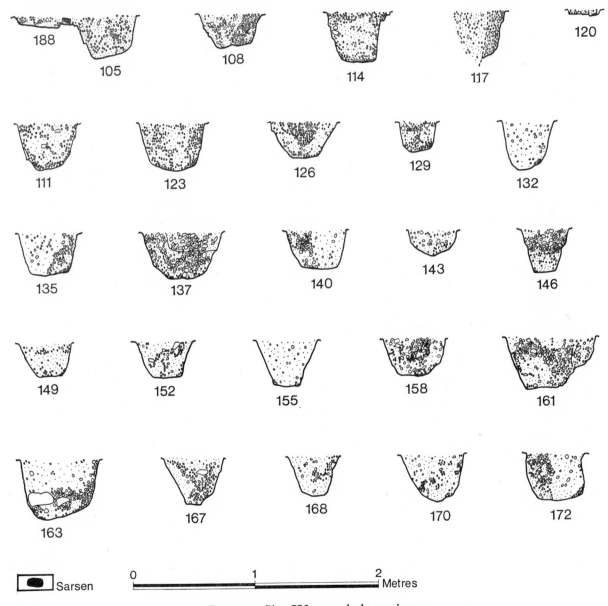

Fig. 15   Site IV: post-hole sections

west and east converge towards the central area. The north–south corridor is 3.00 m. wide and the post-holes flanking it on the west and east (50 and 30, 1 and 26), form straight alignments across the structure. The southern corridor is blocked by a single post-hole (164) where it enters Ring E. The east corridor is 6.00 m. wide at Ring A and narrows to 3.50 m. at the innermost Ring E, the post-holes forming the sides of the corridor pursuing slightly convex alignments. The established width of the western corridor at Ring A is 5.00 m. It narrows to 3.50 m. at Ring E, the post alignments on either side of the corridor pursuing straight alignments.

The post-hole sequences in the rings are fairly complete and the regularity of the latter enables the missing post-holes to be estimated with a reasonable degree of accuracy. Seven post-holes are missing in Ring A, two in Ring B and one in Ring C, Rings D and E being represented in their entirety. Replacement posts are present but are not common, being represented by three in Ring A, two in Ring C and two in Ring E. Because of erosion, the dimensions of the post-holes cannot be regarded as being relevant to their original size and only two post-cores or pipes were recorded. Nevertheless their average dimensions have been provided in Table I and full details in Appendix III. A selection of post-holes has been illustrated (figs. 14, 15; pls. XIa–XIVa). Both the average depth and diameter of the post-holes increase by about 10 cm. from the outer to the innermost rings but it seems unlikely that such a small variation is significant in view of the great amount of chalk that may have been lost through erosion. As only the bases of the post-holes have survived only two pipes were recorded, both in Ring A, which suggest an average post diameter of 28 cm.

Finds from the post-holes are very few and are confined in the main to 279 flint artifacts which include three scrapers. One half of a ring or pendant of fine-grained quartzite was recorded from post-hole 1. Sherds of Grooved Ware were recorded from 14 post-holes.

There follows a detailed account of the individual rings. A discussion of the structure in relation to comparable sites has been reserved for Chapter XVI.

Ring A (post-hole nos. 1–12, 14–38, 40–50)

This ring has over-all diameters of 37.30 m. from north to south and 38.00 m. from east to west. It is composed of four arcs, each originally of 13 post-holes, with radii of 21.80 m. (NE), 16.30 m. (SE), 15.70 m. (SW) and 16.50 m. (NW). These four arcs do not have a common centre but that for the south-east arc is the same as that for Ring B in the same arc. The arcs are separated by four gaps of 3.50 m. in the north facing the causeway across the ditch, 6.00 m. in the east, 3.30 m. in the south and ?5.30 m. in the west. The southern gap or entrance is defined in addition by two post-holes (28 and 29) within the ring which narrow the access to 2.75 m. On account of erosion and later disturbance (e.g. Iron Age pit no. 186), seven posts were missing from the sequence between post-holes 7 and 8, 32 and 33, 37 and 38, 38 and 40 and 40 and 41, but an original total of 52 posts in the ring can be presumed. One post-hole (no. 27) should probably be regarded as a replacement for no. 26 at the southern entrance. The average spacing between the centre of each post-hole in the ring is 2.10 m., a distance which compares well with the average spacing for the separate arcs (NE 2.18 m.; SE 2.10 m.; SW 2.13 m. and NW 2.00 m.). The average diameter of the post-holes is 43 cm. and average depth 26 cm. Only two pipes were recorded, which had diameters of 35 cm. (post-hole 5) and 22 cm. (post-hole 19) respectively.

Ring B (post-hole nos. 51–60, 62–95)

This ring has over-all diameters of 29.50 m. from north to south and 30.80 m. from east to west. It is composed of four arcs, each originally of 12 post-holes, with radii of 15.20 m. (NE), 12.50 m. (SE),

15.20 m. (SW) and 11.30 m. (NW). These four arcs do not have a common centre, but those for the north-east and south-west arcs are the same as those for the corresponding arcs in Ring E, and that for the south-east arc is the same as for the corresponding arc in Ring A. The arcs are separated by four gaps of 3.00 m. in the north, 4.00 m. in the east, ?3.00 m. in the south and 4.50 m. in the west. Two post-holes were missing from the sequence between 57 and 58 and 72A and 73, but an original total of 48 posts in the ring can be presumed. The average spacing between the centres of each post-hole in the ring is 1.93 m. a distance which compares well with the average spacing for the separate arcs (NE 2.00 m., SE 1.90 m., SW 1.85 m. and NW 1.99 m.). The average diameter of the post-holes is 45 cm. and average depth 30 cm. No 'pipes' were seen in section or plan.

Ring C (post-hole nos. 96–131)

This ring has over-all diameters of 24.00 m. from north to south and 24.60 m. from east to west. It is composed of four arcs, each originally of nine post-holes, with radii of 12.80 m. (NE), 10.40 m. (SE), 12.10 m. (SW) and 10.20 m. (NW). The four arcs do not have a common centre but that for the south-west arc is the same as for the corresponding arc in Ring E and the north-east arc shares a common centre with the ring-ditch. The arcs are separated by four gaps of 3.00 m. in the north, 4.00 m. in the east, 3.20 m. in the south and 4.00 m. in the west. On account of erosion, one post-hole was missing from the sequence between post-holes 110 and 111 but an original total of 36 posts in the ring can be assumed. One post-hole (116) should probably be regarded as a replacement for 117, whilst 126A is clearly a replacement for 126. The average spacing between the centres of each post-hole in the ring is 1.98 m., a distance which compares well with the average spacing for the separate arcs (NE 2.00 m., SE 2.00 m., SW 1.97 m. and NW 1.95 m.). The average diameter of the post-holes was 44 cm. and average depth 29 cm. No 'pipes' were recorded in section or plan.

Ring D (post-hole nos. 132–55)

This ring has over-all diameters of 18.30 m. from north to south and 18.20 m. from west to east. It is composed of four arcs. each of which include six post-holes, with radii of 8.70 m. (NE), 7.60 m. (SE), 8.70 m. (SW) and 8.20 m. (NW). These four arcs do not have a common centre but that for the south-east arc is the same as that for the corresponding arc in Ring E. The arcs are separated by four gaps of 3.00 m. in the north, 3.50 m. in the east, 3.00 m. in the south and 3.70 m. in the west. No post-holes in the ring have been destroyed by erosion and no replacement posts were recorded. The average spacing between the centres of each post-hole is 2.21 m., a distance which compares well with the average spacing for the separate arcs (NE 2.18 m., SE 2.16 m., SW 2.26 m. and NW 2.26 m.). The average diameter of the post-holes was 48 cm. and average depth 34 cm. No 'pipes' were recorded in section or plan.

Ring E (post-hole nos. 156–72)

This ring has over-all diameter of 12.20 m. from north to south and 12.50 m. from east to west. It is composed of four arcs, each of which include four post-holes, with radii of 5.80 m. (NE), 5.10 m. (SE), 6.20 m. (SW) and 6.80 m. (NW). These four arcs do not have a common centre but those for the north-east and south-west arcs are the same as those for Ring B in those same arcs and that for the south-east arc is the same as that for the corresponding arc in Ring D. The arcs are separated by four gaps of 3.20 m. in the north, 3.30 m. in the east, 3.10 m. in the south and 3.50 m. in the west. The southern gap has at its centre a single post-hole (164) which it is difficult to see as an original feature. It may therefore have been a replacement post to assist in supporting the roof at its highest point. A second replacement post (165A) was sited next to post-hole 165. No posts were missing from the sequence and an original total of 16 posts in the ring can be assumed. The average spacing between the centres of each post-hole in the ring is 2.11 m., a distance which agrees well with the average spacing

2*

for the separate arcs of 2.10 m. (NE), 2.00 m. (SE), 2.20 m. (SW) and 2.16 m. (NW). The average diameter of the post-holes is 53 cm. and average depth 36 cm. No 'pipes' were recorded in section or plan.

Phase 2: The Stone Cove
(figs. 6, 8–13, 16–17; pls. IIIa–Va, VII, XIVb–XVIIIb)

The timber structure was replaced by a central setting of pits and sarsen monoliths, with similar pits or uprights outlying to the west, north and east, at a stage in the history of the site when the ditch was approximately one-third full of silt and a soil had formed over its contents. On top of this buried soil, whose molluscan fauna indicates a woodland environment, formed a pale loam which at various points in the ditch circuit contained at its base an extensive spread of ash and charcoal, fresh sarsen flakes, stone mauls, flint artifacts, animal bones and numerous sherds of Beaker pottery. Charcoal from this deposit provided a radiocarbon determination of 1680 ± 60 bc (BM-668). The sudden appearance in the ditch silts of such large quantities of knapped sarsen flakes is related to the erection of the stone monoliths within the ditch.

The central structure (fig. 16, pl. Va) is based around four pits set on the corners of a 6.00 m. square (173–6). The sockets for four sarsen uprights were recorded along the west, north and east sides of this square (177–9, 181). These contained numerous fresh sarsen flakes, indicating that the monoliths they originally supported had been broken up *in situ*. In socket 178 was found the actual stump of the original monolith. No such sockets were recorded along the southern side of the square and it has been assumed that this side had remained open with no stone uprights. Two shallow irregular pits (182 and 183) in the vicinity of the cove have been tentatively assigned to this phase.

Outlying the central structure are two pits (13 and 39) sited approximately on the line of the outer walls of the Phase I building; an imaginary line between these two pits bisects the east and west corridors into the latter. Some 1.70 m. east of Pit 39 were the sockets for two sarsen monoliths (190 and 191); no such sockets were recorded in the vicinity of Pit 13. North of the central setting, at a point between Rings A and B of the Phase I building and offset west from the centre of the northern corridor into that structure, was a single stone socket (184). The latter is not equidistant from Pits 13 and 39, nor does there appear to be any geometric significance in the siting of the outlying sarsen uprights and pits. The absence of an outlying monolith to the east in the vicinity of Pit 13 is an anomaly which may be resolved by an examination of the distribution of sarsen flakes within the ditch. These are concentrated in Segments IX, X and X alpha in the vicinity of stone-holes 190 and 191, in Segment XIII related to stone-hole 184 and in Segment IV. The latter is in the vicinity of Pit 13, and may indicate the former presence of a sarsen monolith outlier to the east, whose socket has been destroyed by erosion. The evidence, however, is circumstantial and serves to emphasize the dangers of attributing alignments to stone structures on the basis of their present appearance, even after excavation.

The central setting belongs to that class of structures referred to as 'coves' and will be discussed in a subsequent section of this report. Finds were few and confined to a series of 42 flakes of which 50% were recorded from stone-hole 191. The latter also produced sherds of Grooved Ware.

MOUNT PLEASANT
SITE IV : PHASE 2

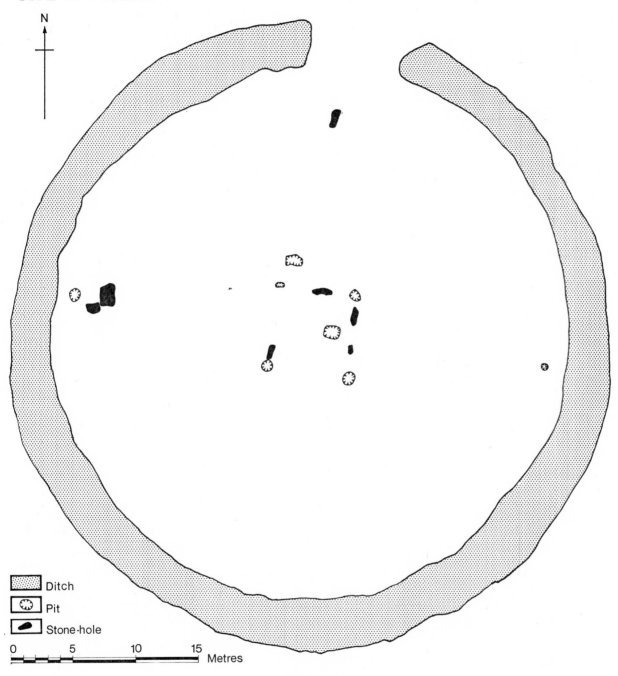

N

Ditch
Pit
Stone-hole

0 5 10 15
Metres

Fig. 16

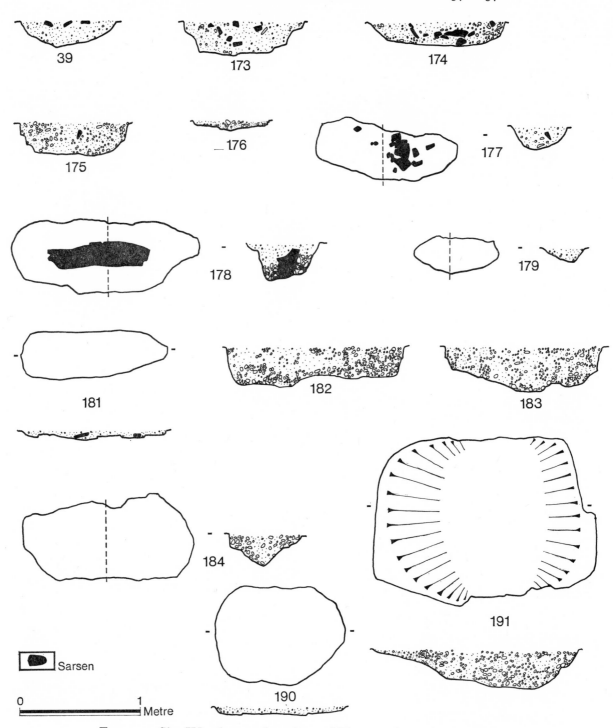

FIG. 17.   Site IV: plans and sections of Phase 2 pits and stone-holes

Large numbers of sarsen flakes were recorded from pits and stone-holes of Phase II and these have been summarized in Tables XVII and XVIII. The details of the features are as follows:

13 (fig. 14). A pit 55 cm. in diameter and 7 cm. deep containing fresh flakes of sarsen.

39 (fig. 17). An oval pit with a maximum diameter of 87 cm. and 20 cm. deep. A scattering of sarsen flakes was recorded from its surface.

173 (fig. 17; pl. XIV*b*). An oval pit with diameters of 1.10 m. and 92 cm. and 19 cm. deep. It contained numerous fresh sarsen flakes.

175 (fig. 17; pls. XVI*a* and *b*). A pit 89 cm. in diameter and 27 cm. deep which contained numerous fresh sarsen flakes.

176 (fig. 17; pl. XVII*a*). An oval pit with diameters of 63 and 44 cm. and 7 cm. deep. Sarsen chippings were found in the filling.

177 (fig. 17; pl. XVII*b*). A stone-hole with dimensions of 38 × 1.15 cm. and 18 cm. deep. A thick scattering of sarsen flakes was found in the top of the hole.

178 (fig. 17; pls. XVIII*a* and *b*). A stone-hole with dimensions of 1.55 × 60 cm. and 26 cm. deep. Beneath a layer of fresh sarsen flakes was the butt of a monolith *in situ*, 89 cm. long, 20 cm. broad and 20 cm. deep which was wedged around at its base with small chalk rubble. The top of the butt was faceted and scarred from the breaking up of the sarsen.

179 (fig. 17). A stone-hole with dimensions of 70 and 28 cm. and 11 cm. deep. The filling contained a few sarsen chippings.

181 (fig. 17). A stone-hole with dimensions of 1.20 × 37 cm. and depth of only 6 cm. The filling contained a few sarsen chippings.

182 (fig. 17). An irregular rectangular pit 1.47 m. × 43 cm. and 32 cm. deep. The pit is not closely dateable.

183 (fig. 17). A pit with a roughly rectangular plan 1.29 × 1.07 m. and 35 cm. deep. This feature is not closely dateable.

184 (fig. 17). A stone-hole with dimensions of 1.40 m. × 70 cm. and 24 cm. deep.

190 (fig. 17). A stone-hole with dimensions of 1.07 m. × 78 cm. and 5 cm. deep. The filling contained a number of sarsen chips.

191 (fig. 17). A stone-hole with dimensions of 1.82 × 1.25 m. and 30 cm. deep. The filling produced fresh flakes of sarsen and sherds of Grooved Ware.

The date of the destruction of the stone setting (and the large quantities of fresh sarsen flakes in the tops of the stone-holes indicate that destruction was deliberate) is hinted at by the presence of over 45 lb. of sarsen flakes from the later silts of the ditch in contexts which are likely to belong to the late first century B.C. It seems likely that the destruction occurred at this time, when the Iron Age settlement described below was founded, and when a hut was sited partially within the confines of the then silted ditch.

The Later Settlement
(figs. 18, 19)

The Iron Age aspects of the later settlement are represented by a gully (188) on average 50 cm. wide and 10 cm. deep (fig. 19), surrounding rather more than one-half of a circular building 11.00 m. in diameter. It seems uncertain as to whether the gully described a full circle in which case it may have held the timber uprights for a wall, or whether it was intended to drain the structure. Associated with it (fig. 18) are two post-holes (61 and 189) which presumably supported structural components related to the roofing arrangements. The gully cut through post-holes 62, 101, 105, 136 of the Phase I timber structure. Five body sherds in a hard, burnished, flint-gritted fabric is the only evidence to assign this hut to the Iron Age. It can be related to five pits (186, 192–4, 196), together with Pit B in Segment IV of the ditch. The details of these pits are as follows (fig. 19):

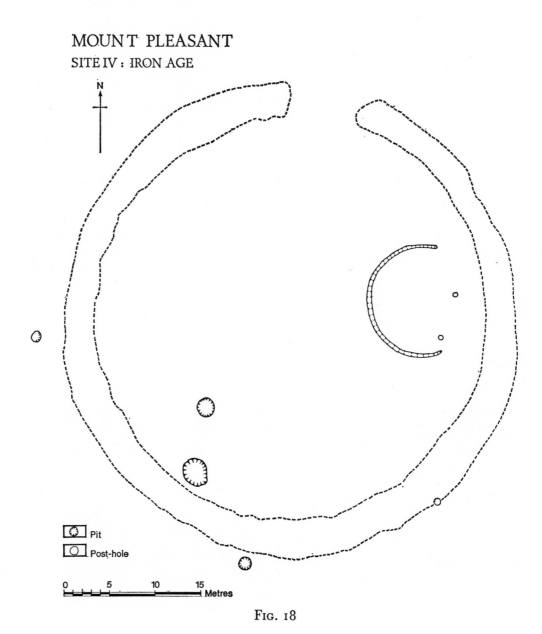

MOUNT PLEASANT
SITE IV : IRON AGE

N

☑ Pit
☐ Post-hole

0   5   10   15
                        Metres

Fig. 18

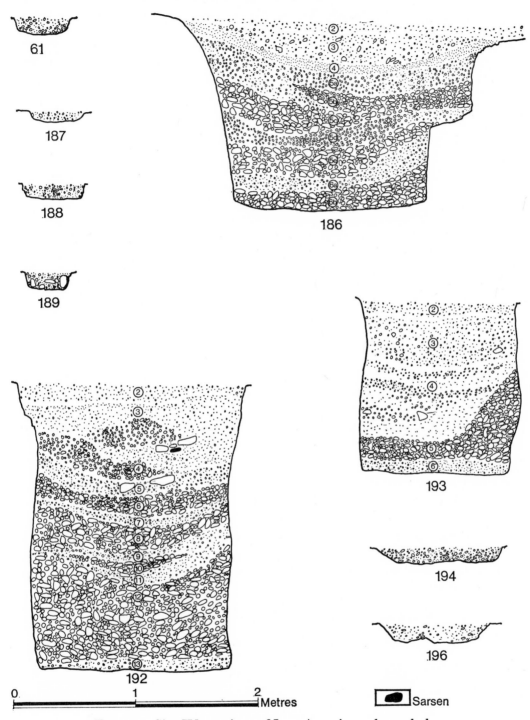

FIG. 19.   Site IV: sections of Iron Age pits and post-holes

186. A cylindrical pit with a ledge on one face, 2.60 m. wide and 1.50 m. deep, filled with alternate layers of chalk rubble and brown humic soil. A total of 16 small body sherds in a hard, black, burnished fabric was recorded from all layers.

192. A large cylindrical pit 1.85 m. in diameter and 2.30 m. deep, filled with layers of chalk rubble and brown humic soil. A total of eight small body sherds of Iron Age type was recorded from all layers.

193. A cylindrical pit 1.30 m. in diameter and 1.35 m. deep filled with small chalk rubble and brown humic soil. One body sherd only was recorded.

194. A shallow pit 1.05 m. in diameter and 10 cm. deep filled with brown loam and small chalk rubble.

196. A shallow pit 90 cm. in diameter and 13 cm. deep filled with brown loam and small chalk rubble.

Romano-British structures are represented by a gully (187) 45 cm. wide and only 7–8 cm. deep, which surrounded a rectangular area 12.00 m. wide from west to east and of unknown length, with a single entrance gap 1.50 m. wide in its south-east corner. The gully was clearly seen to cut across the ditch in Segment XI alpha but had been partially eroded along the east flank of the enclosure. The small quantity of pottery included the everted rim of a bowl in a hard, light-brown, sandy fabric whilst the most significant find is a coin, which if the association is genuine, dates the gully to the fourth century A.D. In addition, a quantity of sherds and other artifacts was recorded from superficial deposits (layers (2) and (3)) from the ditch and testifies to a presence in the late first century B.C. and early centuries A.D.

The latest structure on the site is the Saxon inhumation grave which was partially inserted into the Site IV ditch in Segment XI (fig. 6; pl. XXXIVb). The grave-pit, 1.70 m. long, 50 cm. wide and 20 cm. deep, contained an unaccompanied female adult skeleton with its head to the west. It was lined along its entire southern edge with large flint nodules and along its northern edge were two sarsens and two flint nodules in a broken line. A similar inhumation containing an iron knife and buckle was recorded from the west entrance into the main enclosure. Both graves have been described and discussed by Mr Schweiso in a separate section (p. 181).

III. THE EARTHWORK ENCLOSURE
(figs. 3, 20–28; pls. XIXa–XXIVb)

THE earthwork enclosure is of oval plan with over-all dimensions of 370 m. from west to east and 340 m. from north to south (fig. 20). Of the four entrances, two in the southeast and east can be seen on the ground whilst those in the west and north were discovered as a result of the geophysical survey. The positions of all entrances were checked by this means and the causeway widths between the ditch terminals are west, 5.00 m.; north, 40.00 m.; east, 30.00 m. and south-east, 20.00 m. The bank has been totally destroyed around the northern perimeter of the enclosure especially where the ground falls steeply towards the river Frome. Indeed, at the north entrance there is a strip rather less than 25.00 m. wide between the ditch and the railway cutting (fig. 3), where the ground falls away sharply at an incline of 1 in 4. The bank must have been built on this very steep slope and been very unstable unless there was an effective revetment. Furthermore, it is probable that the enclosure bank, or rather its original site, was truncated by the construction of the railway cutting.

For reasons which have been given in the introduction to this volume, excavations were undertaken at the west entrance in 1970 and at the north entrance in 1971. They have therefore been described in that order. The enclosure bank has been described in a preceding section on the pre-enclosure settlement and the following description therefore concerns itself solely with the ditch.

The West Entrance
(figs. 21–24; pls. XIXa–XXb)

Two cuttings were laid out to investigate a large area around the west entrance (fig. 21). Cutting I, 53.00 m. long and 4.00 m. wide, was designed to obtain a complete section across the ditch and bank. Cutting II, 31.00 m. long with a maximum width of 19.00 m., was designed to cover both terminals and the causeway between them. Cutting I was excavated by hand, whilst the plough-soil was removed from Cutting II by machine. Because of the eroded nature of the bank it was difficult to establish the original width of the berm. It appears, however, to average 15.00 m. wide.

From the plan (fig. 21) and photographs (pls. XIXa, b) it will be apparent that the ditch was extremely irregular and composed of a series of intersecting pits, interspersed with unexcavated spurs and ridges of natural chalk. No one section across the ditch can therefore be regarded as representative, although the sequence of deposits show a degree of consistency. They fall into three main groups (e.g. fig. 22; pl. XXa): a coarse chalk rubble at the base (layers (6) and (7)) overlain by a weathered horizon (layers (4) and (5)), which in turn is sealed by a thick aeolian sediment (layer (3)) and a plough-wash (layer (2)). The irregularity of the ditch can be demonstrated in detail by reference to the sections across its width (figs. 22–4). From a width of 13.50 m. at the southern face of the excavation (Section A), the south terminal of the ditch narrows to a slightly concave terminal nearly 8.00 m. wide. Section B across the ditch 8.00 m. from its terminal exhibits a rather more regular

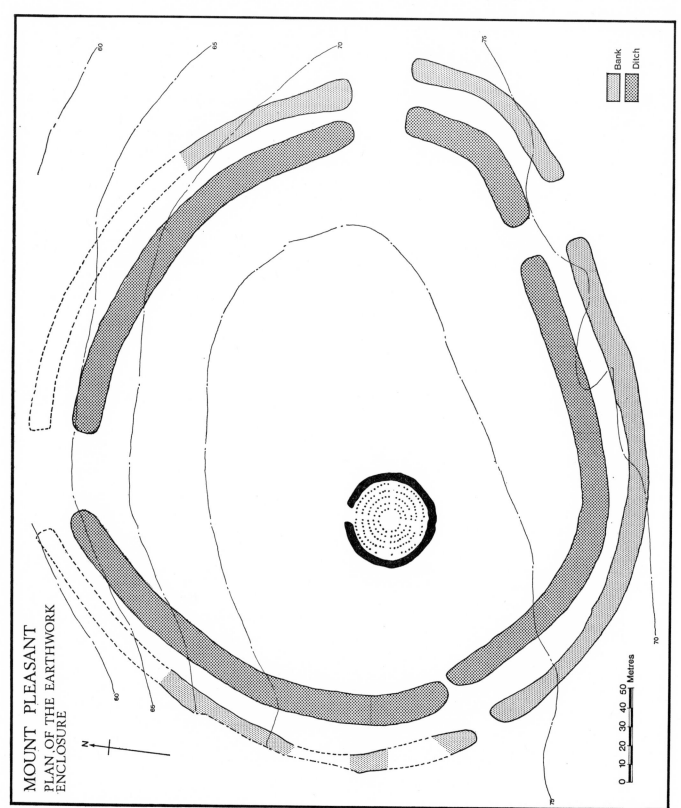

MOUNT PLEASANT

PLAN OF THE EARTHWORK
ENCLOSURE

Bank

Ditch

0 10 20 30 40 50 Metres

FIG. 20

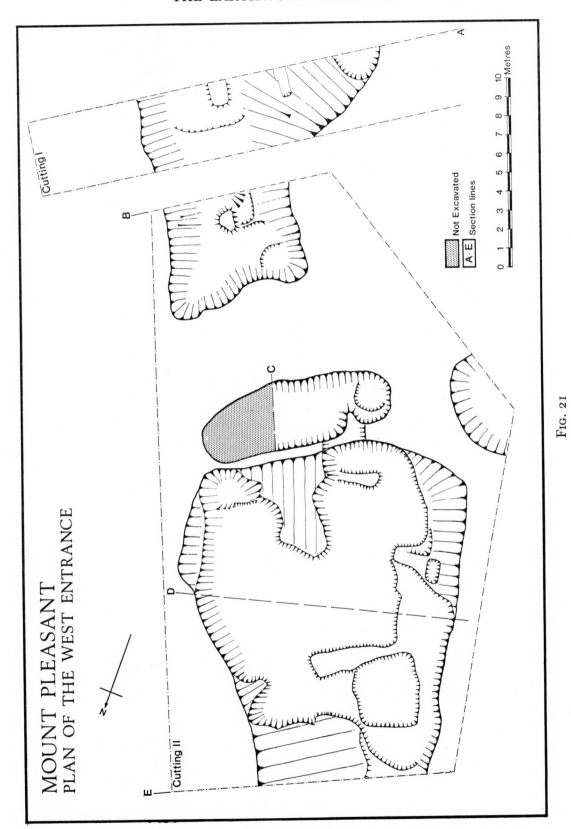

MOUNT PLEASANT
PLAN OF THE WEST ENTRANCE

Not Excavated
A-E   Section lines

0 1 2 3 4 5 6 7 8 9 10   Metres

FIG. 21

profile 7.00 m. wide from lip to lip with a flat, sloping base 4.00 m. wide and 3.20 m. deep from the modern ground surface. The causeway averages 5.00 m. wide and is flanked on the north by an elongated oval pit 10.50 m. long and 3.50 m. wide (identified in this report as the Ditch Terminal Pit). Section C across this feature (fig. 23; pls. XX*a* and *b*) showed that it possessed a classic profile, 3.70 m. wide and 2.00 m. deep, with a flat base 2.50 m. wide.

The north terminal was totally excavated for 17.50 cm. of its length. It is 14.50 m. wide at its terminal and narrows to 9.20 m. at the northern edge of the excavation. It is extremely irregular as is shown both by the plan and by Sections D and E (fig. 24). At the north end of the excavated area the ditch consisted only of a shallow terracing 1.50 m. deep and was clearly never finished at this point. An unexcavated ramp of chalk also occurs at its south terminal and the floor and sides of the ditch are scarred with such ridges and pits. In Section D, midway along the excavated area, the profile is at its most regular, being 14.00 m. wide and 2.70 m. deep with a relatively flat base and steeply sloping sides.

The detailed stratigraphy of the ditch deposits is as follows:

Primary Fill. Coarse angular chalk rubble underlain on occasion by a fine dirty silt (e.g. Sections C and D, layer (8)) which represents the very earliest silting. Two antler picks were selected for radiocarbon dating. They were obtained from the floor of the ditch on either side of the entrance causeway (pl. XX*b*). The antler from the south terminal provided a determination of 1784 ± 41 bc (BM-645) and that from the north terminal 1778 ± 59 bc (BM-646).

Buried Soil. A dark-brown chalky loam with a well-developed crumb structure and occasional bands of coarse chalk rubble (layers (4) and (5)).

Aeolian Material. A thick deposit of pale-brown very compact stone-free loam with occasional bands of chalk rubble (layer (3)). In the south terminal and ditch terminal pit Beaker sherds associated with a spread of charcoal were found at the base of this deposit. A sample of this charcoal from the ditch terminal pit provided a radiocarbon determination of 1460 ± 131 bc (BM-664). In Cutting II a darker horizon was visible within this deposit and may represent a period of stability when a soil was formed.

Plough-wash. A pale-brown chalky loam with numerous chalk lumps which increase towards its base (layer (2)). Within this deposit a number of finer divisions were recognized which are more appropriately described by Dr. Evans in Part III of this report. On the upper edges of the weathering cone of the ditch were a series of criss-cross plough-marks, which were related to similar plough-marks at the base of the plough-soil. Sherds of Romano-British pottery were recorded from this level and the formation of the plough-wash presumably dates from this time.

Modern Plough-soil. Pale grey loam with a few chalk pellets.

The deposits in the southern ditch terminal above the primary chalk rubble were sampled by Dr. Evans and the results have been described by him in Part III of this report. A total of 37 samples was taken from Sections A and B and analysed for land mollusca. In brief, the fauna from the buried soil horizon indicates a shaded environment with a high relative humidity which Dr. Evans argues appertained over the whole site. At this period it seems unlikely that the hill was subjected to either cultivation or grazing stock.

Near the surface of the deposit the fauna indicates some clearance and a decrease in wood-

MOUNT PLEASANT. WEST ENTRANCE

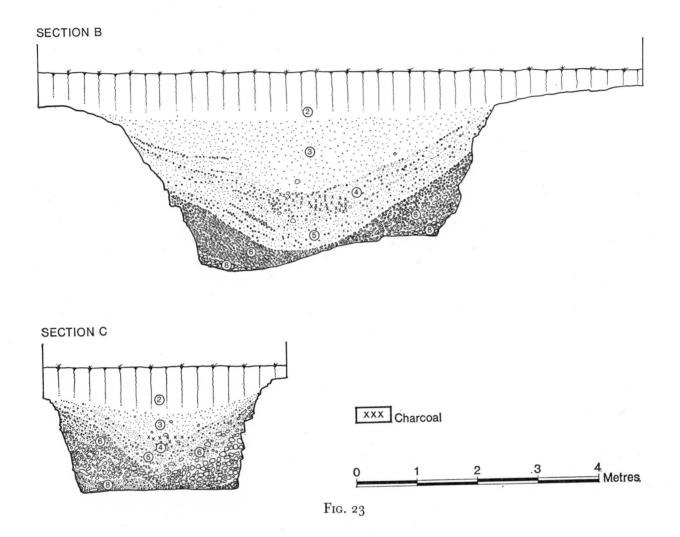

SECTION B

SECTION C

XXX Charcoal

0   1   2   .3   4
                                        Metres.

FIG. 23

land — a process which can be related to ditch sediments at the north entrance, where it is dated by radiocarbon to 1509 ± 53 bc (BM-789) and 1669 ± 55 bc (BM-790) and associated with Beaker sherds and Collared Vessels. The major clearance episode, however, is represented by a deposit of chalk scree sealing the weathered horizon and related to BM-664 (1460 ± 131 bc). Dr. Evans comments on the virtual total eclipse of woodland species and the domination of the fauna by a species which generally favours extremely dry habitats and a broken ground surface. The reasons for this are certainly anthropogenic and possibly due to ploughing. This clearance phase is followed by the aeolian deposit with an open country fauna separated into an upper and lower zone by a soil horizon. The plough-wash deposit is evident on account of its character and the presence of plough-marks but is confirmed by faunal changes typical of prehistoric and Roman cultivation horizons.

The most notable find from the north terminal of the ditch was a flanged bronze axe (fig. 24, Section D) which was recorded 10 cm. above the floor of the ditch and 1.80 m. from its east edge on the surface of a lens of chalk scree (layer (10)). Clearly it is important to establish the time which elapsed between the digging of this part of the ditch around 1800 bc and when the axe was deposited in its silting sequence.

Layer (10) is a component of a series of chalk and clay spills from the east edge of the ditch which at this point was dug through a large solution hole. These deposits (layers (4), (9), (10), (11) and (12)) clearly equate with layers (4), (5), (6) and (8) from the west face of the ditch, of which (6) and (8) are primary rubble. Layers (4) and (5), and possibly (9), represent the buried soil described above, which at the north entrance is associated with Beakers and Collared Vessels and is related to radiocarbon dates of 1509 ± 53 bc (BM-789) and 1669 ± 55 bc (BM-790). The axe occurs in the silting sequence at a point before the formation of this soil and after the digging of the ditch sometime around 1800 bc. The potential range for deposition is therefore between 1800 and 1500 bc in general terms, with the strong probability that it occurred in the century prior to 1500 bc.

Although 1570 flint artifacts were recorded from the deposits of the west entrance as a whole, very few were obtained from the primary rubble. These include flakes, cores, scrapers and one transverse arrowhead. A second transverse arrowhead was obtained from the buried soil but the bulk of the artifacts were recorded from the plough-wash and superficial deposits. The most notable stone artifact is an axe-roughout or chopper made from a chert nodule which was recorded in the buried soil. A single phallus and ball of chalk were recorded in close association from the floor of the ditch to the south of the causeway. Twelve antler picks were recorded, six from the floor of the ditch and six from the primary rubble. Some 110 fragments of animal bones were recorded from primary contexts in the ditch. The minimum numbers of individuals represented are pig (5), *bos* (2), sheep (1), horse (1), dog (1) and red deer (1). A little plain Neolithic bowl pottery was recorded in primary contexts and Grooved Ware from the secondary silts. From a hearth in the aeolian material in the ditch terminal pit came sherds of a Northern/Middle Rhine Beaker.

Two shallow parallel gullies were recorded to the north of the southern bank terminal aligned in a north–south direction (fig. 5). No finds were recorded and their date is unknown. In the same area (fig. 5, pl. XXXIVa) was a shallow grave-pit 2.03 m. broad, 90 cm. wide and 10 cm. deep which contained a single male adult skeleton with its head towards the west–south-west. A small iron knife lay on the pelvis and in its vicinity was a corroded iron buckle. This grave, together with that overlying the Site IV ditch, has been described by Mr. Schweiso in a subsequent section of this report (p. 181).

The North Entrance
(figs. 25–8; pls. XXIIa–XXIVb)

In 1970 both ditch terminals of the west entrance were excavated. Beaker sherds were recorded from the base of the secondary silts, but with the exception of a bronze axe and some stray sherds from the earlier silts the latter were rather sterile. As a result, it was decided in 1971 to investigate the north entrance into the main enclosure to augment the evidence obtained in 1970. A secondary purpose was to confirm the presence of the entrance which was invisible on the ground but which had been indicated by the geophysical survey as being some 40.00 m. wide. Cutting XXVII was therefore positioned to investigate the west terminal and Cutting XXVIII to locate the east terminal (fig. 3; pl. XXXI*a*). In both cuttings the lower silts produced a quantity of Beaker vessels, collared jars, flints and animal bones. Such an association of strata and finds was considered sufficiently rare to justify the excavation of two additional cuttings (XXIX and XXX), to supplement XXVIII at the east terminal.

The west terminal was investigated by a trench 10.00 m. long and 2.00 m. wide aligned west–east (Cutting XXVII). The chalk lip of the causeway was located at the extreme east edge of the cutting and the stratification was complicated by the presence of irregular ridges in the ditch floor (fig. 25). The average depth of the ditch below the modern ground surface

MOUNT PLEASANT NORTH ENTRANCE : CUTTING XXVII

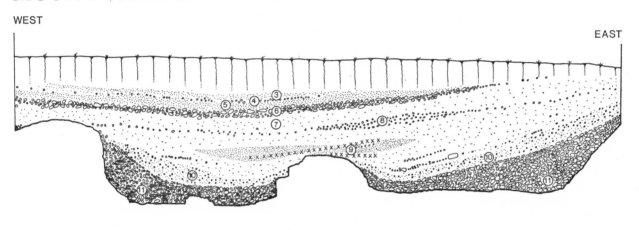

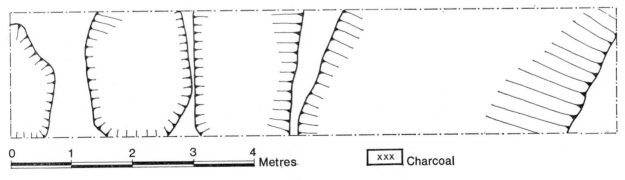

0   1   2   3   4 Metres.   ▢ xxx Charcoal

FIG. 25

was 2.00 m., although this was reduced to 60 cm. by a ridge of natural chalk at the east end of the cutting. The detailed stratigraphy of the ditch deposits in the west terminal is as follows:

Primary Fill. A coarse angular chalk rubble representing the earliest silting of the ditch (fig. 25, layer (11)).

Buried Soil. Thin layers of fine chalk rubble with an admixture of humic material (layer (10)) similar in character to the lower buried soil recorded at the west entrance.

Aeolian Material. A thick deposit of pale brown, very compact loam (layer (7)) with occasional bands of small chalk rubble (layer (8)). In the lower half of the deposit occurred a lens of dark brown silt mixed with comminuted charcoal and a little pellety chalk (layer (9)). This deposit produced animal bones, flint artifacts and sherds of Collared Vessels.

Plough-wash. A pale brown chalky loam with numerous chalk lumps which coalesce into a well-defined layer at its base (layer (6)). The latter is overlain by a soft, light brown soil which appears to represent a period of stability in the aggrading ditch deposits (layer (5)). It is separated by a single line of small chalk lumps (layer (4)) from a second soil horizon (layer (3)) which is a friable brown soil with very few chalk lumps.

Modern Plough-soil. A pale grey loam with a few chalk pellets.

A total of 292 flint artifacts was obtained, mostly from secondary contexts (layer (9)). Of these, ten were recognizable implements (eight scrapers and two blades with edge retouch). Other finds include a carved chalk disc (layer (10)) and bones of pig, *bos*, sheep, horse, dog and red deer. Eighteen fragments of an adult human skull were recorded from layer (10) which, when reconstructed, formed parts of the right and left parietal, occipital and frontal bones. Grooved Ware was recorded from the primary silts and a single Beaker sherd from layer (9). Grooved Ware was present throughout the ditch silts, sherds of Bronze Age fabric appear in layer (9) and include a Collared Vessel.

Three cuttings were sited to investigate the east ditch terminal. A trench 10.00 m. long and 2.00 m. wide (XXVIII) located the east edge of the causeway which proved to be 40.00 m. wide. As a result of the comparatively rich finds in this cutting the excavated area was expanded by the provision of Cutting XXIX (6.00 × 4.00 m. sited 1.00 m. south of Cutting XXVIII), and by Cutting XXX (5.00 × 7.50 m. sited 1.00 m. east of Cuttings XXVIII and XXIX) (fig. 26, pl. XXII*b*). Eventually, the balk between Cuttings XXVIII and XXIX was removed.

The plan, sections and photographs (fig. 26–8; pls. XXII*b*–XXIII*b*) indicate that the ditch is extremely irregular and comprises a series of broad, shallow bays between 2.20 and 2.70 m. deep. No complete section was obtained across the ditch at any point. The stratigraphy of the deposits in the three cuttings is entirely consistent and for purposes of detailed description has been dealt with as one sequence. The largest of the hollows in the floor of the ditch was sectioned by the balk between Cuttings XXVIII and XXIX. It was rectilinear in plan with over-all dimensions of 5.20 and 4.30 m. This hollow was partially surrounded by large stake-holes (fig. 26), some of which were dug through the primary chalk rubble into the bed-rock surrounding the hollow. Where these stake-holes occurred in section, it was apparent that some were cut from the base of layer (8) (*vide* fig. 27) and others from layer (10) and are therefore to be associated with the debris from these levels. Two infant burials found in the ditch silts were also dug from the base of layer (8).

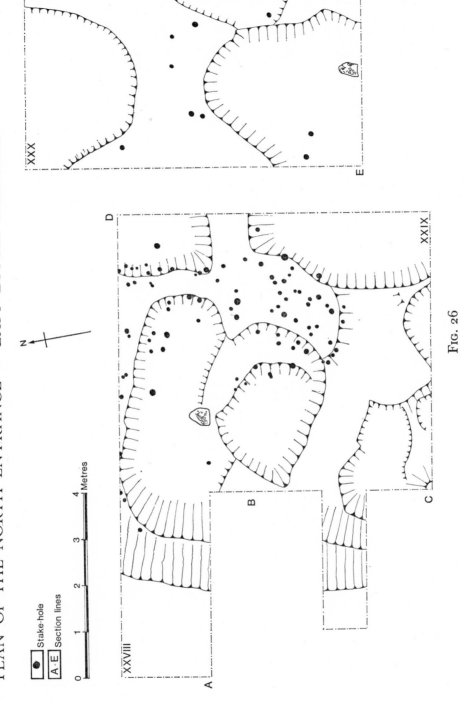

MOUNT PLEASANT
PLAN OF THE NORTH ENTRANCE : EAST DITCH TERMINAL

● Stake-hole
A - E Section lines

0 1 2 3 4 Metres

FIG. 26

It would appear that the hollows in the ditch floor provided shelter for several centuries when the ditch was slowly filling with silt, and these deposits (layers (10) and (6)) produced a quantity of stratified cultural material and a sequence of radiocarbon dates. The detailed stratigraphy of the deposits is as follows (figs. 27–8):

Primary Fill. Small to coarse angular chalk rubble (layer (11)), overlying a localized deposit of ash and dirty rubble (layer (12)) which represents the earliest silting of the ditch. Charcoal samples from layers (12) and (11) were submitted for radiocarbon dating. They produced determinations of 2098 ± 54 bc (BM-793) and 2108 ± 71 bc (BM-792) respectively. These dates are in good agreement and are older by some 200–300 years than those obtained from the floor of the ditch at the west entrance (BM-645, 646), which are also in good agreement with each other. It will have been noted that the north entrance causeway is some 40.00 m. wide whereas that at the west entrance is only 5.00 m. wide. Furthermore, the ditch terminals at the west entrance are in an extremely unfinished state —much more so than at the north entrance. Given that the radiocarbon determinations are valid, and the two groups from the west and north entrances are in good internal agreement, one can conclude that the ditch terminals at the west entrance were extended around 1800 bc, resulting in their unfinished appearance and the reduction of the entrance causeway to its present 5.00 m. The determinations from the north entrance therefore more accurately date the construction of the main enclosure ditch to the century before 2000 bc.

A total of 240 flint artifacts was recorded from layers (11) and (12) of which seven were scrapers. Chalk artifacts include scraped blocks and two fragments of a phallus which was broken in antiquity. Two antler picks were obtained from the floor of the ditch, whilst animal bones include the remains of pig, *bos* and red deer (321 fragments). Fragments of hazel nuts were recorded from layer (11). Grooved Ware occurred throughout the primary silts and Beaker pottery was not recorded in these contexts. Grooved Ware indeed is present in the ditch deposits up to the junction of layers (5) and (6).

Buried Soil. A fine brown soil interspersed with spills of small chalk rubble (layer (10)), which corresponds in its position and character to the lowermost buried soil in the silting sequence at the west entrance. However, it cannot be equated with the latter on account of the disparity of age — a charcoal sample from layer (10) produced a radiocarbon determination of 1941 ± 66 bc (BM-791) — and Dr. Evans would rather make the correlation between the lower buried soil at the west entrance and layers (7) and (8) described below.

Layer (10) sealed stake-holes and clearly the ditch terminal provided some shelter at this time. The chalk lumps became more numerous towards the top of this deposit (layer (9)) and in the bottoms of the hollows the lumps form a discrete layer.

The 773 flint artifacts recorded from layer (10) include scrapers, two transverse arrowheads and the blade of a polished axe. Other artifacts include a carved chalk disc and bones of pig, sheep and *bos*. Beaker pottery first appears alongside the Grooved Ware in layer (10) and continues throughout the sequence up to the junctions of layers (5) and (6).

Aeolian Material. Under this heading have been grouped layers (4)–(8) in ascending order as follows:

Layer (8): a friable ashy grey soil which is less compact than (7) and contains a larger number of small chalk lumps. A number of stake-holes and two infant burials were cut from the base of this layer.

Layer (7): a thick deposit of ashy grey soil which produced a quantity of pottery, stone tools and animal bones.

Layer (6): a compact, light brown loam which is probably in part aeolian material. It was, however, much thinner and less stone-free than the deposit at the west entrance. Samples of charcoal provided radiocarbon determinations from all three layers as follows:

Layer (8): 1669 ± 55 bc (BM-790).
Layer (7): 1509 ± 53 bc (BM-789).
Layer (6): 1556 ± 55 bc (BM-788).

Above layer (6) was a humic buried soil complex (layers (4) and (5)) consisting of alternate bands of stone-free loam and rubble, which is not present at the west entrance and which is regarded by Dr. Evans as being the equivalent to the main bulk of the aeolian deposit in those terminals. The principal basis for this equation is the similarity of the faunal sequence between the two deposits, which indicates mixed woodland and grassland in layer (5) followed by a clearance phase in which grassland species increase.

Two crouched infant burials were found in shallow pits cut from the base of layer (8) (figs. 26–7; pls. XXIVa, b). That from Cutting XXVIII is a possible female who was probably several months old at the time of her death. The skeleton was crouched with the skull towards the south-east. The burial from Cutting XXX was extremely fragmentary, but again the skeleton appears to have been crouched with the head towards the south-east. It was probably that of an infant under one year old. Associated with this burial was a fragment of a long-bone shaft from an older individual. A small piece of an adult parietal bone was recorded from layer (6) in Cutting XXIX.

Some 724 flint artifacts were recorded from layer (8), including nine scrapers and one blade with edge retouch.

Layer (7) produced 1830 flint artifacts including 22 scrapers, two blades with edge retouch, one transverse and one triangular arrowhead. Artifacts of bone and antler include

MOUNT PLEASANT, NORTH ENTRANCE (XXVIII) : SECTION A

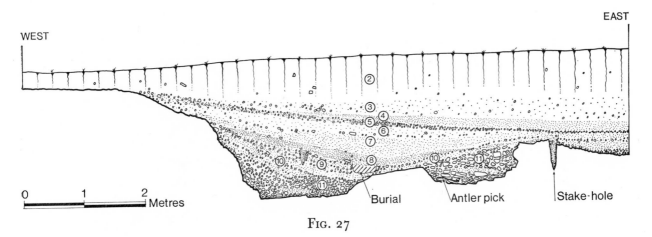

Fig. 27

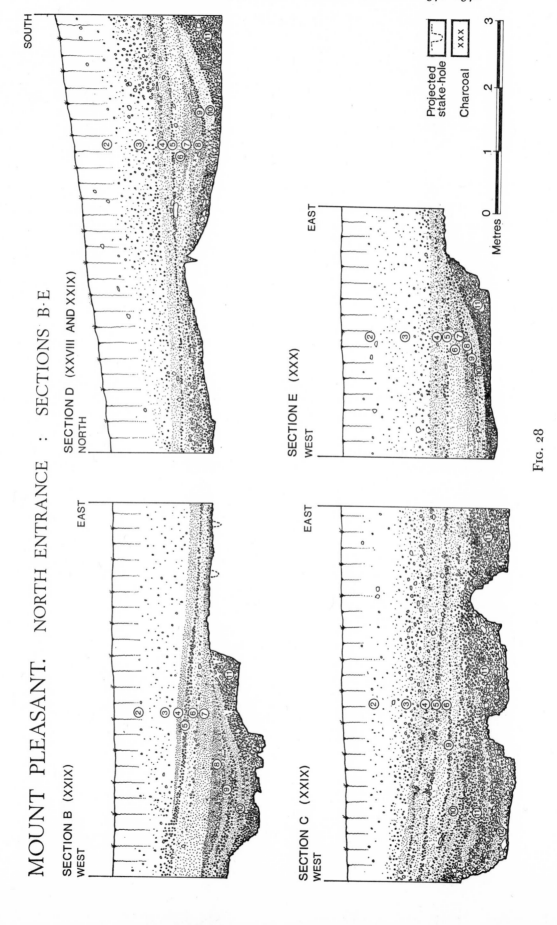

MOUNT PLEASANT.   NORTH ENTRANCE : SECTIONS B·E

SECTION B (XXIX)
WEST

SECTION C (XXIX)
WEST

SECTION D (XXVIII AND XXIX)
NORTH

SECTION E (XXX)
WEST

Projected stake-hole
Charcoal

FIG. 28

awls and pins, a cylindrical bone bead decorated with geometric patterns and a squared peg or fabricator of antler. An antler spatula was recorded from the junction of layers (6) and (7).

Layer (6) produced 1840 flint artifacts including 40 scrapers, one blade with edge retouch, one transverse arrowhead, two awls and one hammerstone. Bone artifacts are represented by a segmented bone toggle, whilst the fauna from layers (6) and (7) include pig, sheep, *bos*, goat and dog.

From layers (7) and (8) sherds of Bronze Age fabric begin to appear alongside the Grooved Ware and Beaker sherds and occur throughout the deposit to layers (3) and (4). Sherds of Food Vessel occur as early as layer (10) but are most numerous in layers (7) and (6) along-side the Collared Vessels. Bucket-shaped vessels are present in layer (4) and may appear in layer (6).

Flint artifacts are less numerous from layers (5) and (4) (345 and 646 artifacts respectively). A single bead-rim of Iron Age type in a thin, hard, burnished fabric was recorded from the top of layer (4) in Cutting XXIX. In layer (3), sherds of Iron Age fabric are more common and in the plough-soil were joined by sherds of seventeenth- and eighteenth-century A.D. date.

IV. THE PALISADE ENCLOSURE
(figs. 3, 5, 29–36; pls. XXV*a*–XXXIII*a*)

INITIAL tests in October 1969 prior to the main geophysical survey on the hill-top revealed what appeared to be a small ditch within and parallel to the main enclosure ditch. A subsequent proton magnetometer survey across the enclosure from west to east showed faint indications of this linear feature inside the main ditch, apparently parallel to it and continuous across the entrances. It was also located in a 30.00 m. square area surveyed within the southern entrance. The elucidation of this linear feature was one of the objectives of the 1970 excavations and to this end a length of it was stripped by machine east of the west entrance into the main enclosure (figs. 3, 5; Cutting III). In addition, subsidiary cuttings (V, VI, VII and VIII) were excavated to establish its plan around the south-west part of the hill. These excavations ascertained that the feature was in fact a palisade trench of variable width and upwards of 3.00 m. deep, which had supported large timber uprights set close together. From the plan which was established it seemed likely that this palisade trench surrounded a substantial part of the hill-top and the investigation of the remainder of its course was one of the main objectives in the 1971 season of excavations. Prior to and during the 1971 excavations, a survey using improved magnetic equipment traced the remainder of the circuit of the palisade trench.

As a result of this survey, a series of cuttings (XII–XXV; XXXIV–XLV) were set out around the perimeter of the palisade trench. The basis for the siting of each trench was the 1971 fluxgate gradiometer survey. Some uniformity was maintained by siting each 5.00 m. trench at 20.00 m. intervals and by aligning the long axis of each cutting along that of the palisade trench. It was not possible to maintain this uniformity at all times (fig. 3) but this lay-out established the plan and history of the enclosure with some degree of confidence. One practical problem was that even the improved magnetic techniques employed in the 1971 geophysical survey were not able to locate the positions of entrances across the trench. It was shown subsequently that the entrance gaps were so narrow that erosion had virtually destroyed any chalk causeway. By good fortune, a trench (XXXVI) which had been sited at the standard 20.00 m. from its neighbours located an east entrance through the palisade trench opposite the east entrance into the main enclosure. Subsequently, long stretches of the palisade trench were examined opposite the north and south entrances into the enclosure (that opposite the west entrance had been examined in 1970). A second entrance was located in the north (XVIII), but no such gap was recorded in the south. Quite clearly, the success of the whole operation was dependent on the reliability of the geophysical survey which enabled the initial trench pattern to be laid out with such accuracy.

The enclosure formed by the palisade trench occupied the highest point of the spur between the 72 and 69 m. contours. To the west and east the enclosure sits astride the spur and there is no natural slope up to its line. To the south, the ground falls away gently but steadily towards the South Winterbourne Valley, whilst to the north the ground falls steeply to the floodplain of the river Frome, presenting a formidable natural obstacle to scaling the

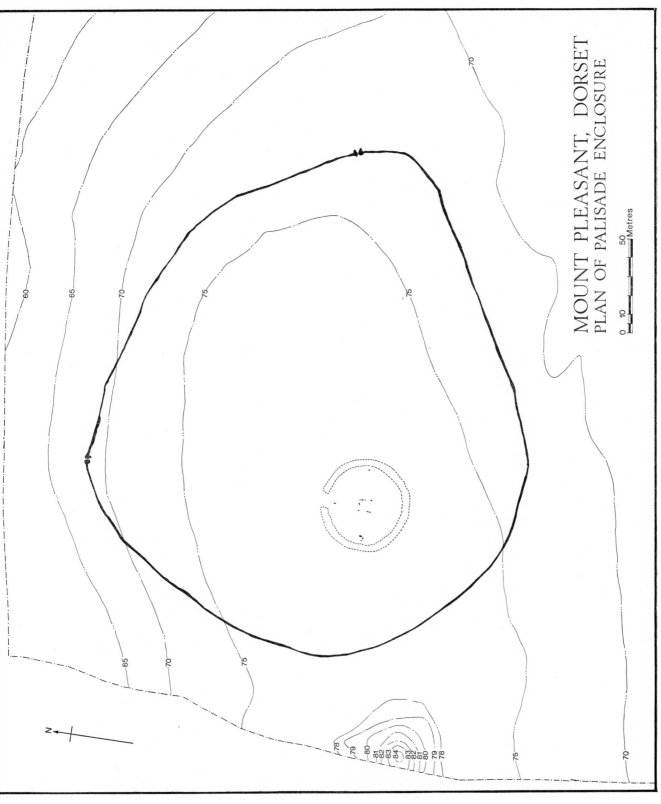

MOUNT PLEASANT, DORSET
PLAN OF PALISADE ENCLOSURE

Fig. 29

hill. The palisade therefore follows a line best suited for defensive purposes in that it takes advantage of the natural contours (figs. 3, 29).

A detailed description of the cuttings across the palisade trench has been provided below and only general comments are given here. The enclosure is illustrated (fig. 29) and consists of a foundation trench of variable width (normally 1.00–2.00 m.) and between 2.50 and 3.00 m. deep, enclosing an oval or egg-shaped area of some 11 acres, 270 m. from west to east and 245 m. from north to south. The line of the trench is consistently within that of the main enclosure ditch (fig. 3) and is breached by two entrances in the north and east opposite entrance causeways across the ditch. Of these entrances, only that in the east was fully investigated. These entrances were extremely narrow, and the gap between the flanking uprights at the east entrance could never have been more than 70 cm. wide. The east entrance was recorded in Cutting XXXVI which has been described in detail below (figs. 30–1; pls. XXXa–XXXIIIa). It is sufficient to record here that the entrance was flanked by two large post-holes with outward facing ramps. These pits held oak posts 1.65 and 1.50 m. in diameter which probably stood to a lesser height than the main wall. A similar northern entrance was recorded in plan in Cutting XVIII.

The normal profile of the palisade trench is straight-sided with a rounded base, the walls of which were frequently scarred with antler pick marks. Under suitable conditions, the 'pipes' or 'cores' of the decayed upright posts could be recognized both in plan and section. Almost invariably the technique had been to ram puddled chalk around the bases of the uprights to provide some stabilization and then to pitch chalk lumps around the posts, together with the occasional antler pick, up to ground level. When this packing was removed in spits the pipes of the decayed or burnt posts were revealed and could be planned. Almost invariably, when all the upper packing had been removed, the casts of post-butts were preserved in the hard puddled chalk packing at the base of the palisade trench. As a result of this preservation it has been possible to estimate that the trench had supported timber uprights of oak, between 30 and 50 cm. in diameter, set close together. The spacing of the posts in fact worked out at an average of two for every metre of trench. Therefore, in a palisade trench 800 m. long, approximately 1600 oak posts would have been employed. In addition, the palisade as excavated was between 2.50 and 3.00 m. deep. To this one must add the unknown amount of chalk surface lost through erosion since the palisade was erected c. 1700 bc and conclude that 3.00 m. is only a minimal estimate. If one assumes that one-third of the post-lengths were embedded in the ground (and this is a guess), then the stockade would have stood 6.00 m. high above ground level and c. 40 cm. thick. The posts would therefore have been 9.00 m. long. No evidence for internal supports for a wall-walk were found inside the line of the main stockade and one must assume that a parapet walk was morticed to the stockade and reached by means of a ladder.

Two radiocarbon determinations were obtained which can be related to the construction of the palisade. Both samples were obtained from Cutting III and produced dates of 1695 ± 43 bc (BM-665) for a charcoal sample and 1687 ± 63 bc (BM-662) from an antler pick. These determinations are in good agreement with each other and with that of 1680 ± 60 bc (BM-668) for the construction of the stone cove within the partially silted ditch of Site IV.

The majority of the associated finds were in a weathered condition and obtained from the

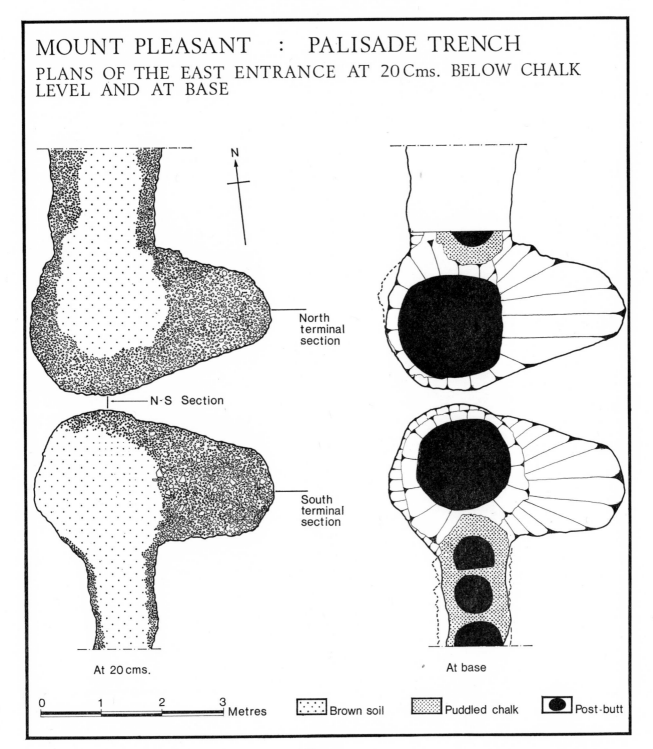

MOUNT PLEASANT : PALISADE TRENCH
PLANS OF THE EAST ENTRANCE AT 20 Cms. BELOW CHALK
LEVEL AND AT BASE

N

North
terminal
section

N·S Section

South
terminal
section

At 20 cms.

At base

0   1   2   3 Metres   Brown soil   Puddled chalk   Post-butt

FIG. 30

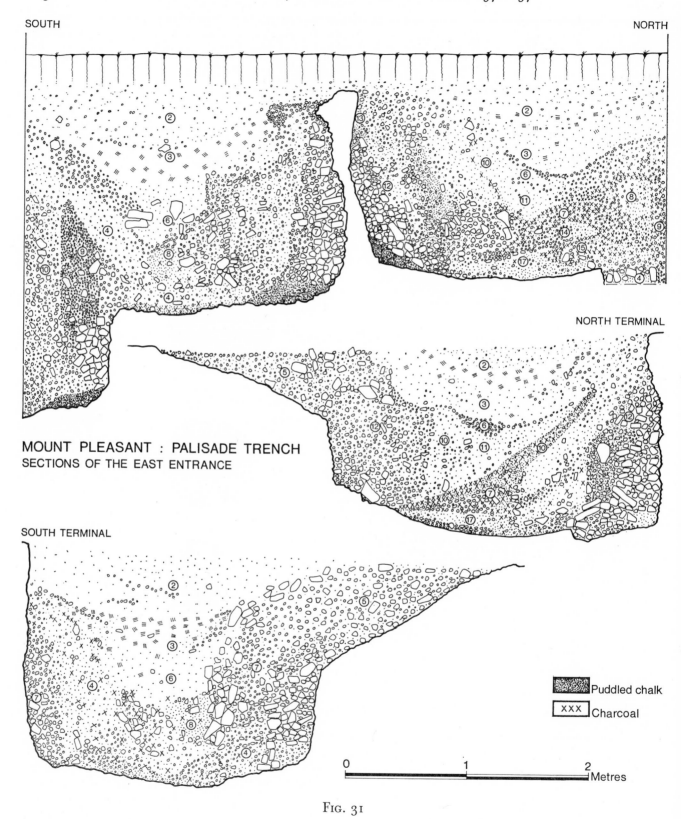

SOUTH

NORTH

NORTH TERMINAL

MOUNT PLEASANT : PALISADE TRENCH
SECTIONS OF THE EAST ENTRANCE

SOUTH TERMINAL

Puddled chalk
xxx Charcoal

0   1   2
Metres

Fig. 31

MOUNT PLEASANT : PALISADE TRENCH

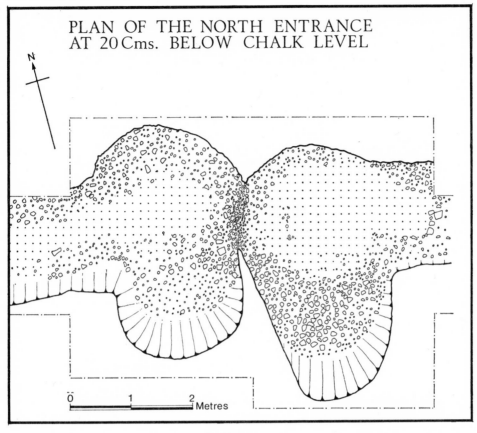

PLAN OF THE NORTH ENTRANCE
AT 20 Cms. BELOW CHALK LEVEL

0   1   2 Metres

FIG. 32

top of the palisade trench (layer (3)) where they had presumably accumulated when the palisade was standing. The pottery includes sherds of Iron Age and Romano-British type from the overlying plough-wash and green-glazed pottery of seventeenth- and eighteenth-century date. The flint artifacts include serrated flakes, blades with edge retouch, transverse arrowheads, fabricators, a polished axe, adzes and awls. The best 'closed' group was obtained from Cutting III, where over 1700 artifacts, including a large collection of scrapers, were obtained from a limited area. In addition to the polished flint axe and two adzes, one complete and one fragmentary greenstone axe were recorded. Carved chalk objects are common and include 30 balls, cylindrical objects of possible phallic significance, carved blocks and a bowl fragment. Some 38 antler picks were recorded from packing around the timber uprights, but bone artifacts were restricted to one pin. The faunal remains include pig, *bos*, sheep, dog, red deer, roe deer, fox and birds (song-thrush, missel-thrush and pintail). Of the identifiable sherds the majority are of Beaker and do not include the AOC vessels. The majority are Wessex/Middle Rhine, finger-pinched or finger-nail decorated or plain Beakers. Other vessel-types include Grooved Ware, Food Vessel forms, a little Peterborough

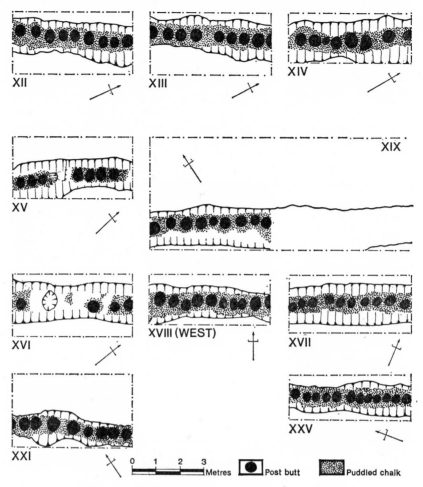

Fɪɢ. 33. Palisade trench: plans of post-butts

Ware and plain Neolithic bowl forms. The palisade trench was extensively sampled and Dr. Longworth points out that the ceramic content is likely to be significant. Therefore it is of interest to note the absence of AOC Beakers and Collared Vessels and the occurrence of the only Peterborough sherds found during the excavations.

The evidence indicates that some sectors of the palisade were destroyed by fire, in other parts the posts were removed (presumably for use elsewhere), and in other places the posts were left to decay *in situ*. The evidence for the destruction of the palisade by fire (Cuttings III, V, VI, VIII, XII, XIII, XVI, XVII, XXII, XXIV, XXV, XXXVI–XLI, XLIV, XLV) consists of spreads of ash and charcoal sealing the top of the trench. Occasionally, careful excavation revealed the actual burnt posts as concentrations of charcoal lumps. In some cuttings the conflagration had been so intense that the posts had smouldered and burnt throughout their length down to the base of the trench and were revealed as cores of ash and burnt chalk. In other cuttings, the posts had been deliberately dug out — presumably for

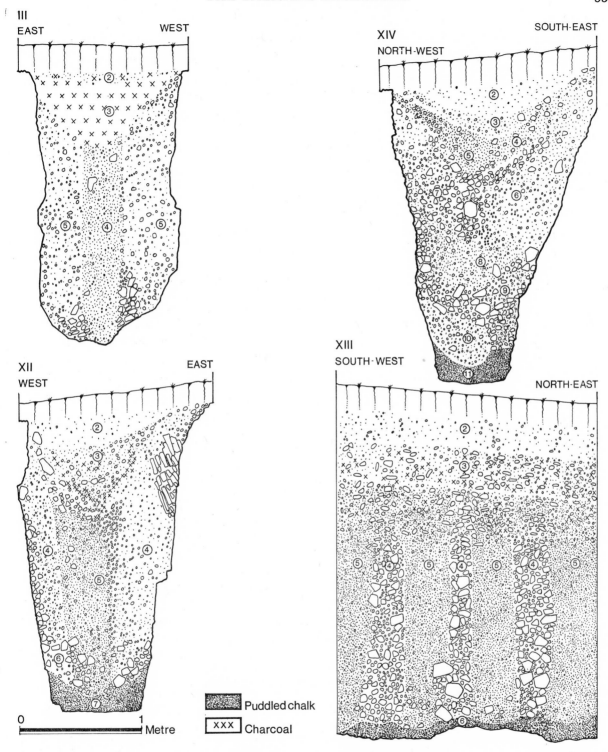

FIG. 34. Palisade trench: sections of cuttings

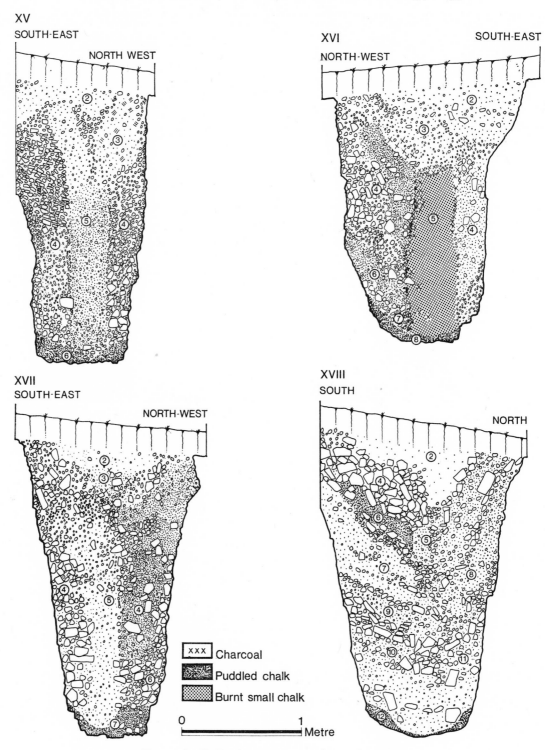

FIG. 35.   Palisade trench: sections of cuttings

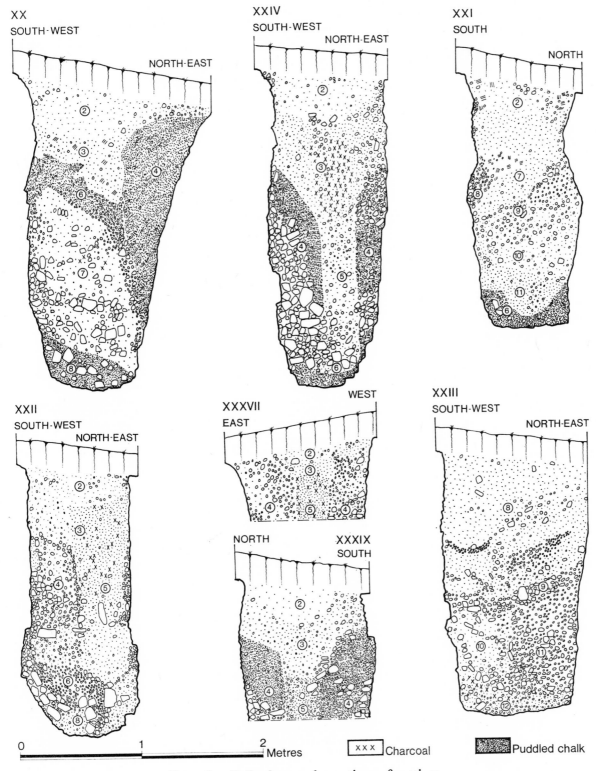

FIG. 36. Palisade trench: sections of cuttings

reuse elsewhere, as seasoned oak posts 9.00 m. long must have been valuable commodities. The evidence for this occurred mainly in the filling of the trench, where the packing material had been removed and then thrown back into the cavity along with other rubbish. The horizontal stratification of the deposits and lack of 'pipes' is evidence for such a process which is confirmed by the occurrence of pits and scoops in the walls of the trench which were produced by the removal of the posts.

In an attempt to obtain a date for this destruction some animal bone was submitted for radiocarbon dating from a refilled cavity in one such cutting (XVIII). However, the date of 2006 ± 45 bc (BM-794) suggests that the trench had been back-filled in part with rubbish from an earlier deposit. In one cutting (XXV) a junction between the burning and removal processes was identified, the timbers having been burnt at the southern end of the cutting and removed at the north end. Finally, in eight cuttings (XII, XV, XVII, XIX–XXI, XXXV and XLII) the posts had been left to decay *in situ*, the 'pipes' being clearly visible at a high level in the palisade trench. In four cuttings, junctions occurred between different processes, so that in Cuttings XII and XVII a transition from burning occurred, and in Cuttings XX and XXI, a transition from post removal. The available evidence does not allow one to ascertain whether the posts which decayed *in situ* were chopped off at ground level so that the stumps remained in the ground, but this must remain a theoretical possibility. In three cuttings (VII, XXIV and XLIII), it was not possible to establish which of the three processes appertained. This evidence for the destruction of the palisade by fire and withdrawal is discussed further in Part IV of this report.

To summarize, it would appear that around 1700 bc some 11 acres of the hill were surrounded in a massive palisade set in a foundation trench at least 3.00 m. deep. The posts of this palisade were of oak and averaged 40 cm. in diameter and a conservative estimate is that it stood 6.00 m. high. Access to this enclosure was by two narrow entrances in the north and east and the structure was ultimately destroyed at an unknown date by fire and dismantling.

Detailed Description of the Cuttings

Cutting III (figs. 5, 34; pls. XXV*b*, XXVI*a* and XXIX*a*)

A cutting with maximum dimensions of 33.00 × 12.00 m., sited to examine the palisade trench within the west entrance to the earthwork enclosure. The trench is of variable width within the cutting but averages 1.25 m. wide and 2.20 m. deep with straight sides and a rounded base. The 'pipes' or 'post-cores' were clearly visible in the packing material (layer (4)). They consisted of a loose humic fill with some small chalk and indicated an average diameter of some 36 cm. for the original timber uprights. The posts were in general set centrally to the foundation trench, the initial stabilization around their bases being provided by large chalk blocks which were probably dropped in from above, judging from the air spaces between them. As the structure was excavated, these blocks when left in place defined the original positions of the timber uprights and on this basis it is possible to calculate that one post occurs every 50 cm. (*vide* fig. 5 and pl. XXIX*a*). The majority of the packing material around the posts consists of hard, rammed puddled chalk (layer (5)) which extends almost up to ground level. Ultimately, the posts along a 15.00 m. length of palisade at the south end of the cutting were destroyed by fire. Evidence for this is represented by a thick deposit of ash and charcoal sealing the top of the palisade trench and by flecks of charcoal which occur in the upper part of the pipe material. This deposit of ash contained a quantity of Beaker sherds, flint artifacts and animal bones. Charcoal from it provided a radiocarbon determination of 1695 ± 43 bc (BM-665) which should relate to the construction of the palisade. This date is supported by a second radiocarbon determination from Cutting III, obtained from an antler pick which had presumably been employed in the excavation of the foundation trench and which had subsequently been utilized as packing material (pl. XXVIa). The date from this pick is 1687 ± 63 bc (BM-662) which agrees well with BM-665 and also with BM-668 from Site IV, which is related to the construction of the stone cove.

Shallow ditches which cross Cutting III at various angles (fig. 5) are undated but are assumed to belong to an agrarian ditch system of Iron Age or Romano-British date.

Cutting V (fig. 5)

A small trench 2.00 × 1.00 m. to confirm the course of the palisade trench. The latter was shown to be 11.0 m. wide and although only excavated to a depth of 30 cm. produced a quantity of charcoal which indicated that the timbers had been destroyed by fire.

Cutting VI (fig. 5)

A cutting 4.00 × 1.50 m. in which the palisade trench was shown to be 1.20 m. wide. It was excavated to a depth of 30 cm. where traces of ash and charcoal indicated that the timbers had probably been destroyed by fire.

Cutting VIII (fig. 6)

A cutting 9.00 × 3.00 m. in which the trench was shown to be 1.20 m. wide. The latter was excavated to a depth of 10 cm.

Cutting VIII

A cutting 10.00 × 2.00 m. in which the palisade trench was shown to be 1.20 m. wide. It was excavated to a depth of 30 cm. where traces of ash and charcoal indicated that the timbers had probably been destroyed by fire.

Cutting XII (figs. 33, 34; pls. XXVIb and XXIXb)

A cutting 2.50 m. wide and 5.00 m. long in which the palisade trench was recorded as being 1.50 m. wide and 2.55 m. deep at the north end of the cutting. It was 2.90 m. deep at the south end. The timber uprights in its northern part had been destroyed by fire — one post had been burnt down to its butt so that its pipe consisted entirely of very loose burnt small chalk mixed with a dark brown soil (layer (5)). Elsewhere, a great deal of ash had accumulated in the upper part of the palisade trench (layer (3)) and also occurred at a low level in the pipes where the posts had smouldered for a considerable part of their length. At the bottom of the palisade trench, all the post-butts were represented in the basal puddled chalk (layer (7), fig. 33, pl. XXIXb). These had an oval shape (a tendency noted in other cuttings) and averaged 35–45 cm. in diameter. Nine such post-butts were recorded. The packing consisted of puddled chalk and larger blocks (layer (4)), in which the outlines of the individual posts were visible at a high level.

Cutting XIII (figs. 33, 34)

A cutting 5.00 m. long and 2.50 m. wide in which the palisade trench was recorded as being 1.15 m. wide and 2.80 m. deep with vertical walls and a rounded base. The traces of eight to nine posts were recorded in the packing material at the base of the trench. In addition, the four posts in the south-west part of the cutting were sectioned longitudinally (fig. 34). Their diameters were fairly regular and ranged from 35 to 40 cm. The butt impressions of the posts were preserved in puddled chalk (layer (6)) but the packing between the posts consisted almost entirely of loosely set chalk blocks with many

3*

air-spaces (layer (4)) which passed into a more confused layer (3) at the top of the palisade trench. The presence of a single burnt post in the centre of the cutting and the percolation of charcoal and ash to a depth of 1.60 m. indicates that in this cutting the timber palisade had been at least partially destroyed by fire.

Cutting XIV (figs. 33, 34)

A cutting 5.00 m. long and 2.00 m. wide in which the palisade trench was recorded as being 2.60 m. deep but of irregular width between 1.40 and 1.70 m. No post-pipes were visible in any section across this cutting. In addition the filling of the palisade trench was variable, consisting of lenses of chalk lumps, deposits of brown soil and lumps of compacted puddled chalk, which had clearly been dumped into the trench and not placed as packing around the timber uprights (fig. 34). The dumps of material frequently formed swags extending across the trench, which resembled a ditch silting profile more than a palisade trench. It has therefore been concluded that the posts were dug out or otherwise removed — possibly for reuse elsewhere, hence the excessive width of the palisade trench in places and its variability. The packing material and soil derived from this process had then been thrown back into the trench. Nevertheless, the basal puddled chalk packing was preserved and a complete set of eight post-butts was recorded (fig. 33). These were of variable size ranging in diameter from 30 to 50 cm. × 60 cm.

Cutting XV (figs. 33, 35)

A cutting 5.00 m. long and 2.50 m. wide in which it was established that the palisade trench was in excess of 1.10 m. wide and between 2.33 and 2.40 m. deep. Seven post-butts were recorded in the basal puddled chalk packing at the bottom of the palisade trench and ranged from 30 to 45 cm. in diameter. The pipes were well preserved, the posts having been packed around with loose rubble and puddled chalk (layer (5)). There was no evidence for the burning of the posts or of their deliberate withdrawal. It therefore seems likely that they decayed *in situ* or were cut off close to ground level.

Cutting XVI (figs. 33, 35; pls. XXVII*a, b*)

A cutting 5.00 × 2.50 m. in which the palisade trench was recorded as being between 1.60 and 1.90 m. wide and 2.20 to 2.25 m. deep. All the posts in the cutting had been burnt and the evidence of a conflagration was very extensive. Illustrative of this is the post-pipe in the north section (fig. 35, pls. XXVII*a* and *b*) where the timber upright had burnt down to its butt. The sides of the pipe were lined with charcoal and burnt powdered chalk, whilst its fill was charcoal and small chips of loose burnt chalk (layer (5)). Elsewhere, the evidence was less dramatic but equally conclusive. Charcoal occurred in all the pipes from top to base and in certain parts it coalesced so as to resemble charred timber stumps. These occurred in the centre of the cutting where two charred stumps of timbers 40 cm. in diameter were traced from the base of layer (3) to a depth of 1.00 m. However, the evidence for butt-casts in the base of the palisade trench was not good and only four were recorded. The posts appear to have had a uniform diameter of 40 cm. and there seems to be no doubt that they were destroyed by a fire of such intensity that the posts smouldered throughout the depth of the palisade trench to their very butts.

Cutting XVII (figs. 33, 35; pls. XXVIII*a*, XXIX*c*)

A cutting 2.30 m. wide and 5.00 m. long in which the palisade trench was recorded as being 1.50 m. wide and between 2.25 and 2.50 m. deep, with steep, mostly vertical walls and a flat base. The complete butt-casts of ten posts were recorded in the puddled chalk at the bottom of the trench and their diameters were uniformly 40 cm. At the north-east end of the cutting the posts had been burnt to a depth of 110 cm. below the present chalk surface. The conflagration had, however, been confined to this part of the cutting. As usual, the timbers had been supported by rammed chalk blocks and puddled chalk (layer (4)).

Cutting XVIII (figs. 32, 33, 35; pls. XXVIII*b*, XXX*a*)

A cutting which was originally 5.00 m. long and 2.00 m. wide and which was later extended east for a distance of 19.50 m. to ascertain whether an entrance existed opposite to the north entrance into the main enclosure. The average width of the palisade trench in this cutting was 1.70 m. and at its east end it was 2.65 m. deep. Where it approached the entrance which was recorded in the extension it was only 1.05 m. wide and 2.50 m. deep. A complete set of nine to ten post-butts was recorded in the puddled chalk packing at the base of the palisade trench. Several were more oval than circular in plan and their diameters ranged from 40 to 50 cm. There was no indication that the posts had been burnt but considerable evidence that they had been removed for reuse elsewhere. All the original packing in the palisade trench down to the puddled chalk at its base had been removed and the derived material thrown back into the trench (*vide* fig. 35, layers (4)–(11)). The upper deposits (layers (3)–(6)) contained a quantity of artifacts and animal bones. A selection of the latter was submitted for radiocarbon assay with the resultant determination of 2006 ± 45 bc (BM-794). This date is earlier by some three centuries than the more reliably associated samples (BM-662, 665) from Cutting III, and it must be assumed that an earlier deposit was disturbed when the palisade trench was back-filled and that some of this material was incorporated in the filling.

An entrance across the palisade trench occurred in the extension to the cutting (fig. 32, pl. XXX*a*). It comprised two large post-holes 2.60 m. in diameter flanking a narrow gap in the palisade trench. These were approached by ramps 1.50 and 2.00 m. long from the inner or uphill side. These post-holes and the adjacent lengths of palisade trench were only excavated to a depth of 20 cm. below natural chalk, so that the packing and tops of the weathering cones were exposed. The spine of natural chalk between the post-holes had broken down into an irregular ridge as a result of collapse into the weathering cones and it is clear that the original entrance must have been very narrow.

Cutting XIX (fig. 33)

A cutting 12.00 m. long and 4.50 m. wide in which the palisade trench was recorded as being of variable width but averaging 1.50 m. wide and 2.60 m. deep. In this cutting the upright timbers appear to have decayed *in situ*. There was no evidence of burning and no indication that the posts had been withdrawn. Where it was fully excavated, the butts of nine posts were recorded in the hard packing at the base of the trench. As usual, these posts were closely set and had an average diameter of 45 cm. The alignment of posts was not central but ran along the northern edge of the palisade trench.

Cutting XX (fig. 36)

A cutting 4.85 m. long and 4.50 m. broad in which the palisade trench was recorded as being 1.45 m. wide and 2.58 m. deep. The picture was confused because of the presence of a hollow which was itself undated but which post-dated the palisade trench. The events concerning the palisade trench are also complicated, as the indications are that at the north-west end of the palisade trench the posts were removed, whereas at the south-east end the posts rotted *in situ*. At the north-west end of the cutting, no pipes were seen in section or plan and the filling consists in the main of a soft brown soil with chalk lumps (layers (3), (6) and (7)) which produced a great quantity of animal bone. The residual packing of rammed small-chalk (layer (4)) does retain a vertical edge, but the filling is consistent with the posts having been removed, the resultant cavity having been filled with rubbish. Four post-butts were, however, preserved in the basal puddled chalk at the north-west end of the trench. Their average diameter was 35 cm.

At the south-east end of the cutting the central pipes were preserved, four post-cores being recorded in the filling of the trench. The posts were on average 35 cm. in diameter and had been packed around in the usual way with compacted chalk lumps. No trace of burning was recorded and the posts appear to have decayed *in situ*.

Cutting XXI (figs. 33, 36; pl. XXVIII*c*)

A cutting 5.00 m. long and 3.00 m. wide in which the palisade trench was recorded as being of variable width (85 cm.–1.10 m.) and as possessing an uneven floor 1.60–2.00 m. below the modern turf-line. A complete series of eight to nine casts of post-butts was recorded in the basal packing of the palisade trench and averaged 45–50 cm. in diameter. There was no evidence for burning in this cutting and a well-preserved pipe in the east section indicates that the posts at that end had decayed *in situ*. This situation altered midway along the cutting so that the west section (fig. 36) could be interpreted in the light of the posts having been removed. The filling consisted of brown soil and nearly horizontally bedded layers of small chalk rubble (layers (7)–(11)) which contained some animal bones and artifacts. This deposit clearly represents possible domestic rubbish obtained from some unlocated site, which was thrown into the cavity produced by the post-robbing. On the south edge of the palisade trench a semi-circular hollow may represent attempts to remove posts or a post at that point.

Cutting XXII (fig. 36)

A cutting 5.00 m. long and 2.00 m. wide in which the palisade trench varied from 1.25 m. wide and 2.50 m. deep at the south-east end of the cutting, to 85 cm. wide and 2.30 m. deep at the north-west end. Only five to six butt-casts were recorded in the bottom of the palisade trench and ranged in diameter from 35 cm. to 45 cm. Evidence for the burning of the timbers was recorded throughout the cutting and charcoal had percolated to depths of 1.25 m. In section, the pipes were clearly defined — that in the north-west section being particularly noteworthy (fig. 36), as it shows the butt of that particular timber lodged in the packing some 37 cm. above the floor of the trench.

Cutting XXIII (fig. 36)

A cutting 5.00 m. long and 2.00 m. wide in which the width of the palisade trench was extremely irregular. In the centre of the cutting the average width was 1.25–1.30 m. and depth 2.10–2.25 m. The posts throughout the length of this cutting had been removed and the cavity back-filled with the old packing material and any other soil and rubbish that had come to hand. These deposits have a more or less horizontal stratification, they were mixed with a great deal of soil and the chalk blocks are weathered. Only one butt-cast was recorded in the puddled chalk in the bottom of the trench as the remainder had been removed when the posts were dug out. The irregular width of the trench, particularly at the ends of the cutting, may well result from the excavations that must have been necessary to get at the posts.

Cutting XXIV (fig. 36)

A cutting 5.00 m. long and 2.00 m. wide in which the palisade trench was recorded as from 1.00 to 1.15 m. wide and 2.68 m. deep. A total of eight to nine posts was recorded in plan in the cutting with an average diameter of 30 cm. However, the usual butt-casts were not present. At the north-west end of the cutting an extensive deposit of ash and charcoal was recorded which extended into several pipes and it is clear that in this cutting the timber uprights had been destroyed by fire.

Cutting XXV (fig. 33)

A cutting 5.00 m. long and 2.00 m. wide in which the palisade trench was recorded as 1.08 m. wide and 2.60 m. deep. A series of well preserved butt-casts was recorded at the base of the palisade trench in the puddled chalk packing. They were noticeably smaller than elsewhere in the circuit and 11–12 posts were recorded. The butt-casts were noticeably oval in plan, the largest being 50 × 30 cm. in diameter, but there was considerable variation in size. At the south end of the cutting there was evidence that the posts had been burnt, but at its north end the posts had clearly been removed and the cavity back-filled with rubble (layer (7)) overlying lenses of compacted chalk (layer (8)), soil and dirty chalk (layers (9)–(11)).

Cutting XXXIV

A cutting 5.00 m. long and 2.50 m. wide in which the palisade trench was of irregular width, varying from 1.12 to 2.00 m. at the north end of the cutting. The deposits had been disturbed by rabbits and badgers for their entire length and the excavation was therefore abandoned at a depth of 90 cm.

Cutting XXXV

A cutting 5.00 m. long and 2.50 m. wide, excavated to a depth of 1.15 m. within which the palisade trench averaged 1.00 m. wide. There was no evidence of burning or withdrawal and the posts appear to have rotted *in situ*.

Cutting XXXVI: The East Entrance (figs. 30, 31; pls. XXXa–XXXIIIa)

This cutting was initially laid out at the standard 5.00 m. from its adjacent trenches and measured 5.00 m. long by 2.00 m. wide. It was later expanded to cover an area 6.00 × 13.00 m. because an entrance into the palisade enclosure occurred at that point. The entrance consisted of two ramped post-holes flanking a narrow gap in the trench. For recording purposes, the post-holes and ramps were divided into quadrants which were so excavated as to provide two sections across each post-hole, one of which included the ramp. The entrance was sited on the axis of the ridge leading into the site from the east and the ramps for the post-holes were aligned to the east away from the enclosure. These ramps were 2.00 m. long and when their use was at an end had been filled with hard-packed chalk rubble (layer (5)). The palisade trench to the north of the entrance was 1.80 m. wide and excavated to a depth of 1.80 m. To the south of the entrance the trench was 85 cm. wide and 2.90 m. deep and tended to broaden towards its base. Three post-pipes were recorded in a length of palisade trench 2.10 m. long. These were respectively 80, 63 and 64 cm. in diameter, that nearest the entrance terminal being semi-circular in plan. The terminal post-holes were massive, the northern being 1.85 m. in diameter and 1.80 m. deep, the southern post-hole being 2.30 m. in diameter and 2.00 m. deep. They had supported massive oak posts — the northern 1.65 m. diameter and the southern 1.50 m. diameter — which were packed around with chalk rubble (layers (7) and (12)) and which had been destroyed by fire.

Great quantities of ash and charcoal were found in the pipes of the entrance post-holes and in the pipes of the adjacent uprights, indicating that the entrance posts had smouldered throughout their length. The entrance post-holes were more shallow than the palisade trench proper and it has therefore been assumed that the posts, although massive in diameter, stood to a lesser height than the main wall. The spine of chalk surviving between the entrance post-holes is only 20 cm. wide and there is no clear evidence of erosion from the post-hole edges. The original entrance gap must presumably be measured between the inner edges of the actual posts and this exercise suggests that the original entrance gap was only 70 cm. wide.

Cutting XXXVII (fig. 36)

A cutting 5.00 m. long and 2.50 m. wide in which the palisade trench averaged 1.00 m. wide. It was excavated to a depth of 80 cm. The posts had been burnt throughout the length of the cutting and at the limit of excavation could be identified as a row of individual timbers.

Cutting XXXVIII

A cutting 5.00 m. long and 3.50 m. wide excavated to a depth of 1.00 m. in which the palisade trench averaged between 1.00 and 1.20 m. wide. Extensive deposits of ash and charcoal indicated that the posts in this cutting had been burnt.

Cutting XXXIX (fig. 36)

A cutting 5.00 m. long and 2.50 m. wide excavated to a depth of 1.25 m. in which the palisade trench averaged 1.00 m. wide. Deposits of ash and charcoal indicated that the posts had been burnt. The pipes of the latter were well preserved and averaged 30 cm. in diameter. Subsequently, the cutting was extended west for a distance of 30.00 m. so as to link up with Cutting XL. The palisade trench was continuous and no gap was present opposite the south-east entrance into the earthwork enclosure.

Cutting XL

A cutting 5.00 m. long and 3.50 m. wide excavated to a depth of 85 cm. in which the palisade trench was 2.30 m. wide. The subsoil in this area was an orange sandy clay with occasional patches of chalk in which it was very difficult to define the edges of the trench. However, the posts in the cutting had been burnt so that the line of the palisade could be traced as a spread of charcoal in the clay. The pipes identified in plan averaged 35–38 cm. in diameter.

Cutting XLI

A staggered cutting 10.00 m. long and 2.00 m. wide in an area where the palisade trench had been dug into a mixture of coarse grey sand and orange brown clay. A slit trench 1.00 m. wide was excavated to the base of the palisade trench at the west end of the cutting. In this the trench was 2.73 m. deep and at its lip was in excess of 2.00 m. wide. However, at a depth of 1.50 m. the walls of the palisade trench were better preserved and it was possible to establish an original width of 1.70 m. A post-butt was recorded in the basal sand which had been packed around with orange brown clay. The upright had been some 40 cm. in diameter and was charred throughout its length. Evidence from elsewhere in the cutting indicated that the other timbers had also been destroyed by fire.

Cutting XLII

A cutting 5.00 m. long and 2.00 m. wide which was excavated to a depth of 50 cm. and in which the palisade trench was recorded as approximately 1.60 m. wide. There was no trace of burning and the top of a single pipe was recorded in the west section. It seems possible therefore that the posts in this cutting had been allowed to decay *in situ*.

Cutting XLIII

A cutting 5.00 m. long and 2.00 m. wide which was excavated to a depth of 50 cm. and in which the palisade trench was recorded as approximately 1.30 m. wide. There was no trace of burning and no indication as to the ultimate fate of the timbers.

Cutting XLIV

A cutting 5.00 m. long and 2.00 m. wide, excavated to a depth of 50 cm., in which the width of the palisade trench varied between 80 cm. and 1.10 m. Extensive deposits of ash and charcoal were recorded in the cutting and it seems likely that the timbers were destroyed by fire.

Cutting XLV

A cutting 5.00 m. long and 2.00 m. wide, excavated to a depth of 50 cm., in which the palisade trench was recorded as being 1.50 m. wide. The presence of ash and charcoal indicates that the timbers were destroyed by fire in this sector.

V. THE CONQUER BARROW
(figs. 37, 38; pl. XXXIII*b*)

THE Conquer Barrow is a large mound built on top of the enclosure bank in its west sector. The barrow is covered by a coppice of trees and there is no record of its having been excavated, although its summit has been much disturbed by modern rubbish pits and the rear gardens of certain houses in Came View have encroached on the western edge of the mound and utilized its slopes as rock gardens. The base of this mound is now much spread but it is still 30.00 m. in diameter and stands 3.00–4.00 m. high above a linear earthwork which is 8.00 m. wide and 4.00 m. high (fig. 37). This earthwork is interpreted as a surviving remnant of the enclosure bank which was constructed at or rather before 2000 bc, although an extension of the ditch at the west entrance in 1800 bc may also have contributed material to it.

During the 1970 excavation of the west entrance into the enclosure (Cutting II), the terminal of a ditch was recorded. In 1971, a series of trenches were excavated (XLVI–LI; figs. 3, 37) to ascertain the character and plan of this ditch, which it was thought might be related to the Conquer Barrow. As a result of these investigations this ditch has in fact been interpreted as that of the Conquer Barrow.

The ditch terminal recorded in Cutting II terminated 2.00 m. south-west of the main enclosure ditch. Augering determined the positions of Cuttings XLVI–LI which are described in detail below. Around the southern and south-eastern perimeter of the Conquer Barrow the ditch was broad and flat-bottomed, 7.00–8.20 m. wide and 2.70 m. deep with steep vertical walls (fig. 38). It was broken by a causeway 6.30 m. wide and continues out of the field into private gardens to the west. The course of the ditch to the north of the barrow mound is less well established but it is thought that its inner edge has been located in Cuttings L and LI (fig. 38) and that it runs out of the field to the west under the modern hedgerow. The suggested plan is therefore that of a barrow mound 4.00 m. high and 30.00 m. in diameter sitting on a remnant of the enclosure bank which is itself 4.00 m. high. It was surrounded to the north and east by a pennanular ditch, the terminals of which stopped short of the main enclosure ditch and which was broken by at least one causeway in the south-east.

An antler pick from the primary rubble of the ditch in Cutting XLVI produced a radiocarbon determination of 2127 $\pm$ 52 bc (BM-795). This date has been discussed in detail below where it has been concluded that the pick must have been derived from an earlier context — probably an adjacent pre-enclosure settlement. Finds from the ditch were very sparse and confined to 306 flint artifacts, including two scrapers and one blade with flat edge retouch. Fragments of bone include pig and *bos* and Iron Age sherds were recorded from the plough-soil. A Beaker sherd was recorded from Cutting XLVI layer (4) and a sherd of Bronze Age fabric from layer (8).

Cutting XLVI (fig. 38, pl. XXXIII*b*)

A cutting 9.00 m. long and 2.00 m. wide to section the ditch which at that point was 7.00 m. wide

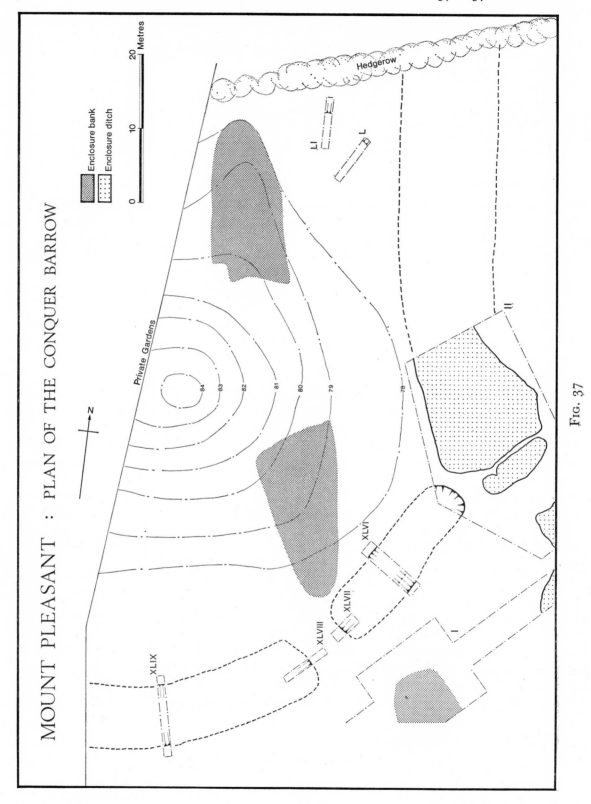

MOUNT PLEASANT : PLAN OF THE CONQUER BARROW

Fig. 37

MOUNT PLEASANT : CONQUER BARROW DITCH

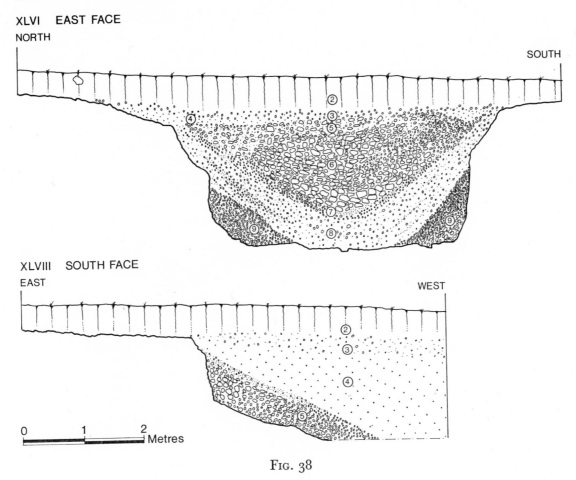

FIG. 38

and 2.70 m. deep with steep sides and a broad, flat base. The basal silt consisted of coarse chalk rubble (layer (9)) overlain by finer chalk silt and bands of small chalk mixed with dark humic material (layer (8)). These early silts were sealed by a buried soil represented by a buff loam containing many very small chalk lumps (layer (7)) which in turn was sealed by a mass of clean angular chalk blocks with many air spaces. An antler pick from the primary rubble produced a radiocarbon determination of 2127 ± 52 bc (BM-795). As the barrow demonstrably post-dates the enclosure bank, which in this sector was probably added to around 1800 bc, the sample pick must be derived from an earlier context. This context may well be the pre-enclosure settlement, which from an area 18.00 m. south of XLVI produced sherds of plain neolithic bowls and charcoal, the latter providing a radiocarbon date of 2122 ± 73 bc (BM-644). Traces of this settlement beneath the enclosure bank may well have been disturbed when the ditch was dug and some materials incorporated in its basal deposits. The mass of chalk blocks filling the upper part of the ditch probably represents a levelling of the enclosure bank at some time in the second half of the second millennium bc, possibly as an aid to cultivation.

Cutting XLVII

A cutting 4.00 m. long and 1.50 m. wide to locate the northern edge of a suspected causeway across the ditch. This was located and the excavation terminated at a depth of 50 cm.

Cutting XLVIII (fig. 38)

A cutting 7.00 m. long and 1.00 m. wide to locate the southern edge of a suspected causeway across the ditch. This was located midway along the cutting which was excavated to a depth of 2.00 m.

Cutting XLIX

A cutting 11.00 m. long and 1.00 m. wide across the ditch south of the causeway. The ditch was 8.20 m. wide at this point and was excavated to a depth of 1.30 m.

Cutting L

A cutting 7.00 m. long and 1.00 m. wide to locate the ditch north-east of the Conquer Barrow. The edge of the ditch was located at the north end of the cutting.

Cutting LI

A cutting 7.00 m. long and 1.00 m. wide to confirm the information obtained from Cutting L. The inner edge of the ditch was recorded 2.00 m. from the north end of the cutting.

VI. THE LATER SETTLEMENT

(fig. 39)

THE evidence for later settlement on the hill-top has in the main been given in previous sections on the structural history of the site. Pottery of the late pre-Roman Iron Age and Romano-British period, and green-glazed wares of seventeenth- and eighteenth-century date occurred in plough-wash deposits at high levels in ditches, where the molluscan fauna indicates intermittent cultivation and grassland.

Shallow gullies recorded in Cuttings I and II are probably related to this process, whilst evidence for a more permanent settlement was obtained from Site IV in the form of a single hut, pits and part of a rectilinear enclosure. The presence of lumps of sarsen at a relevant level in the Site IV ditch indicates that the Stone Cove and its outliers may have been destroyed at that time, possibly to facilitate cultivation. Finally, there are the graves of Saxon date in Cuttings I and IV which have been described in a subsequent section by Mr. Schweiso (p. 181).

A feature not previously described is that recorded in Cutting XXVI which was sited to investigate an anomaly in the geophysical survey. Within a cutting 6.00 m. square was recorded an oval pit 4.70 m. in diameter from north to south and 6.00 m. from west to east with a depth in the centre of 1.70 m. from the modern turf-line. The walls of the pit inclined gently inwards to a flat floor. The fill consisted in the main of a light brown compact soil (fig. 39, layer (2)) separated by a thin layer of small chalk lumps (layer (3)) from a dark brown compact soil with a little small chalk (layer (4)). This deposit was some 40 cm. thick in the centre of the pit, where it rested directly on the chalk floor, becoming more compact towards its base with virtually no chalk content (layer (6)). Near the sides of the pit it was interleaved by spills of chalk lumps (layer (5)) which presumably resulted from weathering processes. Weathered flint flakes were found scattered throughout the filling of the pit and a small quantity of late pre-Roman Iron Age and Romano-British sherds in the upper part of layer (4). A few sherds were also recorded from layer (5).

The purpose of this pit remains obscure. Its diameter is much greater and its depth much less than the normal rubbish pit. Layers (4) and (6) have a waterlogged appearance or at least were formed under damp conditions. It is possible that the pit was dug for the collection of water but mitigating against this view is that there was no indication of any lining to prevent water seepage.

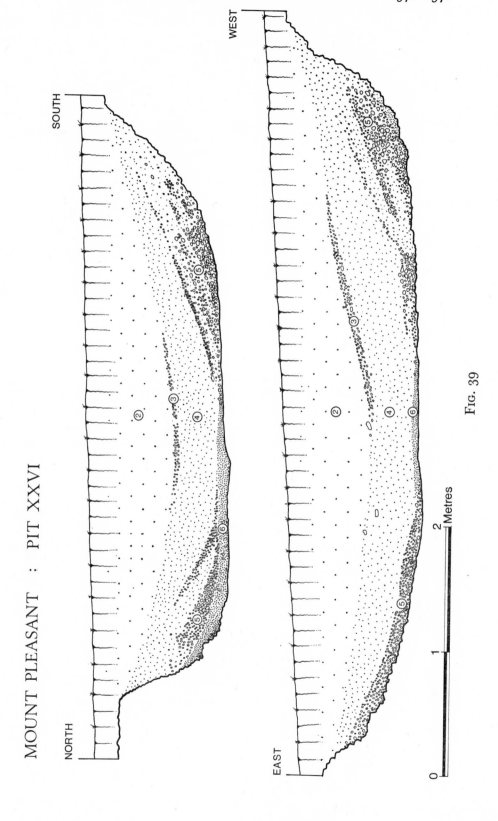

MOUNT PLEASANT : PIT XXVI

FIG. 39

VII. THE WOODHENGE EXCAVATIONS

(figs. 40–43; pls. XXXV*a*–XXXVI*b*)

by J. G. Evans and G. J. Wainwright

INTRODUCTION

WOODHENGE is sited 60 m. south of the Durrington Walls enclosure (SU 15064338) and was listed by the Revd. E. H. Goddard as a disc barrow under 'Durrington 65 b'[1] until aerial observation by Squadron Leader Insall in 1925 revealed a series of concentric rings of dark spots in the wheat within the surrounding earthwork. The area within the ditch was totally excavated by Mrs. Cunnington between 1926 and 1928 and the name 'Woodhenge' coined for the timber structure.[2] The results have since been reinterpreted by Professor Piggott[3] and Mr. Musson[4] and only a brief description of the structure need be repeated here.

The timber structure enclosed by a ditch comprised six concentric rings of post-holes of oval or egg-shaped plan, the outer ring of which has a diameter of 44.1 m. in a north-east/south-west axis and 39.6 m. in a north-west/south-east axis. Mr. Musson has suggested that the remains represent two separate buildings, each with an outward sloping annular roof and with a central court. They were surrounded by a ditch with an external bank, the former occupying a maximum area of 85.3 m. from east to west and 88.3 m. from north-east to south-west. The earthwork was crossed by a single causeway about 9.1 m. wide facing north-east towards the Durrington Walls enclosure (fig. 40). Sherds of Grooved Ware were found on the bottom of the ditch, in the old turf line under the bank and in some of the post-holes. In addition, Windmill Hill ware was found beneath the bank, Beaker sherds from three of the post-holes and sherds of Wessex/Middle Rhine and European Beakers from just beneath the lowest old turf line in the ditch.

Woodhenge was of particular interest to the authors, both of whom were researching into the archaeology and environment of Late Neolithic enclosures in southern England. Firstly, the relationship of Woodhenge to the comparable timber structure excavated in 1967 within the Durrington Walls enclosure was unknown but could be clarified by a radiocarbon determination from the former. Secondly, it was considered desirable to obtain soil samples for molluscan analysis, which it was hoped would yield data relating to the environment before and after the destruction of the enclosure bank, which could then be compared with the data obtained in 1967 from Durrington Walls. Furthermore, it was clear that a radiocarbon determination from Woodhenge was desirable in view of the abundant pottery from the site. In both these aims the excavation was successful.

[1] Goddard, 1913, 48.
[2] Cunnington, 1929.
[3] Piggott, 1940, 207–12, figs 7–9.

[4] Musson, *in* Wainwright and Longworth, 1971, 372–4, fig. 115.

WOODHENGE

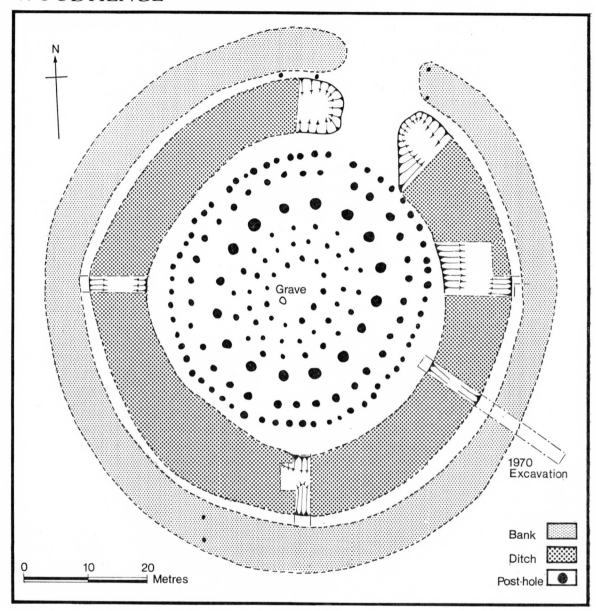

FIG. 40

THE EXCAVATION
(figs. 40–43, pls. XXXVa–XXXVIb)

In June 1970 a single trench 2.00 m. wide and 27.00 m. long was excavated across the bank and ditch of the enclosure in its south-west sector. The position of this cutting relative to those excavated by Cunnington in 1926–8 is shown in fig. 40. The latter are still visible as weed-filled depressions in the turf.[1] A detailed description of the deposits has been reserved for Part III of this report where it accompanies the environmental evidence and only a brief summary of the factual data has been given here.

The Bank and Buried Soil

The bank was preserved to a maximum height of 12 cm., overlain by 25 cm. of plough-wash and modern grassland soil (fig. 41). Its width was approximately 5.00 m. but it survived only as a thin layer of angular chalk rubble, barely visible in places. Denudation due to ploughing had taken place and there was a negative lynchet on the outer side. The buried soil possessed a profile similar to that recorded beneath the bank of Durrington Walls and the land snail data indicates a similar sequence of environmental events prior to the construction of the earthwork. A small quantity of animal bones, flint artifacts and pottery sherds were recorded from the old land surface and have been described in Part II of this report.

The Ditch

The ditch was between 4.4 and 5.1 m. wide and 2.2 m. deep below the level of the old ground surface with a flat base (figs. 42–3, pls. XXXVIa, b). A buttress of unexcavated natural chalk 1.0 m. high extended almost the total width of the cutting. In the outer bay formed by this buttress was a pile of ten antler picks resting on the rock floor of the ditch (pl. XXXVb). A radiocarbon determination of 1867 ± 74 bc (BM-677) was obtained from one of these picks. A small collection of animal bone from the primary chalk rubble silting produced a radiocarbon determination of 1805 ± 54 bc (BM-678). Sherds of Grooved Ware and two transverse arrowheads were obtained from the primary silts.

The silting sequence of the ditch has been described in detail in Part III of this report with reference to the molluscan evidence. It consists essentially of angular chalk rubble at the base (layer (7)), overlaid by the secondary fill of flints and loose chalky loam (layer (6)) which is sealed by a turf-line (layer (5C)). A plough-wash (layer (5B)) overlies this lowermost turf-line and is in turn sealed by a second dark brown turf-line (layer (5A)). An upper chalky loam (layer (4)) represents another plough-wash deposit which in turn is sealed by a third turf-line (layer (3)). This sequence of deposits and turf-lines is sealed by plough-wash and modern turf (layers (2) and (1)) to a level where the ditch is barely visible by surface inspection. The presence of a substantial berm between the ditch and the bank resulted in the coarse silting being derived almost entirely from the ditch sides, although it is possible that a slightly greater quantity of coarse chalk rubble in the outer ditch angle represents some deliberate back-filling of the bank. This suggestion, however, is extremely tentative.

[1] The excavation was executed by the authors with the assistance of J. Jefferies, G. Smith and D. Young.

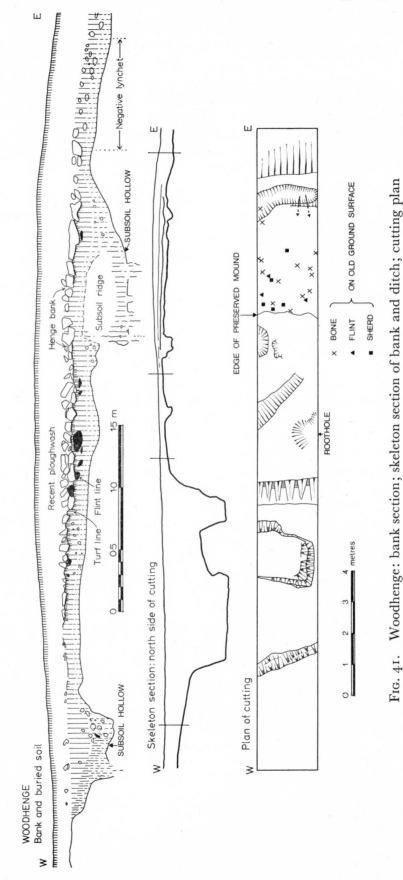

Fig. 41. Woodhenge: bank section; skeleton section of bank and ditch; cutting plan

PART II. THE FINDS
VIII. THE NEOLITHIC AND BRONZE AGE POTTERY
by I. H. LONGWORTH

A TOTAL of 4130 pre-Iron Age sherds[1] was recovered during the course of the excavations of which 3538 can be assigned to individual ceramic traditions with a reasonable degree of confidence. The assemblage thus revealed spans from plain Neolithic bowl pottery to wares characteristic of the mature Bronze Age. The pottery will be described first according to location — occurrence by trench and feature being summarized for ease of reference in Table III — then by individual tradition.[2]

The Fossil Soil Beneath the Enclosure Bank
(trenches I, XXXI, XXXII, XXXIII and SII)

While the vast majority of identifiable sherds from the fossil soil sealed by the enclosure bank are from plain Neolithic bowls (355 sherds), two sherds of Grooved Ware were also recovered from this context in trench I.

Site IV

(a) Primary Silts

With the exception of two sherds of plain Neolithic bowl from segments XIα 10 and XII 7 and two sherds of Beaker from XII 7, the remaining identifiable pottery from the primary silts of the Site IV ditch consisted entirely of Grooved Ware, 59 sherds in all. The sherds of Neolithic bowl, if not derived, would complement the similar association already noted from the fossil soil beneath the main enclosure bank. The two Beaker sherds, one a sherd of AOC Beaker (P139), the other from a plain Beaker (P221) deserve comment. In the case of the AOC Beaker, represented by a total of eight sherds, seven were recovered from the secondary silts in Segment XIII. The sherd from the primary silts in Segment XII actually joins with sherds from the later silts. Since the secondary silts in Segment XII showed extensive rabbit disturbance, it seems highly likely that the sherd from the primary silts is not *in situ* but derived from the upper level. If this is so then it is doubtful whether the fragment of plain Beaker (P221) from the same silt can be accepted as in firm context. Whether this be the case or not it is clear that the digging of the Site IV ditch is to be associated essentially with Grooved Ware users.

(b) Post-holes of the Timber Structure

Of the 19 post-holes from which identifiable sherds were recovered, 14 yielded a total of 16 sherds of Grooved Ware. In addition, post-holes 52 and 128[3] yielded single sherds of Bronze Age fabric and post-hole 75, two small sherds of very weathered Beaker.

---

[1] Excluding sherds less than 1 cm².

[2] I would like to record my warmest thanks to my wife,

Clare, for all her help in sorting and recording this pottery.

[3] Also a sherd of EIA fabric.

(c) *Secondary Silts and Stone Holes*

In the secondary silts the bulk of the identifiable pottery is Beaker (783 sherds), 575 of which were recovered from Segment XIII at the north-western terminal. Grooved Ware is also well represented in these silts, 42 sherds. Of the remaining identifiable sherds, four belong to plain Neolithic bowls, perhaps derived, and eight sherds, which appear to be of Bronze Age Food Vessel fabric, also came from Segment XIII.

The great interest of these secondary silts lies in the variety of Beaker styles represented. In particular the extensive assemblage recovered from Segment XIII, layer (5), indicates contemporaneity on the site during the time span represented by the formation of this layer, of AOC, European, Wessex/Middle Rhine, Northern/Middle Rhine and Southern 4 Beakers together with undecorated, finger-nail, finger-pinched and stroke ornamented forms. This abundance and complexity of Beaker forms is in marked contrast to the preceding layer (layer (6)) which yielded only nine sherds, all from AOC Beaker. A similar, though less extensive, assemblage was recovered from layer (5) in Segment X comprising AOC, First Northern/Dutch, Southern 2–3 and 4. A C14 date of 1680 ± 60 bc (BM-668) derived from charcoal taken from this layer gives some chronological indication of when this assemblage was in contemporary use.

The ceramic evidence offers little further help in the dating and cultural affiliation of the stone settings. Only one feature, F 191, yielded identifiable sherds, but these consisted entirely of Grooved Ware.

(d) *Tertiary Silts*

Not surprisingly, the greatest variety of ceramic traditions are represented in the tertiary silts. While Grooved Ware is all but absent (4 sherds), Beaker pottery remains well represented (77 sherds) and sherds of Food Vessel, Collared Vessel and other Bronze Age wares, totalling 78 sherds, are equally numerous.

In these latest silts, AOC and Wessex/Middle Rhine Beaker forms are certainly represented along with plain and Southern 4 forms. A C14 date of 1324 ± 51 bc (BM-669) from Segment VIIIa, layer (5), in direct association with sherds of Ridged Food Vessel, indicates the approximate chronological horizon.

Main Enclosure Ditch

(a) *Western Entrance* (trenches I, II)

Plain Neolithic bowl pottery was recovered in primary context in the Northern section of trench II, layer (11) (14 sherds). The four sherds of plain bowl from the secondary silts (layer (6)) may indicate the survival of this type of pottery in contemporary use with the Grooved Ware recovered from the same horizon, though the possibility of derivation cannot be entirely ruled out.

Only six identifiable sherds were recovered from the buried soil layers (4) and (5). These comprise three sherds of Beaker (layer (5)), one of Neolithic plain bowl (pit layer (5)), one sherd of Grooved Ware (layer (5)) and one sherd of Bronze Age fabric (layer (4)). From the hearth discovered in the aeolian material in the terminal pit came sherds of a Northern/Middle Rhine Beaker associated with a C14 date of 1460 ± 131 bc (BM-664).

TABLE III

			Neolithic plain bowl	Grooved Ware	Beaker	Peterborough Ware	Bronze Age	Undefined	Total
I	Top of OLS	9	29	2				14	45
II		4					1	1	2
		5		1	3			2	6
		6	4	1				1	6
		8						1	1
		11	14						14
	DTP	3			1				1
	DTP	5	1						1
	DTP	6		1					1
III		3		3	511		5	94	613
	S I	4						2	2
	II	5						1	1
	III	4			1				1
	V	4						1	1
	VI	5						2	2
IV		F2						3	3
		F5						1	1
		F9		1				1	2
		F12						1	1
		F14						1	1
		F16						1	1
		F29						2	2
		F34						2	2
		F38		1					1
		F42						2	2
		F43						1	1
		F45						1	1
		F47		1					1
		F52					1		1
		F56		1					1
		F59						1	1
		F62						1	1
		F64						1	1
		F72		1					1
		F74						1	1
		F75			2				2
		F76		1					1
		F77		1					1
		F78		1					1
		F80		2					2
		F82						1	1
		F83		2				1	3
		F88						1	1
		F89						1	1
		F93						1	1
		F96						1	1

			Neolithic plain bowl	Grooved Ware	Beaker	Peterborough Ware	Bronze Age	Undefined	Total
		F100		1					1
		F106						4	4
		F109						1	1
		F112						1	1
		F113						1	1
		F119						2	2
		F128					1	1	2
		F134						3	3
		F157						1	1
		F159		1					1
		F163						1	1
		F165						1	1
		F168						1	1
		F170		1				1	2
		F172		1				1	2
		F174						1	1
		F178						1	1
		F191		25				3	28
IV	Sg I	3		2	6		5		13
		5		3	1				4
	I α	4			1		1	2	4
		6						6	6
		7		2					2
	II	3			1				1
		7						1	1
	III	3					1		1
		4			1				1
		7		1					1
		8		1					1
	IV	4			2				2
		5					1		1
		7			1				1
		8		3					3
		Unstrat.			26			2	28
	IVα	3						1	1
		4					1		1
		8			2				2
		9		1					1
	V	4			1				1
		7		1				2	3
		8	1					4	5
		9		15					15
	Vα	3					1		1
	VI	3					3		3
		4					14		14
		5						1	1
IV	Sg VIα	4					2		2
	VII	3		1	4		18	4	27
		5			6		13	1	20
		6		5					5

		Neolithic plain bowl	Grooved Ware	Beaker	Peterborough Ware	Bronze Age	Undefined	Total
	7						1	1
	9		4				2	6
VIIα	3					6		6
VIII	4					6		6
	2					1	1	2
	6		4	14			9	27
	7		3					3
VIIIα	3			1		3	1	5
	4						1	1
	5					2		2
IX	4					3	2	5
	5		6	4			2	12
	7		2					2
IXα	2		1			1		2
	4					1		1
	5B		7					7
X	3			1				1
	5		8	26			2	36
	7						1	1
Xα	4			3				3
	5		2	80				82
	6			4			1	5
XI	2			1				1
	5			65				65
	6	3	2	1				6
	7		1					1
	10	1						1
XIα	4			6		1	1	8
	6					2	3	5
	7		7	8			2	17
	8		2				2	4
	9		1					1
	10		9				1	10
XII	6			1			2	3
	7	1	1	2				4
XIII	3			30		9	6	45
	4			15		2		17
	5			566		8	13	587
	6			9				9
	7		1					1
	Dist.			8				8
XIIIα	6a/6b						5	5
IV Ditch	2		1			1		2
XI	5		2					2
XII	4						2	2
XIII	2						1	1

		Neolithic plain bowl	Grooved Ware	Beaker	Peterborough Ware	Bronze Age	Undefined	Total
	3						1	1
	4		1	1			8	10
XIV							3	3
	2		2					2
	4		6	1			5	12
	5		2	1			2	5
XV	3						3	3
XVI	2						2	2
	5			1				1
XVII	2						2	2
	3						1	1
	4		1	1				2
	5	1	3				2	6
XVIII	2		9	1				10
	3		7	3			4	14
	4			1			1	2
	5		3				1	4
	lamp					1		1
XIX						2	15	17
	4					1	1	2
	5						3	3
XX	3			1		4	3	8
	5		1	1		2	2	6
	7		1	1		2	2	6
XXI	3			1	1			2
	7							
	10					1		1
XXII	3	1	1	2	2		11	17
	4				1			1
XXIII	2	1		4		2		7
	3			2	1			3
	5					1	6	7
XXIV	2			5			1	6
	3						1	1
	5		1					1
XXV	3			1	1	3	11	16
	4		1	1		4	1	7
	5	2	1	1		3	4	11
XXVI	4			1				1

		Neolithic plain bowl	Grooved Ware	Beaker	Peterborough Ware	Bronze Age	Undefined	Total
XXVII	5		1					1
	7		11					11
	8		1					1
	9		2	1		5		8
	11		15				2	17
XXVIII	2						2	2
	3	3				72		75
	5					16	6	22
	6					16	1	17
	6/7			2		2		4
	7			1		4		5
	8			2				2
	9		17					17
	10		7	35			2	44
	10/11		1					1
	11		5					5
XXVIII/ XXIX	4					21	3	24
	6		13	12		132	42	199
	6/7		1			11		12
	7		23	5		88	47	163
	8		10	10		43	1	64
	10		12	14				26
	11		2					2
XXIX	3					1		1
	4					1		1
	6		5			40	7	52
	6/7		9	8		52	5	74
	7		3	2		11		16
	8		7	16			4	27
	9			11			2	13
	10	1	257	91		1	19	369
	11	1	16					17
	12		34					34
XXX	3		1					1
	4					14	27	41
	5/6		5	3		40	12	60
	6		6	10		66	23	105
	7			12		1	1	14
	10						1	1
XXXII	1						14	14
	2						3	3
	3	326					7	333
XXXIV	1		3					3
	1/2	1	2					3
	2		1					1

		Neolithic plain bowl	Grooved Ware	Beaker	Peterborough Ware	Bronze Age	Undefined	Total
XXXV	3						2	2
	5						2	2
XXXVI	2			2				2
	3						1	1
	4		2	1				3
	6			1				1
	7		1			1		2
	9		1					1
	10		1					1
	11			1				1
	12		1	1				2
XXXVII	5						1	1
XXXVIII	2						1	1
XL				1			3	4
XLI							3	3
XLII	2					1		1
XLIV	3			1				1
XLVI	4							
	7					1		1
	8							
	9						4	4
XLVIII	5						3	3
Total		391	657	1695	6	781	591	4130

(b) *Northern Entrance* (trenches XXVII, XXVIII, XXVIII/XXIX, XXIX, XXX)

In all sections, the only identifiable pottery from the earliest layer of the primary silts is Grooved Ware — Section XXVII, layer (11) (15 sherds); XXVIII, layer (11) (5 sherds); XXVIII/XXIX, layer (11) (2 sherds) and XXIX, layer (12) (34 sherds) — while a single sherd of plain Neolithic bowl was recovered with a further 16 sherds of Grooved Ware in the upper primary silt layer (11) in trench XXIX.

As recorded, in Sections XXVIII, XXVIII/XXIX and XXIX, Beaker pottery appears alongside Grooved Ware first in layer (10). Trench XXVII differs from this pattern in yielding only a single Beaker sherd (layer (9)) while in trench XXX Beaker appears first in layer (7). While differing in detail from section to section, if the figures for pottery recovered from trenches XXVIII to XXX are combined, it can be seen that Grooved Ware and Beaker pottery occur with no great disparity in frequency throughout the sequence from layer (9) up to the junction of layers (5) and (6). Grooved Ware similarly survives through the sequence up into layer (5) in trench XXVII.

In trench XXIX a sherd of Food Vessel (P245) was recovered from layer (10) and sherds of Collared Vessel (P250) first appear in layer (9) of trench XXVII. Neither form is however well represented until layers (7) and (6) in trenches XXVIII–XXX. Collared Vessel persists through the sequence to the latest silts, 3 and 4, while Bucket-shaped vessels are certainly present in layer (4) and probably by layer (6) in this sequence.

A general picture of the sequence at the Northern Entrance then emerges, with Grooved Ware in primary context, surviving in use well into the secondary silts, being joined by Beaker wares already by layer (10) and sherds of Bronze Age fabric generally by layer (7), and certainly as early as the formation of layer (9) in trench XXVII and possibly layer (10) in trench XXIX.

Unfortunately, some doubt must be entertained regarding the detailed occurrence of pottery from Cuttings XXVIII, XXVIII/XXIX and XXIX within layers (10) to (6)/(7). Sherds almost certainly from a single incised Beaker (P188–190) were recovered from these levels and joining sherds from layers (8) and (9) and from (10) and (6)/(7), respectively, indicate the degree of dispersal to be reckoned with. Since these layers do not appear to represent a single short-lived event, the sherds must be derived but it is now impossible either to re-interpret the evidence to discover the parent layer or to define the area of disturbance involved.

(c) *Trench XI*

Only two pre-Iron Age sherds were recovered from trench XI, both in layer 5, both being Grooved Ware.

Palisade Trench
(trenches III, V–VIII, XII–XXV, XXXIV–XLV)

Of the 650 identifiable sherds from cuttings made through the palisade trench, 550 are Beaker sherds, 55 Grooved Ware, 33 of Bronze Age fabric, 6 of Peterborough Ware and 6 of plain Neolithic bowl. 511 of the Beaker sherds were recovered from trench III.

While the stratigraphy recovered within the cuttings is not in itself significant, it is interesting to note that the content of the trench differs somewhat, ceramically, from the rest of the site. The only Peterborough sherds found during the excavations come from the Palisade and amongst the mass of Beaker sherds from this feature there are none representative of AOC vessels. The majority of identifiable sherds come either from Wessex/Middle Rhine Beakers (e.g. P149, 150, 151 and 155) or from finger-pinched, finger-nail decorated or plain Beakers. Amongst the Bronze Age sherds, Food Vessel forms are present while Collared Vessels, numerous in the secondary and upper silts of the main enclosure, are absent. Since the palisade trench was sampled at many points, it seems unlikely that these variations in the ceramic content are not significant.

The Conquer Barrow Ditch
(trenches XLVI–LI)

Only two of the eight sherds recovered from the barrow ditch could be assigned: one a Beaker sherd from trench XLVI, layer (4), the other of Bronze Age fabric from layer (8).

4

Iron Age Hollow
(trench XXVI)

A single Beaker sherd was recovered from this feature.

NEOLITHIC PLAIN BOWLS

The 391 sherds of Neolithic bowl pottery recovered, principally from the fossil soil beneath the main enclosure bank, are predominantly non-shell gritted, with flint and/or quartz the most frequent additive. The collection consists entirely of simple undecorated round-based forms. Of the 34 rims recovered, 24 are simple, five rolled-over (P31–5), four externally thickened (P21–4), and one (P16) displays a relatively undeveloped 'T'-section. Remains of two horizontally perforated lugs survive (P36–7) and a single imperforate horizontal lug (P26).

The assemblage as a whole can be compared with that from Hembury where, in particular, the high set horizontal lug[1] and horizontally perforated forms[2] are well matched, as is also the carinated bowl (P2).[3] Only the out-flaring rim of the open bowl (P1) seems alien, having more immediate parallels in eastern England.[4]

PETERBOROUGH WARE

Only 6 sherds from the site can be attributed to Peterborough Ware (P38–41). All were recovered from the palisade trench. Of the three rims, P41 certainly, and P39 probably, belong to vessels of the Fengate style while a third appears to be an Ebbsfleet form. Of the three wall sherds, P38 and 40 are likely to come from vessels of Mortlake style.

GROOVED WARE

Though the assemblage is less extensive, comprising only 657 sherds, the Grooved Ware shows striking similarities to that recovered from Durrington Walls, Wiltshire, though lacking some of the rarer elements typical of the substyle there defined.[5] As at Durrington the state of preservation varies considerably, shell and grog being the most frequent tempering materials while flint, quartz, chalk, sand and other grits were at times also employed.

Especially prominent in the collection are sherds carrying vertical plain body cordons, closely spaced (P42, 48 and 56), in pairs (P43 and 45), or widely spaced (P50–4). Less frequent are cordons used to separate panels of body decoration (P62–6). Decorated vertical cordons are confined to Durrington Walls types 7 and 11[6] (e.g. P67–70), the more elaborate forms being absent. A rather greater use appears to be made of diagonal plain cordons

[1] *PDAES* 1931, I, 112, pl. XXVI, P94 and 142.
[2] *PDAES* 1931, I, 112, pl. XXVII, e.g. P73 and 77.
[3] *PDAES* 1932, I, 184, pl. XVIII, P296.

[4] e.g. *inter alia* Broome Heath, *PPS*, xxxviii(1972), P296, 308, etc.
[5] Wainwright and Longworth, 1971, 240–2.
[6] *Ibid.*, fig. 25.

beneath the rim (P73–80) than elsewhere in the substyle,[1] while the use of plain cordons to form geometric patterns in the zone between rim and shoulder cordon (P67) is reminiscent of the similar use of geometric cordons in the Rinyo substyle.[2]

Other traits typical of the Durrington Walls substyle are the use of vertical grooved or incised lines to divide body decoration into panels (P94–8) and the use of incised decoration to form filled triangle patterns (P82). As at Durrington,[3] Marden[4] and Lawford[5] a small number of sherds also carry twisted-cord decoration (P107–9) and a single sherd (P106), more likely to be Grooved Ware than Peterborough, carries a whipped-cord 'maggot' decoration. Plain Grooved Ware is again a feature of the assemblage. Of particular interest here is the plain bowl (P113) which closely resembles pottery recovered both in the recent and in earlier excavations associated with the flint mines at Grime's Graves, Norfolk.

Of other traits typical of the Durrington Walls substyle, incised internal decoration does not appear in the assemblage, nor the rare use of concentric or spiral motifs. Rim forms (fig. 44)[6] tend in the main to belong to the simplest forms.[7] Rounded and flattened rims of types 2 and 3 account for over half of those recovered, and neither internal concave rims of type 13 nor vertically bevelled rims of form 24 are present. The two collared forms recovered (P89 and 91) have closer parallels at Woodhenge[8] than at Durrington Walls.[9] No lugs occur in the collection but rivet holes are present on three sherds.

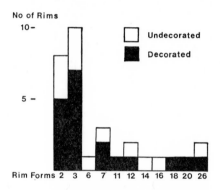

FIG. 44.   Rim form frequencies

Only 2 sherds show a departure from the Durrington Walls substyle, carrying decoration more typical of the Clacton style (P81 and 105).

Three points emerge from the sherds recovered in the ditches of the main enclosure and Site IV (Table IIIA a–c). Firstly, that on the Grooved Ware from the primary silts which appear from the C14 dates to be roughly contemporary, the use of plain and decorated cordons, together with grooved, incised and impressed decoration, is already established in the tradition by this phase; secondly, that the use of plain cordons persisted virtually throughout the span of time that Grooved Ware was being deposited on the site; and thirdly, that the use of twisted cord appears relatively early, is rare and perhaps of short duration.

---

[1] With the possible exception of Yorkshire, cf. Manby, 1974, e.g. Low Caythorpe, fig. 27, Nos. 1–2.

[2] e.g. Childe, 1939, 6–31, pl. XIX.1.

[3] *Op. cit.*, P374–91.

[4] Wainwright, 1971, 51, P13–14, 19, 36–7.

[5] Unpublished. Colchester Museum.

[6] I am indebted to Mr. P. C. Compton for drawing out fig. 44.

[7] *Op. cit.*, fig. 20.

[8] Cunnington, 1929, pls. 26, No. 1; 35, Nos. 70–1.

[9] i.e. *op. cit.*, P29.

TABLE IIIA

Context	Grooved Ware										
	Plain or featureless	Grooved	Incised	Impressed	Twisted cord	Comb	Whipped cord	Rusticated	Stab and drag	Decorated cordons	Plain cordons
IV Ditch											
Primary	48	12	2	1							
Secondary	15	22	2	1							1
Tertiary	2	2									

(a) The Site IV Ditch Sequence

XXVII	5	1										
	7	10										1
	8	1										
	9	2										
	11	3		1	1							11

(b) The Main Enclosure: Sequence at Northern Entrance in Trench XXVII

XXVIII–XXX	3	1										1
	5/6	4										7
	6	15			1			1				4
	6/7	5		1								6
	7	19			1							4
	8	13										6
	9	11			1							
	10	129	5	10	3	2	1		1		8	117
	10/11		1			1						
	11	16		1							1	5
	12	11		2	1						1	20

(c) The Main Enclosure: Sequence at Northern Entrance in Trenches XXVIII–XXX

BEAKER WARES

The Beaker pottery from the site is of particular interest not only for its range and apparent chronological span but also for the multiplicity of traditions apparently in contemporary use on the site. The bulk of the collection derives from two contexts, the secondary and later silts of the Site IV ditch and the palisade. The ensuing analysis follows the divisions put forward by D. L. Clarke in his *Beaker Pottery of Great Britain and Ireland* (1970).

AOC (P131–45)

Spatially, AOC beakers are confined to the Site IV ditch and Northern Entrance of the main enclosure. Chronologically, however, the tradition has considerable depth extending, in the Site IV ditch sequence, through the secondary silts well into the uppermost tertiary silts (Segment XIII 3). The available C14 dates would suggest that such a chronological span is unlikely to have been less than 250 years. Though a considerable range of vessel form is represented, no clear typological succession emerges and the relatively rare technique of using paired cords with the twist set in the same direction appears on sherds from both the secondary and upper silts.

If the single sherd recovered from the primary silt of the Site IV ditch be discounted[1] then AOC beakers are to be associated with the on-going life of the enclosure and Site IV rather than any constructional episode.

European (P164, 175, 177–8)

A small number of sherds, all from the secondary silts of the Site IV ditch, can probably be assigned to European Beakers.

Wessex/Middle Rhine (P146, 148–51, 155, 167 and 179–80; less certainly P152–4, 161, 166 and 171)

A considerable body of sherds mainly carrying simple horizontal lines of comb decoration seems best ascribed to Wessex/Middle Rhine Beakers. The majority of sherds come from the secondary silts of the Site IV Ditch and from the palisade. The form appears to survive on the site sufficiently late to be incorporated also into the tertiary silts of the Site IV ditch.

Northern/Middle Rhine (P157, 169 and ? 168 and 184) and Northern/North Rhine (P147)

Sherds from four vessels appear to belong to Northern/Middle Rhine Beakers: the incised herringbone decorated vessel P157 and probably P184, both from the secondary silts of the Site IV ditch, and the comb-decorated Beakers P168 and 169 from the hearth in the secondary silts of the Western Entrance of the main enclosure.

Sherds of P147, which were also recovered from the secondary silts of the Site IV ditch, could be ascribed equally to the Northern/North Rhine group or to the East Anglian, but clearly stand close to vessels in the Northern Rhineland.

Northern (P159 and 173)

Sherds of a vessel recovered from the secondary silts in two sections of the Site IV ditch belong to a Beaker likely to stand at the beginning of the Northern tradition, P159. Sherds from a further vessel of perhaps typologically more developed form, P173, come from the palisade.

Southern

A greater variety of sherds are attributable to vessels of the Southern tradition. Of these, two Beakers carry bar-chevron decoration, P158 from the secondary silts of the Site IV ditch and P176 from the palisade, and are likely to belong to Phases II–III of the tradition

[1] See p. 75.

while P160, 172 and 165, all from the secondary and later silts of the Site IV ditch, clearly belong to the final stages of that tradition. P160 with its bevelled rim and stroke-decorated shoulder shows strong convergent features with Food Vessel forms.

The remaining sherds, all of incised Beaker, P188–92 and 194–6 have a restricted distribution confined to the secondary silts of the Northern Entrance of the main enclosure and the palisade.

Finger-nail, Finger-pinched and Stroke-decorated (P197–217)

Sherds of lightly applied finger-nail or stroke-decorated Beaker come from the secondary silts of the Northern Entrance of the main enclosure, from the secondary silts of the Site IV ditch and from the palisade. More heavily finger-pinched decorated sherds come from similar contexts in the Site IV ditch (P207) and the palisade (P208) and a single rim with heavy jabbed decoration comes from the secondary silts of the Northern Entrance of the main enclosure. Little contextual distinction can therefore be drawn between heavy and light rusticated sherds from the site.

Plain Beaker (P218–66)

Sherds of plain Beaker were recovered from the secondary and later silts of the Site IV ditch.[1] Of these the only vessel capable of restoration, P218, is a plain version of an AOC or European form.

(?) Foot (P227)

A fragment, possibly from the foot of a polypod Beaker bowl, was recovered from the secondary silts of the Northern Entrance. While no close parallel presents itself, the form appears nearer to the true foot of the Beaker bowl from Inkpen[2] than to the solid polypod foot of the Food Vessel series.[3]

Food Vessels (P228–45)

Sherds from a number of Food Vessels were recovered mainly from the upper and secondary silts of Site IV, the main enclosure ditch and the palisade. The variety of forms represented is considerable. While P230, 232 and 235 are likely to come from vessels of Yorkshire Vase-type, a number of sherds, apparently from relatively large vessels (P229, 231, 233 and 244), come from Ridged Vases whose ancestry lies fairly clearly in rusticated pot Beaker domestic ware. The rim (P240) with its deep internal concave moulding is typical of a series of often undecorated vessels confined to southern and south-western England.[4]

The rims P236, 238–9 and 241 with well-marked internal bevel may come from simple bipartite forms with hollow neck or undifferentiated vase shapes. Sherds P234 and probably 245 appear to belong to vessels best described as Beaker/Food Vessels. The occurrence of P245 in the early silts of the Northern Entrance of the main enclosure ditch demonstrates that Food Vessel forms are already developing at a relatively early date in the Beaker sequence.

---

[1] P224 from Site IV, Segment IV 7, comes from a section extensively disturbed by rabbits. For the context of P221 see p. 75.

[2] Clarke (1971), 306, fig. 204.
[3] See Manby (1969), 273–82.
[4] Cf. Annable and Simpson, 1964, No. 557.

Collared Vessels (P246–96)

Of the sherds of Collared Vessel recovered from the later silts of Site IV and the main enclosure ditch, the vast majority appear to belong to the Secondary series. Owing, however, to the very fragmentary nature of the material, identification cannot be entirely certain.

(a) *Primary Series*. The only sherds which can be placed with any certainty into the primary series are the three rims P246, 247 and 248, the closest parallel for P246 being the sherds recovered from Barclodiad y Gawres.[1] The rims P250 and 251, the collar fragments P260 and 291, and the shoulder P282 may also be assigned to this series but with less certainty.

(b) *Secondary Series*. Of the identifiable fragments the majority are from rims and collars, though sherds of neck, body and base can also be identified. Several of the sherds carry typical features of the South-Eastern style, i.e. point-toothed comb (P277), vertical (P256), horizontal (P258–9, 264, 268, 276–7 and 283), and diagonal (P253 and 265) lines on the collar. Insufficient of any vessel survives to allow complete reconstruction and it is therefore impossible to establish whether the typical bipartite component of this style is present or not.

The occurrence of a number of sherds, e.g. P246 and 271–5, carrying plaited-cord decoration is of interest for this type of corded decoration is not common[2] and these sherds form the first occurrence of such ornament on Collared Vessels in south-west England. Though it is tempting to seek derivation for this type of ornament in the Trevisker culture pottery of the south-west, the present known distribution of its occurrence on Collared Vessels, with concentrations in Suffolk, the east Midlands, Yorkshire and Scotland, makes such a suggestion extremely unlikely.

The presence of undecorated vessels (P286–91) from identical contexts to the decorated vessels underlines the fact that in the Collared as in other ceramic traditions undecorated vessels are likely to form a regular and significant component.

Bucket Urn (P301–9)

A number of recognizable sherds of Bucket Urn type are represented in the later silts. These include a large rim fragment (P309) decorated with a single row of finger-tipping from the Northern Entrance of the main enclosure, the base of a second carrying internal finger-nail decoration (P305), and a third carrying a finger-tip decorated lug (P307). A number of sherds, from one or more vessels (P301–4), again from the Northern Entrance, decorated with roughly scored or deeply incised decoration, probably come from a bipartite vessel. A further fragment (P306) carries finger-nail impressions. The rim P309 probably belongs to a small accessory vessel.

Unattributed

Of uncertain affiliation are a number of sherds carrying twisted-cord decoration (P297–300). The rims P297 and 298 appear to belong to bowl forms. All are likely to be of early Bronze Age date. The strainer base P310 of excessively soft fabric cannot be assigned with confidence to any of the ceramic traditions analysed but its stratigraphic position in the primary silt of the main enclosure ditch would indicate a late Neolithic date.

---

[1] Powell and Daniel (1956), fig. 15.

[2] Longworth (1969), 302, fig. 7.

DISCUSSION

The assemblage of Grooved Ware from Mount Pleasant sheds no new light upon the possible origin of this ceramic tradition, but helps to reinforce conclusions drawn from material recovered from previously excavated sites. By a date of 2000 bc. the Durrington Walls style was well developed with the use of plain and decorated body cordons, grooved, incised and impressed decoration already well established. The rare use of corded decoration is again attested as an early, but not primary, feature of the decorative range implying some incorporation of contemporary AOC Beaker usages. The pottery from the site itself, however, demonstrates that even where the survival of Grooved Ware can be firmly established and where many forms of Beaker are present in the same deposits, the impact of other forms of Beaker usage, so obvious in contemporary late Neolithic and early Bronze Age wares, remains negligible in this tradition.

The Beaker pottery recovered from the site has, on the other hand, considerable implication for both the relative and absolute chronologies of a number of the major groups suggested by Clarke in 1970. The AOC Beaker while amongst the first Beakers to be represented on the site, clearly survives late to be incorporated in the tertiary silts of the Site IV Ditch with a C14 date of 1324 ± 51 bc (BM-669).[1] A straight-sided bipartite form (P162), a form which typologically must fall at the end of the Southern tradition, was recovered from the secondary silts of the Site IV ditch dated by C14 to 1680 ± 60 bc (BM-668). In terms of relative chronology the assemblage of forms recovered from these same secondary silts, including AOC, European, Wessex/Middle Rhine, Northern/Middle Rhine, First Northern/ Dutch, Southern 2–3, Southern 4, plain, finger-nail and finger-pinched, must indicate some degree of contemporaneity between these respective groups. The lasting impression to be gained from this assemblage is that while typological trends may have been correctly identified (Clarke, 1970; Lanting and Van der Waals, 1972), the degree to which these overlapped, began and faded needs to be urgently revised.

Despite the excellent sequences of pottery represented, in only one area does the site shed fresh light regarding ceramic development. In the case of the Ridged Food Vessel there can be little doubt that this developed directly from the cordoned domestic Beaker ware represented at Mount Pleasant by sherds such as P210–12. This is particularly striking when, as in the case of the Food Vessel sherds P231–3, the use of finger-nail or stroke-decoration persists.

In social terms the ditch sequences show that both the main enclosure and Site IV ditch were excavated by Grooved Ware users around 2000 bc at a time when plain bowl pottery was still current.[2] From thenceforth there appears to be little further association of plain bowl users with the site. Grooved Ware continues to be incorporated into the silts high in the main enclosure ditch sequence to be joined first by Beaker and then by Food Vessel, Collared Vessel and other Bronze Age wares. If this survival of Grooved Ware is taken to indicate continuity in the utilization of the site then it seems likely that the users of these later styles took part in that utilization. In contrast, as at Durrington Walls, Marden and Woodhenge, Peterborough Ware is notable for its actual or virtual absence. For the section of later Neo-

---

[1] Contrast this situation with the relatively short life for the comparable AOO 2IIb form in the Netherlands (Lanting, Mook and Van der Waals, 1973).

[2] Unless the bowl pottery sherds are themselves derived.

lithic society which Peterborough Ware appears to represent, these sites at least were of little concern.

TABLE IV

Context		Neolithic plain bowl	Grooved Ware	Bronze Age ware	Undefined	Total
Ditch	⑧	I	I			2
Ditch	⑦		9		2	I I
	⑥		I2		4	I6
OLS	△5		I			I
OLS	△4	I				I
OLS	③	I				I
	△I3		I			I
Plough soil outside Bank				I		I
Total		3	24	I	· 6	34

WOODHENGE

A total of 34 pre-Iron Age sherds was recovered from the cutting made in 1970 through the Woodhenge ditch and bank. Of these three are of plain Neolithic bowl, 24 Grooved Ware, where identifiable, of Durrington Walls style and one of Bronze Age fabric. The remaining six sherds could not be assigned. Table IV summarizes their stratigraphical context.

CATALOGUE
(figs. 45–53, 55)

Neolithic Plain Bowls

P1 Fourteen undecorated sherds including rim of compact paste tempered with a large quantity of grit. Pink throughout. Surfaces eroded.
II (11) DTN

P2 Undecorated wall sherd including shoulder of compact sandy paste tempered with a little shell. Grey externally, brown internally.
I Top of OLS (9)

P3 Undecorated rim sherd of compact paste tempered with fine grit. Grey both faces with brown core. Surface well smoothed.
II DTP (5)

P4 Undecorated rim sherd of compact paste tempered with flint. Grey externally, brown internally. Surfaces eroded.
II (6)

4*

P5   Three undecorated rim sherds of fairly compact paste tempered with grog and grit. Greyish brown both faces with dark grey core.
      XXVIII (3)

P6   Undecorated rim sherd of compact sandy paste tempered with flint grit. Brown both faces with grey core. Weathered.
      IV Segment XII (7)

P7   Undecorated rim sherd of compact sandy paste tempered with a little shell. Light brown both faces with grey core. Weathered.
      XXXII (3)

P8   Undecorated rim sherd of compact paste tempered with large quantity of flint grit. Grey externally, brown internally with grey core. Weathered.
      XXXII (3)

P9   Undecorated rim sherd of compact sandy paste tempered with a little fine grit. Grey externally, brown internally.
      XXXII (3) OLS 4–8 cm.

P10   Undecorated rim sherd of compact sandy paste tempered with large flint grits. Grey externally, grey to brown internally.
      XXXII (3)

P11   Undecorated rim sherd of compact sandy paste tempered with fine grit. Brown both faces with grey core. Weathered.
      XXXII (3) OLS 4–8 cm.

P12   Undecorated rim sherd of compact paste tempered with grit including flint and quartz. Brown externally, greyish brown internally with grey core. Weathered.
      XXXII (3) OLS 4–8 cm.

P13   Undecorated rim sherd of laminated paste tempered with shell. Grey externally, brown internally.
      XXXII (3) OLS 4–8 cm.

P14   Undecorated rim sherd of compact sandy paste tempered with flint grits. Brown to grey externally, grey internally.
      XXXII (3)

P15   Undecorated rim sherd of compact paste tempered with large quantity of fine grit. Grey externally, reddish brown internally. Surface smoothed.
      XVII (5) 160–170 cm.

P16   Undecorated rim sherd of fairly soft paste tempered with a little grit. Grey throughout.
      XXII (3) 70–90 cm.

P17   Undecorated rim sherd of compact sandy paste tempered with flint grit. Grey to brown throughout. Weathered.
      XXXII (3)

P18   Undecorated rim sherd of compact paste tempered with fine flint grit. Grey throughout.
      XXXII (3)

P19   Undecorated rim sherd of compact paste tempered with a little fine grit. Dark grey throughout.
      XXXII (3)

P20   Undecorated rim sherd of compact paste tempered with flint grit. Brown externally, grey internally.
      XXXII (3) OLS 4–8 cm.

P21   Undecorated rim sherd of compact paste. Brown throughout.
      XXXII (3)

P22   Undecorated rim sherd of compact sandy paste. Reddish brown to grey both faces with dark grey core. Weathered.
XXIX (10)

P23   Undecorated rim sherd of compact paste tempered with a large quantity of grit including quartz and flint. Grey to brown throughout.
XXXII (3)

P24   Undecorated rim sherd of compact paste tempered with much flint grit. Greyish brown throughout.
XXXII (3) OLS 4–8 cm.

P25   Rim sherd of compact sandy paste tempered with large quantity of shell. Brown both faces with grey core.
(?) horizontal incised line decoration.
XXXII (3)

P26   Undecorated rim sherd of compact paste tempered with large flint grits. Brown throughout. Remains of horizontal imperforate lug.
XXXII (3) OLS 4–8 cm.

P27   Undecorated rim sherd of compact sandy paste. Brown both faces with grey core. Weathered.
XXXII (3)

P28   Undecorated rim sherd of fairly compact paste tempered with large quantity of grit. Brown both faces with grey core.
II DTS (6)

P29   Undecorated rim sherd of compact sandy paste tempered with a little shell. Light brown externally, grey internally.
I Top of OLS (9)

P30   Undecorated rim sherd of compact sandy paste tempered with some flint. Brown. Surfaces eroded.
I Top of OLS (9)

P31   Undecorated rim sherd of corky paste. Greyish brown throughout. Weathered.
IV Segment V (8)

P32   Undecorated rim sherd of compact paste tempered with flint grit. Greyish brown externally, brown internally.
XXXII (3) OLS 4–8 cm.

P33   Undecorated rim sherd of compact paste tempered with large quantity of flint grit. Grey throughout.
XXXII (3)

P34   Undecorated rim sherd of compact paste tempered with large quantity of flint grit. Grey externally, brown internally.
XXXIV (1)/(2)

P35   Undecorated rim sherd of compact paste tempered with large quantity of flint grit. Patchy grey to brown externally, light brown internally. Grey core.
XXXII (3)

P36   Undecorated horizontally perforated lug of fairly compact paste tempered with flint. Light brown both faces with dark grey core.
IV Segment XI (10)

P37   Fragment of undecorated lug of compact sandy paste tempered with a little grit. Grey throughout.
XXXII (3)

Peterborough Ware

P38   Wall sherd of flaky paste tempered with flint grit. Brown externally, dark grey internally.
Decoration: remains of jabbed decoration.
XXI (3) 30–40 cm.

P39   Rim sherd of fairly compact paste tempered with flint. Grey to brown externally, brown internally with dark grey core.
Decoration: externally, rows of impressions above ? diagonal twisted-cord lines. Internally, short twisted-cord impressions above twisted-cord herringbone.
XXII (3) 100–110 cm.

P40   Wall sherd including shoulder of flaky paste tempered with a large quantity of flint grit. Grey externally, grey to reddish brown internally.
Decoration: remains of short diagonal opposed twisted-cord lines.
XXII (4) 140–150 cm.

P41   Rim sherd of fairly compact paste tempered with much fine grit including shell. Grey externally, brown internally.
Decoration: externally, diagonal twisted-cord lines. On the internal rim bevel, twisted-cord herringbone.
XXV (3) 60–70 cm.

Grooved Ware

P42   Wall sherd of compact coarse paste tempered with grit. Brown externally, brown to grey internally with dark grey core.
Decoration: multiple plain vertical cordons.
XXIX (12)

P43   Wall sherd of fairly compact paste tempered with a little shell. Grey to brown externally, brown internally with dark grey core.
Decoration: horizontal plain cordons from which descend vertical plain cordons.
XXIX (10)

P44   Wall sherd of fairly compact paste. Brown throughout.
Decoration: vertical plain cordons. Weathered.
XXIX (10)

P45   Wall sherd of fairly compact paste tempered with grog and flint. Brown throughout.
Decoration: double vertical plain cordon.
XXIX (10)

P46   Rim sherd of compact paste tempered with some grit. Brown externally, grey to brown internally, with dark grey core.
Decoration: remains of diagonal plain cordons above horizontal plain cordon from which descend vertical plain cordons.
XXVIII (11)

P47   Wall sherd of fairly compact paste tempered with grit. Reddish brown both faces with dark grey core.
Decoration: horizontal plain cordon from which descend three vertical plain cordons. Weathered.
XXIX (12)

P48   Wall sherd of fairly compact paste tempered with grit including grog. Brown both faces with dark grey core.
Decoration: multiple vertical plain cordons.
XXIX (10)

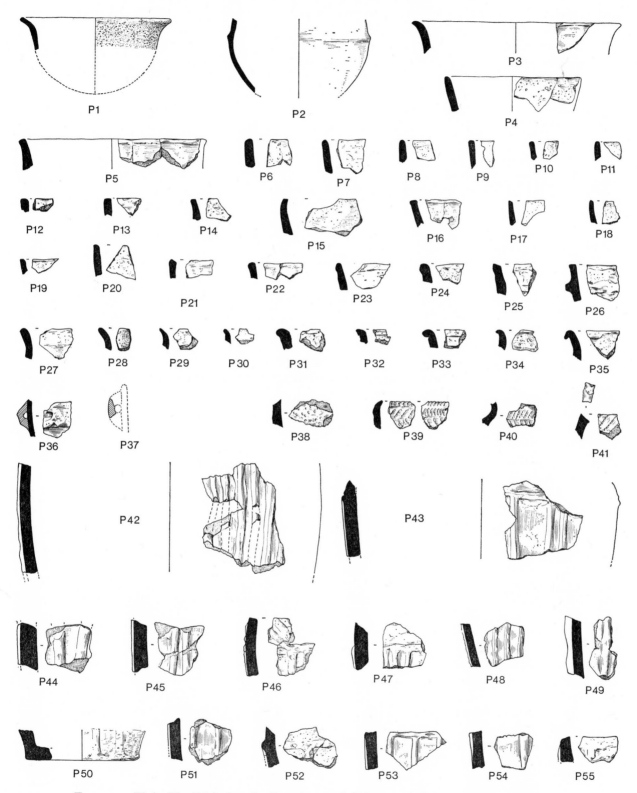

FIG. 45. Plain Neolithic bowls, Peterborough Ware and Grooved Ware. (Scale ¼)

P49   Wall sherd of fairly soft paste tempered with some grit. Patchy grey to brown externally, brown internally with dark grey core.
Decoration: vertical plain cordon.
XXX (6) 0–5 cm.

P50   Base angle of soft flaky paste tempered with grit including quartz. Greyish brown externally, brown internally with dark grey core.
Decoration: remains of vertical plain cordons.
XXIX (10)

P51   Wall sherd of fairly compact paste tempered with some grit. Patchy grey to brown externally, brown internally with dark grey core.
Decoration: vertical plain cordons.
XXVIII (10)

P52   Wall sherd of fairly compact paste tempered with much chalk and grog. Light brown throughout.
Decoration: plain horizontal cordon from which descends a vertical plain cordon.
XXIX (11)

P53   Wall sherd of compact paste tempered with some grit. Reddish brown both faces with dark grey core.
Decoration: horizontal plain cordon from which descend vertical plain cordons.
XXIX (10)

P54   Wall sherd of soft flaky paste. Brown externally, grey internally.
Decoration: undecorated vertical cordon.
XX (7) 120–130 cm.

P55   Rim sherd of compact paste tempered with grit and grog. Light orange both faces with dark grey core.
Decoration: remains of vertical cordon.
XXVIII/XXIX (8)

P56   Wall sherd of fairly compact paste tempered with large quantity of shell grit. Brown throughout.
Decoration: multiple vertical plain cordons.
XXVII (11)

P57   Wall sherd of fairly compact paste tempered with a little shell. Reddish brown both faces with dark grey core.
Decoration: remains of multiple vertical cordons.
XXVIII/XXIX (6)

P58   Base angle of fairly coarse paste tempered with grit including shell and grog. Brown throughout.
Decoration: remains of vertical cordons.
XXIX (10)

P59   Wall sherd of compact paste tempered with a little grit. Light orange both faces with dark grey core.
Decoration: remains of vertical and diagonal plain cordon.
XXVIII/XXIX (8)

P60   Wall sherd of fairly soft paste. Reddish brown throughout.
Decoration: remains of horizontal and vertical cordon.
XVIII (3) 90–100 cm.

P61   Rim sherd of compact paste tempered with a little fine shell. Light orangey brown both faces with dark grey core.
Decoration: ?remains of vertical cordon.
XXVIII (9)

P62   Wall sherd of fairly compact paste tempered with some grog. Greyish brown throughout.
Decoration: vertical plain cordons enclose opposed diagonal roughly scored lines.
XXIX (10) Burnt area

P63   Wall sherd of fairly coarse paste tempered with a little grit. Brown throughout.
Decoration: vertical plain cordon adjoining diagonal incised lines.
XXIX (10)

P64   Wall sherd of compact paste. Brown externally, dark grey internally.
Decoration: remains of vertical plain cordon and diagonal incised lines.
XXIX (12)

P65   Wall sherd of fairly compact paste tempered with some grog. Greyish brown both faces with dark grey core.
Decoration: remains of vertical plain cordon and diagonal roughly scored lines.
XXIX (10) Burnt area
Probably from same vessel as P62.

P66   Wall sherd of compact paste. Brown throughout.
Decoration: vertical plain cordon adjoining incised diagonal lines.
XXIX (10)

P67   Two rim sherds of fairly soft paste tempered with some grit. Brown to grey externally, brown internally.
Decoration: beneath the rim plain vertical applied chevrons are enclosed above by a plain cordon and beneath by a horizontal cordon with finger-tip impressions. From the lower cordon descend vertical cordons with finger-tip impressions.
XXIX (10)

P68   Wall sherd of fairly compact paste tempered with grit. Light brown both faces with dark grey core.
Decoration: remains of vertical cordon decorated with finger-tip impressions.
XXIX (12)

P69   Wall sherd of fairly compact paste tempered with a little grit. Brown throughout.
Decoration: vertical applied cordons decorated with finger-tip impressions.
XXIX (10)

P70   Wall sherd of compact paste. Light brown both faces with dark grey core.
Decoration: vertical cordon with transverse finger-nail impressions and finger-nail impressions to either side.
XXIX (10)

P71   Wall sherd of fairly compact paste tempered with a little grog. Brown both faces with dark grey core.
Decoration: remains of decorated vertical cordon and incised diagonal lines.
XXIX (10)

P72   Rim sherd of fairly soft paste tempered with some grit and grog. Light brown throughout.
Decoration: remains of plain horizontal cordon.
XXIX (10) Burnt area

P73   Rim sherd of compact paste tempered with a little grit. Orange throughout.
Decoration: diagonal plain cordon with finely scored irregular horizontal incised lines to either side.
XXIX (10) Burnt area

P74   Rim sherd of fairly compact paste. Light brown externally, light brown to grey internally with dark grey core.
Decoration: diagonal plain cordon.
XXIX (10)

P75   Rim sherd of fairly soft paste tempered with grit. Brown to grey externally, brown internally.
      Decoration: diagonal plain cordons descend from horizontal plain cordon set beneath the rim.
      XXIX (10)

P76   Rim sherd of fairly compact paste tempered with a little flint. Brown both faces with dark grey
      core. Surface roughly smoothed.
      Decoration: diagonal plain cordon.
      XXIX (10)

P77   Rim sherd of fairly compact paste tempered with a little shell grit. Brown externally, grey
      internally. Surface roughly smoothed.
      Decoration: diagonal plain cordon.
      XXIX (10)

P78   Rim sherd of soft paste tempered with grog. Light brown throughout.
      Decoration: remains of horizontal plain cordon and ? diagonal plain cordon beneath.
      XXIX (10) Burnt area

P79   Wall sherd of soft flaky paste tempered with fine shell. Grey throughout.
      Decoration: slight diagonal plain cordons, beneath remains of horizontal cordon.
      IV Ditch (2)

P80   Wall sherd of fairly compact paste. Grey to brown externally, brown internally.
      Decoration: converging plain cordons.
      XXIX (10)

P81   Wall sherd of fairly compact paste tempered with large quantity of shell. Brown both faces with
      dark grey core.
      Decoration: three broad horizontal grooved lines above slight cordon. Beneath, broad grooved
      line above jabbed impressions.
      IV Segment X (5)

P82   Rim sherd of compact paste tempered with chalk and shell. Orange both faces with dark grey
      core.
      Decoration: groups of opposed incised lines.
      XXIX (10) Burnt area

P83   Two rim sherds of fairly compact paste tempered with grog. Brown to grey externally, light
      brown internally. Surface roughly smoothed.
      Decoration: remains of opposed diagonal incised lines.
      XXIX (10)

P84   Wall sherd of fairly compact paste tempered with a large quantity of shell. Grey to brown
      externally, grey internally with dark grey core.
      Decoration: incised herringbone.
      XIV (4) 55 cm.

P85   Wall sherd of sandy paste tempered with grit including shell. Greyish brown externally, reddish
      brown internally.
      Decoration: remains of horizontal incised lines.
      XXIX (12)

P86   Wall sherd of fairly soft paste tempered with a little grit, including shell. Reddish brown both
      faces with dark grey core.
      Decoration: diagonal below horizontal incised lines.
      XVIII (3) 90–100 cm.

P87   Wall sherd of fairly soft paste. Reddish brown throughout. Surface roughly smoothed.
      Decoration: remains of incised opposed diagonal lines, perhaps part of a filled triangle pattern.
      XXIX (10)

P88   Base angle of compact paste tempered with some chalk and shell. Brown externally, greyish brown internally.
Decoration: remains of opposed diagonal incised lines.
IV Feature 83

P89   Rim sherd of fairly compact sandy paste tempered with shell. Patchy reddish brown to grey both faces.
Decoration: five deep horizontal grooves above beginnings of impressed decoration. Weathered.
IV Feature 191

P90   Wall sherd of fairly compact paste tempered with shell. Reddish brown both faces.
Decoration: horizontal grooved line above diagonal grooved lines. Weathered.
IV Segment IXα (2)

P91   Rim sherd of fairly compact paste. Grey externally, grey to brown internally. Dark grey core.
Decoration: well-executed grooved herringbone.
IV Segment III (8)

P92   Rim sherd of fairly compact paste tempered with large quartz grits. Grey to brown externally, brown internally with dark grey core.
Decoration: multiple vertical grooved chevrons.
XXXVI (4)

P93   Rim sherd of fairly soft crumbly paste tempered with a little grit. Grey to brown externally, reddish brown internally.
Decoration: remains of horizontal lines in(?) grooved technique.
XXIX (10)

P94   Wall sherd of fairly compact paste tempered with much shell. Brown both faces with dark grey core.
Decoration: vertical grooved lines separate panels of diagonal grooved lines, themselves perhaps subdivided by horizontal grooved lines.
IV Segment VII (9)

P95   Wall sherd of compact paste. Brown externally, grey internally with dark grey core.
Decoration: vertical grooved line separates grooved chevrons and diagonal lines.
IV Segment IX (5)

P96   Wall sherd of compact paste tempered with a little shell. Brown externally, grey internally.
Decoration: vertical line separates panels of vertical grooved chevrons. Perforation through the wall drilled after firing.
IV Segment VIII (6)

P97   Four wall sherds of compact paste tempered with shell. Brown both faces with dark grey core.
Decoration: vertical single grooved lines separate panels of grooved diagonal lines, chevrons and filled triangles.
IV Segment XIα (7)

P98   Wall sherd of fairly compact paste tempered with shell. Light brown externally, dark grey internally.
Decoration: remains of two vertical grooved lines adjoining panel of diagonal grooved lines.
XVIII (2)

P99   Two body sherds of flaky paste tempered with much shell. Grey externally, light brown internally with dark grey core.
Decoration: remains of horizontal and diagonal grooved lines.
IV Segment IX (5)

P100   Wall sherd of compact paste tempered with a little shell. Reddish brown to grey externally, reddish brown internally with grey core.

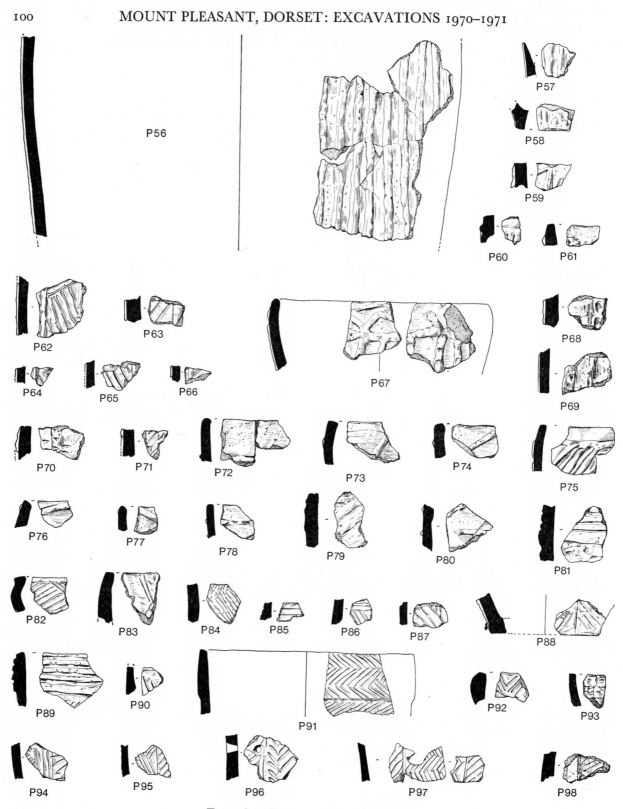

FIG. 46.   Grooved Ware. (Scale ¼)

Decoration: horizontal grooved line separates opposed diagonal grooved lines.

IV Feature 191

P101 Wall sherd of fairly compact paste tempered with shell. Grey throughout, surface roughly smoothed.

Decoration: grooved herringbone.

XXXIV (2)

P102 Wall sherd of fairly soft paste tempered with shell. Reddish brown both faces with dark grey core.

Decoration: diagonal grooved lines.

XXXVI (7)

P103 Wall sherd of fairly compact paste. Reddish brown externally, dark grey internally, surface smoothed.

Decoration: multiple grooved chevrons.

II (5)

P104 Base angle of fairly compact paste tempered with shell. Light brown externally, brown internally.

Decoration: remains of grooved decoration.

IV Segment X (5)

P105 Wall sherd of fairly compact paste. Brown externally, dark grey internally.

Decoration: remains of grooved lines and jabbed filling.

IV Segment IX (7)

P106 Wall sherd of compact paste tempered with large quantity of shell. Grey to brown both faces with dark grey core.

Decoration: remains of whipped-cord maggots.

XXVIII/XXIX (6)

P107 Rim sherd lacking lip of fairly compact paste tempered with large quantity of shell. Brown both faces with dark grey core.

Decoration: four horizontal twisted-cord lines above diagonal opposed grooved lines. Weathered.

XXVIII (10)/(11)

P108 Wall sherd of soft crumbly paste. Brown throughout.

Decoration: remains of horizontal plain cordon with horizontal to diagonal twisted-cord lines beneath.

XXIX (10)

Probably same pot as P109.

P109 Wall sherd of soft crumbly paste tempered with some grog. Brown to grey externally, brown internally.

Decoration: remains of diagonal grooved lines above horizontal plain cordon, with twisted-cord line beneath.

XXIX (10)

P110 Rim sherd of fairly compact paste tempered with flint. Orange to greyish brown externally, orange internally with dark grey core.

Decoration: two rows of jabbed impressions above irregularly placed lunate impressions with a plain horizontal cordon beneath from which descends a vertical plain cordon. A hole drilled from the external surface after firing penetrates halfway through the wall. Remains of perforation through the wall beneath the horizontal cordon, made before firing.

XXIX (10) Burnt area

P111   Rim sherd of fairly compact paste. Brown both faces with dark grey core.
Decoration: a row of jabs underneath the rim.
XXIX Top of (6)

P112   Base angle of coarse paste tempered with grit and grog. Reddish brown externally, brown to dark grey internally.
Decoration: horizontal widely spaced impressions.
XXIX (7)

P113   Fourteen undecorated sherds, plus fragments, of bowl of fairly compact paste. Greyish brown both faces. Weathered and broken at luting.
IV Segment V (9)

P114   Undecorated rim sherd of flaky paste. Grey to brown externally, dark grey internally.
XXXVIN (10)

P115   Undecorated rim sherd of flaky paste tempered with grit. Reddish brown throughout. Surface smoothed.
XXIX (10)

P116   Undecorated rim sherd of compact paste tempered with a little fine grit. Light brown throughout.
XXIX (10)

P117   Undecorated rim sherd of fairly compact paste tempered with grit, including chalk and shell. Light brown externally, brown internally with dark grey core.
XXIX (10)

P118   Undecorated rim sherd of fairly soft paste tempered with fine grit. Brown throughout. Surface roughly smoothed.
XXIX (10)

P119   Undecorated rim sherd of compact paste tempered with a little grit. Orange both faces with dark grey core. Surface roughly smoothed.
XXVIII/XXIX (8)

P120   Undecorated rim sherd of compact paste tempered with a little shell. Patchy grey to brown externally, grey internally.
XXIX (12)

P121   Undecorated rim sherd of fairly compact paste tempered with chalk. Greyish brown throughout.
XXIX (10)

P122   Undecorated rim sherd of soft flaky paste tempered with a little grit. Grey externally, brown internally.
XXIX (10)

P123   Undecorated rim sherd of fairly compact paste tempered with a little shell. Orange with dark grey patches externally, orange to grey internally.
XXIX (11)

P124   Undecorated rim sherd of fairly compact paste tempered with chalk and shell. Light orange throughout.
XXIX (12)

P125   Undecorated rim sherd of soft paste tempered with grog. Brown throughout.
XXVIII/XXIX (8)

P126   Undecorated base angle of soft flaky paste. Reddish brown externally, dark grey internally.
XXIX (7)

P127   Undecorated base angle of soft paste tempered with grit and grog. Reddish brown externally, grey internally with dark grey core.
XXIX (7)

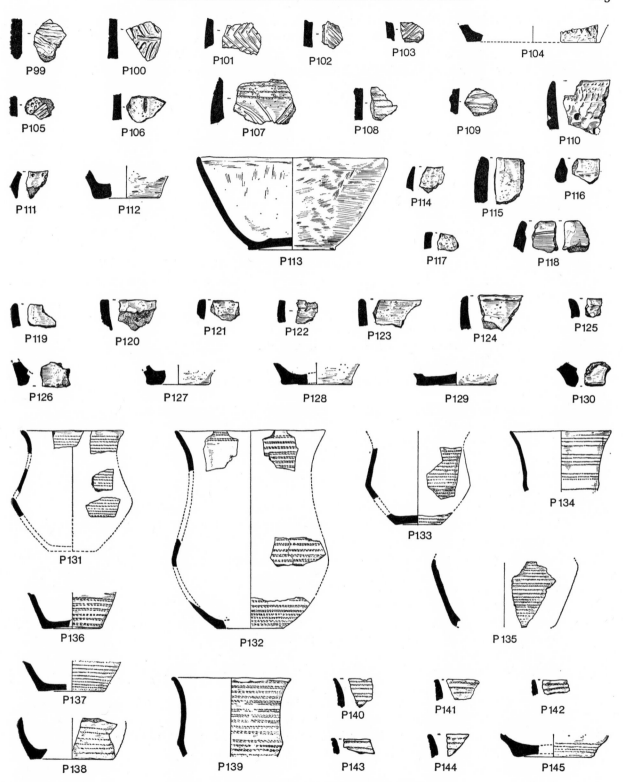

FIG. 47. Grooved Ware and Beaker. (Scale ¼)

P128   Undecorated base angle of compact sandy paste tempered with a little grit and grog. Reddish brown to grey externally, grey internally. Weathered.
XXVIII (10) and XXIX (10)

P129   Base of fairly soft paste tempered with grog and a little grit. Orange throughout.
XXVIII (11)

P130   Undecorated base angle of soft paste. Reddish brown externally, dark grey internally.
XXX (3)

Beaker

P131   Fourteen sherds including rims of fine compact paste. Light brown both faces with dark grey patches, with dark grey core. Surface well smoothed.
Decoration: horizontal fine twisted-cord lines.
IV Segment VIII (6)

P132   Seventeen sherds including rim and base angle of fairly soft sandy paste. Light brown both faces with dark grey core.
Decoration: from rim to base, horizontal pairs of twisted-cord lines, the twists being in the same direction. Internally, beneath the rim, two further horizontal rows of similar impressions.
IV Segment Xa (5)

P133   Nine sherds from the lower two-thirds of a vessel of compact paste. Light brown both faces with dark grey core. Surface well smoothed.
Decoration: horizontal fine twisted-cord lines.
IV Segment XIII (6)

P134   Five sherds including rim of fine compact paste. Reddish brown externally, brown internally with dark grey core.
Decoration: groups of fine twisted-thread lines separated by reserved bands.
IV Segment XIII (5)

P135   Wall sherd, including shoulder, of compact paste. Grey to brown externally, brown internally. Surface smoothed.
Decoration: horizontal lines of twisted-cord impressions.
IV Segment XIII (4)

P136   Base angle of compact paste. Grey externally, reddish brown to grey internally.
Decoration: horizontal pairs of twisted-cord lines, the twists being in the same direction.
IV Segment XIII (3)

P137   Base angle of fine compact paste. Reddish brown both faces with dark grey core. Surface smoothed.
Decoration: horizontal fine twisted-cord lines.
IV Segment XIII (5) (Disturbed)

P138   Base angle of compact paste. Grey to brown externally, grey internally.
Decoration: horizontal twisted-cord lines. Weathered.
IV Segment XIII (5)

P139   Eight sherds from the upper half of a vessel of fairly compact paste. Brown externally, patchy grey to brown internally. Surface roughly smoothed.
Decoration: pairs of horizontal twisted-cord lines, the twists being in the same direction.
IV Segment XIII (5) and IV Segment XII (7)

P140   Rim sherd of fairly soft paste. Reddish brown both faces. Surfaces smoothed.
Decoration: horizontal twisted-cord lines.
IV Segment XIII (5)

P141 Rim sherd of fairly compact paste. Grey both faces.
Decoration: horizontal lines of coarse twisted cord.
IV Segment XIII (3)

P142 Rim sherd of fairly compact paste. Grey throughout.
Decoration: externally, two horizontal twisted-cord lines.
XXIX (7)

P143 Rim sherd of fine compact paste. Brown externally, grey internally with dark grey core.
Decoration: horizontal lines of coarse twisted cord.
IV Segment XIII (5)

P144 Rim sherd of fairly compact paste tempered with a little grit and grog. Grey both faces.
Decoration: horizontal lines of coarse and fine twisted cord.
IV Segment XIII (5)

P145 Base angle of fairly compact paste. Light brown to grey externally, grey internally.
Decoration: horizontal lines of twisted-cord impressions.
IV Segment XIII (5)

P146 Two sherds including rim of compact paste tempered with some grit. Brown externally, grey to brown internally.
Decoration: two narrow horizontal bands, each consisting of four horizontal lines of rectangular toothed-comb impressions.
IV Segment IVa (8)

P147 Fifty-seven sherds from a vessel of compact fine paste tempered with a little grit. Reddish brown both faces with dark grey core. Surface well smoothed.
Decoration: groups of horizontal impressed lines separated by reserved bands.
IV Segment XIII (5)

P148 Rim sherd of fine compact paste. Reddish brown externally, brown internally with dark grey core.
Decoration: five horizontal lines of rectangular toothed-comb stamp impressions externally, beneath the rim. Surface well smoothed.
IV Segment I (5)

P149 Rim sherd of soft paste. Brown externally, grey to brown internally, surface smoothed.
Decoration: deep zone of horizontal rectangular toothed-comb stamp lines incorporating two lines of short spatulate impressions separated by reserved zone from second band of horizontal above vertical rectangular toothed-comb lines.
III (3)

P150 Two rim sherds of compact paste. Reddish brown externally, reddish brown to grey internally with dark grey core. Surface smoothed.
Decoration: two bands of horizontal rectangular toothed-comb stamp lines separated by a reserved zone.
III (3)

P151 Rim sherd of compact paste. Light brown both faces with dark grey core. Surface smoothed.
Decoration: horizontal rectangular toothed-comb stamp lines.
III (3)

P152 Rim sherd of compact paste tempered with a little grit. Light brown both faces with dark grey core.
Decoration: horizontal rectangular toothed-comb stamp.
IV Segment IX (5)

P153 Rim sherd of compact paste. Brown externally, grey internally. Surface smoothed.
Decoration: horizontal lines of rectangular toothed-comb impressions.
IV Segment I (3)

P154 Wall sherd of slightly porous paste. Light brown both faces. Surface smoothed.
Decoration: horizontal rectangular toothed-comb lines.
IV Segment XIII (5)

P155 Wall sherd of compact paste. Reddish brown both faces. Surface smoothed.
Decoration: remains of two zones of horizontal rectangular toothed-comb lines separated by reserved band.
III (3)

P156 Base angle of fairly soft coarse paste. Light greyish brown externally, light brown internally with dark grey core.
Decoration: remains of two lines of horizontal decoration.
IV Segment Iα (4)

P157 Thirty-five sherds including rim of compact paste. Reddish brown to brown both faces with dark grey core.
Decoration: incised herringbone.
IV Segment XIII (5)

P158 About one fifth of a vessel of fairly compact paste tempered with some grog. Light brown externally, light brown to grey internally.
Decoration: in rectangular toothed-comb stamp. Horizontal herringbone split by and bordered beneath by narrow reserved band, outlined with single horizontal lines above complex reserved lozenge pattern, filled by narrow horizontal bands alternately reserved and filled with short vertical lines.

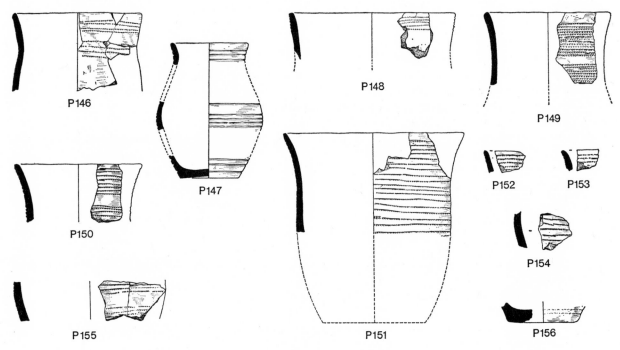

P146　P147　P148　P149

P150　P152　P153

P154

P155　P151　P156

Fig. 48. Beaker. (Scale ¼)

At the base of the neck, a narrow band of diagonal lines bounded above and below by horizontal lines and reserved bands. Over the shoulder and on to the body, reserved bar chevron, the pendant and standing triangles being filled with short horizontal lines.
IV Segment X (5)

P159 Rim sherd of fine compact paste. Light brown externally, grey internally.
Decoration: in the neck, horizontal zones of rectangular toothed-comb stamp vertical chevrons above horizontal chevrons enclosed between discontinuous single horizontal lines.
IV Segment VII (6) and IV Segment X (5)

P160 Two sherds including rim of fairly compact paste tempered with grog. Light brown to grey both faces with dark grey core. Surfaces smoothed.
Decoration: in the neck, coarsely incised multiple zigzag. On the shoulder, short vertical incisions.
IV Segment XIII (4)

P161 Base angle of compact paste. Light brown externally, light brown to grey internally with dark grey core. Surface smoothed.
Decoration: narrow bands of incised lattice.
IV Segment XIII (3)

P162 Fifty-seven sherds of fairly compact paste tempered with fine shell. Light brown to grey both faces with dark grey core.
Decoration: deep bands of impressed herringbone bordered by horizontal impressed rectangular toothed-comb lines and separated by a narrow reserved zone.
IV Segment XIII (5)

P163 Five sherds from base and body of fairly compact paste tempered with some grit. Patchy grey to brown both faces. Surface smoothed.
Decoration: remains of impressed zonal pattern made with (?) broken end of bone. One body sherd carries remains of zone of irregular horizontal scored lines beneath vertical impressions.
IV Segment XIII (5)

P164 Eight sherds including base angle of compact fine paste. Light brown to grey both faces with dark grey core. Surface well smoothed.
Decoration: remains of narrow zones incorporating zigzag, split herringbone and lattice motifs enclosed by horizontal lines, all in rectangular toothed-comb.
IV Segment XIII (5)

P165 Four sherds including rim of fairly compact paste. Light brown externally, brown internally with dark grey core.
Decoration: beneath the rim, incised lattice with a band of confused incised lattice/chevron on the body.
IV Segment X (5)

P166 Nine sherds including rim of compact paste. Grey to brown externally, grey internally. Surface smoothed.
Decoration: narrow horizontal bands of incised lattice.
IV Segment XIII (5)

P167 Two sherds representing most of a vessel of fine compact paste. Patchy grey to reddish brown externally, patchy grey to brown internally. Surface well smoothed.
Decoration: alternate zones of rectangular toothed-comb designs and reserved bands, the uppermost decorated band comprising a confused lattice pattern, the second band herringbone between single rows of lattice, the third zone lattice, the basal zone herringbone bordered above and below by a single row of lattice, the decorated bands in each case being outlined by a horizontal rectangular toothed-comb line.
IV Segment XIII (5)

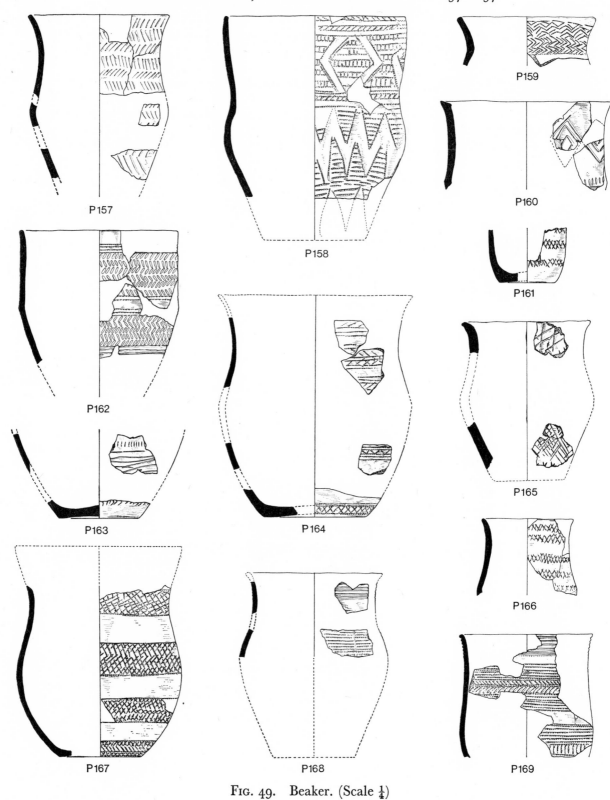

FIG. 49.   Beaker. (Scale ¼)

P168   Ten sherds of compact paste. Reddish brown externally, brown internally with dark grey core. Decoration: zones of horizontal rectangular toothed-comb stamp lines alternating with reserved zones.
II DTP Hearth (3)

P169   Rim sherd extending to belly of compact paste. Brown to grey both faces with dark grey core. Surface smoothed.
Decoration: beneath the rim, a zone of horizontal grooved lines separated from a second zone by a reserved band. The second zone consists of horizontal rectangular toothed-comb lines enclosing a herringbone pattern split by two horizontal lines, all in the same technique. A third zone separated from the second by a reserved band consists of short vertical lines enclosed by horizontal lines, all in rectangular toothed-comb stamp.
II DTP Hearth at base of (3)

P170   Six sherds including rim of compact paste tempered with a little shell. Brown both faces with dark grey core. Surface well smoothed.
Decoration: in rectangular toothed-comb stamp. Below the rim a zone of horizontal lines. Near the belly, a zone of short vertical lines enclosed between groups of horizontal lines separated from further zone of horizontal lines by a reserved band.
III (3)

P171   Rim sherd of compact paste tempered with some grit. Light brown both faces with dark grey core.
Decoration: horizontal rectangular toothed-comb stamp lines and short spatulate impressions.
IV Segment XIα (7)

P172   Rim sherd of compact paste. Brown both faces with dark grey core.
Decoration: horizontal above opposed diagonal lines of rectangular toothed-comb stamp.
XXIX (8)

P173   Rim sherd of compact paste. Brown both faces with dark grey core.
Decoration: narrow zone(s) of irregular rectangular toothed-comb stamp lattice split and enclosed by horizontal rectangular toothed-comb stamp lines.
XXIII (2) 0–10 cm.

P174   Two wall sherds of soft paste. Reddish brown both faces with grey core. Surface smoothed.
Decoration: remains of a pattern made with rectangular toothed-comb stamp, including horizontal and short diagonal lines and vertical chevrons, some separated by a reserved zone.
III (3)

P175   Wall sherd of crumbly paste. Greyish brown both faces.
Decoration: remains of horizontal band of rectangular toothed-comb stamp lattice, bounded above by three rectangular toothed-comb stamp lines.
IV Segment XII (6)

P176   Wall sherd of fairly compact paste tempered with a large quantity of flint grit. Light brown externally, brown internally with dark grey core.
Decoration: reserved bar chevron, the triangles filled with horizontal rectangular toothed-comb stamp lines.
XXIV (2)

P177   Wall sherd of fine compact paste. Light brown both faces with dark grey core.
Decoration: rectangular toothed-comb herringbone split by fine chain-plaited lines.
IV Segment XIII (5)

P178   Wall sherd of fairly compact paste tempered with grit. Grey externally, brown internally. Surface smoothed.

Decoration: narrow band of rectangular toothed-comb lozenges bordered above and below by rectangular toothed-comb lines.

IV Segment XIII (5)

P179 Wall sherd of fairly compact paste. Light brown both faces with dark grey core. Surface smoothed.

Decoration: narrow horizontal band of rectangular toothed-comb impressions bordered above by one, and beneath by three, rectangular toothed-comb lines.

IV Segment XIII (5)

P180 Base angle of compact paste tempered with a little grit. Light brown both faces.

Decoration: remains of pendant triangles filled with horizontal lines outlined by two lines, with a single horizontal line beneath, all in rectangular toothed-comb stamp.

IV Segment XI (6)

P181 Wall sherd of fairly compact paste. Reddish brown externally, brown internally with dark grey core. Surface smoothed.

Decoration: lozenge made with triple lines of jabbed impressions.

II DTN (5)

P182 Wall sherd of fairly compact paste. Reddish brown externally, brown internally with dark grey core. Surface smoothed.

Decoration: diagonal lines made with triple lines of jabbed impressions.

II DTN (5)

Probably same pot as P181.

P183 Two sherds of base angle of fairly compact paste. Reddish brown throughout. Surface smoothed.

Decoration: at the base, short vertical twisted-cord lines.

III (3)

P184 Two sherds including rim of fine compact paste. Brown both faces with dark grey core. Surface smoothed.

Decoration: horizontal rows of short diagonal incised lines.

IV Segment XIα (7)

P185 Rim sherd of compact sandy paste. Reddish brown both faces with grey core. Surface well smoothed.

Decoration: open incised herringbone.

IV Segment Xα (5)

P186 Two wall sherds of compact paste. Reddish brown both faces with dark grey core. Surface well smoothed.

Decoration: impressed herringbone, some of the impressions partially smoothed over.

III (3)

P187 Rim sherd of compact paste. Reddish brown throughout. Surface smoothed.

Decoration: a row of impressions set in herringbone fashion above remains of horizontal rectangular toothed-comb stamp lines.

III (3)

P188 Seven wall sherds similar to P189–90, of compact paste. Grey to brown both faces with dark grey core.

Decoration: incised lattice bounded beneath by a group of horizontal incised lines. On the shoulder, groups of horizontal spatulate impressions. Beneath, a group of horizontal incised lines with incised lattice below.

XXIX (7), (8) and (9)

P189 Wall sherd of compact paste. Dark brown to grey externally, brown internally with dark grey core. Surface roughly smoothed.

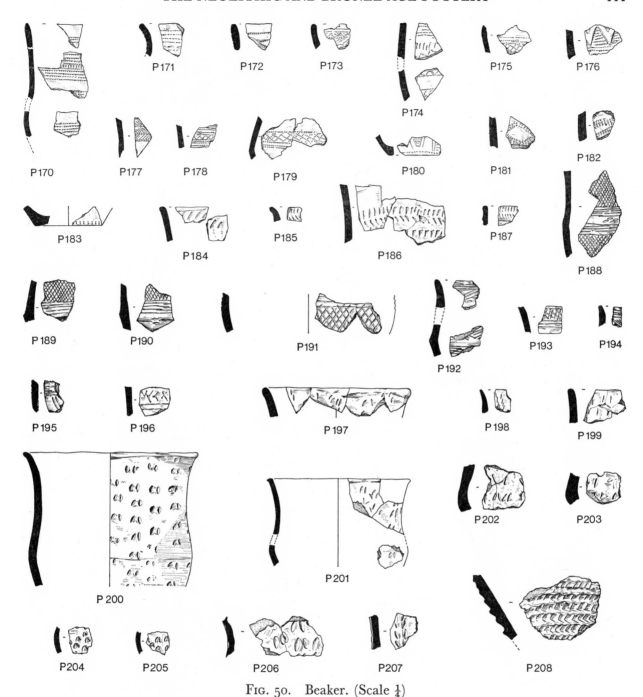

FIG. 50. Beaker. (Scale ¼)

Decoration: a zone of incised lattice above a band of horizontal incised lines.
XXVIII/XXIX (10)
Joins with sherd from XXVIII (6)/(7) (P190)

P190   Three sherds of fairly compact paste tempered with some grit. Reddish brown to brown externally, reddish brown to grey internally with dark grey core.
Decoration: remains of incised lattice above a group of horizontal incised lines. Beneath the shoulder, horizontal spatulate impressions.
XXVIII (6)/(7) and (7) and XXIX (8)

P191   Three sherds of fairly compact paste tempered with some grit. Grey to brown externally, brown internally with dark grey core.
Decoration: zone of incised horizontal lines bordering deep band of incised lattice.
XXX (7) 10–15 cm.

P192   Two sherds including rim of fairly compact paste tempered with some grit. Light brown to grey externally, brown to grey internally with dark grey core. Surface smoothed.
Decoration: beneath the rim, groups of horizontal incised lines above diagonal lines with remains of impressions beneath. At the shoulder, remains of opposed groups of incised lines above and horizontal incised lines beneath.
XXVIII (8)

P193   Three sherds of fairly soft paste. Light brown both faces with dark grey core.
Decoration: narrow zone of rectangular toothed-comb lattice bordered by horizontal rectangular toothed-comb lines.
IV Segment XIII (5)

P194   Rim sherd of compact paste. Grey both faces with dark grey core.
Decoration: groups of finely incised horizontal above diagonal lines.
XXIX (10)

P195   Wall sherd of fairly compact paste tempered with grog. Reddish brown externally, grey to brown internally with dark grey core.
Decoration: roughly executed horizontal incised lines above diagonal opposed incised lines.
XXVIII (6)/(7)

P196   Wall sherd of compact sandy paste. Brown both faces with grey core.
Decoration: roughly executed incised herringbone above two incised horizontal lines.
III (3)

P197   Rim sherd of compact paste. Reddish brown throughout. Surface smoothed.
Decoration: light vertical finger-pinching.
III (3)

P198   Rim sherd of rather soft paste. Brown externally, reddish brown internally, with dark grey core. Surface smoothed.
Decoration: diagonal rows of short incisions, perhaps made with finger-nail.
IV Segment XIII (5)

P199   Rim sherd of fairly compact paste. Brown both faces with reddish brown core. Surface roughly smoothed.
Decoration: irregular finger-nail impressions.
III (3)

P200   Upper half of a vessel of fairly compact paste tempered with grog. Patchy reddish brown to grey externally, brown to grey internally. Surface smoothed.
Decoration: vertical rows of finger-pinching.
XXXVI (4) and (6)

P201   Four sherds including rim of fairly compact paste. Light brown both faces with dark grey core. Surface well smoothed.
Decoration: light finger-pinching.
IV Segment XIII (5)

P202   Wall sherd of coarse paste. Greyish brown both faces with dark grey core.
Decoration: irregular finger-nail impressions.
XXVIII (10)

P203   Two wall sherds including shoulder of fairly compact paste tempered with grit. Reddish brown to grey both faces with dark grey core.
Decoration: remains of impressions probably made with the finger-nail.
XXVIII/XXIX (8)

P204   Wall sherd of compact paste tempered with flint grit. Brown to grey both faces with dark grey core.
Decoration: finger-pinching.
XXXIV (2)

P205   Wall sherd of fairly compact paste tempered with grog. Brown to grey externally, grey internally.
Decoration: finger-pinching.
XXXVI (2)

P206   Two wall sherds of compact paste. Greyish brown externally, grey to brown internally, dark grey core. Surface smoothed.
Decoration: coarse finger-pinching.
IV Segment IV (4)

P207   Two sherds of rather coarse paste tempered with grit. Grey to brown both faces with dark grey core.
Decoration: coarse vertical finger-pinched ridge.
IV Segment XIII (5)

P208   Wall sherd of coarse paste tempered with flint grit. Reddish brown externally, grey internally.
Decoration: horizontal ridges formed by rustication.
III (3)

P209   Twenty-nine sherds including rim of soft coarse paste tempered with large quantity of grog and grit. Light reddish brown externally, light brown to grey internally. Surface smoothed.
Decoration: on the outer edge of the rim, round-based impressions. On the body, short vertical to diagonal round-based strokes.
IV Segment XIII (5)

P210   Rim sherd of fairly soft paste tempered with some grog. Grey throughout.
Decoration: above and below pinched-out cordon, vertical jabbed impressions.
XXIX (8)

P211   Rim sherd of fairly compact paste. Reddish brown to grey both faces. Surface smoothed.
Decoration: above and below pinched-out cordon, rows of short vertical impressions.
III (3)

P212   Rim sherd of compact paste. Light brown throughout. Surface smoothed.
Decoration: rows of short vertical impressions.
IV Segment XIII (5)

P213   Five sherds perhaps from the same vessel, including base and rim, of fairly compact paste. Brown externally, grey to brown internally. Surface smoothed.
Decoration: rows of triangular-shaped impressions.
IV Segment XIII (5)

P214 Two rim sherds of fairly compact paste. Reddish brown externally, reddish brown to grey internally with dark grey core.
Decoration: single row of jabbed impressions below the rim.
III (3)

P215 Wall sherd including shoulder of fairly compact paste tempered with grog. Light brown externally, greyish brown internally with dark grey core. Surface roughly smoothed.
Decoration: irregularly placed impressions.
III (3)

P216 Wall sherd of fairly compact paste tempered with some grit. Brown externally, brown to grey internally.
Decoration: diagonal incised strokes.
XXX (7)

P217 Rim sherd of sandy paste tempered with a little grog. Brown externally, grey internally. Surface roughly smoothed.
Decoration: a single row of (?) bone impressions set some way beneath the rim.
IV Segment XIII disturbed

P218 Thirty-nine sherds including rim and base angle from an undecorated vessel of fine compact paste. Light brown both faces with dark grey core. Surface roughly smoothed.
IV Segment XIII (4) and (5)

P219 Two undecorated rim sherds of fairly compact paste. Reddish brown both faces with dark grey core.
IV Segment XIII (5)

P220 Undecorated rim sherd of compact sandy paste. Red externally, red to grey internally with dark grey core. Surface roughly smoothed.
IV Segment XIII (4A)

P221 Undecorated rim sherd of compact paste. Light brown both faces with grey core. Surface roughly smoothed.
IV Segment XII (7)

P222 Undecorated base angle of fairly compact paste. Light brown both faces with grey core. Surface smoothed.
IV Segment XIα (7)

P223 Undecorated base angle of flaky paste. Greyish brown externally, brown internally. Surface smoothed.
IV Segment X (5)

P224 Undecorated base angle of fairly compact paste. Brown externally, grey internally. Surface smoothed.
IV Segment IV (7)

P225 Undecorated base angle of compact paste tempered with grog. Brown externally, grey internally.
IV Segment XIII (3)

P226 Undecorated base angle of compact paste. Brown externally, grey internally with dark grey core. Surface roughly smoothed.
IV Segment XIII (4A)

Polypod Bowl

P227 Undecorated fragment of foot of well-fired compact paste. Reddish brown throughout.
XXX (6)

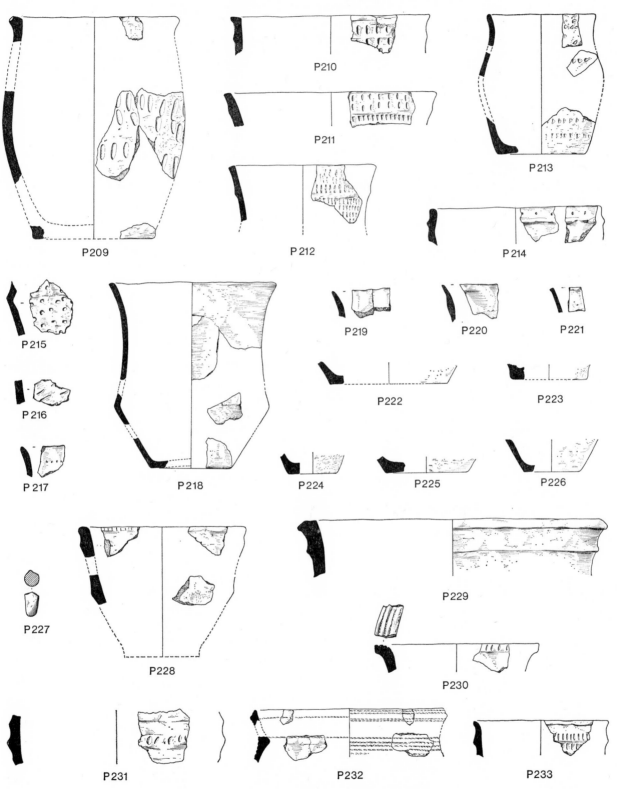

Fig. 51. Beaker and Food Vessel. (Scale ¼)

Food Vessel

P228   Three sherds including rim, of coarse paste. Grey to brown both faces with dark grey core. Decoration: a row of vertical finger-nail impressions on the internal edge of the rim. One sherd carries slight boss.
    IV Segment XIII (5)

P229   Undecorated rim sherd of coarse paste tempered with grog. Patchy grey to brown both faces.
    IV Segment XIII (4)

P230   Rim sherd of fairly soft paste tempered with grog. Brown externally, greyish brown internally. Decoration: on the internal surface of the rim, three twisted-cord lines. On the external rim bevel, short diagonal impressions.
    IV Segment V (3)

P231   Wall sherd of fairly compact paste tempered with some grog. Light brown externally, brown internally. Surface smoothed.
    Decoration: jabbed impressions on central cordon.
    IV Segment XIII (4)

P232   Nine sherds including rim of soft crumbly paste. Greyish brown externally, grey internally. Decoration: on the internal rim bevel, remains of two twisted-cord lines. On the external surface, horizontal twisted-cord lines.
    IV Segment VII (5)

P233   Rim sherd of fairly soft crumbly paste tempered with a little grit. Brown both faces. Decoration: above and below pinched-out cordon, short vertical incisions.
    IV Segment VIIIα (5)

P234   Four sherds including rim and shoulder of fairly compact paste. Light brown to grey externally, light brown internally with dark grey core. Decoration: on the neck, rows of jabbed impressions.
    XXVIII (6)/(7) and (7)

P235   Undecorated rim sherd of fairly compact paste tempered with grit. Light brown externally, light brown to grey internally. Surface roughly smoothed.
    IV Segment VIIIα (3)

P236   Rim sherd of fairly soft paste tempered with grog. Reddish brown both faces with dark grey core. Decoration: externally and on the internal rim bevel, impressions made with the end of a bone or twig.
    XX (5)

P237   Four rim sherds of fairly compact paste. Reddish brown externally, reddish brown to grey internally with dark grey core. Decoration: on top of the rim, short diagonal incised lines. On the upper edge of the rim, a row of blobs.
    III (3)

P238   Rim sherd of flaky paste tempered with grog. Light brown both faces with dark grey core. Decoration: on the edge of the everted rim, vertical finger-nail impressions.
    XXIX (6)/(7)

P239   Undecorated rim sherd of fairly soft paste. Light brown throughout.
    XXIX (6)/(7)

P240   Two undecorated rim sherds of fairly compact paste tempered with some grog. Brown externally, grey to brown internally with dark grey core. Surface roughly smoothed.
    XXVIII (7)

P241 Undecorated rim sherd of fairly compact paste tempered with grit. Brown externally, greyish brown internally.
XXIX (6)/(7)

P242 Undecorated base angle of fairly soft paste tempered with grog. Greyish brown externally, grey internally.
XX (3)

P243 Rim sherd of fairly soft paste tempered with a little fine grit. Grey externally, brown internally.
Decoration: remains of impressions on the rim.
XXIX (6)

P244 Undecorated wall sherd of fairly compact paste tempered with fine grog and a little grit. Grey externally, light brown internally with dark grey core.
IV Segment VII (3)

P245 Wall sherd of flaky paste. Greyish brown both faces with dark grey core. Surface roughly smoothed.
Decoration: rows of circular impressions.
XXIX (10)

Collared Vessel

P246 Two fragments including rim of fairly soft paste tempered with shell. Reddish brown to grey externally, grey internally.
Decoration: on the collar, short diagonal impressions enclosed between single plaited-cord lines. On the internal moulding, remains of horizontal plaited-cord lines.
XXVIII (6) and XXIX (6)

P247 Fragment of collar of fairly compact paste. Patchy grey to brown both faces.
Decoration: remains of twisted-cord hurdle pattern.
XXVIII (6)

P248 Rim sherd of fairly compact paste tempered with some grit. Grey externally, dark grey internally.
Decoration: horizontal twisted-cord lines.
XXIX (6)

P249 Three rim sherds of compact paste. Greyish brown externally, grey internally.
Decoration: on the collar, rough twisted-cord herringbone bordered above by two twisted-cord lines. On the internal rim bevel, short diagonal twisted-cord lines.
XXIX (6) and (7)

P250 Rim sherd of fairly soft paste. Brown externally, dark grey internally.
Decoration: on the internal rim bevel, three twisted-cord lines. On the collar, twisted-cord hurdle pattern bounded above by two twisted-cord lines.
XXVII (9)

P251 Rim sherd of compact paste. Grey to brown externally, brown internally.
Decoration: remains of twisted-cord lines above diagonal twisted-cord lines. On the internal rim bevel, a single twisted-cord line.
XXX (6)

P252 Rim sherd of fairly compact paste tempered with a little grit. Reddish brown throughout.
Decoration: remains of horizontal twisted-cord lines externally above beginnings of vertical lines. On the internal rim bevel, two horizontal twisted-cord lines.
XXX (6)

P253 Rim sherd of fairly soft paste. Brown externally, grey internally.
Decoration: on the internal rim bevel, horizontal twisted-cord lines. Externally, remains of

diagonal twisted-cord lines.

IV (2) Plough-soil

P254 Rim sherd of fairly compact paste tempered with a little grit and grog. Grey to brown both faces with dark grey core.

Decoration: on the internal rim bevel, remains of two to three twisted-cord lines.

IV Segment IX (4)

P255 Rim sherd of fairly coarse paste tempered with grog. Greyish brown both faces with dark grey core.

Decoration: on the internal rim bevel, two twisted-cord lines.

IV Segment VIIIa (3)

P256 Rim sherd of fairly compact paste tempered with a little grit. Grey externally, brown internally with dark grey core.

Decoration: externally, remains of vertical twisted-cord impressions. On the internal rim bevel, a single twisted-cord line.

XXIX (6)/(7)

P257 Rim sherd of compact paste. Light brown both faces with dark grey core. Surface roughly smoothed.

Decoration: remains of twisted-cord decoration externally and on the internal rim bevel.

XXIX (7)

P258 Rim sherd of flaky paste. Grey to brown externally, brown internally with dark grey core.

Decoration: on the internal rim bevel, two twisted-cord lines. Externally, beneath the rim, three horizontal twisted-cord lines.

XXIX (7)

P259 Fragment from the upper part of a collar of fairly compact paste. Light brown both faces with dark grey core.

Decoration: on the collar, horizontal twisted-cord lines. On the internal rim bevel, two twisted-cord lines.

XXIX (6)

P260 Wall sherd probably from a collar of fairly compact paste tempered with a little grit. Patchy grey to brown externally, brown internally with dark grey core.

Decoration: remains of vertical twisted-cord lines.

XXIX (6)

P261 Fragment from a base of a collar of fairly compact paste. Greyish brown externally, brown internally with grey core.

Decoration: remains of blurred twisted-cord lines.

XXVIII (6)

P262 Fragment from the base of a collar of fairly compact paste. Brown both faces with dark grey core.

Decoration: remains of two horizontal twisted-cord lines.

XXIX (6)

P263 Fragment from the base of a collar of compact paste. Orangey brown to grey externally, with dark grey core.

Decoration: horizontal twisted-cord line.

XXX (6)

P264 Fragment from the base of a collar of fairly compact paste tempered with grit. Brown externally, grey internally with dark grey core.

Decoration: on the collar, horizontal twisted-cord lines.

XXIX (3)

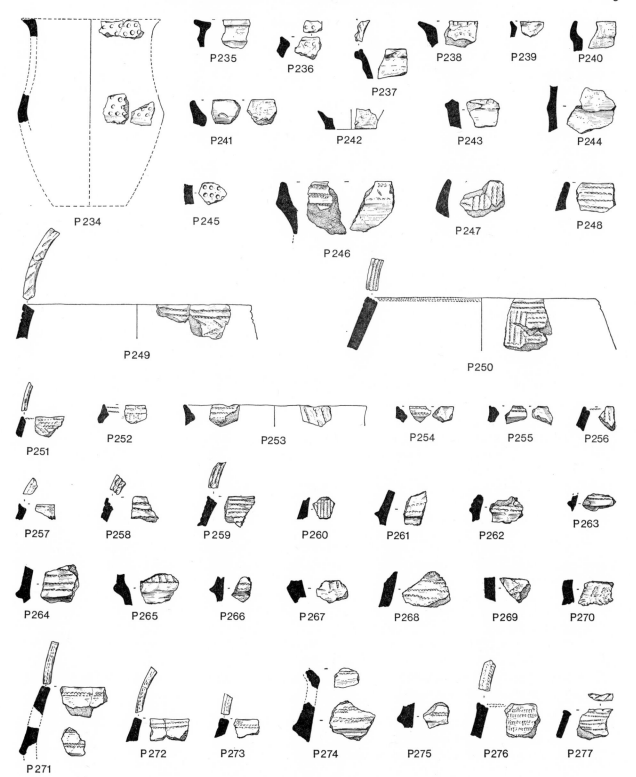

FIG. 52. Food Vessel and Collared Vessel. (Scale ¼)

P265 Fragment from the base of a collar of fairly coarse paste tempered with grog and grit. Light brown externally, dark grey internally.
Decoration: remains of diagonal twisted-cord lines bordered by a single horizontal twisted-cord line beneath.
IV Segment IV (5)

P266 Two sherds from the base of a collar of fairly compact paste tempered with some shell. Reddish brown externally, grey internally.
Decoration: at the base of the collar, two horizontal twisted-cord lines.
XXX (6)

P267 Fragment of shoulder of fairly soft paste tempered with shell. Reddish brown to grey externally, grey internally.
Decoration: remains of diagonal twisted-cord lines.
XXIXB (6)

P268 Wall sherd of coarse paste tempered with grit. Greyish brown both faces with dark grey core.
Decoration: remains of irregular horizontal twisted-cord lines.
XXVIII (6)/(7)

P269 Wall sherd of compact paste tempered with grit. Brown externally, grey internally. Surface roughly smoothed.
Decoration: remains of opposed twisted-cord lines.
XXVIII/XXIX (7)

P270 Wall sherd of rather crumbly paste tempered with a little grit and grog. Light brown both faces with dark grey core.
Decoration: remains of indefinite herringbone, perhaps made with cord impressions.
XXVIII (6)

P271 Five sherds including rim of fairly soft paste tempered with some grog. Grey to brown both faces with dark grey core.
Decoration: beneath the rim and at the base of the collar, horizontal plaited-cord lines. On top of the rim, a single plaited-cord line.
XXIX (6)/(7) and (7)

P272 Rim sherd of fairly compact paste. Greyish brown externally, brown internally with dark grey core.
Decoration: remains of one to two plaited-cord lines beneath the rim with remains of a single similar line on top of the rim.
XXIX (6)

P273 Rim sherd of fairly compact paste tempered with grog. Reddish brown throughout. Surface smoothed.
Decoration: beneath the rim externally, a single plaited-cord line with remains of a similar line on top of the rim.
XXIX (6)

P274 Three sherds of fairly compact paste tempered with grog. Patchy grey to brown both faces with dark grey core.
Decoration: on the internal rim bevel, remains of a horizontal plaited-cord line. On the collar, remains of plaited-cord lines.
XXIX (6)

P275 Fragment from the base of a collar of fairly soft paste tempered with some shell. Reddish brown both faces with dark grey core.
Decoration: a single horizontal plaited-cord line.
XXX (6)

P276   Two rim sherds of fairly soft paste tempered with grit. Reddish brown externally, greyish brown internally with dark grey core.
Decoration: remains of roughly horizontal lines of coarse toothed-comb impressions. On the internal rim bevel, a further two rows of similar impressions.
XXVIII/XXIX (6)

P277   Rim sherd of a ? collared vessel of fairly compact paste tempered with grit. Patchy grey to light brown externally, grey internally.
Decoration: on top of the rim, short diagonal point toothed-comb lines. On the collar, discontinuous horizontal point toothed-comb lines.
IV Segment VII (3)

P278   Fragment from the base of a collar of fairly compact paste. Brown both faces with dark grey core.
Decoration: rows of jabbed impressions on the collar.
XXX (4)

P279   Fragment of collar of fairly compact paste tempered with large grits. Brown externally, greyish brown internally with dark grey core.
Decoration: on the collar, all-over jabs.
XXVIII (6)

P280   Fragment from the base of a collar of fairly compact paste. Reddish brown externally, grey internally.
Decoration: remains of jabbed impressions.
XXX (6)

P281   Rim sherd of coarse paste tempered with a little grit. Grey externally, brown internally with dark grey core.
Decoration: on the internal rim bevel, lightly incised lattice. On the external surface, remains of indistinct impressions.
IV Segment Iα (4)

P282   Two wall sherds including shoulder of fairly coarse paste. Reddish brown both faces with dark grey core.
Decoration: on the neck and on to the shoulder, stabbed herringbone.
XXIX (7)

P283   Wall sherd of crumbly paste tempered with grit. Brown externally, grey internally with dark grey core.
Decoration: remains of whipped-cord lines.
XXVIII/XXIX (4)

P284   Wall sherd of fairly compact paste. Light brown externally, brown internally with dark grey core.
Decoration: twisted-cord horseshoes.
XXIX (6)

P285   Wall sherd of fairly compact paste. Brown externally, brown to grey internally with dark grey core.
Decoration: remains of twisted-cord horseshoes.
XXIX (6)

P286   Fragment from the upper part of an undecorated Collared Vessel. Reddish brown externally, brown internally with dark grey core.
XXIX (6)

P287   Undecorated rim sherd of fairly soft paste tempered with grog. Orange throughout.
XXX (5)/(6)

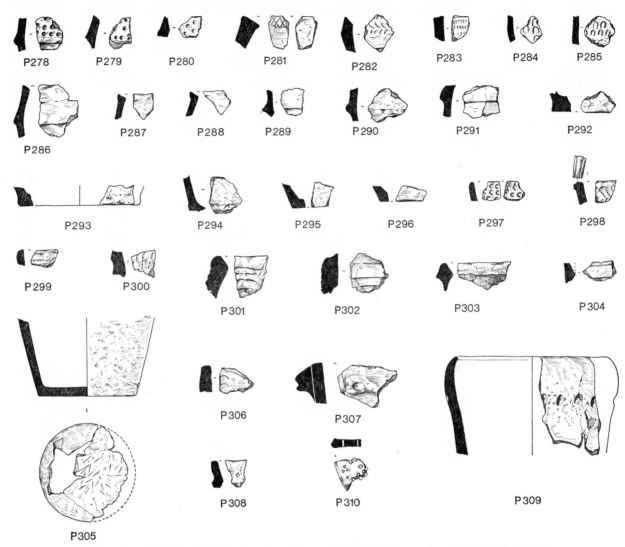

FIG. 53.   Collared Vessel, Bucket Urn and other Bronze Age wares. (Scale ¼)

P288   Undecorated rim sherd of fairly compact paste. Reddish brown externally, brown internally
with dark grey core.
XXIX (6)

P289   Undecorated fragment of collar of compact paste tempered with a little grog. Light brown both
faces with dark grey core.
XXVIII/XXIX (4)

P290   Undecorated fragment of collar of soft flaky paste tempered with grit. Brown to grey externally,
brown internally with dark grey core. Surface roughly smoothed.
XXVIII/XXIX (7)

P291   Undecorated base of collar of fairly compact paste. Light orange/brown externally, grey internally with dark grey core. Surface smoothed.
XXIX (7)

P292   Undecorated base angle of crumbly paste tempered with grog. Reddish brown externally, brown to grey internally with dark grey core.
XXVIII/XXIX (7)

P293   Undecorated base angle of fairly compact paste tempered with fine flint grit. Reddish brown externally, grey internally.
XXIX (6)

P294   Undecorated base angle of compact paste tempered with a little grit. Light reddish brown externally, dark grey internally.
XXVIII/XXIX (4)

P295   Undecorated base angle of fairly compact paste tempered with a little grog. Reddish brown externally, grey internally.
XXIX (6)

P296   Undecorated base angle of compact paste. Dark orange externally, brown internally with dark grey core.
XXX (6)

Bucket Urn and other Bronze Age Wares

P297   Rim sherd of compact paste tempered with grit. Light brown externally, greyish brown internally.
Decoration: externally and internally, twisted-cord horseshoes.
XXVIII (6)

P298   Rim sherd of fairly coarse paste. Brown externally, dark grey internally.
Decoration: on top of the rim, remains of two twisted-cord lines. Externally, remains of diagonal, twisted-cord lines.
IV Segment VI (3)

P299   Rim sherd of compact paste tempered with some grit. Brown both faces with dark grey core.
Decoration: remains of horizontal twisted-cord lines.
XXIX (7)

P300   Wall sherd of fairly soft paste tempered with some grit. Brown both faces with dark grey core.
Decoration: remains of diagonal twisted-cord lines.
XXVIII (5)

P301   Two rim sherds of compact paste. Greyish brown throughout.
Decoration: roughly scored horizontal to diagonal lines. The remains of a hole drilled after firing pierces halfway through the wall from the external surface.
XXIX Top (6)
Probably same vessel as P303.

P302   Wall sherd of compact but laminated paste tempered with some grit. Greyish brown both faces with dark grey core.
Decoration: deeply incised horizontal lines.
XXVIII/XXIX (6)
? Same pot as P304.

P303   Four rim sherds of compact paste tempered with grit. Patchy grey to brown.
Decoration: remains of incised horizontal line.
XXVIII/XXIX (6), XXIX (6), XXX (5)/(6) and (6)
Probably same pot as P301.

P304   Wall sherd of compact paste. Greyish brown throughout.
Decoration: remains of incised lines.
XXIX (6)

5*

P305 Base of fairly compact paste tempered with grit. Brown externally, grey to brown internally with dark grey core.
Decoration: internally, finger-nail impressions over base and on lower part of wall.
XXVIII/XXIX (6)

P306 Wall sherd of fairly compact paste tempered with grit. Greyish brown externally, dark grey internally.
Decoration: remains of finger-nail impressions.
XXX (4)

P307 Wall sherd of compact sandy paste. Reddish brown to grey externally, dark grey internally. Remains of imperforate lug carrying finger-tip impression. Weathered.
XXX (4)

P308 Undecorated rim sherd of compact paste tempered with grit. Reddish brown throughout.
XXIX (6)

P309 Rim sherd of fairly compact paste tempered with some grit. Greyish brown externally, grey internally.
Decoration: a row of finger-tip impressions set 5 cm. below the rim.
XXIX (4)

P310 Fragments of strainer base of fairly soft paste. Grey throughout.
XXIX (9)

Woodhenge

Neolithic Plain Bowls

P342 Undecorated rim sherd of compact paste tempered with a few large flint grits. Grey externally, brown internally.
Ditch layer (8)

P343 Undecorated rim sherd of compact paste tempered with grit. Grey throughout, surface smoothed.
OLS Below Bank /3\

Grooved Ware

P344 Two wall sherds of compact paste tempered with shell. Brown externally, greyish brown internally, with dark grey core.
Decoration: horizontal grooves above jabbed impressions.
Ditch layer (7)

P345 Base angle of fairly compact paste tempered with a little grit and grog. Brown externally, grey internally.
Decoration: remains of horizontal grooved lines.
Ditch layer (8)

P346 Base angle of compact paste tempered with a little shell. Reddish brown externally, grey internally.
Decoration: remains of impressions.
Ditch layer (6)

P 342   P 343   P 344   P 345   P 346

FIG. 54.   Woodhenge: plain Neolithic bowls and Grooved Ware. (Scale ¼)

IX. THE IRON AGE AND ROMANO-BRITISH POTTERY
(fig. 55)

A SMALL quantity of later prehistoric and Romano-British pottery was recorded from superficial deposits in Neolithic and Bronze Age contexts and from contemporary structures, indicating a sporadic occupation of that date on the hill-top.

Site IV: Plough-soil

Some 96 sherds were recorded when the surface of the chalk was trowelled following the removal of the plough-soil by machine. An unknown quantity of material was lost in this latter process. Those recorded comprise weathered sherds of a hard, black, gritty fabric and include a bead-rim, the everted rim of a cooking pot and the flanged rim of a pie-dish. In addition, a small number of body, rim and base sherds of coarse, earthenware bowls and pans of seventeenth- and eighteenth-century date were recorded. They are in a brick-red, buff or pinkish buff fabric and covered on both surfaces by a green or yellowish-green glaze.

Site IV

Five sherds were recorded, including the rim and upper wall of a bead-rim bowl in a hard, black, burnished fabric (P311).

Site IV: Pit (186)

Sixteen small sherds in a hard, black, burnished fabric were recorded from all layers.

Site IV: Rectilinear Enclosure (187)

Twelve sherds were recorded, including the everted rim of a bowl in a hard, light brown, sandy fabric (P314).

Site IV: Iron Age Hut (188)

Five small body sherds were recorded in a hard, black, flint-gritted fabric which was occasionally burnished.

Site IV: Pit (192)

Eight small body sherds in a hard, flint gritted fabric were recorded from all layers.

Site IV: Pit (193)

One thin-walled, hard, flint-gritted sherd with traces of external burnish was recorded.

Site IV: Superficial Ditch Deposits

A quantity of sherds was obtained from superficial deposits of the Neolithic ditch, amongst which the following vessels are represented:

P312   Rim of a simple dish in a hard flint gritted fabric (Segment I alpha layer (2)).

P313   The rim and wall of a bead-rim bowl in a hard, black fabric (Segment I alpha layer (2)).

P315   The rim and upper wall of a bead-rim bowl in a hard, black sandy fabric (Segment II layer (2)).

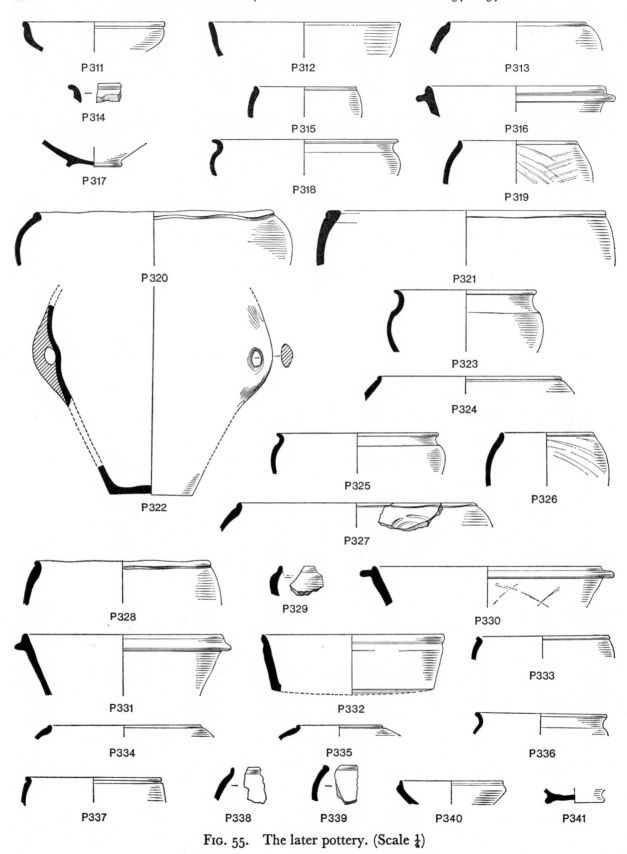

Fig. 55.   The later pottery. (Scale ¼)

P316 The rim of a flanged pie-dish in a dark grey fabric with a black, burnished surface (Segment III layer (2)).

P317 A base with footring in a hard, light-grey fabric, burnished black on both faces (Segment IV layer (2).

P318 The rim and shoulder of a small bowl with hollow neck and everted rim in a hard, thin, flint-gritted fabric (Segment IV, layer (2)).

P319 Rim-sherds of a bead-rim bowl in a thin, hard, flint gritted fabric decorated with a lightly burnished lattice pattern (Segment IX layer (2)).

P320 Fragments of a bead-rim bowl in a hard, thin, sandy fabric (Segment V layer (4)).

P321 A flat-rimmed jar in a hard sandy fabric (Segment VI layer (3)).

P322 Twenty-four sherds, including lugs and base, of a jar with two countersunk lug handles in a thick, hard, black fabric which is burnished externally (Segment V layer (4)).

P323 A bowl in a hard, fine burnished fabric with everted rim, hollow neck and well-defined shoulder (Segment VI layer (3)).

P324 A bead-rim bowl in a hard, flint-gritted fabric (Segment VI layer (3)).

P325 A bowl with a short everted rim and hollow neck in a fine, sandy fabric (Segment VIII layer (2)).

P326 A bead-rim bowl in a hard, flint-gritted fabric (Segment VIII layer (2)).

P327 A bead-rim bowl in a light grey to pink, hard gritty fabric and impressed eye-brow motifs on the shoulder (Segment VIII layer (3)).

P328 A bead-rim bowl in a hard, flint gritted fabric (Segment VIII alpha layer (3)).

P331 The rim and upper wall of a flanged bowl in a hard, black fabric with a burnished exterior (Segment XII layer (2)).

The Enclosure Ditch

P329 A bead-rim bowl in a hard, black, flint-gritted fabric (Cutting II layer (2)).

P330 The rim of a flanged bowl in a hard, flint-gritted fabric (Cutting II layer (2)).

P332 The beaded rim of a straight-walled platter (Cutting II layer (2)).

P333 A bead rim in thin, hard, burnished fabric (Cutting XXIX layer (4)).

In addition, a number of body sherds from similar vessels was recorded, together with rim, body and base sherds of coarse, earthenware bowls and pans. At the north entrance, sherds of Iron Age and Romano-British type were recorded from layers 1–4.

The Palisade Trench

P334 A bead-rim bowl in hard, black, flint-gritted fabric (Cutting XXIII layer (1)). A small quantity of weathered body sherds and green glazed pottery of seventeenth- and eighteenth-century date were recorded from the top of the palisade trench.

Conquer Barrow

P335 A bead-rim in a hard, black, flint-gritted fabric (Cutting XLVI layer (3)).

P336 The everted rim of a lightly burnished bowl in a thin, buff fabric (Cutting XLVI layer (3)).

P337 A bead-rim in a hard, flint-gritted fabric (Cutting XLVI layer (3)). In addition, body sherds of similar fabric and green glazed sherds of later date were recorded.

Iron Age Hollow (XXVI)

P338 A bead-rim in hard, flint-gritted fabric (layer (1)).

P339 A bead-rim in a hard flint-gritted fabric slightly burnished (layer (1)).

P340 A bead-rim bowl in a hard, flint-gritted fabric (layer (4)).

P341 A base with a low footring in a black, burnished, flint-gritted fabric (layer (4)).

X. THE BRONZE AXE FROM MOUNT PLEASANT: DESCRIPTION, COMPOSITION AND AFFINITIES

(figs. 56–9)

by D. BRITTON

Description

THE axe blade is complete and intact. Parts of the surface are covered by a green, slightly rough, encrustation. Everywhere else the surface shows a smooth and even patina of a dark brownish green. The butt of the axe is narrow, arched, and thin. The faces widen from the butt to the cutting-edge, at first gradually and then more markedly close to the cutting-edge itself. Across each face there is a horizontal bevel: on face 1 it is 4.9 cm. from the butt and rather faint, and on face 2, 5.3 cm. from the butt and more distinct. Another bevel runs across each face parallel to the cutting-edge and about 1 cm. above it. The margins of each face have very slight flanges which extend from near the butt to the cutting-edge. The sides are divided along their length into two facets by a bevel which fades out close to the butt. Most of each face is covered by incised decoration of the kind sometimes called 'rain pattern'. This consists of indentations which are lenticular in plan, concave in cross-section, and more or less elongated. All are oriented more or less vertically and set close together, but they do not form lines or other distinct groupings. On face 1 the decoration starts about 1.8 cm. from the butt, and on face 2 about 2.5 cm. On both it continues, covering the whole width of the face, almost to the bevel which sets off the cutting-edge.

Length 12.2 cm. Width across the cutting-edge 6.7 cm. Maximum thickness 1.05 cm. Weight 202 g. (fig. 56, BR2).

Composition

A small sample from the interior of the axe was analysed by the British Museum Research Laboratory, using a combination of emission spectroscopy, atomic absorption spectroscopy, and cathode-ray polarography. Their report states that 'the metal is a bronze (copper/tin) alloy. . . . The quantitative composition is as follows: copper 91.0%; tin 8.62%; iron 0.11%; silver 0.06%; nickel 0.04%; cobalt 0.02%; cadmium 0.09%.' Arsenic was present but it was not possible to obtain an accurate quantitative figure for this. (R.L. File No. 3086. 24 August 1971.)

Classification and Comparisons

The form and composition of the Mount Pleasant axe place it unambiguously within the broad category of 'flat and flanged bronze axes'. These are characteristic of the Early Bronze Age in the British Isles, and are often regarded as one of the criteria by which that period may be defined.[1] Among such axes that from Mount Pleasant approximates to Dr. Coles's Type B Scottish axes, and to Dr. Harbison's Ballyvalley type among axes from Ireland. In terms of Megaw and Hardy's classification of decorated axes, it belongs to their type 1.[2]

[1] *Vide* e.g. Evans, 1881, 36–69; Britton, 1963, 263f.; [2] Megaw and Hardy, 1938.
Coles, 1968–9, 3f.; Harbison, 1969.

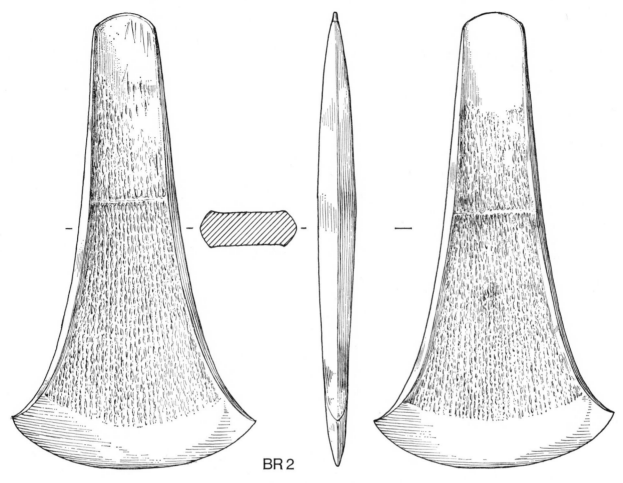

BR 2

FIG. 56.   Bronze axe. (Scale 1/1)

There are many finds from the British Isles of axes more or less like that from Mount Pleasant, but to bring some degree of precision into our discussion of comparable axes, we should specify the similarities that we intend to take into account. In terms of form, the axes most similar are those with a thin and more or less narrow butt, a blade which widens gradually from butt to cutting-edge, and only slight flanges or no flanges at all. In terms of decoration, we shall consider all those which have a rain pattern on the faces. Axes which meet these criteria both of form and decoration might be classified in various ways: the division into three groups used here is at least simple to apply and convenient for the immediate purpose.

In *Groups 1A and 1B* rain pattern is the only form of decoration.

Group 1A. Rain pattern occurs extensively on both the upper and lower parts of the faces: often it nearly covers both parts.

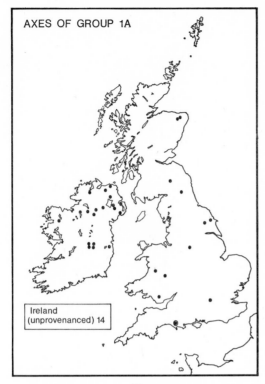

FIG. 57

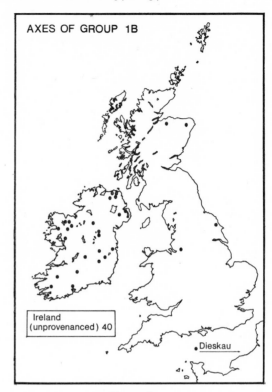

FIG. 58

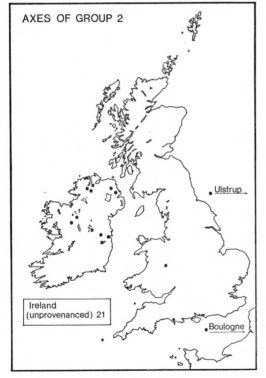

FIG. 59

FIG. 57.   Distribution of axes of group 1A.
FIG. 58.   Distribution of axes of group 1B
FIG. 59.   Distribution of axes of group 2
N.B. figs. 57–59. For Ireland, the data are
abstracted from P. Harbison (1969) and
are comprehensive. For Britain, a few
examples only are mapped for illustration

Group 1B. Rain pattern occurs extensively, but only on part of the faces, usually only on the lower part.

In *Group 2* rain pattern occurs on the faces, but in combination with other forms of decoration.

Axes of these three groups are widely distributed in the British Isles and a few have been reported from continental Europe. Most are single finds, but at least one comes from a burial and a number of others from hoards. The material from Ireland is included in Dr. Harbison's fully illustrated and documented catalogue.[1] Using this as a basis, I have attempted to list the Irish finds and to map their distribution (Appendix 1, p. 134ff.; figs. 57–9). These data are also summarized in Table V. For Britain, no comparable catalogue is available and I have merely been able to indicate on the maps and in Appendix 1 a few examples of such axes, which serve to show that all three groups are represented here. The continental finds known to me are very few: they consist of a Group 1B axe in a hoard from Dieskau near Halle, in East Germany (on this, see below p. 138); and two axes of Group 2, one from Boulogne in northern France,[2] and the other from Ulstrup in Jutland.[3]

TABLE V

Axes of Groups 1A, 1B, and 2 from Ireland

Group	Total	N	C	S	NP
1A	34	*	*	—	14
1B	77	*	*	*	40
2	34	*	*	—	21

N, C, S refer to the northern, central, and southern regions of Ireland. NP = no provenance known.

Moot Low, Derbyshire: a Burial with an Axe of Group 1A

In 1845 T. Bateman excavated a round barrow, Moot Low, and at its centre he found 'a large cist' cut into the rock. At the west end of the cist 'lay the skeleton of a middle-sized man, whose legs were drawn up; near his head lay a fine bronze celt of novel form; it was placed in a line with the body with its edge upwards'. The account suggests a typical Early Bronze Age inhumation, possibly the primary burial beneath the barrow. The axe is a good example of Group 1A, slightly flanged and with vertical rain pattern covering most of the faces. In form, size, and decoration, it has much in common with the axe from Mount Pleasant. No other object was recorded as accompanying the burial, except, possibly, the lower jaw of a small pig. (Further details and references are given below, p. 136.)

[1] Harbison, 1969.
[2] Megaw and Hardy, 1938, 306, fig. 15(b) on 228.
[3] Butler, 1955 and 1963, *vide* index.

Hoards with Axes of Groups 1A, 1B and 2

Axes of all three groups are known from hoards. Although at least 11 finds have been published as authentic or possible hoards of this character, their documentation varies greatly in quality. Here mention is made only of the seven for which the evidence seems reasonably strong. (Appendix 3, p. 136ff., gives details.)

Five hoards out of the seven include, as Table VI shows, axes which belong (like that from Mount Pleasant) to Group 1A. They are associated with axes of Groups 1B and 2, and with others of generally similar form but either plain or else decorated in different ways. Table VII gives more details of the axes in the same five hoards, and compares them with the axe from Mount Pleasant. It shows the association of slightly flanged axes with axes that have no flanges; the wide occurrence of bevels across the faces and near the cutting-edges of different forms of axe; and the varied treatment of the sides of the axes.

Of the two remaining hoards, that from Low Glenstockdale has one Group 2 axe associated with a plain axe that is generally similar to plain axes in some of the other hoards. The Dieskau hoard by contrast has one axe of Group 1B and a large quantity of characteristically Central European metalwork. It may be doubted whether it is relevant to mention this find at all. But just possibly a link is provided by the Willerby Wold hoard, since that shows an association of axes of Group 1A (as Mount Pleasant) and Group 1B (as Dieskau). The Mount Pleasant and Dieskau axes are also fairly similar in general form and size, and both have bevels across the face and setting off the cutting-edge.

TABLE VI

Hoards with axes of Groups 1A, 1B, and 2

Hoards	Axes					Other items
	1A	*1B*	*2*	*D*	*P*	
County Donegal: Glenalla	1	—	1	—	2	
County Offaly: Tullamore	2	—	—	—	—	
County Wicklow: Ballynasculloge	1	—	—	—	—	Artificially rounded stone
Yorks.: Wold Farm, Willerby	1	1	—	1	1	
Banffshire: Colleonard Farm	2	1	—	3	1	Pot
Wigtowns: Low Glenstockdale	—	—	1	—	1	
East Germany: Dieskau	—	1	—	—	—	Únětice metalwork, amber beads and pot

D = decorated, but no rain pattern. P = plain.

These seven hoards may all be attributed to the Early Bronze Ages respectively of Ireland, Britain, and Central Europe.[1] The question to be considered now is whether they can be dated any more closely.

The Irish finds consist only of axes (apart from the 'artificially rounded stone', now lost, from Ballynasculloge Lower), and these are all of Dr. Harbison's Ballyvalleyt ype.[2] Hoards

[1] *Vide* e.g. Harbison, 1969; Britton, 1963; Coles, 1968–9; von Brunn, 1959; Gimbutas, 1965, for the general background.

[2] Harbison, 1969, 32f.

TABLE VII

Details of axes in hoards which have Group 1A axes, compared with the axe from Mount Pleasant

Hoard		1	2	3	Treatment of sides
(Mount Pleasant	1A	*	*	*	Bevelled along length)
Glenalla	1A	—	*	—	Lozenge facets
	2	—	*	—	Convex cross-section
	P	—	—	—	Flattish (unfinished)
	P	—	—	—	Flattish (unfinished)
Tullamore	1A	—	—	—	
	1A	—	—	—	
Ballynasculloge	1A	—	—	—	Slightly convex in cross-section
Wold Farm, Willerby	P	—	*	*	Bevelled along length
	1A	*	*	*	Double bevel (three facets)
	1B	*	*	*	Rounded in cross-section
	D	*	*	*	Slightly convex in cross-section
Colleonard Farm	1A	—	—	—	Bevelled along length
	1A	—	—	—	Bevelled along length
	D	—	—	—	Bevelled along length
	D	—	—	—	Bevelled along length
	D	—	—	?	Flat in cross-section
	1B	*	—	—	Rounded in cross-section
	P	*	?	—	Rounded in cross-section

D = decorated, but no rain pattern. P = plain. 1 = slight or very slight flanges. 2 = bevel across middle part of faces. 3 = bevel near cutting-edge. * denotes feature present, — denotes feature absent.

with such axes, together with other finds of similar material, characterize a component within the Early Bronze Age metalwork of Ireland. This component is linked by Dr. Harbison with two others to define a Frankford–Killaha–Ballyvalley Period. He discusses the evidence for the chronology of this period, and concludes that the three components may indeed indicate three successive horizons, although at present rigid internal divisions are not easy to prove.[1]

For Scotland, we have two hoards. That from Colleonard Farm is used by Dr. Coles to exemplify one of three 'phases of industrial activity' within the Scottish Early Bronze Age, and the hoard from Low Glenstockdale should belong to the same 'phase'.[2] In his study he suggests that these phases may at least have started at successive times, in the order: Migdale, Colleonard Farm, Gavel Moss. But a postscript (p. 110) refers to a reconsideration of this view, and suggests instead that the Colleonard Farm and Gavel Moss phases may really

[1] Harbison, 1969, 70–82.   [2] Coles, 1968–9, 68–76.

have begun at a similar time, although the Migdale phase may still have started earlier than either. It may be added that the pot which contained the Colleonard Farm axes does not appear to help in any closer dating.

The only hoard from southern Britain is the Willerby find, consisting of four axes (of Groups 1A, 1B, and two others). Unfortunately, in contrast to Ireland and Scotland, no recent critical study has been published which deals with the Early Bronze Age metalwork from southern Britain from the point of view of chronology. This being so, it seems to me premature to suggest a closer dating for the Willerby hoard within that period. It might however be hoped that in this case further indications of date might be given by the context of the find. Greenwell found the four axes as a single, isolated deposit in his excavation of a round barrow, Barrow CCXXXV. They do not appear to have been grave goods, at least in the usual sense, since they were 8 ft. away from the shaft at the centre of the barrow in which the burials had been placed. These burials seem to have been a succession of at least three deposits, the latest an inhumation with an All-Over-Corded Beaker and a flint scraper. Greenwell's account is summary and lacks plans or sections. His own view was that the axes were 'deposited where they were found at the time of the erection of the mound'. However it is doubtful whether we have the evidence which would show the true relations between the burials, the construction of the barrow, and the deposit of the axes.

The last hoard to be considered is that from Dieskau, with its axe of Group 1B. This axe has long been regarded as the work of an Irish or British smith, whether it was made locally or imported.[1] The Dieskau hoard is a notable example of a group of Early Bronze Age finds which are concentrated in this region of East Germany, as well as in Brandenburg, Silesia, western Poland, and Bohemia.[2] They illustrate one aspect of the Únětice Culture (using the term in a very broad sense), and on Professor Gimbutas's arrangement of the material they are characteristic of its middle or 'Classical' stage.[3] In terms of the traditional Reinecke system they belong to Bronzezeit A, and more specifically to a developed phase of Bronzezeit A1. In addition to the hoards, there is a related group of unusually elaborate and rich burials under monumental round barrows. Two of these are of particular interest for the present review since they have provided material for radiocarbon dating. At Helmsdorf in East Germany (Kreis Hettstedt) oak from the 'funerary bed' (Totenbett) gave a date (Bln 248) of 1663 ± 160 bc.[4] From the other site, Łęki Małe in western Poland (district of Kościan), comes a date (GrN 5037) of 1655 ± 40 bc, derived from wood which was part of the roof of the main grave (Grave A).[5] (Both dates are given on the basis of a half-life of 5570 ± 30 years.)

APPENDIX 1. AXES OF GROUPS 1A, 1B, AND 2

IRELAND

These lists are based on information in P. Harbison, *The Axes of the Early Bronze Age in Ireland* (Prähistorische Bronzefunde IX.1) (München, 1969), and the numbers are those of his catalogue.

[1] *Vide* e.g. Megaw and Hardy, 1938, 285, 290; Butler, 1963, index, 276; Waterbolk and Butler, 1965, 249.

[2] For general accounts, see e.g. von Brunn, 1959; Gimbutas, 1965, esp. 267–8.

[3] Gimbutas, 1965, 260–70.

[4] Kohl and Quitta, 1966, 29.

[5] Bakker, Vogel and Wiślański, 1969, 15–16.

GROUP 1A

Co. Antrim: Ballymontenagh (841), Bushmills (854), Lisburn (967). *Co. Cavan:* Mullaghmore (985), Rinn (993). *Co. Derry:* Cool Glebe, Coolyvenny Upper (888). *Co. Donegal:* Glenalla (936). *Co. Down:* Drumlough (906), Scrabo Hill (998), Strangford (1006). *Co. Fermanagh:* Faughard (925). *Co. Leitrim:* Garvagh (934). *Co. Mayo:* Carrowleeken (860). *Co. Offaly:* 'near Edenderry' (917, 918), Tullamore (1013, 1014). *Co. Tipperary:* unknown provenance (1009). *Co. Tyrone:* Benburb (850). *Co. Wicklow:* Ballynasculloge Lower (842). *Unknown provenances:* 521, 1029, 1036, 1045, 1076, 1114, 1128, 1151, 1176, 1184, 1188, 1198, 1201, 1223.

GROUP 1B

Co. Antrim: Brownstown, near Ballymoney (852), Portrush (992), unknown provenances (816, 817). *Co. Carlow:* Tinriland (1008). *Co. Clare:* unknown provenance (870). *Co. Cork:* Famlough, near Bandon (923), Glengariff (941), unknown provenances (892, 894). *Co. Derry:* Altduff (815), Coleraine (882). *Co. Donegal:* Cloghan (871). *Co. Down:* Guiness (945), Scrabo Hill (999). *Co. Dublin:* Clontarf (877). *Co. Kerry:* Cordal (889). *Co. Leitrim:* Ardrum (819). *Co. Limerick:* Lough Gur (972), unknown provenances (963, 966). *Co. Mayo:* 'neighbourhood of Achil' (812), Ballina (824), 'near Ballina' (825), Carrowleeken (862), Carrowmore (864), Garracloon (931), 'near Westport' (1017). *Co. Offaly:* Clongarrett (1682). *Co. Tipperary:* Clonoura (875), Rockforest (994). *Co. Tyrone:* unknown provenance (1016). *Co. Westmeath:* Ballinderry Lake (827), The Downs (903). *Co. Wicklow:* Kilcoagh (951), unknown provenance (1021). *Northern Ireland (unknown provenance):* 1027. *Unknown provenances:* 1044, 1046, 1047, 1051, 1054, 1066, 1072, 1077, 1083, 1087, 1091, 1097, 1099, 1106, 1108, 1118, 1129, 1136, 1137, 1138, 1141, 1153, 1164, 1168, 1169, 1173, 1177, 1180, 1181, 1197, 1199, 1216, 1219, 1220, 1794, 1797, 1824, 1826, 1832, 1841.

GROUP 2

Co. Antrim: Ballymena (836), Connor (884). *Co. Derry:* near Garvagh ? (933). *Co. Donegal:* Buncrana (853), Carrowen (859), Glenalla (937). *Co. Dublin:* Clontarf (878), unknown provenance (909). *Co. Galway:* Beby, near Castlerea (847). *Co. Kildare:* Dysart Carbury (914), Kilkea (954). *Co. Roscommon:* Emlagh, near Elphin (921). *Co. Westmeath:* Mullingar (986). *Unknown provenances:* 1040, 1065, 1086, 1088, 1103, 1127 1130, 1139, 1150, 1161, 1189, 1202, 1203, 1213, 1224, 1795, 1798, 1799, 1822, 1853, 1854.

BRITAIN

A *few examples only* are cited, to illustrate that axes of all three groups occur.

GROUP 1A

England
Derbyshire: Moot Low. From grave, see p. 136.
Dorset: Mount Pleasant.
Lancs.: Gleaston Castle. *Cumb. and West. . . . Arch. Soc.* xv (1899), 161–4.
London: Stepney. *British Assoc. Card Catal. of Bronze Impls.*
Northumberland: Ryall. British Museum (WG 1809).
Shropshire: Clunbury. *Shrop. Arch. Trans.* (4th S) xii (1929), 62–4.
Yorkshire: Leppington. *British Assoc. Card Catal. of Bronze Impls.*
Wold Farm, Willerby. In hoard, see p. 137.

Wales
Glamorgan: Ystradowen. *British Association Card Catal. of Bronze Impls.*
Montgomery: Twr Gwyn Waun, near Carno. *British Assoc. Card Catal. of Bronze Impls.*

Scotland
Banffshire: Colleonard Farm. In hoard, see p. 137.
Roxburgh: near Eildon. *PSAS* ci (1968–9), 13.

GROUP 1B

England
Lancs.: Risdon, near Warrington. *VCH Lancs.* I (London, 1906), pl. 4.
Yorkshire: Wold Farm, Willerby. In hoard, see p. 137.

Scotland
Banffshire: Colleonard Farm. In hoard, see p. 137.
Morayshire: near Darnaway. *PSAS* ci (1968–9), 10.

GROUP 2

England
Dorset: Preston Down, near Weymouth. J. Evans, *The Ancient Bronze Implements. . . .* (London, 1881), 46.
Shropshire: Clee Hill, Titterstone Clee. *Shrop. Arch. Trans. (4th S)* x (1926), 233.

APPENDIX 2. MOOT LOW, DERBYSHIRE:
A BURIAL WITH AN AXE OF GROUP 1A

Site: round barrow; at time of excavation about 90 ft. across, about 4 ft. high, level on top; known as Moot Low; located about half-way between Alsop Moor and Dovedale.

Excavation: by T. Bateman, 2 June 1845. *Group 1A axe:* found near head of skeleton of 'middle-sized man'; slightly flanged; sides rounded in cross-section; vertical rain pattern on faces from butt to about 3.5 cm. from cutting-edge. L. 13.0 cm. *Museum:* Sheffield City Museum (axe). *Publication:* T. Bateman, *Vestiges of the Antiquities of Derbyshire* (London, 1848), 66; J. Evans, *The Ancient Bronze Implements, . . .* (London, 1881), 44, f.3 on 44; E. Howarth, *Catalogue of the Bateman Collection of Antiquities in the Sheffield Public Museum* (London, 1899), 82; *J. Derbyshire Archaeol. and Nat. Hist. Soc.* lxxv (1955), 90, 113.

APPENDIX 3. HOARDS WITH AXES OF GROUPS 1A, 1B, AND 2

IRELAND

Co. Donegal: Glenalla
Four *flat axes:* (1) Lozenge facets along sides; bevel across faces; vertical rain pattern over whole of one face, and on other wherever original surface survives. L. 19.65 cm. Harbison, 936. (2) Sides rather convex in cross-section; bevel across faces; vertical rain pattern on upper part of faces, and on lower part design built up from vertical and oblique strokes. L. 18.6 cm. Harbison, 937. (3) Unfinished (edge blunt); sides flattish. L. 15.4 cm. Harbison, 1582. (4) Unfinished (edge blunt); sides flattish. L. 15.2 cm. Harbison, 1583. *Discovery:* 'These axes were found lying on the surface of the ground under a large rock on the high land near the border dividing Glenalla and Oughterlin townlands' (*PRIA* xliic (1935), 162). *Museum:* National Museum of Ireland, Dublin (1933. 1225–8). *Publication:* *PRIA* xliic (1939),

161–3, 188–90; *PPS* iv (1938), 303; *PRIA* lxviic (1968) 50, 77; P. Harbison, *The Axes of the Early Bronze Age in Ireland* (Prähistorische Bronzefunde IX.1) (München, 1969), 1–2, 37, 53, 71, pl.42, pl.66. *Analyses:* chemical, for all four: tin–bronze (*PRIA* xliic (1935), 188–90).

Co. Offaly: Tullamore

Two *flat axes:* (1) Approximately vertical rain pattern over most of faces. L. 17.2 cm. Harbison, 1013. (2) Vertical rain pattern over most of faces. L. 17.2 cm. Harbison, 1014. *Discovery:* Found together at Tullamore, according to the Day Collection Catalogue. *Collections:* (2) Hunt Collection, Howth; (1) ?. *Publication: Catalogue of the Sale of the Collection of Robert Day* (1913), lots 204–5, pl. 8; *PRIA* lxviic (1968), 57, 91; P. Harbison, *The Axes of the Early Bronze Age in Ireland* (Prähistorische Bronzefunde IX.1) (München, 1969), 1–2, 39, 71, pl. 45.

Co. Wicklow: Ballynasculloge Lower

One *flat axe:* Sides slightly convex in cross-section; vertical rain pattern over most of faces. L. 12.25 cm. Harbison, 842. One *artificially rounded stone. Discovery:* Details unknown. *Museum:* Axe in National Museum of Ireland, Dublin (1934: 10, 869); stone lost. *Publication: PPS* iv (1938), 305; *PRIA* lxviic (1968), 42, 63; P. Harbison, *The Axes of the Early Bronze Age in Ireland* (Prähistorische Bronzefunde IX.1) (München, 1969), 1–2, 34, 71, pl. 38.

ENGLAND

Yorkshire (East Riding): Wold Farm, Willerby

One *flat axe:* Sides bevelled; faint traces of bevel across faces, and bevel setting off cutting-edge. L. 16.5 cm. Three *axes with very slight flanges:* (1) Three facets along sides; bevels across faces and setting off cutting-edge; vertical rain pattern on upper and lower parts of faces. L. 18.7 cm. (2) Sides rounded in cross-section; bevel across faces, and faint bevel setting off cutting-edge; vertical rain pattern on lower part of each face, which (at least on one face) extends above bevel a little way along the margins of the face. L. 14.8 cm. (3) Sides slightly convex in cross-section; bevels across faces and setting off cutting-edge; design on faces of rows of vertical strokes, lines, chevrons, and zigzags. L. 14.8 cm. *Discovery:* In excavation of Barrow CCXXXV by W. Greenwell, on Wold Farm, Willerby. *Museum:* British Museum, London (WG 1805–8). *Publication: A* lii (1890), 2–4; *PPS* iv (1938), 283–5; *PPS* xxix (1963), 272, 302, 314; cf. D. Clarke, *Beaker Pottery of Great Britain and Ireland* (Cambridge, 1970), I, 67, II, 285.

SCOTLAND

Banffshire: Colleonard Farm

Four *flat axes:* (1) Sides bevelled; vertical rain pattern over whole of faces. L. 13.3 cm. (2) Sides bevelled; vertical rain pattern at least over middle and lower parts of faces (upper part corroded). L. 13.5 cm. (3) Sides bevelled; vertical fluting on faces; small notches along angles between faces and sides. L. 15.0 cm. (4) Sides bevelled; vertical fluting on faces. L. 14.2 cm. One *middle part of flat axe:* Sides flat in cross-section; vertical fluting on faces. One *axe with very slight flanges:* Sides rounded in cross-section; vertical rain pattern over middle and lower parts of faces. L. 17.0 cm. One *lower part of axe with very slight flanges:* Sides rounded in cross-section. One *pot:* Coarse brownish ware; conical with slightly splayed foot and flat base; row of impressions below rim; below this, scratched zigzag pattern; above middle, obliquely slashed cordon. Height 17.8 cm. *Discovery:* In 1857; axes in pot, which was about 1 ft. below surface. *Museum:* National Museum of Antiquities of Scotland, Edinburgh (DA. 19–24, EA.18). *Publication:* S. Piggott and M. Stewart, *Inventaria Archaeologica: Great Britain.* 5th Set (London, 1957), GB.29 (with refs.); *PSAS* ci (1968–9), 104, etc. *Analyses:* All metalwork, by optical spectroscopy: tin–bronze (*PSAS* ci (1968–9), 95, with ref.).

Wigtownshire: Low Glenstockdale

Two *flat axes:* (1) Lozenge facets along sides; bevel across faces and setting off cutting-edge; vertical rain pattern on upper part of faces, irregular chevron pattern on lower part. L. 16.9 cm. (2) Sides convex in cross-section; bevel setting off cutting-edge; faces plain. L. 14.3 cm. *Discovery:* In peat-cutting, at depth of 4 ft. *Museum:* Stranraer Museum. *Publication: Trans. Dumfries and Galloway Nat. Hist. and Antiq. Soc.* xxvi (1947), 124; xlii (1965) 68; *PSAS* ci (1968–9), 14, 109.

EAST GERMANY

Saalkreis: Dieskau

One *axe with slight flanges:* Bevels across face and setting off cutting-edge; vertical rain pattern on lower part of faces. L. 12.8 cm. Two *shaft-hole axes:* 'Pick-axe' form. Two *metal-shafted halberds.* One *halberd blade,* with part of metal shaft. Three *rivets* and other *fragments,* from one or more metal-shafted halberds. Eleven *halberd blades.* Ten *neck-rings with recoiled ends.* Four *massive penannular rings (oval),* perhaps large armlets. Four *massive annular rings (oval),* perhaps large armlets. One *penannular 'leech' ring,* round in cross-section. One *penannular 'leech' ring,* faceted in cross-section. Seven *penannular armlets* with slightly expanded ends. Two *arm spirals.* Twenty-three *small coils* (Spiralröllchen). One hundred and six *amber beads.* One *pot,* of which only sherds survive. *Discovery:* In 1904; metalwork and amber beads in pot. *Museum:* Halle Museum (45:38). *Publication:* W. A. von Brunn, *Die Hortfunde der frühen Bronzezeit aus Sachsen-Anhalt, Sachsen und Thüringen* (Berlin, 1959), 55–6, with refs., Taf. 12–19, index, 80; J. J. Butler, *Bronze Age Connections across the North Sea* (Palaeohistoria 9) (Groningen, 1963), index, 276. *Analyses:* Many items, by optical spectroscopy; among them, decorated axe (tin–bronze): H. Otto and W. Witter, *Handbuch der ältesten vorgeschichtlichen Metallurgie in Mitteleuropa* (Leipzig, 1952), 128, no. 397.

The following finds may represent hoards, but the evidence seems inconclusive at present.

Ireland

Co. Antrim: Connor. *PRIA* lxviic (1968), 46, 72; P. Harbison, *The Axes of the Early Bronze Age in Ireland* (Prähistorische Bronzefunde IX.1) (München, 1969), 1–2, 35, 71, pl. 40.

Co. Down: Scrabo Hill. *PRIA* lxviic (1968), 55–6, 89; P. Harbison, *ibid.,* index, 103.

Co. Mayo: Carrowleeken. *PRIA* lxviic (1968), 44–5, 67; P. Harbison, *ibid.,* 1–2, 34, 71, pl. 39.

Denmark

Jutland: Ulstrup (Vellev Parish, Hovlberg Herred). *KUML* (1955), 36–45; J. J. Butler, *Bronze Age Connections across the North Sea* (Palaeohistoria 9) (Groningen, 1963), 31–3, 46, 207–8, 210, pl. 3.

XI. THE OTHER FINDS

FLINT
(figs. 60–73)

The Pre-Enclosure Settlement

FLINT artifacts were recorded from four of the cuttings that were excavated to examine the fossil soil beneath the enclosure bank and the distribution of artifacts within these cuttings is shown in Table VIII. The raw material was very weathered but appeared to be a chalk flint of fair quality, wh'lst a few flakes of Portland chert were also present. Amongst the collection, 62 artifacts were obtained from the ploughsoil and can therefore be regarded as unstratified. They include a single short-end scraper and a plano-convex knife (F11). Seventeen flakes and one long-end scraper were obtained from the bank material and the remaining 1084 artifacts derived from the old land surface beneath the bank. In Cutting XXXII the old land surface was divided arbitrarily into 4 and 8 cm. spits for recording purposes and these divisions are shown in Table VIII.

Of the seven cores recorded, four are single platform cores of A2 type (*vide* Wainwright and Longworth, 1971, 156–81, for artifact classifications), two are multi-directional and one keeled (F1). A sample of 592 complete waste flakes from Cuttings I (layer (9)) and XXXII (layer (3)) was measured for length and breadth and breadth–length ratio.[1] The results have been portrayed in histogram form (fig. 60) which indicates that 79% of the flakes are between 20 and 49 mm. long, with a peak of 35% between 30 and 39 mm., and that 83.6% are between 10 and 39 mm. broad with a peak of 35% between 20 and 29 mm. The majority of flakes have breadth–length ratios between 2:5 and 5:5 (2:5 18.6%; 3:5 28%; 4:5 25%

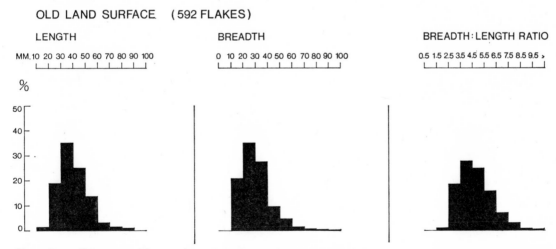

OLD LAND SURFACE (592 FLAKES)

FIG. 60. Diagram illustrating the dimensions of flakes from the secondary silts of the Site IV ditch

[1] Cf. Smith, 1965; Wainwright and Longworth, 1971, figs. 67, 68.

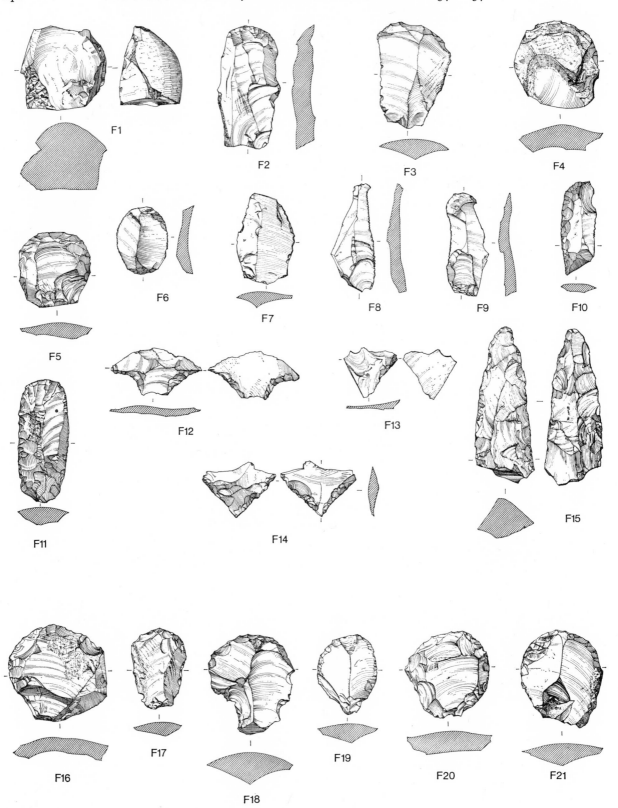

FIG. 61.   Flint artifacts. (Scale ½)

TABLE VIII

Pre-enclosure phase: distribution of flint artifacts

Provenance	Flakes	Cores	Scrapers	Serrated flakes	Blades with flat edge retouch	Blades with steep edge retouch	Transverse arrowheads	Polished axes	Flaked axes	Plano-convex knives	Totals
I (9)	247	4	5	I	I	—	I	—	I	—	260
XXXI (1)	13	—	I	—	—	—	—	—	—	—	14
XXXII (1)	47	—	—	—	—	—	—	—	—	I	48
XXXII (2)	8	—	I	—	—	—	—	—	—	—	9
XXXII (3) top	549	3	6	4	—	—	2	—	—	—	564
XXXII (3) 4–8 cm.	219	—	2	I	—	I	—	I	—	—	224
XXXII (3) 8–16 cm.	9	—	—	—	—	—	—	—	—	—	9
XXXIII (2)	9	—	—	—	—	—	—	—	—	—	9
XXXIII (3)	27	—	—	—	—	—	—	—	—	—	27
Totals	1128	7	15	6	I	I	3	I	I	I	1164

and 5:5 15.9%). Only 19.3% are blade-like in that their breadth–length ratio is not more that 2:5 as compared with 45.4% from Broome Heath[1] and 41% from Windmill Hill,[2] the industries from which have been dated to the mid-third or late fourth millennia B.C. More similar to the Mount Pleasant pre-bank assemblage are the flake industries from Durrington Walls[3] and the Late Neolithic occupation site on the West Kennet Avenue[4] where the blade-like flakes were 11 and 20% respectively. The tendency of flake industries in later Neolithic times to assume broad, squat outlines has been demonstrated at several sites and it is therefore of interest to note that at Broome Heath and Windmill Hill flakes in excess of 30 mm. wide total 21% in the earlier Neolithic, whereas at Mount Pleasant and Durrington Walls the comparable percentages are 44 and 56% respectively. The technological evidence therefore suggests a date towards the end of the second millennium bc for the flake industry from the Mount Pleasant pre-enclosure phase.

Scrapers (F2–7). Amongst the implements found in and on the fossil soil, scrapers are the most numerous. They have been grouped as follows:[5]

Class A. End scrapers	(i) Long (F2–3)	7
	(ii) Short (F4–5)	3
Class B. Double-ended	(ii) Short (F6)	1
Class D. Side (F7)		1
Class E. On broken flakes		1
Total		13

The numbers involved are too few to allow for any form of statistical analyses.

[1] Wainwright, 1972, 50.
[2] Smith, 1965, fig. 38.
[3] Wainwright and Longworth, 1971, figs. 67, 68.
[4] Smith, 1965, fig. 38.
[5] Wainwright and Longworth, 1971, 164.

Serrated flakes (F8–9). Six serrated flakes were recorded. Three complete serrated blades and the tip of a fourth were found in close proximity on top of the old land surface in Cutting XXXII.

Blades with flat edge retouch (F10). A blade with uniserial bifacial flat edge retouch.

Blades with steep edge retouch. A blade with steep edge retouch was recorded from within the fossil soil in Cutting XXXII.

Transverse arrowheads (F12–14). Three transverse arrowheads of Clark's Class D were recorded from Cuttings I (F14) and XXXII (F12, 13).[1] Seven such arrowheads of varying forms were recorded from the old land surface under the bank of the Durrington Walls enclosure.[2]

Polished axe. A flake from a polished axe was recorded from within the old land surface in Cutting XXXII.

Flaked axe (F15). The heavily patinated tip of a flaked axe or pick was recorded from the old land surface in Cutting I.

Site IV: Phase 1

Very few artifacts were recorded from the Phase 1 contexts of the structure — 349 from primary layers in the ditch and 283 from the post-holes of the building. Amongst the former were 336 flakes and seven cores — all of single platform type. Insufficient flakes prevented any attempt at statistical analyses. Seven scrapers were recorded in addition, five of which are short-end type (F16–18) and one discoidal (F19). The artifacts are mainly fresh and included three flakes of Portland chert.

From the post-holes, 279 flakes, one core and three scrapers were recorded. These artifacts are more weathered and were evenly distributed in the filling of most post-holes. A keeled core was obtained from post-hole 31, a disc and short end scraper from post-hole 82 (F20–21) and a single discoidal scraper from post-hole 169.

Site IV: Phase 2

A total of 3017 artifacts was recorded from the secondary silts of the Site IV ditch in contexts which are considered to be contemporary with the stone cove. Of these, 102 (3%)

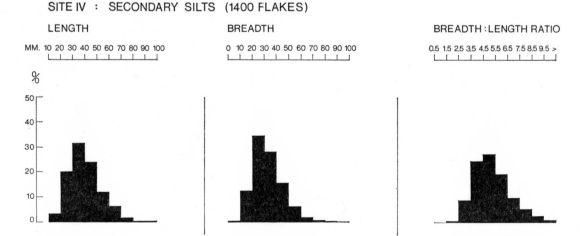

Fig. 62. Diagram illustrating the dimensions of flakes from the secondary silts of the Site IV ditch

[1] Clark, 1934.   [2] Wainwright and Longworth, 1971, 16.

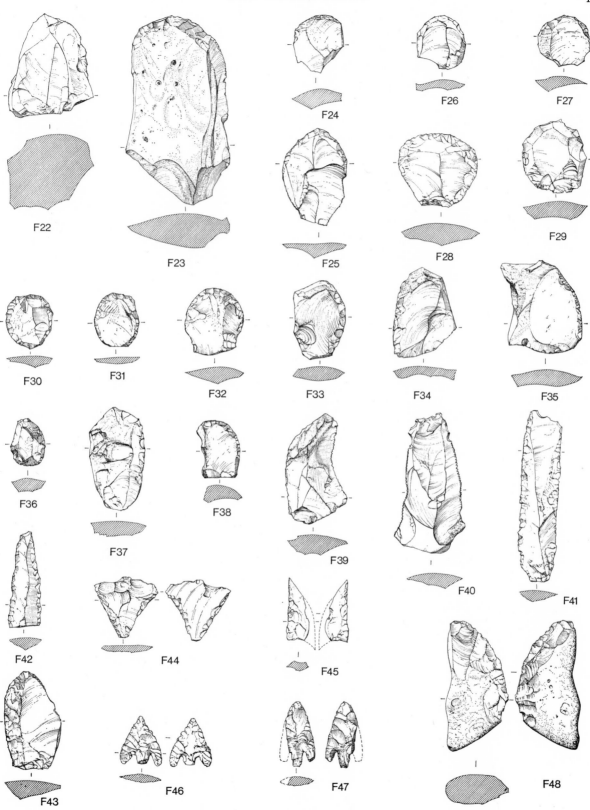

FIG. 63. Flint artifacts. (Scale ½)

are implements and the remainder waste products. The greatest concentration of artifacts undoubtedly occurred in Segment XIII, west of the entrance causeway, which produced 1246 artifacts or 41% of the total.

In Table IX the distribution of artifacts in terms of segment and layer number is portrayed, with the exception of those segments that produced only flakes and cores. The raw material includes 23 flakes, one core and one blade with flat edge retouch of Portland chert.

Of the eight cores recorded, seven were of the single platform type variety (F22) and one possessed two parallel platforms. A sample of 1400 complete waste flakes was measured for length and breadth and breadth–length ratios, in the same way as those from the fossil soil beneath the enclosure bank. The results have been portrayed in histogram form (fig. 62), which indicates that nearly 80% of the flakes are between 20 and 49 mm. long with a peak of 31.7% between 30 and 39 mm. and that 75% are between 10 and 39 mm. broad, with a peak of 34.6% between 20 and 29 mm. In these respects the flakes confirm the trend noted previously from the fossil soil beneath the enclosure bank. Only 9.4% of the flakes are blade-like in that their breadth–length ratios are not more than 2:5 compared with 19.3% from the fossil soil and clearly this later industry from the Site IV ditch is composed of flakes which are very broad and squat. Indeed, 52% of the flakes are in excess of 30 mm. broad.

Scrapers (F23–38). The 89 scrapers that were recorded have been typed according to the system employed in the Durrington Walls report. An additional category of scraper that was retouched across the long axis and down one lateral edge has been created to allow for the inclusion of a specific group.

Class A.	End scrapers	(i) Long (F23)	(3)	
		(ii) Short (F24–8)	(34)	37
Class C.	Discoidal (F29–32)			15
Class D.	Side scrapers	(i) Long		—
		(ii) Short (F33–6)		23
Class E.	On broken flakes			7
Class G.	End and side scrapers (F37–8)			7
Total				89

A homogeneous group of 58 scrapers from Segment XIII layer (5) was measured for length, breadth and thickness and the results have been portrayed in histogram form (fig. 64). The preferred length for the scrapers was between 30 and 49 mm. (67.3%), although 24% are between 20 and 29 mm. long, and preferred breadth 20–39 mm. (81%). Furthermore, only 8.6% of the scrapers are over 50 mm. long and only 15.5% in excess of 40 mm. broad. The preferred thickness is a more variable factor: the highest percentage of scrapers are between 9 and 11 mm. thick. The trend towards increasingly small scrapers in Beaker contexts already demonstrated at Broome Heath in Norfolk,[1] at the West Kennet Avenue and at Belle Tout in Sussex[2] is therefore confirmed. The scraper types are consistent with those normally represented at sites of this period, with high percentages of short end and side varieties.

Serrated flakes (F39–40). Three serrated flakes were recorded, one of which possesses bilateral retouch.

Blades with flat edge retouch (F41–3). Four blades with flat edge retouch were recorded and include a particularly fine example of Portland chert (F41).

Blades with steep edge retouch. One such implement was recorded but has not been illustrated.

[1] Wainwright, 1972, fig. 39.　　　　　　[2] Bradley, 1970.

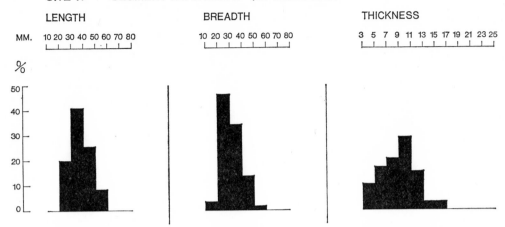

FIG. 64. Diagram illustrating the dimensions of scrapers from the secondary silts of the Site IV ditch in Segment XIII

Transverse arrowheads (F44–5). Two transverse arrowheads were recorded and are representative of Classes D (F44) and G respectively (F45).

Barbed and tanged arrowheads (F46–7). Two barbed and tanged arrowheads were recorded from layer (5) in Segment XIII. The tang of one specimen had been broken in antiquity.

Chopping tool (F48). A bifacially worked chopping tool was recorded from Segment XIII layer (5).

Only 42 flakes were recorded from pits and stoneholes related to Phase 2 of Site IV. Of these, over 50% were recorded from feature 191.

Site IV: The Later Silts

The artifacts included in this section were derived from the upper silts of the Site IV ditch in contexts which may have been contaminated in late prehistoric or Romano-British times. For this reason no attempt has been made at any metrical analysis of the implements or by-products. Table XI portrays the distribution of the artifacts in terms of ditch segment and layer, omitting those segments which only produced flakes and cores. A total of 2059 artifacts was recorded from these layers of which 1978 are by-products and 71 (3.5%) are implements. Amongst the former are four cores, three of which are single platform types, whilst the fourth possesses two platforms at oblique angles. The raw material is mainly flint but includes 28 flakes and three scrapers of Portland chert.

Scrapers (F49–56). The scrapers have been classified according to the system employed throughout this report:

Class A.	End scrapers	(i) Long (F49)	(4)	
		(ii) Short (F50–4)	(47)	51
Class B.	Double-ended (ii) Short			1
Class C.	Discoidal (F55)			4
Class D.	Side (ii) Short (F56)			5
Class E.	On broken flakes			3
Total				64

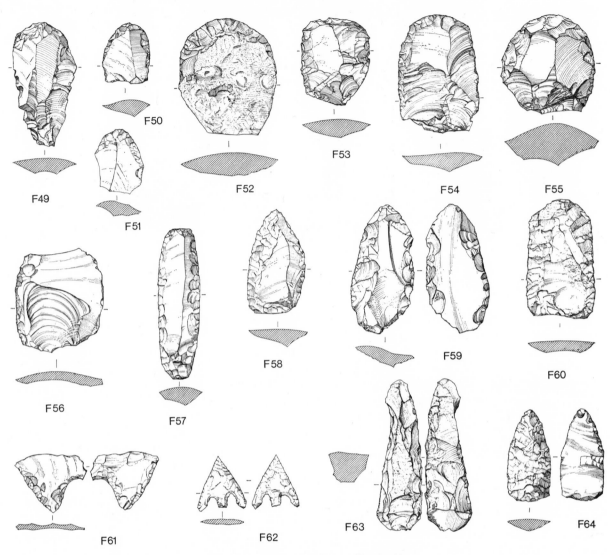

FIG. 65.   Flint artifacts. (Scale ½)

The scrapers are the predominant implement type and comprise 85% of the total assemblage. Amongst the group, short end scrapers are the most common variety.

Serrated flakes. One serrated flake was recorded but not illustrated.

Blades with flat edge retouch (F57–60). Nine good examples of this implement type were recorded, two on leaf-shaped flakes and one on a broad flake which is approaching a plano-convex form.

Blades with steep edge retouch. Two blades with steep edge retouch were recorded but have not been illustrated.

Transverse arrowheads (F61). A single transverse arrowhead of Class E was recorded from layer (3) in Segment IX.

Barbed and tanged arrowheads (F62). A single barbed and tanged arrowhead with a straight-sided triangular outline was recorded from layer (4) in Segment III.

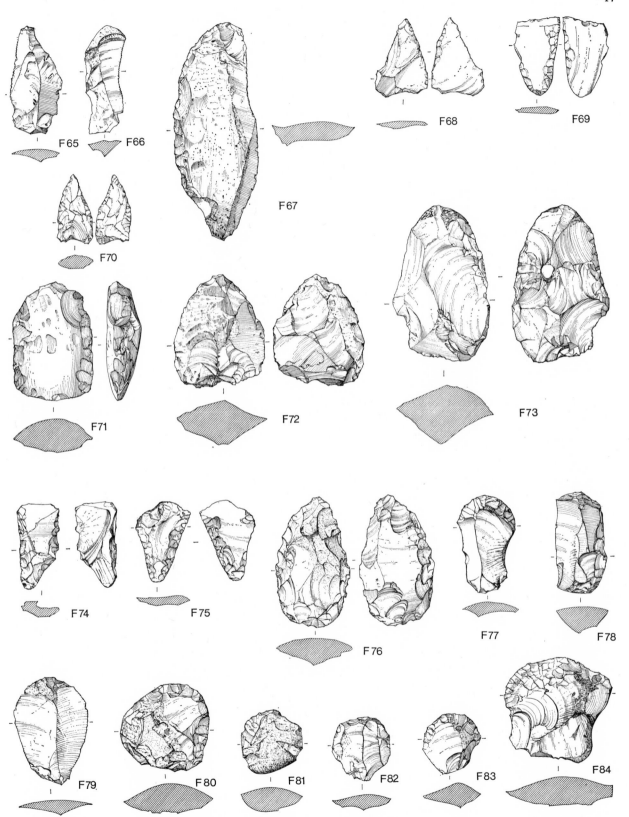

FIG. 66. Flint artifacts. (Scale ½)

TABLE IX

Site IV: Phase 2: distribution of flint artifacts in the ditch segments

Provenance	Flakes	Cores	Scrapers	Serrated flakes	Blades with flat edge retouch	Blades with steep edge retouch	Transverse arrowheads	Barbed and tanged arrowheads	Chopping tool	Totals
Iα (5)	6		1							7
Iα (6)	17			1						18
V (7)	127		1							128
Vα (5)	28	2	1							31
VI (5)	63		3							66
VII (6)	91		2							93
VIIIα (6)	59		1							60
IX (5)	97	1				1				99
IXα (5)	122		2		1					125
X (5)	144	1	5							150
X (6)	24		2							26
Xα (5)	63	1	4							68
Xα (6)	12		1							13
XI (5)	54		2							56
XI (6)	36				1					37
XIα (7)	70			1	1					72
XIα (8)	100	1	2		1		1			105
XII (6)	238							1		239
XIII (5)	1180		62	1				2	1	1246

TABLE X

Site IV: Distribution of flint artifacts from the later features

Provenance	Flakes	Scrapers	Fabricator	Totals
185 (Saxon grave)	2			2
186 (Iron Age pit)	33	1		34
187 (R-B ditch)	20	1		21
188 (Iron Age gully)	33			33
189	1			1
192 (Iron Age pit)	34	1	1	36
193 (Iron Age pit)	42	3		45
196 (Iron Age pit)	1			1
Totals	166	6	1	173

Fabricator (F63). A single fabricator or strike-a-light was recorded in mint condition.

Awl. A single awl was recorded but not illustrated.

Plano-convex knife (F64). A fine and complete example of a plano-convex knife on a leaf-shaped blade was recorded from layer (4) in Segment XIII.

In addition to the flint artifacts from the later silts of the ditch, a small number of by-products and implements were recorded from features related to the later settlements. These have been summarized in Table X.

TABLE XI

Site IV: The later silts: distribution of flint artifacts

Provenance	Flakes	Cores	Scrapers	Serrated flakes	Blades with flat edge retouch	Blades with steep edge retouch	Transverse arrowheads	Barbed and tanged arrowheads	Fabricator	Awl	Plano-convex knife	Totals
I (3)	205	1	8	1	2							217
Iα (2)	18		1		1							20
Iα (3)	5					1						6
II (2)	11		1		2							14
III (4)								1				1
V (3)	40		2									42
V (4)	21				1							22
VI (3)	14		2									16
VII (2)	7		2									9
VII (3)	35		1									36
VII (5)	178	1	4		1							184
VIIα (4)	7									1		8
VIIα (5A)	7					1						8
VIII (2)	86		2						1			89
VIII (5)	18		2									20
VIIIα (2)	16		1									17
VIIIα (5)	20		2									22
IX (3)	19		1				1					21
IX (4)	15		1									16
IXα (3)	7		1									8
IXα (4)	34		4									38
X (2)	36		2									38
X (3)	31		1									32
X (4)	53		4									57
Xα (3)	21	1	2									24
XIα (2)	25				1							26
XIα (4)	120		3									123
XIα (5)			1									1
XIα (6)	73		1		1							75
XII (2)	59	1	1									61
XIII (2)	75		2									77
XIII (3)	181		7								1	189
XIII (3A)	16		3									19
XIII (4)	57		2									59

The Enclosure Ditch: The West Entrance

The excavation of the west entrance (Cuttings I and II) produced 1570 flint artifacts (Table XII). Of these, recognizable implements totalled 49 or 3% of the whole. Insufficient flakes were recorded from any one deposit to enable any form of metrical analysis and the most prolific layers ((2), (3) and (4)) were superficial and subject to contamination. The cores from all layers totalled 11, of which four were single platform and seven of keeled varieties. The relationship of the implement classes to the ditch stratification may be obtained from Table XII. On account of the restricted numbers of artifacts involved the material has been described on a functional basis.

Scrapers. As is normal, scrapers comprise the most numerous implement type. Twenty-five examples were recorded, which include end (18), side (5), and hollow (2) varieties.

Serrated flakes (F65, 66). Seven serrated flakes were recorded, of which two are illustrated.

Blades with flat edge retouch. Four blades with flat edge retouch were recorded, none of which are illustrated.

Blades with steep edge retouch (F67). One long blade retains cortex over most of its upper surface and possesses bold steep retouch down one curved edge.

Transverse arrowheads (F68–70). Three transverse arrowheads were recorded, two of Class D (F68, 69) and one of Class G (F70).

Fabricator. One heavily utilized fabricator or strike-a-light, manufactured from a thick rod of flint.

Polished axe (F71). A small, chipped and polished flint axe, patinated a matt white. The implement may originally have been larger and had its fractured end flaked to a thinned butt.

Flaked axes (F72, 73). Three small flaked axes were recorded from superficial deposits in the ditch.

Very little material which can be regarded as primary to the ditch was recorded. It consists of a few flakes and a single transverse arrowhead (F70). The bulk of the material was obtained from superficial deposits (layers (2), (3) and (4)) where it may be in a derived position.

The Enclosure Ditch: The North Entrance

(i) The West Terminal. A total of 292 artifacts was recorded from Cutting XXVII. Of these, ten were implements, comprising eight scrapers, one blade with flat edge retouch and one blade with steep edge retouch. The majority of the artifacts were derived from what can be regarded as a secondary context (layer (9)).

(ii) The East Terminal (Cuttings XXVIII, XXIX and XXX). Three cuttings were excavated to explore the east terminal of the north entrance. The deposits in the terminal were consistent and the layers in the three cuttings have therefore been harmonized. Furthermore, the majority of the strata produced human refuse and a stratified sequence of materials which covered virtually the whole of the second millennium bc was obtained. This stratified sequence has been supported and documented by six radiocarbon determinations. To emphasize this rarely obtained sequence the artifacts have been illustrated in their layer groupings and not on a morphological basis.

The raw material was largely flint of poor quality with a small admixture of Portland chert. From the east terminal, 7934 artifacts were recorded, of which 157 (nearly 2%) were recognizable implements. Of the 7777 by-products, cores total 93 or 1.5% of the whole. There is little variation in the distribution of core types throughout the deposits (Table XIX). The predominant type is the single platform blade core (58 examples), next in frequency are the keeled cores (23 examples), with other varieties providing only minor percentages of the whole.

Samples of complete waste flakes from layers (6), (7), (8) and (10) were measured for length and breadth and breadth–length ratio and the results portrayed in histogram form (fig. 67). These indicate that those flakes between 20 and 49 mm. long total 76.8% (layer (10)), 77.7% (layer (8)), 77.2% (layer (7)), and 83.1% (layer (6)) respectively. However, 31.7% from layer (8) are between 20 and 29 mm. long, as opposed to 22.9% from layer (10) and this change of emphasis is reflected in layers (7) and (6) (27.7 and 26.3% respectively). Similarly those flakes between 10 and 39 mm. broad comprise 78.1% (layer (10)), 85.7% (layer (8)), 84.1% (layer (7)) and 86.5% (layer (6)). The differences in flake sizes between the various layers is therefore not marked but shows a definite tendency towards a shorter and broader profile, a trend which has already been remarked upon from elsewhere. As is normal, the majority of flakes have breadth–length ratios between 2:5 and 5:5. Those flakes that are blade-like, in that their breadth–length ratio is not more than 2:5, total 11.3% (layer (10)), 10.7% (layer (8)), 9.9% (layer (7)) and 6.8% (layer (6)). The trend towards a short squat outline for the flakes is therefore confirmed by comparison between layer (10) (Grooved Ware and a radiocarbon date of 1941 ± 66 bc), and layer (6) (collared vessels and a radiocarbon date of 1556 ± 55 bc), where the percentage of blade-like flakes is extremely low in the latter. It is of interest to compare the percentage of blades from layer (10) with the broadly contemporary assemblage from Durrington Walls where 11% of the flakes fall into this category.

Scrapers (F77–90, 96–99, 101–103, 109). The occurrence of scraper types and their distribution relative to the layer sequence is shown in Table XIII. Of the 128 scrapers from the east terminal, 40 (31%) were recorded from layer (6) and 22 (15.5%) from layer (7). The most common form is the end scraper which comprises 72% of the whole, followed by side scrapers (8%) and scrapers on broken flakes (8%). Represented in small numbers are double-ended, discoidal and hollow scrapers (long end scrapers F77, 78, 101; short end F79–85, 96, 97, 102, 103, 109; double-ended F86; discoidal F87, 98; side scrapers, F88, 89, 99; hollow, F90).

Blades with flat edge retouch (F91, 104). Ten blades with flat edge retouch were recorded, all from secondary contexts in the ditch.

Blades with steep edge retouch. One such blade was recorded from layer (10).

Transverse arrowheads (F74, 75, 92, 100, 107, 108). Of the six recorded transverse arrowheads, two of classes D and F were obtained from layer (10) (F107, 108), two Class B types from layers (7) and (6) (F92, 100) and two of Class D from layers (3) and (1) (F74, 75).

Triangular arrowhead. A single bifacially worked triangular arrowhead was recorded from layer (7).

Fabricator: A single fabricator or strike-a-light was recorded from layer (3) where it may be in a derived position.

Polished axe (F105). The blade of a polished flint axe patinated a matt white was obtained from layer (10). The artifact was broken in antiquity and subsequent flaking suggests that attempts were made to convert it into a core.

Flaked axe (F76). A small flaked axe with retouch extending over the whole of one surface was obtained from layer (4).

Awls (F93–95). Three awls were recorded from layers (6) and (6)/(7).

Hammerstones. Four flint hammerstones were distributed in layers (2), (4), (6) and (10).

Miscellaneous (F106). A keeled blade with flat edge retouch around its whole perimeter was obtained from layer (10). It is worn and polished at its tip through scraping some resistant substance.

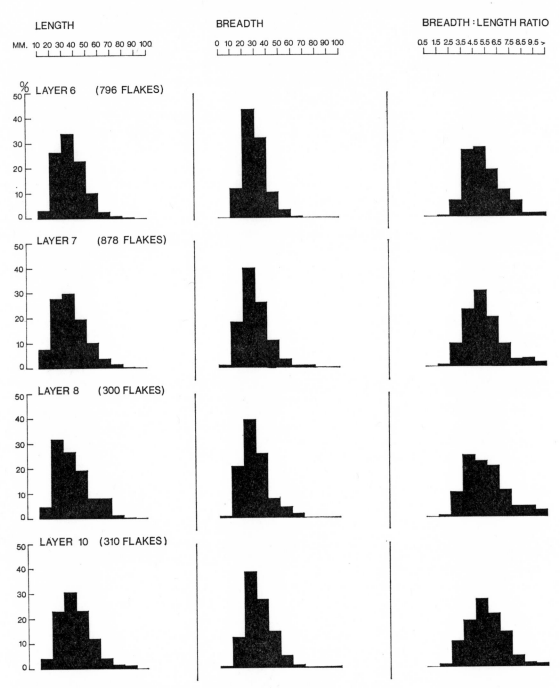

FIG. 67.   Diagram illustrating the dimensions of flakes from the enclosure ditch at the north entrance

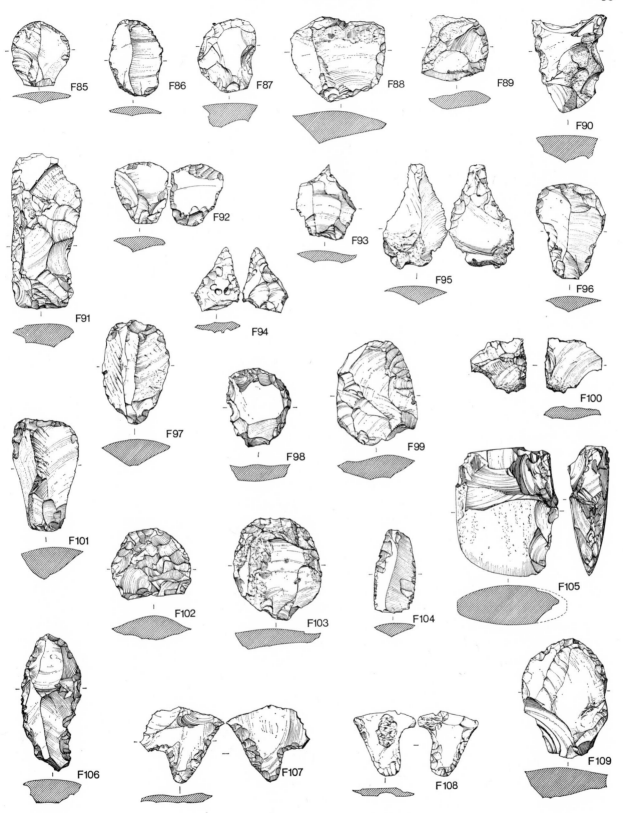

F85
F86
F87
F88
F89
F90
F91
F92
F93
F95
F96
F94
F97
F98
F99
F100
F101
F102
F103
F104
F105
F106
F107
F108
F109

FIG. 68. Flint artifacts. (Scale ½)

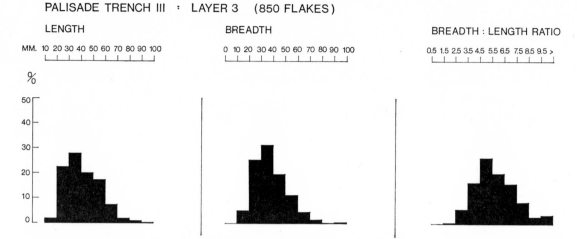

PALISADE TRENCH III · LAYER 3 (850 FLAKES)

FIG. 69.   Diagram illustrating the dimensions of flakes from the palisade trench in Cutting III

The distribution of artifacts according to the layers in the ditch have been given in Table XII but can be summarized as follows. The base of the ditch (layers (10) and (11)) produced only cores, flakes and a few scrapers (F109) along with the associated Grooved Ware. However, layer (10) in addition yielded a blade with edge retouch, two transverse arrowheads and the blade of a polished axe (F105–8). Layer (7) produced similar artifacts with the addition of a triangular arrowhead (F96–100), as did layer (6), from which was obtained the largest collection of scrapers (F77–94). Quantities of flakes were also recorded from the upper silts where the artifacts included two transverse arrowheads and a flaked axe (F74–6).

The Palisade Trench

In Table XV the flint artifacts from the palisade trench are portrayed in relation to the excavated segments without reference to the stratification in the latter. The reasons for this presentation are firstly that to include details of flint artifacts in each layer of every segment would be both tedious and prohibitively lengthy; secondly, that by virtue of its function it cannot be conclusively established that the artifacts in the foundation trench are in fact contemporary with that feature and not coincidentally incorporated in its packing. The bulk of the artifacts were obtained from the top of the palisade trench (layer (3)), where they had presumably accumulated around the base of the palisade whilst it was still standing. Because of these uncertainties few general conclusions can be drawn, but an exception has been made in the case of Segment III (layer (3)) where a total of 1738 artifacts, including a large collection of scrapers, was recorded in a burnt deposit at the top of the trench which produced a radiocarbon determination of 1695 ± 43 bc (BM-665). Because of the close association of this group, metrical analyses were made of the flakes and scrapers contained within it.

A total of 5733 artifacts was recorded from the palisade trench of which 171 were recognizable implements. The bulk of the raw material was flint with a small admixture of Portland chert. Of the 56 cores, over 50% (34 examples) were of the single-platform variety (Class A2) and 12 were keeled forms (Class D). Of the remainder, five were varieties of the

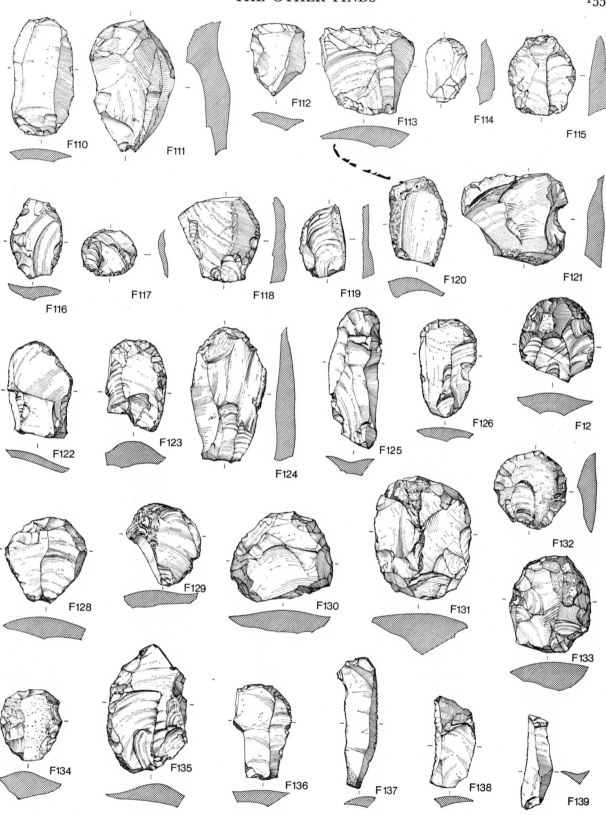

FIG. 70. Flint artifacts. (Scale ½)

6*

TABLE XII

Flint artifacts related to deposits of the enclosure ditch

Provenance	Flakes	Cores	Scrapers	Serrated flakes	Blades with flat edge retouch	Blades with steep edge retouch	Transverse arrowheads	Leaf-shaped arrowheads	Triangular arrowheads	Fabricators	Polished axes	Flaked axes	Adzes	Awls	Denticulated flakes	Hammerstones	Plano-convex knives	Miscellaneous
I (1)	24		2		1													
I (2)	61		2								1							
I (3)	50	2	1		1							1						
I (4)	12																	
I (5)	2																	
II (2)	440	2	7	2	2		1					2						
II (3)	331	4	6	2		1				1				2				
II (4)	285	2	3	2			1							1	1			
II (5)	56		2															
II (6)	211	1	1	1														
II (7)	8		1															
II (8)	3						1											
II (9)	20																	
II (10)	7																	
XXVII (2)	12																	
XXVII (5)	6																	
XXVII (7)	25		1															
XXVII (8)	5																	
XXVII (9)	117	1	7		1	1												
XXVII (10)	116																	
North Entrance: East Terminal																		
(1)	65	1	1				1											
(2)	473	3	11													1		
(3)	258	3	8		2		1			1								
(4)	614	23	7									1				1		
(5)	336	2	5		2													
(6)	1783	10	40		3		1							2		1		
(6)/(7)	507	3	10											1				
(7)	1793	11	22		2		1		1									
(8)	707	7	9		1													
(9)	182	3	1															
(10)	738	22	7			1	2				1					1		1
(11)	212	4	7															
(12)	16	1																
Totals	9475	105	161	7	15	3	9	—	1	2	2	4	—	6	1	4	—	1

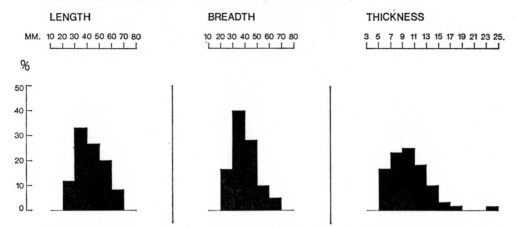

PALISADE TRENCH III : LAYER 3 (60 SCRAPERS)

LENGTH   BREADTH   THICKNESS

FIG. 71. Diagram illustrating the dimensions of scrapers from the palisade trench in Cutting III

TABLE XIII

Scraper classes related to deposits of the main enclosure ditch

Provenance	Class									Totals
	A(i)	A(ii)	B(i)	B(ii)	C	D(i)	D(ii)	E	F	
West Entrance										
I (1)		1							1	2
I (2)		2								2
I (3)	1									1
II (2)		6							1	7
II (3)	1	2					3			6
II (4)		2					1			3
II (5)		2								2
II (6)							1			1
II (7)		1								1
North Entrance										
XXVII (7)							1			1
XXVII (9)	1	4			1		1			7
XXVIII, XXIX, XXX:										
(1)		1								1
(2)	1	9					1			11
(3)	2	3						2	1	8
(4)	1	6								7
(5)		4					1			5
(6)	5	20		2	4		4	4	1	40
(6)/(7)	1	7						2		10
(7)	2	11			1		6	2		22
(8)	2	7								9
(9)		1								1
(10)		4						3		7
(11)		6					1			7
	17	99	—	2	6	—	20	13	4	161

TABLE XIV

Core types related to deposits in the east terminal of the north entrance

Layer No.	Core types								Totals
	A1	A2	B1	B2	B3	C	D	E	
(1)		1							1
(2)		3							3
(3)	1						1	1	3
(4)	2	11			2		6	2	23
(5)		2							2
(6)		8			1			1	10
(6)/(7)		1					1	1	3
(7)	1	5			1		1	3	11
(8)		3		1	1		1	1	7
(9)		2		1					3
(10)	2	11	1	4			4		22
(11)		4							4
(12)		1							1
	6	52	1	6	5	—	14	9	93

two platform type-and the remainder were unclassifiable. These percentages are confirmed by the small collection of 11 cores from Segment III (layer (3)). A sample of 850 complete waste flakes from the latter context was measured for length and breadth and breadth–length ratio. The results have been portrayed in histogram form (fig. 69) which indicates that 70.6% of the flakes are between 20 and 49 mm. long and that 62.2% are between 10 and 39 mm. broad. Only 5.8% of the flakes are blade-like in that their breadth–length ratios are not more than 2:5, and as many as 69% of the flakes are more than 30 mm. broad. The proportion of blade-like flakes is very low and compares best with the broadly contemporary flake assemblages from the secondary silts of the Site IV ditch (9.4%), and layer (7) from the east terminal of the enclosure ditch at its north entrance (9.9%).

Scrapers (F110–36). A total of 131 scrapers was recorded and they are the most common implement type. Morphologically they have been classified as follows:

Class A.	End scrapers	(i) Long (F110, 124–6)	(7)	
		(ii) Short (F111–14, 127–31)	(61)	68
Class C.	Discoidal (F115–17, 132–4)			13
Class D.	Side	(ii) Short (F118–20, 135)		29
Class E.	On broken flakes (F136)			12
Class F.	Hollow (F121)			1
Class G.	End and side (ii) Short (F122–3)			8
Total				131

The 64 scrapers from the burnt deposit in Cutting III (layer (3)) formed a distinctive and homogeneous group and a selection of 60 artifacts was measured for length, breadth and thickness. The results have been portrayed in histogram form (fig. 71), from which it is clear that the preferred length of the scrapers is between 30 and 59 mm. (80%) and preferred breadth between 30 and 49 mm. (85%). Slightly more than 28% are more than 50 mm. long and 43% in excess of 40 mm. broad. The preferred thickness is rather variable but appears to lie between 5 and 12.9 mm. (83%) although a high proportion (25%) are between 9 and 10.9 mm. thick. One may compare these details with the broadly contemporary collection of 58 scrapers from the secondary silts of the Site IV ditch. Of this group, 8.6% are only 50 mm. long and only 15.5% in excess of 40 mm. broad, as compared with 28 and 43% respectively from the palisade trench. Quite clearly, the latter are on average much larger than those from the Site IV ditch but the significance of this distinction is at present obscure.

For ease of reference the scraper assemblage from Cutting III has been illustrated as a group (F110–23) and the implements have been categorized as follows:

Class A.	End Scrapers	(i) Long (F110)	(1)	
		(ii) Short (F111–14)	(21)	22
Class C.	Discoidal (F115–17)			9
Class D.	Side	(ii) Short (F118–20)		19
Class E.	On broken flakes			5
Class F.	Hollow (F21)			1
Class G.	End and side (F122–3)			8
Total				64

Scrapers on the ends of flakes are still the dominant form, but side-scrapers with retouch carried down one lateral edge are unusually numerous.

Amongst the discoidal scrapers over 50% have a narrow butt and pointed tip. A specific group which also occurs in the secondary silts of the Site IV ditch are end and side-scrapers in which the retouch is carried across the end of the flake and down one lateral edge.

Serrated flakes (F137–40). Twelve serrated flakes and blades were recorded, of which seven were obtained from Cutting III layer (3).

Blades with flat edge retouch (F141). Of the seven blades with flat edge retouch, three were recorded from Cutting III layer (3).

Blades with steep edge retouch. Only one blade with steep edge retouch was recorded and this has not been illustrated.

Transverse arrowheads (F142–9). Eight transverse arrowheads were recorded, one Class A (F142, Segment XLVI layer (2)); one Class B (F143, Segment III layer (4)); two Class D (F144), Segment XXV layer (4); F145, Segment XXIV layer (2)); three Class G (F146, Segment XX layer (8); F147, Segment XXIV layer (2) and F148, Segment XXXVI layer (9)) and one Class H (F149, segment XXXV layer (5)). The arrowhead F148 is an unusually elongated type with bifacial flat retouch along one edge, across its flat base and obliquely at the tip.

Leaf arrowhead (F150). A fragmentary and lightly patinated leaf-shaped arrowhead was recorded from layer (2) of the north post-hole at the east entrance (Segment XXXVI N). This is probably a derived position.

Fabricators (F151–2). Three fabricators or strike-a-lights were recorded, of which two have been illustrated.

Polished axe (F153). The cutting edge of a polished flint axe from which flakes have subsequently been removed was recorded from layer (2) in Segment XVII.

Flaked axe (F154). The pointed butt of a large flaked axe was recorded from layer (2) in Segment XXIII. It was broken in antiquity and is patinated a matt white.

Adzes (F155–6). Two probable adze tools were recorded, both from layer (5) in Segment XX. The first is a bifacially worked core tool, with a thick triangular section, and broken across its width (F156); whilst the second is the reworked butt of a flaked axe-head in which steep retouch at the fractured surface has converted the implement into an adze-like tool (F155).

Awls (F157). Two awls were recorded, one of which has been illustrated.

Denticulated flakes. One denticulated flake was recorded but has not been illustrated.

Hammerstones. One hammerstone was recorded but has not been illustrated.

TABLE XV

Palisade trench: distribution of flint artifacts

Provenance	Flakes	Cores	Scrapers	Serrated flakes	Blades with flat edge retouch	Blades with steep edge retouch	Transverse arrowheads	Leaf arrowheads	Fabricators	Polished axes	Flaked axes	Adzes	Awls	Denticulated flakes	Hammerstones
III	1906	14	64	7	3		1								
XII	16				1										
XIII	103	1	2	1											
XIV	50		4						1						
XV	163	3	3												
XVI	45		1		1										
XVII	157	2	4	1						1					
XVIII	250	1	3												
XIX	334	1	7						1						
XX	214	3	10				1					2	1		
XXI	138	2		1											
XXII	361		6		1								1		
XXIII	162	5	4		1						1			1	
XXIV	312	9	4	1			1								
XXV	105	4	5	1			1								
XXVII	7		1												
XXVIII	38														
XXXIV	61		3				1								
XXXV	71						1								
XXXVY IS	209	3	3												
XXXVY IN	314	3	5				1	1							
XXXVII	41		1						1						
XXXVIII	38														1
XXXIX	97	3	2												
XL	192	1	2												
XLI	10		1												
XLII	7														
XLIII	8														
XLIV	10														
XLV	8	1													
XLVI	79					1	1								
	5506	56	131	12	7	1	8	1	3	1	1	2	2	1	1

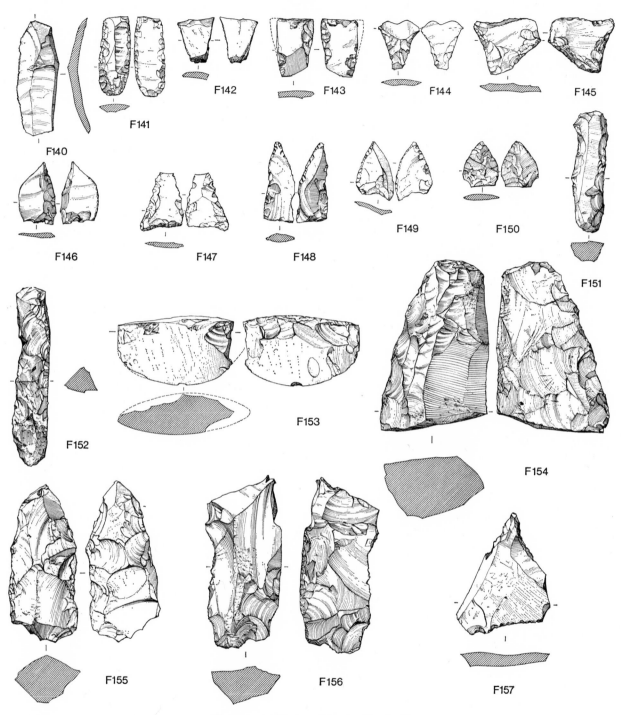

F140 F141 F142 F143 F144 F145
F146 F147 F148 F149 F150 F151
F152 F153 F154
F155 F156 F157

FIG. 72.   Flint artifacts. (Scale $\frac{1}{2}$)

Conquer Barrow Ditch

A total of 366 weathered flint artifacts was recovered from all levels in the Conquer Barrow ditch. Of the five cores (trench XLVIII layers (4) and (9)), three are of single platform and two are keeled types. The three recognizable implements are two scrapers (trench XLIX layers (1) and (4)), of short-end and side types respectively, and one blade with flat edge retouch (trench XLVIII layer (6)).

Iron Age Hollow (XXVI)

A total of 311 weathered flint artifacts was recorded from all layers in this hollow. The recognizable implements comprise two short end scrapers and one serrated blade.

Woodhenge (F158–63)

A subsoil hollow beneath the bank. A slightly calcined core-trimming flake of Mesolithic type was recovered from a subsoil hollow beneath the old ground surface. Such hollows are interpreted as the casts of ancient tree-roots and the example from Woodhenge produced a molluscan fauna of woodland type together with abundant flecks of charcoal, suggesting the activities of hunter–gatherer communities.

The old land surface (F158). A total of 132 flakes, one side-scraper and four cores were recorded from this context. All the artifacts were patinated white.

The ditch (F159–63). A total of 19 waste flakes was recorded from the primary rubble in the ditch (layer (8)); they were in a slightly fresher condition than the remainder of the assemblage. From the finer chalk rubble (layer (7)) were obtained 67 flakes, one short-end scraper (F159) and two transverse arrowheads of classes G (F160) and H (F161). Waste flakes only were recorded from layers (6) (6B), (5C) (5), (5B) (3) and (4) (two specimens). The uppermost layers in the ditch (layers (1)–(3)) produced 21 flakes, a single platform blade-core (F163) and a side-scraper (F162).

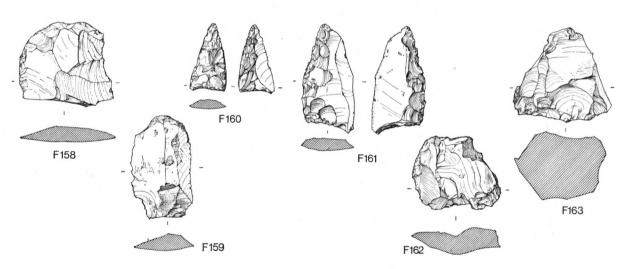

FIG. 73.   Flint artifacts from Woodhenge. (Scale ½)

To these artifacts should be added the arrowheads of transverse, barbed and tanged and leaf type, fabricators, awls, knives, projectile points, denticulated flakes, scrapers, an adze and the butt of a flaked flint axe recorded from the 1926–8 excavations. Most of these were obtained from the fossil soil beneath the bank.

STONE
(fig. 74)

The Pre-Enclosure Settlement

No stone artifacts were recorded from the fossil soil beneath the enclosure bank. Items of foreign stone include five sarsen flakes and 15 water-rolled quartzite pebbles which average 3 cm. in diameter.

Site IV: Phase 1

No sarsen flakes were recorded from post-holes attributable to Phase 1 of the timber structure and only ten fragments (3 lb. 4 oz.) from the primary silts of the surrounding ditch (vide Table XVII). This material includes a single flake weighing 2 lb. from Segment III.

S1 One half a ring or pendant of fine-grained quartzite which is circular in section and has the internal aperture smoothed from wear (post-hole 1).

Site IV: Phase 2

A large quantity of sarsen flakes was recorded from the secondary silts of the ditch. Their distribution and quantities have been recorded in Table XVII. Rather more than 300 lb. (1452 fragments) of sarsen flakes were recorded and were concentrated most especially in Segments IV, IX, X alpha and XIII. Many flakes were large and fresh. They frequently retained the cortex of the original sarsen block on one face and showed clear percussion bulbs where they had been struck off. A small percentage had been subjected to intense heat and this process may have played a part in the shaping of the monolith. The flakes, combined with the evidence of the mauls described below, provide clear evidence for the shaping and preparation on the site at a period which has been ascertained by BM-668 as 1680 ± 60 bc. Similarly, the quantities of sarsen flakes from features within the excavated area of Site IV have been summarized in Table XVIII, which is self-explanatory. The quantities of fresh sarsen flakes from the pits and stone-holes of the central setting in particular confirm their contemporaneity with the relevant phase in the ditch sediments and relate the latter conclusively to the construction of a stone cove within the confines of the partially silted ditch.

S2 A maul of sarsen which is flaked and battered partially around its perimeter through use (Segment V layer (7)).
S3 A sarsen pebble chipped and fractured through use as a maul (Segment IV layer (4)).
S4 A sarsen pebble utilized as a maul (Segment VII layer (5). Not illustrated are two comparable mauls from superficial deposits in the ditch (Segments VIIIα layer (2) and IXα layer (3)) and two burnished pebbles (Segments IXα layer (5) and XI layer (5)).

The Enclosure Ditch: The West Entrance

A small quantity of sarsen fragments (5 lb.) which do not include any struck flakes, were recorded from layers (2), (3), (5) and (6) in the enclosure ditch.

S5   An axe-roughout or chopper manufactured from a nodule of chert with foraminifera (cf. *The Implement Petrology Survey of the South West*, Dorset 113, ser. No. 1456). The implement is of simple type with flakes removed bifacially around its perimeter and cortex retained in the middle of both broad surfaces. The intention may have been to complete the implement by polishing but it could have functioned as a chopper with no further retouch (Cutting II layer (5)).

The Enclosure Ditch: The North Entrance

A few sarsen fragments were recorded from the west terminal of this entrance (Cutting XXVII) and rather more from the east terminal. The fragments from the latter have been summarized in Table XVI below, from which it will be seen that a concentration of fragments occurs in layer (6). Only a few flakes are fresh, the majority are weathered lumps of stone.

TABLE XVI

The enclosure ditch: distribution of sarsen fragments from the east terminal of the north entrance

Cutting	Layer numbers (weight in lb.)											
	1	2	3	4	5	6	7	8	9	10	11	12
XXVIII	—	1–10	0–2	—	0–2	4–3	0–10	0–2	0–8	0–2	0–14	—
XXIX	—	1–8	2–0	2–0	—	11–0	0–10	0–4	—	5–12	1–0	0–8
XXX	—	3–0	1–8	2–8	0–2	1–0	—	—	—	0–2	—	—
Totals	—	6–2	3–10	4–8	0–4	16–3	1–4	0–6	0–8	6–0	1–14	0–8

S6   A flat pebble 10 cm. long, with one surface smoothed and worn, possibly through use as a whetstone (Cutting XXVIII layer (6)).

Not illustrated is one half of a flat quartzite pebble smoothed and burnished on its two flat surfaces.

The Palisade Trench

Small quantities of weathered sandstone lumps were recorded from the palisade trench, chiefly from the superficial deposits. No fresh flakes were recognized.

S7   A weathered stone axe 13 cm. long with a pointed butt. Near the latter the implement is round in section but it becomes more oval near its blade (Cutting XII layer (3)). *The Implement Petrology Survey of the South West* (Dorset 118, ser. No. 1582) describes it as a light green coloured greenstone of medium grain which weathers to a rough surface, the exact source of which is unknown. 'Plagioclase prisms are full of small grains of horneblende. Brownish augite is also present, surrounded by bluish green horneblende in needles and irregular masses. Also some large irregular crystals of black iron ore.'

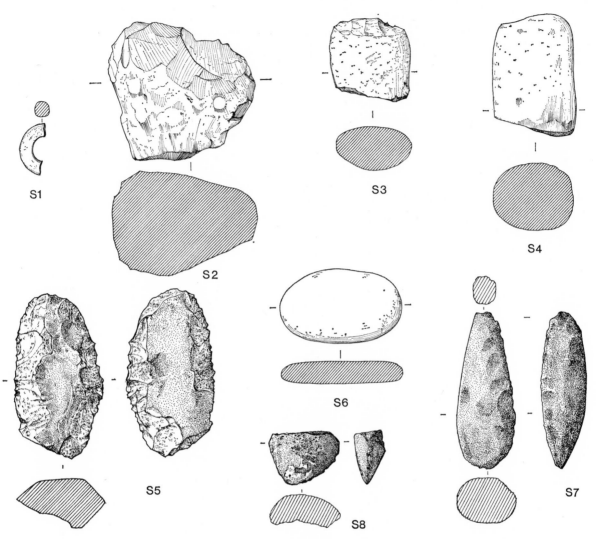

FIG. 74.   Stone artifacts. (Scale ⅓)

S8   Three fragments of a stone axe, the largest fragment of which has been illustrated and which represents the much weathered tip of an asymmetric blade (Cutting XIII layer (4), at a depth of 2.30–2.50 m. below the natural chalk surface). *The Implement Petrology Survey of the South West* (Dorset 117, ser. No. 1581) describes it as a light green coloured greenstone, weathering rough with a coarse grain. It is a thermally altered greenstone, composed of altered felspar and green horneblende with unaltered cores of brownish augite, together with much brown mica in overlapping scales. Black iron ore is also present. The exact source of the stone is unknown.

Not illustrated is a fragment of ferruginous sandstone 5 × 4 cm. with one flat polished surface.

TABLE XVII

Site IV: distribution of sarsen fragments from the ditch

Segment	Primary		Secondary		Tertiary	
	Weight in lb.	No. of fragments	Weight in lb.	No. of fragments	Weight in lb.	No. of fragments
Iα	—	—	3–2	13	5–0	13
III	2–0	I	—	—	—	—
IV	0–2	I	78–0	249	0–8	2
IVα	0–8	I	3–8	8	3–0	8
V	—	—	8–0	13	—	—
Vα	—	—	9–8	19	0–2	I
VI	—	—	0–8	3	—	—
VIα	—	—	6–0	8	4–0	7
VII	0–8	6	10–0	14	1–4	9
VIIα	—	—	—	—	2–8	8
VIII	—	—	—	—	0–2	3
VIIIα	—	—	8–8	24	5 0	14
IX	—	—	52–0	358	1–2	3
IXα	—	—	8–0	22	7–0	29
X	—	—	36–0	353	5–10	31
Xα	—	—	47–8	285	3–2	6
XI	—	—	7–0	14	0–8	I
XIα	0–2	I	5–4	21	6–4	20
XIII	—	—	21–8	48	0–6	4
Totals	3–4	10	304–6	1452	45–8	159

TABLE XVIII

Site IV: distribution of sarsen fragments in the features

Feature number	Function	Weight in lb.	Fragments
13	Pit	2–0	13
39	Pit	13–0	95
173	Pit	18–8	56
174	Pit	34–8	90
175	Pit	0–10	24
176	Pit	0–8	6
177	Stone-hole	6–0	44
178	Stone-hole	27–8	167
179	Stone-hole	1–0	5
181	Stone-hole	1–0	2
183	Pit	0–2	I
185	Saxon grave	0–2	I
186	Iron Age pit	0–2	I
189	Iron Age post-hole	1–0	10
191	Stone-hole	2–0	33
193	Iron Age pit	0–2	3

CHALK
(figs. 75–7)

Site IV: Phase 1

C1   A single chalk ball some 5 cm. in diameter with a smoothed surface (Segment VI layer (7)).

The Enclosure Ditch: the West Entrance

C2   A carefully worked phallus 11 cm. long, the surface of which exhibits longitudinal striations. Along with the chalk ball (C3) this artifact was recorded from the floor of the ditch to the south of the chalk causeway (Cutting II layer (8)).

C3   A ball some 7 cm. in diameter with a scraped surface and one segment missing (Cutting II layer (8)).

The Enclosure Ditch: the North Entrance

C4   A scraped cylinder, the longitudinal striations being particularly well preserved. One terminal of the cylinder has been scraped to a rough butt, the other terminal has not been scraped but exhibits percussion marks (Cutting XXIX layer (12)).

C5   Two fragments of a phallus which was broken in antiquity, the two parts being recorded in close proximity on the chalk floor of the ditch. When joined, the object is 8 cm. long and carefully worked with a scraped and smoothed surface, the base of the phallus expanding to an enlarged and neatly cut butt. The tip of the phallus is missing, having been broken off in antiquity (Cutting XXVIII layer (11)).

C6   A smoothed but otherwise featureless chalk block 15 × 9 × 6 cm. with an unretouched flat base, on which it can stand unsupported. The entire surface of the block has been scraped, the striations almost invariably being aligned along the long axis of the object (Cutting XXIX layer (11)).

C7   A thick disc with crudely fashioned flat surfaces and a deep broad groove partially around its circumference (Cutting XXVIII layer (10)).

Not illustrated is a small and irregular lump with one fluted surface.

The Palisade Trench

By far the most numerous artifacts associated with the palisade trench are the chalk balls, of which 30 examples were recorded — principally from the packing material which had been placed around the posts. (Segments XII, (5) (two examples); XIII (4) (one example), XIV (4) (four examples); XV (5) (one example); XVI (3) (one example); XVI (4) (one example); XVII (5) (one example); XVIII (3) (two examples); XVIII (4) (two examples); XVIII (5) (eight examples); XX (8) (one example); XXII (4) (two examples); XXIII (5) (one example); XXIV (4) (one example); XXV (5) (two examples).) From this list of contexts it is apparent that 12 examples were recorded from Segment XVIII and four from Segment XIV, thus accounting for over 50% of the whole. The objects appear to have been first pecked and then scraped (possibly with a flint blade) into the required shape. An appreciable number were broken in antiquity. Carved chalk balls, occasionally with phalli, have been recorded at many prehistoric sites, including contexts attributable to the third and early second millennia bc.[1] They could be representative of a concern with fertility or could also have been missiles, or even have resulted from the idle scraping of chalk lumps (C8–14).

[1] *Vide* Smith, 1967, 474; Wainwright and Longworth, 1971, 203.

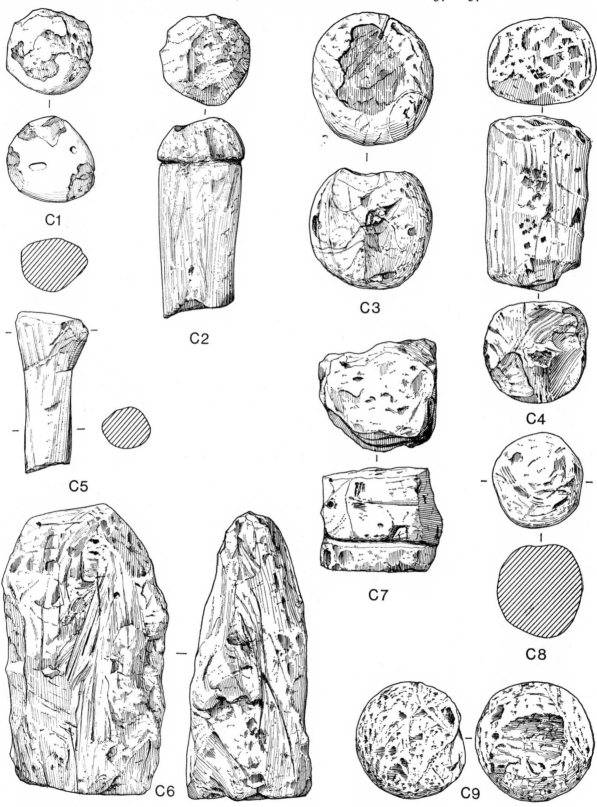

C1

C2

C3

C4

C5

C6

C7

C8

C9

Fig. 75.   Chalk artifacts. (Scale $\frac{1}{2}$)

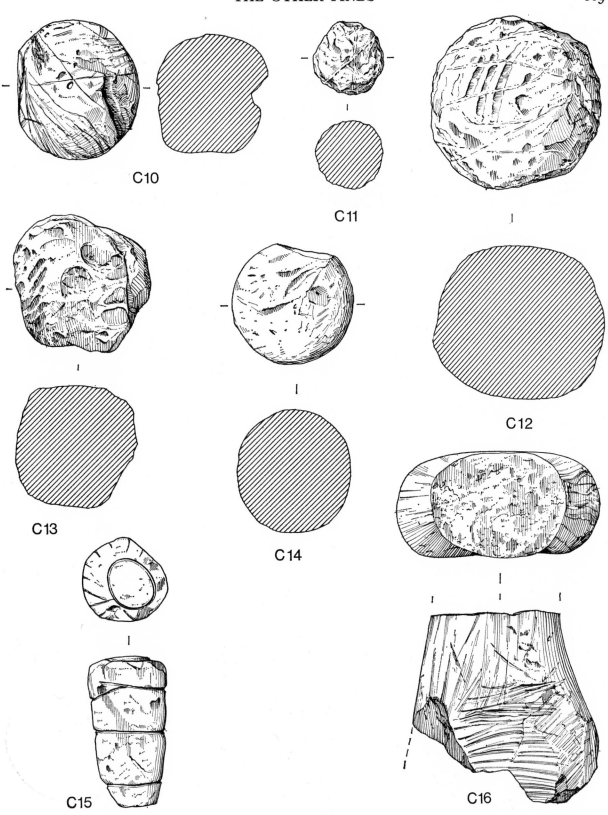

C10

C11

C12

C13

C14

C15

C16

FIG. 76.   Chalk artifacts. (Scale ½)

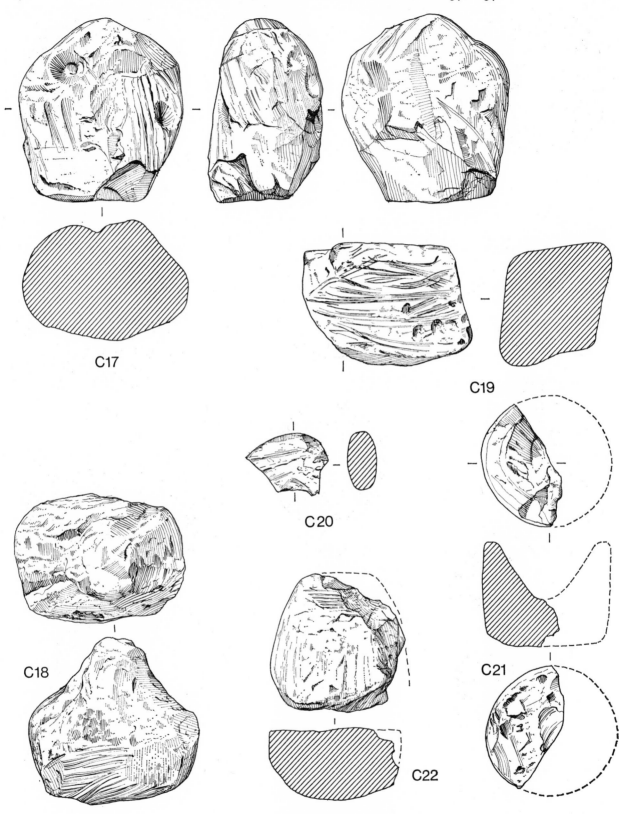

FIG. 77.   Chalk artifacts. (Scale ½)

C15 A tapering object 8 cm. long with an irregularly circular section 45 mm. diameter at the broad end and 25 mm. at the narrow. Possibly of phallic significance, the object has been scraped into the required shape, the longitudinal striations being visible in part on its roughly finished surface. Around its girth are three deeply incised grooves and a crude circle is inscribed on the face of its broader terminal (Cutting III layer (4)).

C16 A section from near the base of a carefully carved cylindrical object. Its surface is smoothed and scraped but the original nature of the artifact cannot be ascertained (Cutting XII layer (5)).

C17 A carved lump with over-all dimensions of 9 × 9 × 5 cm., fashioned into a trapezoid shape. Some care was taken in the working of the surface with the exception of one flat face which has been left rough and unsmoothed (Cutting XII layer (5)).

C18 A carved block 10 × 6 cm. with squared ends, a scraped surface and a lateral protuberance. The latter is rather weathered and its original dimensions cannot now be established. Marks of pecking occur at the junction of the protuberance and the chalk block (Cutting XIV layer (4)).

C19 A squared block, scraped on its six flat surfaces and trapezoid in section (Cutting XVI layer (4)).

C20 A fragment of carved chalk, curved in outline and oval in section. The surface of the object is carefully finished but not enough of it has survived to enable the shape of the parent object to be determined (Cutting XVIII layer (5)).

C21 Part of the rim, wall and base of a circular bowl or cup standing 50 mm. high and 68 mm. in external diameter at the lip. The top of the rim, external wall and base of the vessel are well finished and smoothed. However, the interior of the vessel is in a rougher condition and the marks of the preliminary carving are still visible (Cutting XVIII layer (3)).

C22 A chalk object with four carefully smoothed and scraped surfaces which is probably part of a trapezoidal block similar to that recorded from Cutting XII layer (5) (Cutting XVIII layer (5)).

Not illustrated: chalk lumps which showed marks of antler picks were not uncommon but only a few were retained owing to their bulk. In addition, the following objects were recorded:

(i) A block with a roughly triangular section 11 cm. long and 7 cm. thick. The flat surfaces and terminals have been scraped, the marks of this process being clearly visible on the chalk surface (Cutting XVIII unstratified).

(ii) A crudely worked elongated block of chalk 16 cm. long. Intermittent scraping and smoothing occurs on all four surfaces and the two terminals. A small irregular hole on one flat face may represent an unfinished attempt to perforate the block (Cutting XXV layer (4)).

(iii) An uneven and apparently freshly quarried chalk lump with one half of a cylindrical perforation 2 cm. in diameter preserved in one edge (Cutting XXXVI layer (4)).

(iv) A heavy carved disc 11 cm. in diameter and 7 cm. thick with a fragment broken from its perimeter. The surface of the artifact is uneven and scraping marks are visible upon it (Cutting XXVI layer (12)).

ANTLER
(figs. 78–9)

Site IV: Phase 1

A minimum number of 11 antler picks was recorded from primary contexts in the Site IV ditch (segments I, IV, VI, VI alpha, VII (one example from each), XII and XIII (three examples)). One pick from Segment VII layer (10) was submitted for radiocarbon assay (BM–666) and two have been illustrated (A1–2). They were presumably employed in the

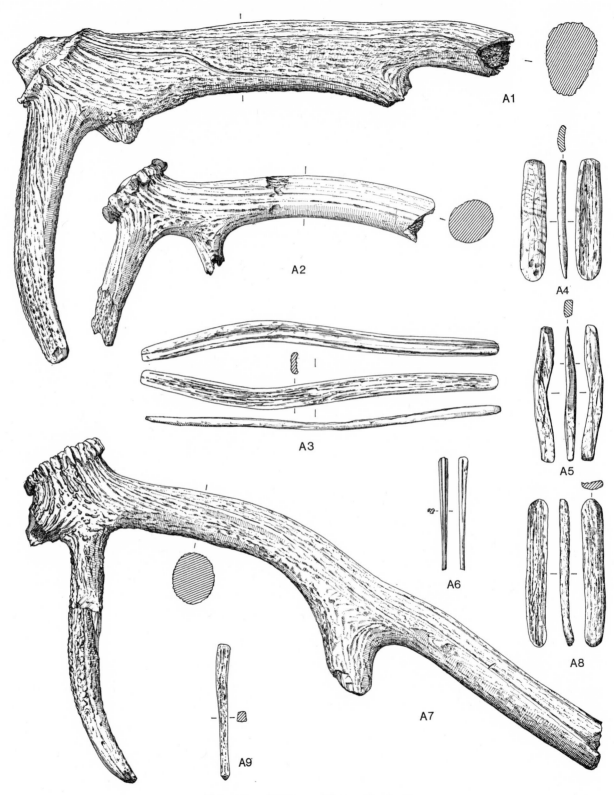

Fig. 78.   Antler artifacts. (Scale ⅓)

excavation of the ditch and all have worn tines with occasional signs of battering behind the burr. All the antlers had been shed.

Site IV: Phase 2

Two picks (Segments VII layer (6) and XI layer (6)), fragments of an antler beam (Segment XII layer (6)) and a roe deer antler (Segment V layer (8)) were recorded from secondary contexts in the Site IV ditch. It is possible that the picks were used to excavate the stone holes and pits of the Phase 2 structure. All the antlers had been shed and the picks showed signs of wear.

A3   An antler artifact 30 cm. long and with an average width of 16 mm. The artifact is sinuous in outline, describing a crude curve, the long edges being smoothed and bevelled. One end is blunt, squared and smoothed from use on both flat surfaces. The other end has been thinned to a chisel edge and is worn from use. The artifact is intermittently smoothed throughout its length and gives the impression of being well worn. When found, it was in three fragments, the breaks having occurred in antiquity (Segment XIII layer (5)). The artifact falls into an implement category commonly referred to as spatulae, although this particular example is unusually elongated. Other examples from the site include A4, A5 and A8, to which the following comments also refer. A discussion of antler, bone and stone spatulae has been undertaken by Smith and Simpson[1] in respect of tools obtained from an interment under Barrow G66 on Overton Hill in north Wiltshire. They conclude that the tools were used for softening and burnishing leather, are found in the final phases of the Beaker culture and overlap in time with Collared Vessels and ogival daggers.

Dr. Clarke[2] has given more precision to the Beaker associations of the artifacts by noting that they do occur with WMR graves but more particularly with Beakers of the southern series (S1 and S2). Of the six sexed graves in which they are found, all are male. The artifacts and their associations at Mount Pleasant confirm these assessments made by Smith, Simpson and Clarke.

A4   A complete antler spatula 9.7 cm. long and 2 cm. broad. The long edges are bevelled and worn. The artifact narrows slightly towards its butt which is blunt and bevelled. The broader end is spatulate and much worn and polished from use. The upper surface of the implement portrays faint traces of broad, shallow, transverse grooves which may indicate the former presence of a binding agency which secured it to a haft (Segment XIII layer (5)).

A5   A much-worn artifact which is probably of antler. It is 11 cm. long with an average width of 13 mm. and is curved in one plane. The long edges of the artifact show traces of the cutting and scraping by which this shape was achieved. One end of the implement is thick and squared and worn smooth for some 200 mm. on one surface. The second and slightly narrower end has been thinned to a chisel edge and is also worn on one surface (Segment XIII layer (5)).

It is clear that these three implements (A3–5) form a group, not only on account of their physical resemblances but also because they were recorded from broadly the same area in the enclosure ditch.

A6   A sliver of antler 9 cm. long. Two grooves run parallel with the long edges and a central groove is also present on the under surface. The sliver resembles a by-product from the 'groove and splinter' technique of working antler.

[1] Smith and Simpson, 1966, 134–41.   [2] Clarke, 1970, 448.

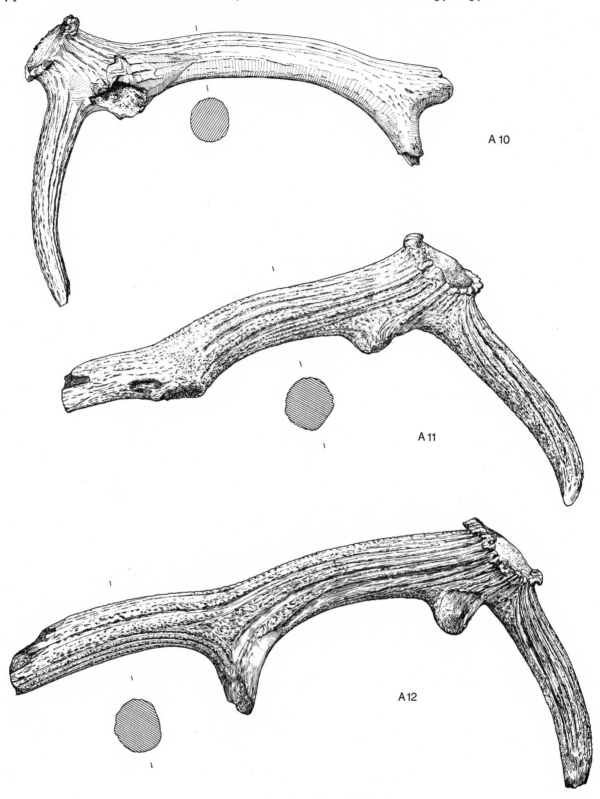

FIG. 79.   Antler picks. (Scale ⅓)

The Enclosure Ditch: the West Entrance

Twelve antler picks were recorded at the west entrance (Cutting II), either from the floor of the ditch (six examples) or from the rapid chalk silts (six examples). Two picks from the rock floor of the ditch on either side of the narrow causeway were sent for radiocarbon assay (BM-645–6) and one example has been drawn (A7). All picks save one were shed antlers and show signs of intensive use. A single pick and antler fragments were recorded from the slower silts (layers (3), (4) and (5)).

The Enclosure Ditch: the North Entrance

Two picks and the fragments of two tines were recorded from the chalk rubble (layer (11)) at the bottom of the east ditch terminal. Two tines were also recorded from layer (7) in the same ditch silts.

A8   Two fragments of a spatula 16 mm. wide and bevelled at both ends. One fragment has a curved profile and is worn as if from use (Cutting XXVIII layer (6)/(7)). This implement belongs to the same category as those from Segment XIII layer (5) in the Site IV ditch (A3–5).

A9   A squared peg or fabricator 11 cm. long and 8 mm. thick. The surface of the artifact shows cut and scrape marks, the butt end is squared and neatly finished and the narrower end has been fashioned with a blunt point. The tip does not show any signs of wear and it would appear that whatever its original purpose, the artifact was not used (Cutting XXIX layer (7)).

The Palisade Trench

A total of 38 complete antler picks was recorded from the palisade trench, almost invariably from the chalk rubble packing which had been placed around the timber uprights. (Cuttings III (4) (four examples); III (5) (seven examples); XIV (4) (one example); XV (5) (one example); XVI (3) (one example); XVI (4) (three examples); XVIII (5) (two examples); XVIII (6) (one example); XIX (4) (one example); XX (4) (four examples); XXI (6) (one example); XXI (10) (one example); XXII (3) (one example); XXII (5) (one example); XXIV (5) (one example); XXIV (6) (one example); XXV (5) (two examples); XXXVI (4) (two examples), XXXVI (7) (two examples); XXXIX (4) (one example).) The majority were recorded from near the base of the trench. They had clearly been used to excavate the latter and then thrown back in to augment the packing material. Most were in a worn condition and some were abraded behind the burr. One pick from the base of the trench in Cutting III was used as sample material for a radiocarbon assay (BM-662) and one example has been illustrated (A10). Single tines from picks were recorded from Cuttings III layers (4) and (5); XIX layer (4) and XXII layer (4), and fragments of antler beam from Cuttings III layer (4); XIX layer (4); XX layer (8) and XXXVI layers (4) and (12). All the antlers had been shed.

The Conquer Barrow

A single antler pick was recorded from the base of the Conquer Barrow ditch in Cutting XLVI and used as a sample for radiocarbon assay (BM-795).

Woodhenge

A collection of ten antler picks was recorded from the floor of the ditch (pl. XXXV*b*). All the antlers had been shed and the tips of the tines were smoothed from use. One pick showed signs of battering behind the burr as if it had been hammered into the chalk. The picks had presumably been used to excavate the enclosure ditch and then dropped in a pile when the work was completed. A similar, though much larger, pile of antler picks was recorded from the floor of the Durrington enclosure ditch.[1] Two specimens have been illustrated (A11–12).

BONE
(fig. 80)

The Pre-Enclosure Settlement

Ten fragments of animal bone were recorded from the old land surface beneath the enclosure bank. They include remains of *bos* (2) and sheep (1).

Site IV: Phase 1

Some 228 fragments of animal bones were recorded from the primary contexts of Site IV, principally from the rapid silts of the ditch. The minimum numbers of individuals represented are pig (3), *bos* (2), sheep (1), dog (1), red deer (1), fox (1), badger (1) and bird (common crane).

B1   The calcined tip of a bone pin or awl (Segment VII layer (9)).

Site IV: Phase 2

Some 879 fragments of animal bones were recorded from the secondary contexts of Site IV, principally from the slower silts of the ditch. The minimum numbers of individuals represented are *bos* (8), pig (7), sheep (6), dog (2), red deer (2) and birds (greylag and pintail). No bone artifacts were recorded.

The Enclosure Ditch: West Entrance

Some 110 fragments of animal bones were recorded from primary contexts of the main enclosure ditch at the west entrance. The minimum numbers of individuals represented are pig (5), *bos* (2), sheep (1), horse (1), dog (1) and red deer (1).

TABLE XIX

Distribution of animal remains in the deposits of the north entrance terminals

Context	Minimum no. of species							No. of fragments
	Bos	*Bos* sp.	*Pig*	*Sheep*	*Red deer*	*Goat*	*Dog*	
Layers (11)–(12)	2	1	10	—	1	—	—	321
Layers (8)–(10)	2	—	13	4	—	—	—	400
Layers (6)–(7)	2	—	4	3	—	1	1	440

[1] Wainwright and Longworth, 1971, 22.

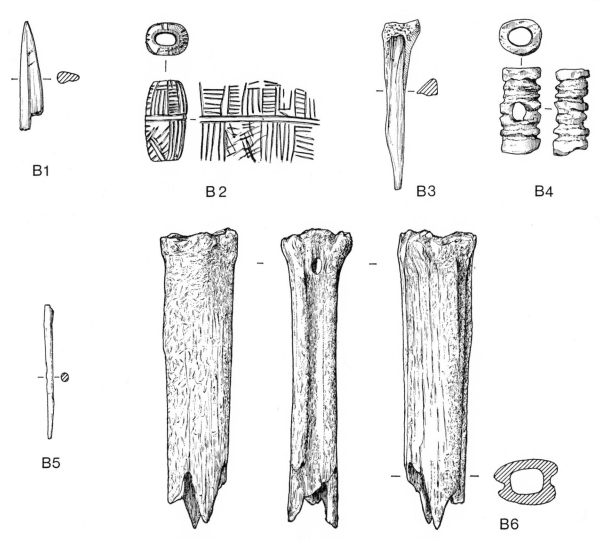

FIG. 80.   Bone artifacts. (B1, B2, B4, B6 (Scale 1/1); B3, B5 (Scale ½))

The Enclosure Ditch: North Entrance

The animal bones from the ditch terminals of the north entrance have been tabulated below. From this summary it is clear that pig bones are very much in the majority in the early part of the second millennium bc.

B2   A cylindrical bone bead 20 mm. long with an oval perforation. The external surface of the bead is decorated overall with delicately incised geometric patterns (XXVIII layer (7)). The bead is similar in type to an undecorated example from the Wessex Early Bronze Age bowl barrow Upton Lovell G2(a).[1]

B3   A bone awl with the tip missing and the articular surface preserved at the butt (XXIX layer (7)).

[1] Annable and Simpson, 1964, 253.

B4   A very fragile bone toggle 21 mm. long and 8 × 10 mm. in diameter which was broken in antiquity and found in two pieces. The longitudinal perforation is oval as is the single transverse perforation, the toggle being expanded slightly where the latter occurs in order to receive it. The
external surface of the toggle is decorated with six deeply incised grooves (XXX layer (6)). In
form the toggle is not unlike the six segmented bone beads which were possibly associated with the
primary cremation in the Warminster G10 bowl barrow[1] but in function it is more akin to the
bone toggle associated with part of a stone bracer which may have come from a disc barrow near
Bishops Cannings, Wilts.[2]

Also from layer (7) but not illustrated came the tip of a polished bone pin or awl (XXVIII), a
similar object being recorded from the junction of layers (6) and (7) (Cutting XXIX). A weathered
long bone fragment which was cut transversely was recorded from layer (6) (XXIX).

The Palisade Trench

A total of 664 fragments of animal bones was recorded from deposits in the palisade
trench, almost invariably from layer (3). The minimum numbers of animals represented
are pig (17), *bos* (8), sheep (3), *bos* (2), *bos* sp. (1), red deer (1), roe deer (1), fox (1) and birds
(song-thrush, missel-thrush and pintail).

B5   The only artifact recorded was a polished bone pin 7 cm. long with a simple head (Cutting XXV
layer (5), at a depth of 1.50 m.).

The Conquer Barrow

Eleven fragments of bone were recorded from all deposits in the Conquer Barrow ditch
and include remains of pig (2) and *bos* (1). No artifacts were recorded.

Iron Age

A total of 454 fragments of bone were recorded from all Iron Age and later deposits.
The minimum numbers of animals represented are *bos* (8), sheep (7), pig (5), horse (2),
red deer (2), goat (1), badger (1) and fox (1). No artifacts were recognized.

Woodhenge

Thirteen fragments of animal bone was recorded from the old land surface under the
bank, to which should be added 48 fragments from the primary silts of the ditch. The
minimum numbers of animals represented are pig (3), *bos* (2), sheep (1), and goat (1). The
earlier excavations produced remains of dog, deer, fox, cat and weasel in addition.

B6   A weathered bone artifact was recorded in the main body of the soil profile below the enclosure
bank in a context where it could have pre-dated the latter by an unknown margin. It is a weathered
long-bone 7.25 cm. long, which has been worked into a crude comb by means of a series of incisions at one terminal. It may be compared with examples in antler from mid-third millennium
bc contexts at Windmill Hill, Wilts.[3]

---

[1] Annable and Simpson, 1964, 279–84.   [3] Smith, 1965, fig. 53.
[2] Annable and Simpson, 1964, 447–8.

BRONZE
(fig. 81)

Site IV

BR1   A bronze brooch of 'Dolphin' type with ornamented bow, hinged pin and solid catch plate (Segment VII layer (2)).[1]

The Enclosure Ditch: West Entrance

BR2   A bronze axe 12.2 cm. long which was recorded from the ditch sediments near the west entrance. Dr. Britton has made it the subject of an intensive study which appears as Chapter X of this report.

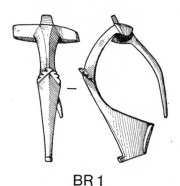

BR 1

FIG. 81.   Bronze brooch. (Scale 1/1)

SHALE
(fig. 82)

Site IV

Fragments of shale were recorded from Pit B in the enclosure ditch (Segment IV) in an Iron Age or Romano-British context.

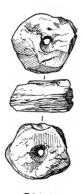

SH 1

FIG. 82.   Shale roundel. (Scale 1/1)

[1] Cf. Hawkes and Hull, 1947, pl. XCII.

The Enclosure Ditch: West Entrance
SH1   A roundel of shale 3 cm. in diameter with a central hour-glass perforation (Cutting II layer (2)).

BAKED CLAY
(fig. 83)

BA 1

FIG. 83.   Baked clay ball. (Scale $\frac{1}{2}$)

Site IV
Fragments of burnt clay, some bearing imprints of wattle, were recorded from the ditch (Segments IV layer (2), VI layer (3) and XI layer (2)). In addition, a piece of baked clay from Pit 186 is an angle fragment from an oven or possibly a loomweight. Its external surface is covered with impressions which were identified as grass by Dr. A. M. Evans of the Department of Applied Biology, University of Cambridge. Spikelets of *Bromus* spp. and probably *Avena* spp. were identified.

Palisade Trench
BA1   One half of a ball of baked clay 25 mm. in diameter (Cutting XXXVI layer (12)).

GLASS

Site IV
A small spherical bead of blue glass with a central perforation was found unstratified in the plough-soil.

THE COINS
by P. CURNOW

Site IV
VRBS ROMA, wolf and twins on reverse, $\overline{\text{PLG}}$ Lyons mint A.D. 330–5. LRBC I cf. 190 (unstratified above 187).

Enclosure Ditch: West Entrance
DN VALENS PF AVG, reverse SECVRITAS REIPVBLICAE Victory l, TCON Arles mint A.D. 367–78, LRBC II 528/32 (Cutting II layer (2)).

XII. THE ANGLO-SAXON BURIALS

by J. Schwieso

TWO graves were found during the excavation: Grave 1 lay near the western entrance of the main enclosure whilst Grave 185 was partially cut into the fill of the ditch of Site IV.

Description

Grave 1. A shallow, subrectangular pit, dug with near vertical sides, which measured 2.03 m. in length, 0.90 m. in breadth and was cut 0.10 m. into the chalk which was overlain by about 0.20 m. of plough-soil. The grave was aligned with the head end to the west–south-west and the foot end to the east–north-east. It contained the skeleton of an elderly man (*vide* Appendix I) extended on its back, face to the north, with the left arm lying on its side and the right arm slightly bent with the hand resting upon the right pelvis. Ploughing had removed most of the skull.

A small iron knife (fig. 84) lay between the pelvis halves, point to the east. Immediately east from it lay a corroded iron buckle (pl. XXXIV*a*).

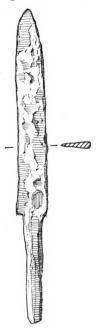

FIG. 84. Iron knife. (Scale ½)

Grave 185. A shallow pit measuring 1.70 m. in length, 0.50 m. in breadth and dug 0.20 m. into the chalk and into the upper fill of the ditch, here overlain by 0.22 m. of plough-soil. In it lay the skeleton of a woman, aged between 17 and 25, head to the west and feet to the east. The skeleton lay extended upon its back with the right arm bent at right angles across the body and the left arm bent sharply across the body so that the hand lay upon the right shoulder. Along the south edge of the grave, between the body and the wall, was a packing of large flints and one sarsen. On the north side lay two flints and two sarsens (pl. XXXIV*b*). There were no grave goods.

Finds from Grave 1
Knife Iron, length 16.6 cm., blade length 11.0 cm., blade width 1.6 cm., approximately parallel sided for most of its length with a slightly bevelled tang (fig. 84).
Buckle Iron, length 3.5 cm., width 1.0 cm., very poor condition with no sign of a belt chape.

Discussion

The material from Grave 1 shows that it is of Anglo-Saxon date and the proximity and general nature of Grave 185 suggests a similar date for it — a conclusion which will be seen to be supported by comparative evidence. Dorset lies on the western edge of the area in which pagan Saxon graves occur, and within the county two distinct cemetery groups exist; an eastern one extending from Cranbourne Chase into southern Somerset and Wiltshire and a much smaller south-western one along the chalk downs. There are four burial groups in the latter; secondary burials in a barrow at Hardown Hill, dated A.D. 450–550,[1] a flat cemetery of unaccompanied burials at Toller Fratrum which may be of Romano-British date,[2] the Mount Pleasant burials, which, it is suggested, are seventh century; and the Maiden Castle burials. These produced a scramasax and knife in a shallow grave which Evison[3] dates to the second half of the seventh century and a mutilated body of a man dated by radiocarbon to the seventh century.[4] The Mount Pleasant graves can be seen to resemble their neighbours at Maiden Castle in both style of burial and date.

Comparative Evidence

Although the Mount Pleasant burials have few local parallels, by the late pagan period Anglo-Saxon grave goods had become relatively standardized all over southern and eastern England so parallels may be sought in these areas.

The Graves. Many Anglo-Saxon burials are shallow, and carelessly laid in the grave whether their accompanying goods are rich or poor.[5] A lining of flints is occasionally found either forming a cist-like structure[6] or placed at the feet, thighs and head as if to support an overlying bier.[7] At Petersfinger,[8] grave 12 had a row of flints along one side, and a few on the other, very like Grave 185 at Mount Pleasant. This parallel makes the proposed Anglo-Saxon date for Grave 185 highly probable. At Winnall[9] many of the bodies lay in similar positions to those at Mount Pleasant and were aligned approximately east to west. This particular alignment does not necessarily imply that the graves are Christian, whereas the presence of grave goods in Grave 1 need not exclude its being Christian.[10]

[1] Evison, 1968, 230.
[2] Meaney, 1964, 82.
[3] Evison, 1968, 238.
[4] Brothwell, 1973, 240.
[5] Hawkes and Meaney, 1970, 29.

[6] Akerman, 1853, 265.
[7] Leeds and Riley, 1942, 65.
[8] Leeds and Shortt, 1953.
[9] Hawkes and Meaney, 1970, 29.
[10] Hawkes and Meaney, 1970, 52.

The Finds. Most late cemeteries contain numbers of sparsely furnished or unfurnished graves and where grave goods do occur they are commonly limited to a knife, belt buckle or other personal adornments. No exact parallels could be found for either knife or buckle but several similar examples are quoted below.

Knife. Not of Evison's characteristic late pagan type with groove along back or curved back. Parallels are Petersfinger, fig. 9, Nos. 115, 171 and 179 and Winnall, fig. 13–3.[1]

Buckle. Most buckles of this size are more oval at the ends and possess a belt chape. Perhaps such a chape had been present but had decayed. A similar chapeless buckle from Chamberlins Barn[2] was supposed to have lost its chape. Other similar examples are Petersfinger,[3] Burwell[4] and Uncleby.[5]

Summary

Two poorly furnished graves can be seen to belong to a sparse group of Anglo-Saxon burials spread over south-western Dorset. They can be dated to the seventh century and are thus of a similar date to their nearest members of the group, the graves from Maiden Castle. Whether they belong to settlers or odd raiding parties cannot be determined, though the woman's grave suggests that they are settlers. Evison[6] suggests that there is little evidence for permanent Saxon occupation in much of Dorset previous to the 650s which would suggest that these burials should be in the second half of the seventh century.

---

[1] Leeds and Shortt, 1953; Hawkes and Meaney, 1970.
[2] Hyslop, 1963, fig. 7.
[3] Leeds and Shortt, 1953, pl. VII, 180, LX, 116.
[4] Lethbridge, 1931, fig. 22, 12.
[5] Mortimer, 1905, pl. LXXXVII, fig. 668.
[6] Evison, 1968.

PART III. ENVIRONMENT AND CHRONOLOGY
XIII. RADIOCARBON DATES FOR MOUNT PLEASANT

by Richard Burleigh
Research Laboratory, The British Museum

INTRODUCTION

A SERIES of 19 radiocarbon dates has been obtained for the successive construction and occupation phases at Mount Pleasant. These radiocarbon determinations have provided dates for the pre-enclosure settlement (one date), phases of the timber structure (five dates), construction of the palisade trench (two dates) and phases of the enclosure ditch (nine dates, comprising six from the north entrance and three from the west entrance). Additionally, two other dates were obtained for samples from the Conquer Barrow ditch (BM-794) and the palisade trench (BM-795) but appear to relate to materials derived from occupations earlier than these structures.

Eleven of these dates, based on samples obtained during the excavations in 1970, have already been published (BM-644 to BM-646 and BM-662 to BM-669).[1] The remainder (BM-788 to BM-795) are additional dates based on samples from the 1971 excavations and have not been previously published. Thus the dates are presented together as a complete series for the first time in this report (Table XX). The exact provenance and associations of the samples which provided these dates and some of the implications of the dates, and their relationships to other relevant radiocarbon dates, are fully discussed elsewhere in the report. The 11 dates previously published have also been discussed in relation to dates for other Late Neolithic enclosures in southern England and their associated wares, at Durrington Walls, Marden and Woodhenge.[1] This section of the report is therefore concerned almost exclusively with the methods by which the dates were obtained, technical matters relating thereto and with the limitations of the dates and, in the interests of greater absolute accuracy, their possible equivalent ages in calendar years so far as this can be ascertained at present.

METHODS

Twelve of the dates were obtained from samples of wood charcoal (*Quercus robur* L, identified by G. C. Morgan, now at the University of Leicester); six were obtained from the antlers of red deer (*Cervus elaphus* L) and one from domestic animal bone (*Bos* sp., identified by R. Harcourt). Apart from strictly archaeological considerations, because of their well-established provenances these samples provided a further opportunity for the comparison of dates from bone and, in particular, antler with those obtained from charcoal as part of a continuing programme for assessing the reliability of antler and bone as dating materials.[2] Whole bone and antler are not usually reliable for radiocarbon dating because

---

[1] Burleigh *et al.*, 1972.

[2] Evans and Burleigh, 1969; Burleigh, 1971a, b; Burleigh *et al.*, 1972.

the carbonates which they contain tend to undergo exchange with bicarbonates in ground water, generally leading to dates which are too young. To overcome this the organic protein collagen, the other major component of both bone and antler, is freed of these carbonates (and, at the same time, inert phosphates) by prolonged elution with a dilute mineral acid. Where there has been a substantial risk of contamination over the period of burial by (generally younger) humic material, the separated collagen may also be treated with dilute alkali to remove these substances as well. Due to the highly calcareous soil conditions at Mount Pleasant secondary treatment with alkali was not found to be necessary. Similarly it was only necessary to treat the charcoal samples with dilute acid for removal of carbonates. Following this chemical pretreatment, itself followed by careful washing and drying of the cleaned samples, it is reasonably certain that all the materials dated were completely free of age contaminants. The internal agreement of the sequence of Mount Pleasant dates and that of the dates for the different kinds of sample materials, each of which has a different susceptibility to contamination, lends strong support to this assertion.

The pretreated sample materials were converted via a series of controlled steps of preparative chemistry to the organic liquid benzene and the C_{14} activity of each benzene sample was then measured by liquid scintillation counting. The radiocarbon dates obtained from these measurements are given in Table XX below. These various procedures, which have been described in more detail elsewhere,[1] are more or less standard among radiocarbon dating laboratories.

RESULTS

In Table XX the dates, which were calculated by computer from the C_{14} measurements, have been given on the basis of the conventional Libby half-life for C_{14} of 5570 ± 30 years as recommended by the journal *Radiocarbon* but using lower case notation[2] to indicate radiocarbon years; A.D. 1950 is the accepted standard year of reference for dates before present. The dates have been corrected for isotopic fractionation from mass spectrometer measurements of the abundance ratios of the stable carbon isotopes C_{13} and C_{12}. These measurements were all within the normal range expected and no large age corrections were needed. Some of the dates are derived from the weighted means of separate counting runs (of any one sample) which were individually in good agreement. The need or otherwise for repeat measurements depends on the size of the sample available for measurement and the limits that are acceptable for the associated error terms. The error terms, which are based on counting statistics alone, are equivalent to plus or minus one standard deviation.

As already indicated above, the dates generally form an internally consistent series irrespective of the different kinds of sample materials used for the determinations and are consistent also, with the exceptions already noted of BM-794 and BM-795, with the stratigraphic sequence of the features and structures to which they relate. Where two or more dates relate to the same feature, or to features which are stratigraphically close in time, the dates are indistinguishable statistically.

---

[1] Burleigh, 1972.   [2] *Antiquity* xlvi, 265.

TABLE XX

Mount Pleasant radiocarbon determinations

(Dates are in radiocarbon years based on the conventional 5570 year half-life for C14 and are grouped by provenance)

Provenance	Date	Lab. No.
Pre-enclosure settlement	**4072** ± **73** bp (*c.* **2122** bc)	BM–644
Enclosure ditch: west entrance		
Primary (II (8) DTS)	3734 ± 41 bp (*c.* 1784 bc)	BM–645
Primary (II (8) DTN)	3728 ± 59 bp (*c.* 1778 bc)	BM–646
Secondary (II DTPN (3))	**3410** ± **131** bp (*c.* **1460** bc)	BM–664
Enclosure ditch: north entrance		
XXIX/XXVIII (6)	**3506** ± **55** bp (*c.* **1556** bc)	BM–788
XXIX (7)	**3459** ± **53** bp (*c.* **1509** bc)	BM–789
XXVIII/XXIX (8)	**3619** ± **55** bp (*c.* **1669** bc)	BM–790
XXIX (10)	**3891** ± **66** bp (*c.* **1941** bc)	BM–791
XXVIII/XXIX (11)	**4058** ± **71** bp (*c.* **2108** bc)	BM–792
XXIX (12)	**4048** ± **54** bp (*c.* **2098** bc)	BM–793
Timber structure: Site (IV)		
Primary (Seg. VII (10))	**3911** ± **89** bp (*c.* **1961** bc)	BM–663
Primary (Seg. VII (10))	3941 ± 72 bp (*c.* 1991 bc)	BM–666
Primary (Seg. VII (10))	3988 ± 84 bp (*c.* 2038 bc)	BM–667
Secondary (Seg. X (5))	**3630** ± **60** bp (*c.* **1680** bc)	BM–668
Tertiary (Seg. VIII alpha (5))	**3274** ± **51** bp (*c.* **1324** bc)	BM–669
Palisade trench (construction)	3637 ± 63 bp (*c.* 1687 bc)	BM–662
	3645 ± **43** bp (*c.* **1695** bc)	BM–665
Palisade trench (Pit XVII)	3956 ± 45 bp (*c.* 2006 bc)	BM–794
Conquer Barrow ditch (XLVI)	4077 ± 52 bp (*c.* 2127 bc)	BM–795

The dates obtained from charcoal are printed in bold face figures. All the other dates were obtained from collagen separated from antler with the exception of BM–794 for which collagen separated from animal bone was used. Fuller details of the sample materials used for these measurements are given in the text above.

DISCUSSION

Natural C14 Variations and their Effect on Radiocarbon Dates

The occurrence in past millennia of natural C14 variations is now well attested[1] and it is generally recognized that, as a result, dates expressed in radiocarbon years are not always directly equivalent to the same period of time in calendar years. As is also well known great effort has been expended by certain radiocarbon dating laboratories (notably Arizona, La Jolla and Pennsylvania) in trying to establish a correlation between radiocarbon and calendar years by measuring the C14 content of a large number of sequential wood samples

[1] Olsson (ed.), 1970.

of known age established by ring counting, from certain long-lived tree species, particularly the bristlecone pine (*Pinus aristata*, Engelm).

In summary this work has shown that, going back in time from about the middle of the second millennium B.C., radiocarbon dates are increasingly too young in comparison with calendar ages up to a maximum of about 700 years or so around 5000 B.C. There is evidence also for another kind of variation, the occurrence of short-term fluctuations which have become respectably known as 'wiggles' or 'kinks' in the long-term trend. Generally speaking the long-term trend is not in dispute though there is some doubt as to whether the actual bristlecone curve can be extrapolated for use in more distant regions since, when this is done, there appears to be some tendency for over-correction of dates. At present it is not clear whether this arises from errors in the curve or is the result of small but real differences between geographic regions. There is less agreement about the exact timing and amplitude of the shorter-term 'wiggles', although beyond reasonable doubt some of these have indeed occurred. Their main interest from the dating point of view is that they may render insensitive some sections of the so-called calibration curve although it is not yet completely clear how serious this effect is in practice.

It is not appropriate here to discuss the possible causes of the variations in detail but they probably result mainly from changes in the production rate of $C14$ in the earth's atmosphere due to gradual changes in the intensity of the cosmic radiation, by the indirect action of which $C14$ is formed. These in turn may have been brought about by systematic geomagnetic changes and changes in solar activity, and climatic change may also have played a part by modifying the behaviour of parts of the $C14$ exchange reservoir (amount of water in the oceans, size of the biomass, etc.). Exactly how much each of these possible mechanisms and others at present unknown may have contributed to the observed total effect or what the interactions of the proposed mechanisms may have been is not known with any certainty.

Eventually a series of radiocarbon measurements similar to those for the bristlecone wood should be available for European material. There is probably no other material of longevity comparable with the bristlecones but abundant individual trees, principally oaks, preserved in Irish peat bogs and some other deposits elsewhere in western Europe are known from radiocarbon check measurements to span collectively a similar period of time. When the dendrochronology of this material has been thoroughly worked out it should afford an opportunity for critical comparisons with the bristlecone data in particular to test the idea of the over-all applicability of the generalized bristlecone curve.

Meanwhile conversions of radiocarbon dates into dates in calendar years, while possessing greater absolute accuracy than the 'raw' dates must nevertheless be considered as tentative and approximate. For most purposes it will usually be better to compare dates with one another in terms of radiocarbon years before present (bp) and this will remain so until there is final agreement among radiocarbon dating laboratories on a more exact empirical relationship between radiocarbon and calendar years.

Conversion of Radiocarbon Dates into Dates in Calendar Years

A considerable number of calibration curves (or tables) have already been published, mostly differing in detail. Some of these curves have a pronounced 'wiggle' structure while others are much smoother (and in some cases may be over-smoothed). The recently published

7*

MASCA calibration tables[1] bring together all the results of measurements made over a period of some 15 years by the three laboratories mainly concerned (up to 1973). It is from these tables that the 'corrected' dates given in Table XXI and used elsewhere in this report have been taken.

It will immediately be seen from Table XXI that some of the Mount Pleasant dates fall into those regions of the calibration curve apparently corresponding to a more or less extended period of time in calendar years and not to a single date (not considering here the standard deviations of the radiocarbon dates). Eleven of the 19 dates fall into this category and in about half these cases the uncertainty of the calibrated date is somewhat more than 100 years (in addition to the associated error of the corresponding uncalibrated dates).

Due to random errors the scatter of the data from which the MASCA tables were calculated may partly conceal the form of the age corrected curve of C14 variation with time. Only a very much greater number of calibration measurements than are at present available, and, as discussed above, measurements also of material from other regions, can resolve this point. Thus while in general it can be said that the use of calibrated radiocarbon dates undoubtedly produces more accurate chronological relationships, these are still, for the time being, approximations.

TABLE XXI

Calibration of Mount Pleasant radiocarbon dates in calender years

The method by which these calibrated dates have been derived is described in the text above. As explained more fully there the calibration data used for conversion of radiocarbon dates into dates in calendar years are still subject to various uncertainties. The calendar dates given in the table should therefore be considered as no more than approximate. The dates are listed in laboratory number order and, following archaeological convention, the uncalibrated dates are given in years bc (i.e. in years bp minus 1950) although strictly speaking uncalibrated dates should only be expressed in radiocarbon years before present (bp).

Lab. No.	Radiocarbon date	Calendar date or date range
BM–644	2122 ± 73 bc	2690–2800 (± 85) B.C.
BM–645	1784 ± 41 bc	2180 ± 52 B.C.
BM–646	1778 ± 59 bc	2170 ± 71 B.C.
BM–662	1687 ± 63 bc	2120–2140 (± 75) B.C.
BM–663	1961 ± 89 bc	2490–2540 (± 102) B.C.
BM–664	1460 ± 131 bc	1770–1870 (± 145) B.C.
BM–665	1695 ± 43 bc	2120–2140 (± 54) B.C.
BM–666	1991 ± 72 bc	2560 ± 84 B.C.
BM–667	2038 ± 84 bc	2600 ± 97 B.C.
BM–668	1680 ± 60 bc	2110–2130 (± 72) B.C.
BM–669	1324 ± 51 bc	1640 ± 63 B.C.
BM–788	1556 ± 55 bc	2020–2040 (± 67) B.C.
BM–789	1509 ± 53 bc	1920–1950 (± 65) B.C.
BM–790	1669 ± 55 bc	2110 ± 67 B.C.
BM–791	1941 ± 66 bc	2480 ± 78 B.C.
BM–792	2108 ± 71 bc	2690–2800 (± 83) B.C.
BM–793	2098 ± 54 bc	2650–2780 (± 66) B.C.
BM–794	2006 ± 45 bc	2560 ± 56 B.C.
BM–795	2127 ± 52 bc	2700–2820 (± 64) B.C.

[1] Ralph, Michael and Han, 1973.

ACKNOWLEDGEMENTS

The work of chemically pretreating the raw sample materials, synthesis from these of pure samples for radiocarbon measurement and measurement of the prepared samples by liquid scintillation counting was painstakingly carried out by Mr. N. D. Meeks and Mrs. M. A. Seeley at the British Museum Research Laboratory. Thanks are also due to Dr. G. J. Wainwright for his patient and helpful advice throughout the course of the programme for dating samples from henge monuments and related sites and for the excellent quality of the critical sample materials he has supplied and the exemplary manner in which these have always been documented.

NOTE ADDED IN PROOF

This report on the radiocarbon dates obtained for Mount Pleasant was written in July 1974. Since then these dates have also been reported in *Radiocarbon*[1] and, among other advances, another calibration curve for radiocarbon dates has been published. This is based on a new analysis by R. M. Clark of all the available bristlecone pine measurements.[2] When re-calibrated from Clark's data the Mount Pleasant dates are still in reasonable agreement with those obtained by the use of the MASCA curve as listed in Table XXI of this report, the substance and conclusions of which therefore remain essentially unaltered.

[1] Burleigh, R., Hewson, A. and Meeks, N., 1977. 'British Museum natural radiocarbon measurements VIII'. *Radiocarbon* **18**, 16–42.

[2] Clark, R. M., 1975. 'A calibration curve for radiocarbon dates'. *Antiquity* xlix, 251–66.

XIV. MOUNT PLEASANT AND WOODHENGE: THE LAND MOLLUSCA

by J. G. Evans and Hilary Jones

SINCE 1966 excavations have taken place on a number of Neolithic 'henges' in southern England. These have provided an unrivalled opportunity for reconsidering not only the archaeological significance of these monuments but their environmental context as well. The sites are Durrington Walls,[1] Marden,[2] Mount Pleasant and Woodhenge (this publication), Avebury (the late Mrs. F. de M. Vatcher, unpublished) and the Devil's Quoits, Stanton Harcourt (Mrs. M. Grey, unpublished). The palaeo-environment of Durrington Walls, Marden and Avebury[3] has already been described in full, and it is the object of this report to deal with Mount Pleasant and Woodhenge. The material from the Devil's Quoits has not yet been analysed and the site will be referred to, therefore, only incidentally.

The main sequence at Mount Pleasant and Woodhenge covers the late Neolithic and Bronze Age periods, and since much of our work has previously been confined to the earlier Neolithic, the opportunity of studying these deposits was welcomed. The existence in the fill of the main enclosure ditch at Mount Pleasant of a thick layer of wind-blown material has led us to discuss the question of the climate of southern England during the Bronze Age. The main technique used was molluscan analysis. Radiocarbon dates have provided a full time scale, and the abundant pottery recovered has enabled the successive horizons to be fitted into the archaeological record.

It is fitting at this point to acknowledge with gratitude the debt which we owe to Dr. G. J. Wainwright who has enabled us to make these environmental studies. His hospitality on site, his willingness to explain the archaeological context of the various horizons, and his silent endurance of the devastation we have wreaked on his beautiful sections can go unrecorded no longer.

METHODS

The molluscan analyses were done using the method described by Evans.[4]

The results have been presented as tables (Tables XXII–XXV) and in histogram form (figs. 85–9). Two methods of graphical presentation have been used. In figs. 85, 86, 88–9 the results are in terms of relative abundance, each species being plotted as a percentage of the total fauna (excluding *Cecilioides acicula*). Fig. 87 is an additional plot of the sequence from the Mount Pleasant main enclosure ditch shown in fig. 86 but in terms of absolute abundance.

Relative histograms are the more usual form of presentation since they bring out clearly the predominant elements in an assemblage and facilitate comparison from one layer to the next (cf. the Limacidae in fig. 86 with fig. 87, 0–15 cm.). They negate changes in the abund-

[1] Wainwright and Longworth, 1971.
[2] Wainwright *et al.*, 1971.
[3] Evans, 1972.
[4] Evans, 1972.

ance of the fauna as a whole, some of which may be due to environmental factors (e.g. the massive increase at 162.5 cm. in fig. 87), others to the dilutory effect of stones in the sediment (e.g. at 125 cm., Trench I, in fig. 86). Absolute histograms, on the other hand, bring out salient features in the general suitability of the environment for molluscan life, whatever the immediate nature of the habitat. This is quite clearly shown in fig. 87 where the effects of clearance (at 200 cm.), although drastically altering the composition of the fauna in terms of species, do not adversely affect the total abundance of mollusca. However, peaks of general abundance are not necessarily to be equated with buried soil surfaces or standstill phases.

In constructing fig. 87 the effects of dilution by stones have, in fact, been allowed for and removed. This has been done by calculating the number of shells per 1.0 kg. of sediment less the weight of all stones in each sample (mainly quartz and chalk) greater than 0.5 mm. The following formula was used:

$$\frac{A}{B-C} \times B = x$$

where A = number of shells counted
       B = air-dry weight of sediment (generally 1.0 kg.)
       C = weight of stones greater than 0.5 mm.
       x = number of shells plotted.

The weights of stones in two size grades (0.5–2.00 mm. and greater than 2.00 mm.) have been plotted alongside the sediment columns in figs. 86, 88 and 89 in order to bring out certain stratigraphical changes more clearly.

The mollusca have been grouped into three broad ecological categories — woodland, intermediate and grassland. These terms are generalized and do not necessarily imply woodland or grassland as such, or habitats intermediate between these two. *Pomatias elegans* has been kept separate as being a species requiring broken ground, but at the same time a certain degree of moisture and/or shade. It is a particularly good indicator of the onset of clearance (figs. 85, 86, 88 and 89).

The interpretation of the histograms in terms of past environments is complicated by our lack of knowledge about a number of factors. In the first place, quantitative data on modern molluscan faunas, particularly those from unshaded habitats, is almost entirely absent.[1] Furthermore, certain species are almost certainly favoured by different environmental factors under different general environments. This applies, for example, to the two species of *Cepaea*. On the lower slopes of the Chilterns near Rickmansworth *C. hortensis* is widespread while *C. nemoralis* is largely restricted to woods; higher up on the Chiltern plateau *C. nemoralis* is common in open habitats.[2]

A second and probably related factor is the interaction of molluscan species with each other in the habitat. We do not know whether mollusca occupy a habitat in the same way that plants do, each species competing with another for components such as food and shelter, or whether they are independent of each other. This has an important bearing on the inter-

[1] But see Chappell *et al.*, 1971.   [2] Cameron, 1969, 107.

pretation of the histograms of relative abundance. For example, in fig. 86 there is a marked peak of *Helicella itala* between 87.5 and 95 cm. (Trench II), but in fig. 87, the absolute diagram, this is barely registered. Are we to consider the peak in the relative diagram, which is controlled by a decline in other species and the maintenance of a constant abundance of *H. itala*, to be an indication of a habitat change in favour of *H. itala*, or are we to ignore it and accept the absolute diagram as reflecting a constant state in the factors affecting this species?

Thirdly, changes of abundance may not be related to immediate changes in habitat factors such as shade, disturbance or relative humidity. They may reflect cyclical variations in abundance which all species undergo, and which are linked to a complex of factors, such as weather, disease and predators (see discussion of this problem in snails and slugs in Evans, 1972, 122). For example, *Pupilla muscorum* in fig. 86 shows a general increase at 200 cm. in response to woodland clearance, and a gradual decline subsequently from 155 to 0 cm. Superimposed on this pattern is a series of minor fluctuations which may have no immediate origin in terms of land use or vegetation.

A fourth complication is of a technical nature and concerns the question of identification. This applies particularly to the Limacidae which constitute a conspicuous element in the fauna at Mount Pleasant. The Limacidae are a group of slugs represented subfossil only by their internal shell. These are not specifically identifiable, and since the various species in the group occupy widely differing habitats the curve in fig. 86 may be made up of more than one species. Indeed this is likely, and we can suggest that the shells in the lower levels of the ditch (185–237.5 cm.) belong to one of the woodland species such as *Limax maximus*, while those in the upper levels of the plough-wash (0–65 cm.) probably belong to *Agriolimax reticulatus*, the grey field slug.

WOODHENGE

The background to the 1970 Woodhenge excavation has been described in a previous chapter. Both the buried soil beneath the bank, and the ditch deposits were sampled for molluscan analysis.

The Buried Soil beneath the Bank

The buried soil beneath the bank showed the following stratigraphy (fig. 41):

Depth below buried
soil surface (cm.)

0–3	Old turf-line. Dark brown chalky loam devoid of stones; formed by earthworm sorting.[1]
3–5	Line of flints; the product of earthworm sorting.
5–15	Main body of soil. Dark brown chalky loam with numerous angular chalk fragments. In deeper parts becoming pale grey and less stony.
15–20 (max.)	Subsoil hollows. Irregular hollows containing pale brown chalky loam with many chalk lumps and a few flints; zones of dark, less stony earth in places. These are probably the casts of ancient tree roots.[2] Much charcoal.

[1] Atkinson, 1957.   [2] Evans, 1972, 219.

Depth below buried
soil surface (cm.)

15/50+   Subsoil. Horizontally alternating coarse chalky rubble and patches of finer, buff-
                    coloured material. The latter is probably of periglacial (aeolian) origin.[1]

This profile is similar to that recorded beneath the bank of Durrington Walls[2] and the
land snail sequence indicates a similar sequence of environmental events prior to the construction of the earthwork.

Five soil samples were taken as follows (fig. 85(b)):

Depth below buried soil surface (cm.)	Horizon	Weight (less stones greater than 1.0 cm.) (kg.)
0–3	Turf-line	2.8
3–5	Flint-line	1.5
5–15	Main body of soil	3.0
15–35	Subsoil hollow	5.0
35+	Subsoil	3.0

The results have been presented in tabular form (Table XXII) and as a histogram of
relative abundance (fig. 85(b)). The following environmental sequence is indicated.

The subsoil yielded no mollusca, but it is probable that, at the time the buff-coloured
material was being deposited, a tundra environment obtained.[3] At Durrington Walls
nearby, material of this kind beneath the buried post-glacial soil yielded a fauna of late-
glacial type.

The fauna from the subsoil hollow is a woodland one, grassland species (excluding *Vallonia
costata* which is not confined to open ground) amounting to only 4%. This fauna, taken
together with the subsoil hollows which are probably the casts of ancient tree roots, is clear
evidence for the former presence of woodland on the site. A Mesolithic flint and abundant
charcoal in the subsoil hollow suggest the activities of hunter–gatherer communities.[4]

There then followed a forest clearance phase (3–15 cm.) indicated particularly by a sharp
rise in the abundance of *Pomatias elegans*. This was recognized too at Durrington Walls. The
date of the phase is uncertain, but at Durrington it was tentatively ascribed to the middle of
the third millennium (*c.* 2600–2400 bc) and considered to be entirely of anthropogenic
origin.

Finally there was a period of dry grassland (0–3 cm.) when the environment was free of
woody vegetation, and probably maintained as such by sheep grazing. The duration of this
period cannot be ascertained, but its inception was prior to 1800 bc when the henge was
constructed. The molluscan fauna of this final grassland phase is characterized by the two
species of *Vallonia*, *V. costata* and *V. excentrica*, in roughly equal abundance, with *Helicella
itala* and *Pupilla* as the other major elements. The rare xerophile, *Truncatellina*, also occurs.
This is a species which has been recorded from several Neolithic and Bronze Age sites in the
Stonehenge area[5] but which is today extinct in Wiltshire.

[1] Evans, 1968.
[2] Wainwright and Longworth, 1971.
[3] Evans, 1968.

[4] Smith, 1970.
[5] Evans, 1972, 140.

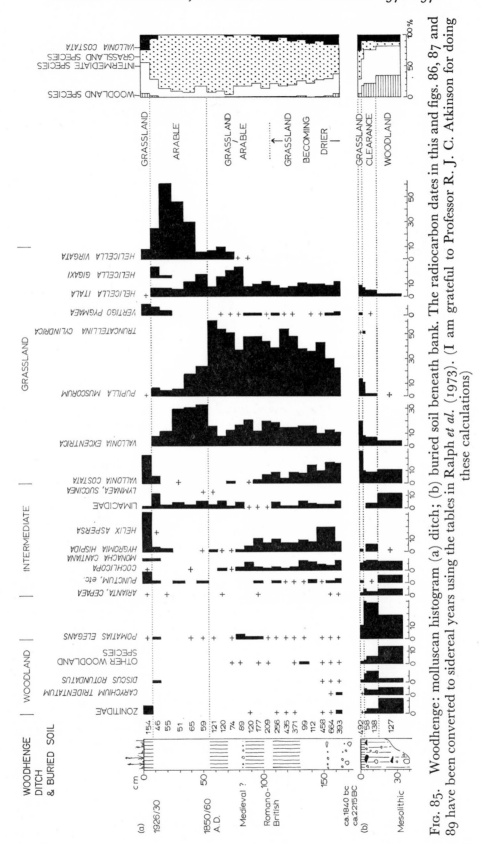

FIG. 85. Woodhenge: molluscan histogram (a) ditch; (b) buried soil beneath bank. The radiocarbon dates in this and figs. 86, 87 and 89 have been converted to sidereal years using the tables in Ralph *et al.* (1973). (I am grateful to Professor R. J. C. Atkinson for doing these calculations)

The Ditch Deposits

A series of samples (each weighing 0.5 kg., air-dry) was cut from the south section (fig. 43) and analysed for land molluscs. The stratigraphy of the deposits at the point sampled was as follows (fig. 85(a)):

Depth below surface (cm.)		
0–8		Modern turf. Dark brown/black stone-free loam under a vegetation cover of grass; not grazed, but maintained by the Department of the Environment with occasional mowing. Layer 1.
8–55		Plough-wash. Pale brown chalky loam with numerous chalk pellets, particularly on the bank side; becoming darker at the base. Layer 2.
55–70		Turf-line. Dark brown stone-free loam. Layer 3.
70–85		Chalky loam with numerous small chalk pellets. Layer 4.
	70–77.5	Pea-grit zone. Material brought down by earthworms' activity to line their hibernation chambers.[1]
	77.5–85	(?) Plough-wash. No pea-grit.
85–100		Turf-line. Dark brown stone-free loam. Layer 5A.
100–107		Plough-wash. Chalky loam with numerous small chalk pellets; weakly humified. Layer 5B.
107.5–130		Turf-line. Dark brown stone-free loam. Layer 5C.
130–165		Secondary fill. Layer 6.
	130–152.5	Flinty and loose chalky loam, with a line of stones at the base. Layer 6A.
	152.5–165	Compact fine grey chalky loam, more or less stone free. Layer 6B.
165–210		Primary fill. Coarse angular chalk rubble with intermixed turfs and humic material derived from the old ground surface. Fine in the upper levels (layer (7)), becoming coarser with depth (layer (8)).

The results of snail analysis (Table XXII) have been presented in terms of relative abundance (fig. 85(a)). The faunal and stratigraphical evidence suggests the following sequence of environmental changes.

After the ditch had been dug it was left to silt up by natural means. As Mrs. Cunnington pointed out,[2] the presence of a substantial berm between the ditch and bank resulted in the coarse silting (layers (7) and (8)) being derived almost entirely from the ditch sides, and evidence from the experimental earthwork on Overton Down[3] suggests that a period of not more than ten years was involved in the accumulation of this material.

The secondary fill (layer (6)) is much finer and probably accumulated under gentler conditions of rainwashing than did the primary fill, and over a longer period of time. The overlying soil horizon (layer (5C)) merges insensibly into the secondary fill and represents the final stages of the natural infilling when processes of physical weathering (frost action and rainwashing) had given way entirely to processes of chemical weathering (dissolution of calcium carbonate and the release of iron from acid insoluble residues) — in fact soil formation.

[1] Atkinson, 1957.
[2] Cunnington, 1929.

[3] Jewell and Dimbleby, 1966.

The molluscan fauna reflects open conditions throughout the phase of secondary infilling and soil formation. There is a slightly higher percentage of woodland species in the lowest sample, and an increase in grassland species from the base of the lowest turf-line up to its surface (107.5 cm.), but there is no question of scrub or even tall dank grass ever having grown in the ditch bottom. This is in marked contrast to the situation at Mount Pleasant (fig. 89), and suggests that the environment was being kept open, from the time the henge was constructed, by some artificial means — possibly by the grazing of stock. It is arguable of course that clearance in the area was so extensive that refuges for shade-loving species of snail had been destroyed and that, although scrub may have regenerated into the ditch, no snails were present in the vicinity to colonize the habitat. However, this is not the case, for almost all the woodland species present in the buried soil prior to the construction of the henge occur in the lowest level of the secondary fill, and their condition of preservation — particularly that of the fragile Zonitidae and *Carychium* — is such as to indicate that they are not derived from earlier deposits. In other words, the species were present in the area, but through environmental factors intrinsic to the site (and not necessarily its surroundings) were unable to attain their optimum abundance.

Certain differences between the fauna in the lowest ditch turf-line (107.5–130 cm.) and that in the turf-line beneath the bank must be commented on. Both faunas clearly reflect dry grassland, probably kept as such by grazing stock. The main differences are the absence of *Pomatias elegans*, the paucity of *Vallonia costata* and the high abundance of *Pupilla* in the ditch, and it is not immediately obvious to what these differences are due. Similar trends, particularly the rise of *Pupilla* and the decline of *Vallonia costata*, have been recorded from other sites, e.g. South Street in north Wiltshire,[1] Wayland's Smithy in Berkshire (M. P. Kerney, personal communication) and Mount Pleasant (p. 198), and I have suggested[2] that climatic dryness during the Bronze Age may have been responsible for these changes. But this is an explanation which is not at all satisfactory, and until we have the relevant modern ecological data the problem must remain unsolved.

The age of the fauna at the top of the lowest turf-line (107.5–130 cm.) is probably Romano-British for Mrs. Cunnington recorded pottery of this date from this level.

Subsequent infilling is of man-made origin and, as discussed by Mrs. Cunnington, was probably brought about by cultivation of the land around, and subsequently over, the site. There were three such episodes of cultivation (100–107.5, 70–85 and 7.5–55 cm.), and after each a turf-line formed. During this sequence the fauna was basically similar to that below, but becoming increasingly impoverished; by 45 cm. *Pupilla* at 61% has assumed almost total dominance, with *Vallonia excentrica*, *Helicella*, the Limacidae and *Hygromia hispida* as the only major elements, suggesting an environment which had become very dry, and possibly impoverished of organic matter.

The introduction of *Helicella virgata* at about 80 cm., and later of *Helicella gigaxi*, was probably brought about by man for these species are unknown in Britain prior to medieval times.

The final phase of cultivation on the site, represented by the plough-wash deposit between 7.5 and 55 cm., is dated historically from its inception in the middle of the nineteenth century (1850/1860) to 1926 when the Cunningtons' excavation took place. The most

[1] Evans, 1972, 330.   [2] Evans, 1972, 149.

notable faunal changes during this time are the increase of *Helicella virgata* (foreshadowed in an earlier cultivation horizon (70–80 cm.) by a rise of *Helicella itala*) and the decline, and ultimately the virtual extinction of *Pupilla*. These changes probably reflect an increase in the intensity and duration of cultivation by comparison with that of earlier times.

From 1930 onwards the site has been under grass and maintained by the Department of the Environment. The faunal changes, probably in response to this management change, are marked. *Pupilla* and *Vallonia excentrica* have become virtually extinct, and the species of *Helicella* reduced to less than 10%. *Vallonia costata* makes a dramatic comeback attaining an abundance equal to that of pre-henge times, and *Vertigo pygmaea* becomes prominent for the first time. Other changes — the rise of the Zonitidae and the *Punctum pygmaeum* group — suggest an increase in the moisture-retaining capacity of the soil and the relative humidity of the environment, and a decrease in the amount of mechanical disturbance received.

MOUNT PLEASANT

Four positions were sampled for land molluscan analysis: the buried soil beneath the main enclosure bank; the main enclosure ditch (south-west entrance terminal); the buried soil in the main enclosure ditch (north entrance terminal); the ring ditch.

The Buried Soil beneath the Enclosure Bank

The buried soil beneath the enclosure bank was revealed in trench XXXII. It consisted of a surface turf-line of dark brown humic loam varying from 2 to 5 cm. in thickness, underlain by 10–15 cm. of humic stony material, paler in colour (fig. 86). The turf-line, as at Woodhenge, was probably formed by earthworm sorting. The immediate subsoil consisted of fine buff-coloured material in pockets and channels, in a matrix of coarser chalky debris. This extended to at least 60 cm. below the base of the buried soil. Identical deposits occur in many places on the chalk[1] and are considered to be of periglacial origin.

Three samples from the buried soil were analysed for mollusca as follows (fig. 86, Table XXIII):

Depth below surface of buried soil (cm.)	Air-dry weight (kg.)
0–2.5	1.0
2.5–5.0	1.0
5.0–15.0	2.0

The assemblages are dominated by grassland and intermediate species, with other woodland species (mainly *Clausilia bidentata*) as an important component. The low absolute numbers and the fact that the assemblage is almost certainly in part residual (due to the differential preservation of certain species) make interpretation difficult. Thus virtually all the examples of *Clausilia bidentata*, *Pomatias elegans* and *Cepaea* are worn apical fragments, not fresh specimens; apices of these species are resistant to destruction and they are probably the remnants of a fauna whose other elements have been destroyed. The grassland species, on the other hand, are in better condition, complete adult specimens being frequent, and there

[1] Evans, 1968.

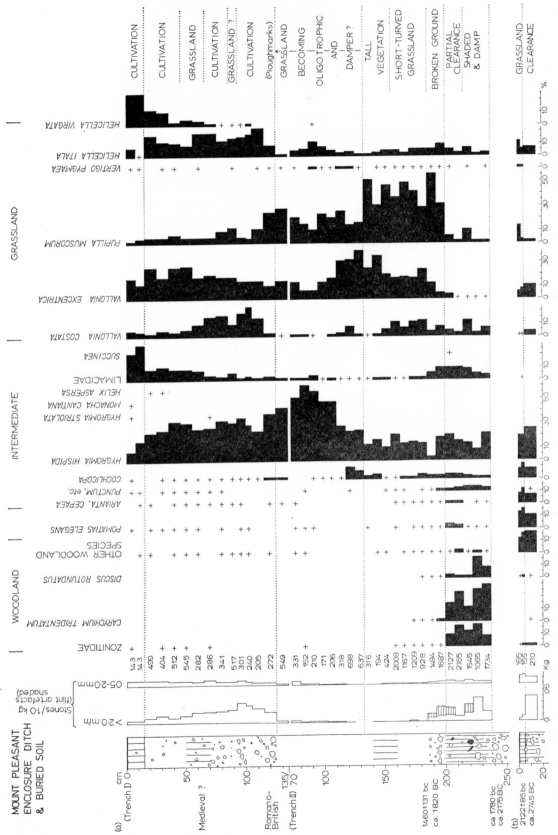

Fig. 86. Mount Pleasant: molluscan histogram through (a) enclosure ditch deposits; (b) buried soil beneath enclosure bank

seems little doubt that the fauna at the time of burial reflects an environment of dry grass-land. Charcoal from within the buried soil associated with Neolithic sherds of plain bowls yielded a C14 determination of *c.* 2100 bc (*c.* 2690–2800 B.C.).

The Main Enclosure Ditch

There were three main deposits in the fill of the enclosure ditch: a plough-wash at the top of the section (layer (2)), a wind-blown sediment in the middle (layer (3)), and a buried soil at the base (layers (4) and (5)). The underlying coarse chalk rubble (layers (6) and (8)) was not sampled, for such material is generally devoid of shells.

In order to obtain as long a sequence as possible, the deposits were sampled in two lots. The greatest thickness of plough-wash occurred in the south-east section (Section A) of Trench I, and the samples were accordingly taken from this section. Trench I had not, however, been taken down below the surface of the wind-blown deposit, and it was there-fore necessary to sample the lower deposits in the adjacent trench II (Section B). In the following account, figures for depth measurements which fall in the overlap zone (70–135 cm.) are suffixed by the trench number where the situation is not otherwise clear.

The detailed stratigraphy of the deposits sampled is as follows (fig. 86):

Depth below
surface (cm.)
Trench I

0–15		Modern plough-soil. Pale grey loam with a few chalk pellets.
15–125		Plough-wash. Pale-brown chalky loam with numerous chalk lump (layer (2)). Becoming more stony with depth. A number of finer divisions were recognized:
	50–70	Slightly darker horizon, probably a soil formed during a standstill phase in the accumulation.
	85–92.5	Zone of finer material; coarse chalk lumps sparse.
	92.5–100	Zone of coarser material; chalk lumps numerous.
		At the base of the plough-wash there were lines of chalk pellets passing obliquely up into the deposit (fig. 86). These are thought to be plough-marks in cross section. Coincident with this level, and running down into it from the weathering ramps of the ditch was a series of criss-cross plough-marks. Sherds of Romano-British pottery were recorded from the base of the plough-wash and it is to this period that the plough-marks and the inception of plough-wash formation probably belong.
125+		Wind-laid material (layer (3)).

Trench II

0–70		Modern plough-soil and plough-wash (layers (1) and (2)).
70–185		Wind-laid deposit. Pale brown, very compact stone-free loam (layer (3)). Wormholes penetrate to 102.5 cm.
	140–160	Darker horizon; probably a soil formed during a standstill phase in the accumulation.
185–200		Pale brown loam with abundant coarse chalk rubble. Band of coarse scree at *c.* 195 cm. (base of layer (3)). Radiocarbon assay of charcoal from this horizon gave a date of 1460 ± 131 bc (*c.* 1770–1870 B.C.) (BM-664).

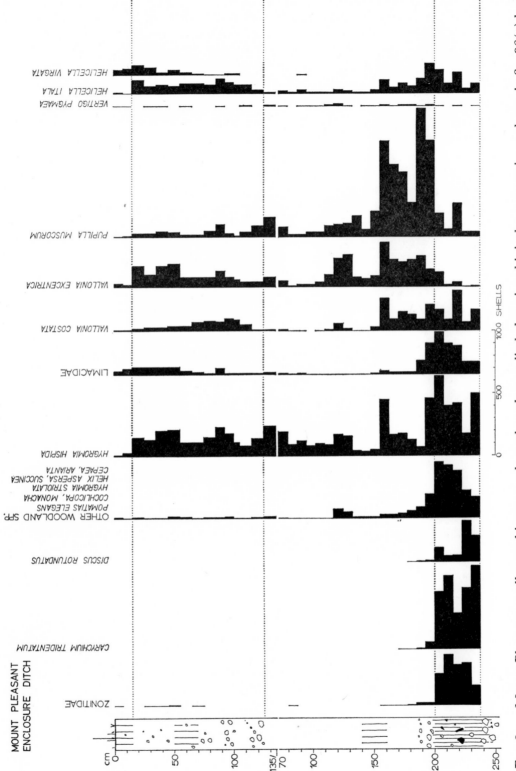

FIG. 87.   Mount Pleasant: molluscan histogram through enclosure ditch deposits; this is the same series as shown in fig. 86(a) but constructed on an absolute basis

Depth below
surface (cm.)

200–245   Buried soil. Dark brown chalky loam with a well-developed crumb structure;
                 occasional bands of coarse chalk rubble (layers (4) and (5)).

245+   Primary fill. Coarse angular chalk rubble (layers (6) and (8)). Antler picks from
                 the base of the ditch gave C14 determinations of *c.* 1780 bc (*c.* 2175 B.C.)
                 (BM-645–6).

Thirty-seven soil samples were cut from these two sections as indicated in Table XXIII and
fig. 86. Each weighed 1.0 kg. (air-dry). They were analysed for land mollusca and the results
were plotted in terms of relative (fig. 86) and absolute (fig. 87) abundance. A total of 25,325
shells was extracted.

The fauna from the buried soil horizon (200–237.5 cm.) indicates a shaded environment
with a high relative humidity. The Zonitidae (*Oxychilus, Retinella* and *Vitrea*) and *Carychium*
are groups which are fastidious in their requirements for undisturbed conditions. It is,
however, difficult to be certain as to the exact structure of the vegetation. Tall grasses and
the absence of grazing animals create conditions almost equal in their suitability for woodland species to those engendered by deep leaf litter under a tree cover. But the high abundance of shells and the well-developed crumb structure of the soil argue for a considerable
length of time for this period, during which woody species might be expected to become
established in the absence of grazing stock. Radiocarbon dates indicate a period of between
300 and 400 years.

It is not possible to ascertain the extent of this environment over the site as a whole.
However, the wide and shallow profile of the ditch would probably not have made for the
extreme micro-climatic conditions of moisture and shelter which obtain in a relatively
deeper and more constricted situation, and it is thus possible that this environment prevailed over the entire site. At the corresponding levels in the north entrance (trenches
XXVII–XXX) and in the lower buried soil of the small ring ditch (fig. 89, 65–135 cm.)
similar conditions obtained. There was quite clearly, therefore, a period in the later centuries
of the third and earlier centuries of the second millennia B.C. when the site was subjected
to neither agriculture nor grazing stock.

The presence of a significant proportion of grassland species in this horizon, particularly
Pupilla and *Helicella*, suggests a certain amount of intermittent disturbance, and this is
confirmed by the bands of chalk rubble which occur throughout the soil.

In the surface two samples (200–215 cm.) the over-all increase in grassland species and the
decrease in woodland species indicates a more general opening up of the environment, and
this is strongly supported by the rise in abundance of the clearance indicator, *Pomatias elegans*.
Many of the examples of this species were adult and well preserved with the operculum (a
detachable shelly valve which closes the aperture) in place. Clearly these shells were unmoved
from their position of death, unlike those from the buried soil beneath the enclosure bank.
This episode may be related to the Bronze Age (Beaker/Collared Vessels) occupation recorded
from an equivalent stratigraphical position in the sediments of the north entrance ditch
terminals where it is dated by C14 to *c.* 1920–2110 B.C. (BM-789 and 790).

The major clearance episode, however, was sudden and total. It took place at 200 cm.
and involved the deposition of a rush of chalk scree into the ditch, which resulted in the

burial of the soil. The date of this episode is 1460 $\pm$ 131 bc (c. 1770–1870 B.C.) (BM-664) as indicated by C14 assay of charcoal from the base of layer (3).

The faunal changes at 200 cm. were dramatic, there being a virtually total eclipse of all woodland species. The open-country fauna which succeeds is dominated by *Pupilla*, a species which generally favours extremely dry habitats and a broken ground surface. This change is not due to ploughing across the ditch; the surface profile at this level is too steep and the scree bands too discrete. Ploughing would have caused some admixture of the underlying soil, and neither the fauna nor the stratigraphy indicated that this has taken place. In fact we cannot be certain of the cause of the chalk scree horizon other than saying that it is probably of anthropogenic origin and associated with the subsequent phase of open country. It is possibly due to ploughing along the edge of the ditch, or an attempt at partial levelling of the bank.

But it is the origin of the subsequent layer, the wind-laid deposit, which is the most contentious. We have not carried out a mechanical analysis of this material but its silty texture (as determined by hand tests in the field) and the virtual absence of particles greater than 0.5 mm. (fig. 86) argue for an aeolian origin. Hillwashes, even if laid down under very gentle conditions, invariably contain a sizeable coarse grit component.

The fauna is an open-country one, and the sequence falls into three phases corresponding to the three stratigraphical divisions of lower wind-laid material (160–185 cm.), soil horizon (140–160 cm.) and upper wind-laid material (125 (trench I)–140 cm.).

The first phase is characterized by a high absolute abundance of snails. *Pupilla* predominates and *Hygromia*, *Vallonia* and *Helicella* are all common. A dry environment of short grasses is indicated and the large snail populations are probably a reflection of a high lime content, brought about by the continuous deposition of wind-borne dust.

In the second phase, the buried soil, there is a drop in abundance, of all species, and a relative decline of *Vallonia costata* and *Helicella*. The environment appears to have become less suitable for mollusca, probably due to a decrease in the lime content, itself a reflection of the cessation of the deposition of wind-borne material. It is possible too that there was a change to taller grasses and a locally higher relative humidity as indicated by the decline of *Vallonia costata* and *Helicella itala*, but this is not so certain. Both these species (and in particular *H. itala*) are generally found in dry short-turfed grass, and *H. itala* is an obligatory calcicole (i.e. it must have a high lime content in the environment). This suggests that a dense mat of semi-rotted plant material may have formed at this stage thus preventing access to the underlying chalk and creating conditions which were almost anaerobic; bacterial decay and consequently the turnover of organic matter would have been reduced and an oligotrophic situation (i.e. one poor in nutrients) obtained. This is a situation which often arises today in chalkland habitats which are not grazed and are reverting to scrub.

In the third phase, the absolute numbers of snails increases initially and there is a temporary rise in *V. costata* and *H. itala*, coincident with the renewed deposition of aeolian material. However, the former species soon becomes virtually absent and there is a general decline in the abundance of most species. Otherwise, the characteristic feature is the predominance of *Hygromia hispida* which may reflect an increase in the relative humidity of the local environment — perhaps brought on by the relaxation of grazing pressure and the growth of tall grasses. But the interpretation of the environment at this stage is made difficult by the apparent incompatibility of a fauna which suggests extreme oligotrophy with a situation in which the continued deposition of wind-borne material was taking place and which might have been expected to have maintained the soil and vegetation in a eutrophic (nutrient-rich) and highly calcareous state.

It is in the interpetation of the molluscan assemblages from the wind-laid deposits that we feel most strongly the lack of quantitative data on modern populations. If this were available the ancient environment at each successive level could be reconstructed with a greater degree of certainty and accuracy.

The uppermost of the three main horizons in the ditch sequence is a plough-wash deposit (15–125 cm.), formed by ploughing right across the ditch. This is clear from the massive increase in coarse chalk rubble, the mixed nature of the material and the presence of ploughmarks at the base of the layer. The increase in both *Vallonia costata* and *Helicella itala* in the fauna indicates a drying out of the environment and a rise in the lime content. Both these species, and particularly *H. itala* are typical of prehistoric and Roman cultivation horizons. The presence of Romano-British pottery in the lower levels is indicative of a Roman or possibly post-Roman date for the onset of ploughing.

Between 50 and 70 cm. there is a soil horizon indicating a pause in the accumulation, and it is to be noted that the faunas above and below this horizon are not identical. In the lower zone, *Vallonia costata* is well represented and shows a peak between 92.5 and 105 cm. coincident with the maximum concentration of coarse chalk rubble. Between 85 and 92.5 cm. where there was a noticeably fine zone, *V. costata* declines while most other species, particularly *Pupilla*, increase. The exact ecological significance of these slight changes is uncertain but there may have been a short standstill phase in the accumulation between 85 and 92.5 cm. when a vegetation cover of grasses spread over the area. Certainly the slight changes at 85 cm. foreshadow the more permanent changes which begin at *c.* 65 cm. and which are associated with a definite pause in the accumulation. This horizon is coincident with a drop in absolute numbers. In the upper zone, Limacidae and *Vallonia excentrica* increase; *Vallonia costata* and *Pupilla* show a decline. *Helicella itala* maintains its abundance and *H. virgata* increases, representing an increase in the genus *Helicella* as a whole; the two species are closely similar in their requirements and there is probably a competitive effect between them. These changes reflect an environment becoming increasingly dry, and one in which the turnover of organic matter within the soil is probably declining as the intensity of cropping increases. The Limacidae (probably mostly *Agriolimax reticulatus*, a species common in arable habitats today) are probably living on fresh plant material.

The medieval introduction, *Helicella virgata*, is consistently present from about 75 cm. upwards suggesting an historical date for the upper plough-wash zone. The few examples of this species below 75 cm. are probably derived from earthworm burrows which were seen in section to penetrate down into the wind-blown deposit; it is impossible to avoid all these when sampling.

In the modern plough-soil, snails are few and the predominant elements three — the Limacidae, *Vallonia excentrica* and *Helicella virgata* — a reflection of the very severe conditions of dryness, absence of shelter and low organic-matter turnover presented by the arable environment of today. The sharp break at 15 cm. emphasizes the antiquity of the underlying deposit and demonstrates that the process of deposition is no longer going on.

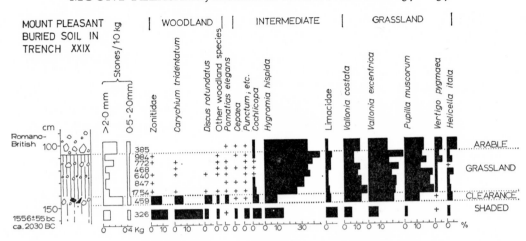

FIG. 88. Mount Pleasant: molluscan histogram through the upper buried soil in Cutting XXIX

The Buried Soil in Trench XXIX

The sequence of events just described took place in the vicinity of the south-west entrance of the main enclosure under the shadow of the Conquer Barrow (see site plan, fig. 3). Cuttings through the deposits of the north entrance ditch terminals showed a different situation (see Section C, trench XXIX). In the first place, there were traces of actual settlement in the form of stake circles (huts) which penetrated into the ditch fill from a level equivalent to the surface of the lowest buried soil (200 cm. in fig. 86). These were overlaid by layers of fine chalk rubble with an admixture of humic material (layers (7) and (8)), followed by a layer (6), which is probably in part wind-blown material. The latter was, however, much attenuated in thickness and not as pure as the magnificent deposit in the south-west terminals. Above was a well-humified buried soil complex consisting of alternate bands of stone-free loam and rubble (layers (4) and (5)). This was not represented at all in trenches I and II and is taken to be equivalent to the main bulk of the wind-blown deposit, a conclusion which is supported by the similarity of the faunal sequences in the two. Finally there is the plough-wash deposit (layers (2) and (3)).

The detailed stratigraphy of the buried soil (layer (4)) was as follows (fig. 88):

Depth below modern
surface (cm.)

0–107		Modern soil and plough-wash (layer (3)).
107–141		Buried soil (layer (4)). Dark brown loam with alternate zones of stone-free turf and chalk rubble.
	107–112	Turf-line.
	112–117	Stone-line, mainly chalk fragments.
	117–122	Turf.
	122–127	Stone-line, mainly chalk fragments.
	127–141	Turf.
141–148		Stone-line. Chalk fragments and flints (layer (5)).
148+		Pale stony loam (layer (6)). A radiocarbon date of 1556 ± 55 bc (c. 2030 B.C.) (BM-788) was obtained for this horizon.

The following series of nine samples was analysed for mollusca (fig. 88, Table XXIV):

Depth below modern surface (cm.)	Air-dry weight (kg.)	Number of shells per 1.0 kg.
97–107	0.5	770
107–112	0.5	1968
112–117	0.5	1544
117–122	0.25	1872
122–127	0.25	2560
127–135	0.25	3388
135–141	0.5	3508
141–148	0.5	918
152–160	0.5	652

The sequence (fig. 88, Table XXIV) is virtually identical to that from the south-west entrance (fig. 86) although very much compressed. In layer (5) (152–160 cm.) there is a mixed fauna of woodland and grassland species, the latter comprising about 20% of the total. Then follows a clearance zone in which there is a marked increase in chalk and flint debris; woodland species decrease, grassland species (60%) increase, and *Pomatias elegans* reaches its maximum.

In the buried soil, open-country species with *Hygromia hispida* predominate. *Vallonia costata* and *Pupilla* show an over-all gradual decline as in the wind-blown deposit; *V. excentrica* and *Hygromia* show a slight increase while *Helicella* is more or less constant. The sequence is interrupted by two stone lines which are probably of composite origin. In part they may have been caused by disturbance on the edge of the ditch (possibly very short periods of cultivation, or over-grazing) causing chalk rubble to spill down across the contemporary soil surface; and in part they may be due to worm-sorting under grassland, a process which we met with first in the buried soil beneath the enclosure bank (fig. 86). Similar processes can be seen going on today at the nearby site of Maiden Castle. Grazing sheep cause breaks in the turf on the sides of the hill-fort ditches with the result that the chalk is exposed and spreads of rubble spill down into the ditch bottom. In a few years these become totally buried by earthworm action, and the grass cover renewed. It is noticeable that these slight changes in the stratigraphy at Mount Pleasant are reflected in the molluscan assemblages. *Vallonia excentrica* shows marked peaks of abundance in the stone-free zones while *Pupilla* and *Helicella* (but not *V. costata*) are more prevalent in the rubble zones.

If we are to equate the upper turf-line (107–112 cm.) with a specific zone in the wind-blown deposit in the south-west terminals it must be with the upper levels (70–120 cm.). The similarity of the faunas probably reflects broadly similar environments, but the far greater number of snails in the buried soil by comparison with their paucity in the wind-blown deposit is not easy to explain. In part we may be seeing a reflection of different sedimentation rates, but this need not be the whole story. It is possible, for example, that the environment of the wind-blown deposit was one of dank grasses and low organic-matter turnover as suggested by the pale colour and low humic content. In the buried soil, however, there is a much higher humic content and a better developed crumb structure, and it is likely that this reflects an environment of short-turfed grassland grazed by sheep in which organic-matter turnover was high — manuring by sheep and the closeness to the surface

TABLE XXIV

Mount Pleasant, land mollusca, buried soil in main enclosure ditch,
trench XXIX, South section

	cm.								
	152–160	141–148	135–141	127–135	122–127	117–122	112–117	107–112	97–107
	Air-dry weight (kg.)								
	0.5	0.5	0.5	0.25	0.25	0.25	0.5	0.5	0.5
Pomatias elegans (Müller)	2	12	4	6	3	1	4	—	2
Carychium tridentatum (Risso)	77	34	7	—	2	1	1	—	—
Cochlicopa lubrica (Müller)	4	2	20	—	—	—	—	3	1
Cochlicopa lubricella (Porro)	—	6	2	8	3	1	—	—	1
Cochlicopa spp.	18	17	26	6	2	2	6	14	4
Vertigo pygmaea (Draparnaud)	1	2	32	18	14	10	47	29	23
Pupilla muscorum (Linné)	7	53	407	174	144	65	142	112	62
Acanthinula aculeata (Müller)	4	1	1	—	—	—	—	1	—
Vallonia costata (Müller)	19	64	310	113	67	60	62	69	52
Vallonia excentrica Sterki	26	95	367	193	117	112	135	263	60
Ena montana (Draparnaud)	—	2	—	—	—	—	—	—	—
Ena obscura (Müller)	—	—	1	—	—	—	—	—	—
Marpessa laminata (Montagu)	1	—	—	—	—	—	—	—	—
Clausilia bidentata (Ström)	2	7	7	—	2	1	3	4	—
Cecilioides acicula (Müller)	—	—	—	—	—	—	2	—	19
Arianta, Cepaea spp.	6	2	3	1	—	2	—	3	5
Hygromia hispida (Linné)	55	48	433	267	234	171	304	407	135
Helicella itala (Linné)	6	19	51	21	32	7	31	19	30
Punctum pygmaeum (Draparnaud)	—	1	3	2	2	2	—	12	1
Discus rotundatus (Müller)	9	29	5	—	1	—	—	—	—
Vitrea crystallina (Müller)	3	—	—	—	—	—	—	—	—
Vitrea contracta (Westerlund)	11	6	1	1	—	—	—	—	—
Oxychilus cellarius (Müller)	8	7	5	1	2	—	—	cf.1	—
Retinella radiatula (Alder)	5	2	10	5	1	2	1	—	—
Retinella pura (Alder)	10	16	4	—	—	—	cf.2	—	—
Retinella nitidula (Draparnaud)	14	13	6	2	—	—	—	—	—
Vitrina pellucida (Müller)	7	1	2	4	—	—	1	2	—
Limacidae	31	20	47	25	14	21	33	45	9

cf. = Probable identification.

allowing free aeration of the soil and a high bacterial population (i.e. a eutrophic environment).

In the plough-wash, the main faunal changes are the increase of *Vallonia costata* and *Helicella* and the decline of *V. excentrica* and *Hygromia*.

The Ring Ditch of the Timber Structure

The fill of the ring ditch showed the following sequence (fig. 89):

Depth below surface (cm.)	
0–15	Modern plough-soil.
15–35	Plough-wash. Pale brown stony loam with numerous angular chalk fragments. Romano-British pottery (layer (1)).
35–65	Buried soil. Dark brown loam with a pronounced stone line at 55 cm. (layers (3) and (4)).
65–95	Pale loam with an ash and charcoal zone between 75 and 85 cm. (layer (5)). A hearth from the surface of this layer yielded a C14 date of 1324 ± 51 bc (*c.* 1640 B.C.) (BM-669) and was associated with sherds of Collared Vessels and Food Vessels. In the ash and charcoal zone the majority of associated sherds were from Beakers. Charcoal yielded a C14 date of 1680 ± 60 bc (*c.* 2110–2130 B.C.) (BM-668) for this zone.
95–135	Buried soil. Dark brown stony loam with numerous bands of chalky rubble (layer (6)).
135–170	Primary fill. Coarse chalk and flint rubble (layer (7)). C14 dates from the bottom of the ditch fall around 2000 bc (*c.* 2490–2600 B.C.) (BM-663, 666 and 667); associated pottery is Grooved Ware.

A series of samples, each weighing 0.5 kg. (air-dry) was cut from this section at 10 cm. intervals and analysed for mollusca. The results are presented in Table XXV and fig. 89, the latter being a histogram of relative abundance. The sequence is quite straightforward.

In the lower buried soil (95–135 cm.) a woodland fauna prevails, open-country species, with the exception of a low percentage of *Helicella*, being virtually absent. This horizon is

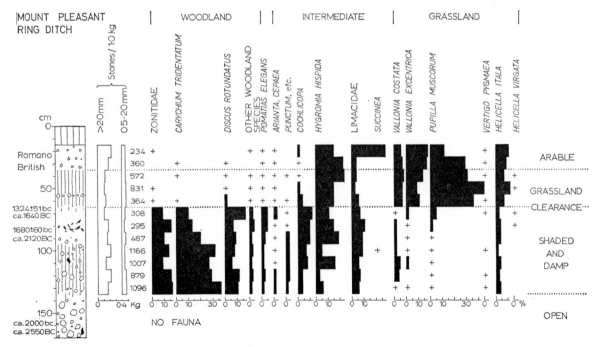

FIG. 89.   Mount Pleasant: molluscan histogram through the deposits of the Site IV ditch

roughly equivalent to the lower buried soil in the main enclosure ditch (fig. 86, 200–245 cm.) but on the whole is probably slightly earlier.

In the subsequent deposit (65–95 cm.), which is contemporary with the destruction of the timber building and the erection of the stone cove, the woodland environment is generally maintained, although the increase of *Pupilla*, *Vallonia excentrica* and *Pomatias elegans* in the upper two samples indicates some disturbance.

Clearance at 65 cm. is sudden and total, and again it is *Pupilla* which is first to predominate. Other grassland species are nevertheless common, and an environment of short-turfed grassland is probable at this stage. Equivalence with the wind-blown deposit (fig. 86) and buried soil in the north terminals of the main enclosure ditch (fig. 88) seems likely.

Finally, ploughing in Romano-British times led to the formation of a thin layer of ploughwash (15–35 cm.) and the same faunal changes which we saw in trenches I and II — the rise of the Limacidae, *Vallonia excentrica* and *Helicella*, and the decline of *Hygromia*, *Vallonia costata* and *Pupilla* — take place.

DISCUSSION

At both sites the earliest deposit is the buried soil beneath the enclosure bank. The longest sequence is that at Woodhenge where there is evidence for periglacial conditions followed by a woodland environment, then an episode of clearance, and ultimately a grassland regime. At Mount Pleasant the sequence is less complete, but it is likely that this is due simply to the vagaries of preservation. Periglacial structures were present at the surface of the subsoil, and the lower levels of the overlying buried soil contained vestiges of a shade-loving fauna. The presence of open-country species in this lower horizon indicates disturbance, possibly by tillage; and the fauna in the surface turf-line was undoubtedly one of grassland.

In Wiltshire, additional evidence for late-glacial and post-glacial environmental conditions up to the period of Neolithic forest clearance comes from a number of sites, among which are the henge monuments, Durrington Walls, Marden and Avebury; the sequence at the latter is exceptionally complete.[1] The main episodes on these sites are summarized in Table XXVI.

In Dorset too, there is evidence to support the former prevalence of woodland and its clearance in Neolithic times. At Litton Cheney (SY 912905), 16 km. due west of Mount Pleasant, pollen analysis of a peat deposit yielded evidence of woodland during the Atlantic period in which hazel was a prominent species. At the level of the elm decline (*c.* 3000 bc) there was an increase in non-tree pollen suggesting clearance. This site was on Greensand and only about 170 m. from the edge of the chalk.[2] On Black Down, Portesham (SY 613875), 11 km. west-south-west of Mount Pleasant, pollen analysis of a buried soil beneath a Bronze Age barrow showed 'an early period of forest conditions, including mainly oak with some lime, elm, birch and occasionally pine' which gave way to more open country in which bracken, grass and weeds of cultivation were the main flora.[3] This site was on gravel overlying the chalk. 22 km. to the east, just north of Wareham and well away from the chalk (SY 922893), pollen analysis of a valley peat demonstrated a vegetation cover of woodland in

[1] Evans, 1972.
[2] Sidaway, 1963.
[3] Dimbleby, *in* Thompson and Ashbee, 1957.

TABLE XXVI

Main environmental events on the chalk of Wiltshire and Dorset in the late-glacial and post-glacial periods

Period	Environment
Medieval/Romano-British/ Iron Age	Intermittent cultivation and grassland. Formation of ploughwash deposits.
Bronze Age	Open environment of grassland or arable. Cultivation/grazing intermittent. Formation of wind-laid material.
Late Neolithic	Woodland regeneration. Not at Woodhenge.
Late Neolithic	Construction of large henge monuments.
Neolithic	Long period of grassland, probably maintained by grazing.
Neolithic	Woodland clearance. Ploughing and possibly other forms of tillage. Ploughmarks at Avebury.
(Mesolithic) Atlantic(?)	Dense woodland. Recorded only at Avebury, but probable at most sites.
Mesolithic Boreal(?)	Open woodland. Evidence of fire and possible influence of Mesolithic man (Evans, 1972, 219, 256).
(Upper Palaeolithic) Late-glacial	Subarctic environment, probably tundra. Formation of periglacial structures and wind-lain material.

Boreal and Atlantic times.[1] This was followed by an elm decline (although the exact position of this in the diagram is debatable) and a marked increase in heaths (Ericales) and grasses; plantains (*Plantago lanceolata* and *P. coronopus*) come in at this level for the first time and other weeds of cultivation, notably the Chenopodiaceae, become consistently present.

The molluscan evidence from the nearby site of Maiden Castle is unsatisfactory in that no provenance is given for the Neolithic fauna.[2] However, the series of well-marked turf-lines of Neolithic and Bronze Age date — one associated with the causewayed enclosure, one overlying the ditch of the enclosure but sealed by the bank of the long mound and a third sealed by the Iron Age rampart — attests to the early establishment and persistence of grassland.[3] From the buried soil beneath the Neolithic long barrow on Thickthorn Down (ST 971123) a molluscan fauna of open-country was recovered.[4]

Turning to later episodes we find that at Mount Pleasant the environment reflected by the fauna in the buried soil immediately above the primary coarse fill in the ring ditch and main enclosure was probably one of woodland. We have already discussed the problems of

[1] Seagrief, 1959.
[2] Kennard, *in* Wheeler, 1943, **372.**
[3] Wheeler, 1953, pl. V; Godwin and Tansley, 1941.
[4] Kennard, *in* Drew and Piggott, 1943.

interpreting the exact nature of this environment, and whether it was confined to the ditches or extended over the entire area of the site. But the important point is that at this stage, which corresponds approximately to the late third or early second millennium B.C., the site was neither cultivated or grazed. This is in marked contrast to the situation at Woodhenge where the environment of the ditch remained open throughout its history.

It is possible that this period of agricultural inactivity is of more than local significance (in spite of Woodhenge). Thus woodland regeneration during Late Neolithic and Beaker times has been recorded from a number of sites on the chalk in southern England.[1] At Black Down, Portesham (see above), regeneration of alder and hazel took place after a cultivation phase. As a working hypothesis it might be useful to consider these episodes as a reflection of a general trend at this time.

More difficult to interpret are the upper prehistoric deposits in the ditches at Mount Pleasant and Woodhenge, and we must discuss here the question of Bronze Age climate. The period begins around 1500 bc (c. 1770–1870 B.C.) and is represented by a variety of deposits. At Woodhenge the relevant horizons are the lowest turf-line ((5c) in fig. 43) and the underlying loams ((6a) and (6b)). At Mount Pleasant the period is represented by either a fine silty loam (the wind-laid material) as in the west entrance ditch terminals or a soil horizon as in the north entrance ditch terminals and the ring ditch of the timber structure. In all cases the deposits are overlaid by a Romano-British plough-soil.

Two conditions are essential for the formation of wind-laid material. One is that the vegetation cover be broken thus exposing the bare soil to erosion; the other that dry and windy conditions prevail, and coincide, for at least a part of the year. The main work on Bronze Age soils as evidence for climate was done by Dr. I. W. Cornwall in 1953. His conclusions, relating to Bronze Age sites in the Oxford region, are as follows: 'For wind to be an important agency in filling artificial pits and ditches requires a climate at least seasonally dry and a cover of only sparse vegetation, so that bare soil is exposed to wind-erosion. These conditions do not ever obtain at the present day, but it appears as if they did so during at least part of the Bronze Age.' A similar argument was put forward to explain the silty texture of the infilling of the Y-holes at Stonehenge. However, since this paper was written new facts have become available. For example, in eastern England the present trend of removing hedges and creating larger fields has led to wind erosion of soil.[2] In Yorkshire massive stripping of the surface soil took place in the spring of one year when exceptional meteorological conditions obtained — low rainfall, above average temperatures and a very high frequency of gale-force winds. Similar phenomena have been recorded from East Anglia where dust storms are a not uncommon sight. The key factor in the inception of wind erosion is not necessarily climatic change but land-use change — the removal of hedges, the intensification of tillage, or massive overgrazing by sheep or cattle.

The evidence from Mount Pleasant supporting this hypothesis for wind-laid deposits is not everywhere present. It is possible, for example, that cultivation was confined to the western part of the site (wind-laid material was present as a thick layer in the Conquer Barrow ditch), and that on the summit (ring ditch) and to the north, grazing of stock prevailed. The absence of wind-laid material from the ring ditch can be explained either by the shallow depth of the ditch or, more likely, by suggesting the presence of a field boundary between the

[1] Burleigh et al., 1973.   [2] Radley and Simms, 1967.

western entrance of the enclosure and the ring ditch. The virtual absence of wind-laid material in the north entrance terminals may likewise be due to the existence of a fence or hedge, or to the fact that the area was not directly to the windward of the fields.

Likewise in the Stonehenge area, wind-laid material is present in a Bronze Age context at Durrington Walls[1] and Stonehenge[2] but not at Woodhenge. We can assume therefore that during the Bronze Age, tillage took place close to the south-east entrance of Durrington Walls and around Stonehenge, but not around Woodhenge. Here we must assume grazing in view of the open nature of the environment.

Similar deposits have been recorded from sites in Derbyshire,[3] Yorkshire (the henge monument Thornborough Rings) and Oxfordshire.[4] Mr. Don Benson (personal communication) has synthesized the archaeological contexts of the Oxfordshire examples, and finds that there is a red-brown, stone-free deposit in many Late Neolithic and Bronze Age ditches which can be dated to the Middle/Late Bronze Age to Iron Age periods. This is never as thick as the chalkland deposits and at some sites, for example the Devil's Quoits, Stanton Harcourt, is more loamy than silty (Dr. Susan Limbrey, personal communication); but at other sites the deposit shows definite sorting in the silt component.[5]

At the present day, wind erosion of soil from agricultural land appears to be confined to the east of England and does not, as far as we know, take place in Oxfordshire, Wiltshire or Dorset. Perhaps the necessary conditions of large expanses of exposed soil surface are not available but this is unlikely, for the removal of hedges in Wiltshire and the ploughing up of unenclosed downland has reached the stage where cultivated land often stretches to the horizon, unbroken by any form of boundary. It is much more probable that suitable climatic conditions do not now obtain. What this implies is that during the Bronze Age climatic conditions were suitable for the wind erosion of soil further west than today, as Dr Cornwall concluded, but only where the surface was exposed. But exposure itself through the removal of the surface vegetation is probably not caused by climate but by agriculture — tillage or possibly overgrazing. This is the only way that we can explain the intermittent distribution of wind-laid material in closely adjacent sites.

Within the period covered by the wind-laid deposit and the main upper buried soil of the enclosure ditch at Mount Pleasant, intermittent agriculture and/or overgrazing are indicated by the layered nature of the deposits. Thus there is a soil horizon within the wind-laid material (fig. 86, 140–160 cm.) indicating a standstill phase in the deposition; and in the main buried soil (fig. 88, 107.5–141 cm.) there are two stone horizons (at 115 and 125 cm.), indicating disturbance of the soil surface. But there is no indication in the molluscan assemblages of scrub or woodland regeneration during the periods of surface stability. We can see a parallel to this situation in the Sub-Boreal pollen record at Wareham, a site already referred to.[6] Farming is indicated by peaks of grasses coincident with peaks of *Plantago*, and these alternate with maxima in the Ericales curve, indicating that the farming was intermittent.

What is the duration of this period of wind erosion? At Mount Pleasant the beginning of deposition is dated to 1460 ± 131 bc (BM-664). Other relevant dates are 1324 ± 51 bc

---

[1] Wainwright and Longworth, 1971.
[2] Cornwall, 1953.
[3] Cornwall, *in* Lomas, 1962.

[4] Cornwall, 1953.
[5] Cornwall, 1953.
[6] Seagrief, 1959.

8

(BM-669) for the base of the upper buried soil in the ring ditch, and possibly 1556 ± 55 bc (BM-788) for the base of the upper buried soil (layer (6)) in the main enclosure ditch. We have argued that both these buried soils are equivalent in age to the wind-laid deposit. There is a C14 date of 1240 ± 105 bc (I-2445) from the bottom of Y-hole 30 at Stonehenge[1] and the Oxfordshire sites (see above) indicate a Middle/Late Bronze Age to Iron Age context on archaeological evidence. When corrected, these dates fall within the first half of the second millennium B.C. Wind transport had certainly ceased by Romano-British times, but how much earlier than this is uncertain. It is unlikely, however, that conditions were dry enough for wind transport after the climatic deterioration of the first millennium bc, dates for which range from c. 1300 bc to as late as c. 250 bc.[2] Taking the earliest of these we can define the period of wind transport as terminating around 1600 B.C. (corrected date) and thus occupying a span of not more than 400 years.

But it appears that the climatic deterioration took place in a series of stages and that between c. 1200 and 500 bc there could have been a return to drier conditions when wind deposition resumed. Certainly the evidence from Swedish bogs points this way, and the British dates for recurrence surfaces also cluster into an early and a late group.[3] It is probably rash to suggest that the buried soil (140–160 cm.) within the wind-laid deposit at Mount Pleasant represents a climatically damp period (c. 1200 bc?), but the possibility must at least be entertained. We certainly have two phases of wind-deposition with an intervening standstill phase.

Other periods when wind-deposition of sediments took place on the chalk are known. I. W. Cornwall[4] on the evidence of the mechanical analyses of a layer in the ditch of the Nutbane long barrow, Hampshire, suggested one such as having taken place between the digging of the ditch at 2730 ± 150 bc (BM-49) and a horizon containing Beaker pottery dated archaeologically (but with reference to the C14 chronology) to c. 1800 bc. Corrected, these dates give a possible range between c. 3400 and 2200 B.C., a range which is earlier than that of the Mount Pleasant episode.

Yet earlier phases took place during the late-glacial period[5] and it is probable that the infilling of the periglacial involutions at Durrington Walls, Woodhenge, Mount Pleasant, Avebury and other sites is in part of aeolian origin.

The episodes of Romano-British and medieval agriculture need little further discussion. Such episodes are frequently represented by plough-wash deposits in prehistoric ditches. The closest site to Mount Pleasant documented by molluscan analysis is Badbury Earthwork about 30 km. to the north-east;[6] and in Wiltshire there is a plough-wash deposit in the ditch of the South Street long barrow (about 27 km. north of Woodhenge) which is largely of medieval origin.[7] At both Mount Pleasant and Woodhenge, periods of tillage alternated with periods of grassland as they did in prehistoric times. At Durrington Walls the plough-wash deposit in the upper levels of the ditch was of Iron Age and Romano-British origin, but this was not investigated by molluscan analysis.

It is worth pointing out that the deposition of these plough-wash deposits took place mainly

[1] Atkinson, 1967.
[2] Godwin, 1966; Turner, 1970, 101; Piggott, 1972.
[3] Godwin, 1966, 10.
[4] In Morgan, 1959, 49.

[5] Perrin, 1956; Evans, 1968.
[6] Evans, 1972, 337.
[7] Evans, 1972, 328.

by subaerial processes involving mechanical disturbance of the soil and rainwashing,[1] and that these processes contrast markedly with the mode of deposition of the aeolian material. Moreover they were taking place in a period when precipitation was higher than previously. But again we find it difficult to distinguish between the effects of man and the effects of climate, and while a higher rainfall may well have favoured plough-wash formation, there is no doubt that the shallower profile of the ditch, which was brought about by the deposition of wind-borne material, enabled cultivation to take place right across the ditch instead of simply around it as had previously been the case. Nevertheless plough-wash deposits of pre-Iron Age origin are virtually unknown.

The entire sequence of environmental events at Woodhenge, Mount Pleasant and the other henges recently investigated is summarized in Table XXVI.

[1] Evans, 1972, 282.

XV. THE ANIMAL BONES

by R. A. HARCOURT

INTRODUCTION

THE collection, comprising nearly 3500 identified specimens, is made up of material from seven different archaeological features which fall chronologically into four separate groups: Late Neolithic (*c.* 1800 B.C.), Beaker (*c.* 1700 B.C.), Bronze Age (*c.* 1400 B.C.) and Iron Age (*c.* 100 B.C.) and it is on this basis that the material has been described.[1]

No attempt has been made to express age in years, because to do so without the knowledge of when various epiphyses fused and teeth erupted in the prehistoric and early historic periods gives a spurious impression of precision. It is probable, however, that the sequence in which these events occurred was the same as that in modern animals.[2] The preferred approach has been that of establishing age groups for each species in which the sample is large enough. To do this the long bone epiphyses were divided into early and late fusing moieties, the number of fused and unfused specimens in each being expressed as a percentage of the total. The unfused epiphyses in the early fusing group then indicate the percentage of juveniles in the population and the fused specimens in the late fusing group, the percentage of fully mature adults and aged animals. The intermediate group of young adults is derived by subtraction.

All measurements are in millimetres and the extremities of long bones are measured across the articular surfaces.

DESCRIPTION OF MATERIAL

I. *Late Neolithic*

(630 specimens identified)[3]

The material from this period was very well preserved. The domestic species present, with the minimum number of individuals of each in brackets, were cattle (8), sheep (4), goat (1) — not certainly identified — pig (17) and dog (2). The wild species were horse (1), red deer (2), aurochs (1), wild boar (1), fox (1) and birds. All parts of the skeleton were about equally represented with the exception of skulls.

Domestic Species

Cattle. The measurable bones indicate large cattle typical of the Neolithic although the complete metacarpal is that of an animal at the lower end of the size range.[4]

The sample was small but from the evidence of the epiphyses the bones of the fully mature comprised 52% of the total and those of juveniles 8%. Several of the lower third molars present were heavily worn suggesting animals of an advanced age.

---

[1] The bird-bones were kindly identified by D. Bramwell.
[2] Silver, 1969.

[3] This figure includes the material from Woodhenge.
[4] Harcourt, 1971a, b; Jewell, 1963.

Sheep. Because of the small amount of material all that can be said of this species is that it was there.

Goat. The presence of this animal in the Neolithic is well attested[1] but on this site is not certain, the evidence being the somewhat intuitive identification of an incomplete juvenile tibia.

Pig. The bone dimensions of this species closely match those of the pigs at Durrington Walls and by comparison with Pitt-Rivers' test animal the tallest probably stood about 170 cm. (28 in.) at the shoulder.[2] The biggest age group was that of the young adults, 47% of the total; the juveniles and mature adults comprised, respectively, 31 and 22%.

Dog. There were only six specimens from the Neolithic levels and only one of note. This was a lower first molar (21 mm. length) similar to that of a modern female Alsatian in size but in fact probably from a smaller dog because primitive dogs tended to have large teeth relative to skull and body size.[3]

Wild Species

The total number of specimens from horse, red deer and fox was 16 and only one was of note, a complete metacarpal of red deer (263 tl, 37 pw, 24 msd, 40 dw). It is thought that the horse was wild in the Neolithic largely perhaps because there is no evidence to the contrary.[4]

Aurochs (Bos primigenius). In the main enclosure ditch was found the proximal part of a massive radius and ulna and the distal extremity, probably of the same animal, of a radius (98 pw, 80 dw). The areas of muscle attachment in both these were particularly well marked, a criterion sometimes used to distinguish wild and domestic individuals and sometimes to differentiate between male and female.

Wild Boar (Sus scrofa). Also from the main enclosure ditch came a much damaged but recognizable very large scapula and the distal extremity of a humerus (47 dw). This measurement comes within the range reported by Clason[5] for the wild boar in Holland and is also exactly the same as that of the mounted specimen in the British Museum (Natural History). A distal humerus identified as wild boar but with a width of only 39 mm. is on display in Salisbury Museum.

Birds. The single specimen found was from a common crane (*Grus grus*) in the Site IV ditch.

II. *Beaker*
(1946 specimens identified)

The domestic species represented were cattle (18), sheep (12), pig (35) and dog (3) and the dimensions of all measurable bones are shown in Table XXVIII. The wild species were aurochs (2), wild boar (1), red deer (2), roe deer (1), fox (1) and birds.

Cattle. A comparison of Tables XXVII and XXVIII shows that the Neolithic and Beaker cattle on this site were of very similar size as is to be expected in view of the short time

[1] Grigson, 1965; Harcourt, 1971a; Jackson, 1934.   [4] Harcourt, 1971a; Zeuner, 1963.
[2] Pitt-Rivers, 1887.   [5] Clason, 1967.
[3] Personal observation.

interval. The fully mature age group comprised 54% of the total but the early fusing group of epiphyses were so few that they provided an inadequate sample. Twenty-two lower third molars, a later erupting tooth were found. Three (13%) had the third cusp unworn, in four (18%) it was just in wear, while in 15 (68%) all three cusps were well worn, indicating fully mature, even old animals.

Sheep. The only specimens suitable for ageing purposes were eight lower third molars and seven temporary lower third premolars. One of the latter group which showed no wear at all must have come from a lamb while the degree of attrition on the others indicated young

TABLE XXVII

Measurements of bones of domestic species — Neolithic

Cattle	
Humerus	dw 73–78 (2). Radius pw 68–73 (4)
Tibia	dw 47–50 (2). Astragalus lateral length 60
Metacarpal	l 202. pw 54. mds 30. dw 57*
Pig	
Humerus	tlh 170–190 (4). dw 29–35 (17)
Astragalus	lateral length 39–41 (2)
Scapula	width of neck 24–35 (3)

tl = total length. tlh = total length to head. pw = proximal width. msd = midshaft diameter. dw = distal length. Figures in brackets indicate the number of specimens measured.

* The msd index (msd 100/tl) is 14.8% suggesting this was a cow[1] so the length is multiplied by 6, giving an approximate shoulder height of 121 cm. (47 in.).[2]

adults. Four of the eight molars were heavily worn. The dimensions of the bones are closely akin to those of the Soay, a small slender animal.

Pig. Fully mature animals formed 31%, juveniles 27%, and young adults 44% of the total. Just as with the cattle, no change is apparent in the size compared to those of the earlier period. In the main enclosure ditch were found three lower third molars showing a remarkable amount of wear. The occlusal surfaces were completely flat and worn right down to the roots so that these teeth, judging from their size, probably came from very old breeding sows.

Wild Species

Aurochs. The evidence for the presence of this species consists of a distal humerus, a lower third molar and two astragali. The astragali had a lateral length of 78 and 87 mm. respectively. From the data presented by Grigson[3] the larger may have been from a bull but

[1] Howard, 1963.
[2] Fock, 1966.
[3] Grigson, 1965.

the 78 mm. specimen is smaller than those recorded from any European country except Hungary where, the evidence suggests, there was a smaller race. However the total she records from Britain is 12 specimens and the difference between those and that from this site is only 2 mm. and between it and one from Sweden 1 mm. An astragalus of 79 mm. tentatively identified as aurochs was found at Marden.[1] The largest astragalus of Neolithic or Bronze Age cattle in Britain known to the author from published and unpublished data is one of 72 mm. from Durrington Walls[2] which is itself slightly longer than any previously

TABLE XXVIII

Measurements of bones of domestic species — Beaker

	tl	pw	msd	dw
Cattle				
Humerus	—	—	—	67–78 (9)
Radius	257	68	38	61
	—	62–82 (6)	—	59–63 (3)
Metacarpal*	203	53	30	57
	—	63–66 (3)	—	63
Astragalus, lateral length. 63–68 (8)				
Lower third molar, greatest length, 35–43 (20)				
Sheep				
Humerus	—	—	—	24
Radius	149	27	15	23
Lower third molar	20–22.5 (6)			
Pig				
Humerus	—	—	—	30–35 (9)
Tibia	189	49	22	24
	—	—	—	22–24 (11)
Astragalus	41–44 (8)	—	—	—
Lower third molar	32–40 (7)	—	—	—

* msd index 14.8%. Shoulder height 122 cm. (48 in.) approx. See note Table XXVII.

recorded. There can be little doubt that there was a gradation in size between domestic cattle, those in the process of being domesticated, and wild bovids[3] and thus any specimen not at the extreme of the size range will be difficult to identify with certainty. The humerus was a massive bone; the distal articular surface had a width of 102 mm. and the thickness of the cortical bone, where it was broken 12 cm. above the condyles, was 17.5 mm. The lower third molar had a length of 46 mm. which puts it within the size range of *Bos primigenius*.[4] Three specimens were from the palisade trench and one from the Site IV ditch.

[1] Harcourt, 1971b.
[2] Harcourt, 1971a.
[3] Grigson, 1969.

[4] Degerbol, M., cited by Higgs, E. S. (1960) *in* Alexander, J., Ozanne., P. C. and Ozanne, A. *Proc. Prehist. Soc.*, **26**, 263.

Wild Boar. By the usual criterion of size two specimens, both from the Site IV ditch, were thought to belong to this species, an astragalus and a portion of tusk. The astragalus had a length of 54 mm. which is larger than all but one of the seven astragali ascribed to wild boar at the Iron Age site of Heuneberg[1] and bigger than most of those figured by Clason.[2] The tusk, of which only a short portion remained, must have been formidable in life. The dimensions of the three sides were 25, 20 and 13 mm. The remaining wild species, red deer, roe deer and fox do not merit individual mention.

Birds. In the palisade trench were three bones of song-thrush (*Turdus philomelos*), one of missel-thrush (*T. viscivorus*) and one of pintail (*Anas acuta*). From the Site IV ditch came one bone each of either greylag or bean goose (*Anser anser* or *A. arvensis*) and one from a pintail (*Anas acuta*).

III. *Bronze Age*
(454 specimens identified)

The material from this period was very poorly preserved with many of the fragments being recognizable only anatomically and to species because of their comminuted state and providing no other information. There were, for example, numbers of split bovine teeth. The domestic animals were cattle (3), sheep (3), goat (1) and pig (5) and dog (1). The wild species were red deer, fox and badger, one individual of each.

Cattle. Four lower third molars had lengths of 35–37 mm., a tibia with a distal width of 50 mm. and the proximal width of a metatarsal was 49 mm.

Sheep and Goat. There are three measurable bones, tibiae with distal widths of 22–23 mm., identified as sheep. The goat remains consisted of a complete metatarsal of 115 mm. length and an msd index of 10.4%. This is markedly shorter and broader than any of the more than 100 complete metatarsals from numerous different sites identified by the writer as being those of sheep and is in accordance with the general statement that goat metapodials tend to be shorter and broader than those of sheep.[3]

Pig remains do not merit special mention. Dog was represented only by a right upper first molar, from an animal of about terrier size.

Wild Species

The remains of red deer consisted of 25 teeth, including two lower third molars of 31 mm., probably those of a fairly large stag and an antler from a killed or dead animal. There was also the ulna of a very young fox and that of a young badger.

IV. *Iron Age*
(454 specimens identified)

The domestic species present were cattle (6), sheep (5), goat (1), pig (3), horse (2), dog (1), and the wild species red deer (2), fox (2) and badger (1).

Cattle. The measurable bones were a humerus with a dw 60 mm., two tibiae of dw 50 mm., three lower third molars ranging from 32 to 35 mm. and a complete radius with a damaged

[1] Geringer, 1967.
[2] Clason, 1967.

[3] Boessneck, 1969.

distal extremity (318 tl, 83 pw and msd 48). These, except for the radius which is bigger than any other so far recorded from the Iron Age, are similar to those from other contemporary sites. The longest radius from Little Woodbury was 237 mm.[1] and from Longbridge Deverill was 260 mm.[2] Another noteworthy specimen was a skull, much damaged, but of which enough remained to show it was from a hornless animal.

Sheep and Goat. A total of 68 specimens, from sheep, mostly teeth, provided very little useful information. The presence of a radius with fused distal epiphysis and lower third molars showing much wear attested to survival well into maturity. Goat provided only one bone.

Pig. All that can be said of this species is that there was a tibia of 24 mm. dw and an astragalus with a length of 44 mm.

Horse. The only complete bone, out of some 12 specimens, a metacarpal (202 tl, 41 pw, 28 msd and 42 dw), indicated a pony of about 12½ hands (130 cm.), the size regularly found on Iron Age sites.[3]

Dog. The only bone of note was part of a mandible in which the lower first molar measured 22 mm. in length.

Wild Species

These were red deer, fox and badger, represented by a total of only 20 specimens.

The Meat Contribution of Wild and Domestic Species

The survival rate, that is, the ratio of individuals represented on a site to the number originally present, can never be known so it is better to think in terms of relative meat contributions rather than absolute weights. The size of the sheep shows very little variation throughout the archaeological period and is close to that of the modern Soay of which the dressed carcase weight is about 30 lb. (14 kg.). One sheep therefore is taken as unity and the weight of other species, derived from estimated statures, bone dimensions and for deer the information available about the weight of modern animals, is expressed as a ratio of this. Inevitably no great precision can be claimed for such a method but in view of the nature of the material it is probably the best available.

TABLE XXIX

Percentage meat contributions of wild and domestic species

	Cattle	Sheep	Pig	Goat	Horse	Wild species
Neolithic	60	2	16	1	—	21
Beaker	67	5.5	16	—	—	10.5
Bronze Age	68	6	15	2	—	9
Iron Age	59	5	5	1	20	10

The ratio for a particular species is multiplied by the minimum number of individuals to give the number of 'meat units' contributed by that species (mu). This value is then ex-

[1] Jackson, 1948.
[2] Harcourt, in preparation.
[3] Harcourt, in preparation.

pressed as a percentage of the total meat units provided by all species combined (MU). Then

$$\text{Percentage meat contribution} = \frac{mu}{MU} \cdot 100.$$

The ratios used for the various species were cattle 12 (10 in the Iron Age), pig 1.5, goat 1, red deer 5, aurochs 20, wild boar 3, roe deer 1 and horse 10.

The fox and badger were excluded even though there is every probability that members of both species would have gone into the cooking pot but their relative contribution was regarded as negligible. There is indeed no reason to suppose that dogs were not eaten as well. Because hunted animals are likely to be killed at a distance from the settlement they are liable to be underrepresented and a paucity of remains need not necessarily mean that only a few were eaten. This is because the usual practice for hunters when a kill is made is to skin the carcase, often leaving the lower limb bones still attached to the skin, then to remove the meat from the other bones which are left on the site of the kill. The skin and the meat are taken away but, of course, disappear without trace.

Such practices, although known to be widespread,[1] were not invariable as is clearly shown by the presence, for example, of a humerus and radius of aurochs on this site. The evidence for the presence of red deer, however, antlers apart, consisted only of a few lower leg and foot bones and teeth.

The presence of the duck, goose and crane bones suggests that wildfowling provided a small but no doubt useful contribution to the larder. It is possible that the bones of the thrushes may be explained in the same way.

DISCUSSION

From Table XXX can be seen the way in which the relative numbers of the various domestic species altered during the time span of this site, nearly 2000 years. Cattle increased slightly, sheep showed a two-fold increase and the pig, a three-fold decrease. The alteration in the numbers of these two species can presumably be attributed to forest clearance and the consequent reduction of habitat suitable for the pig. It must be borne in mind, however,

TABLE XXX

Numbers and percentages of domestic species

	NSI	Cattle (%)	Sheep (%)	Pig (%)	Horse (%)	Goat (%)
Neolithic	630	27 (8)	13 (4)	57 (17)	—	3 (1)
Beaker	1946	28 (18)	18 (12)	54 (35)	—	—
Bronze Age	454	25 (3)	25 (3)	42 (5)	—	8 (1)
Iron Age	454	35 (6)	29 (5)	18 (3)	12 (2)	6 (1)

Figures in brackets: minimum number of individuals.
NSI: Number of specimens identified.

[1] Perkins and Daly, 1968; Wheat, 1967.

that on an important centre such as this one, the relative proportions of the species present may not reflect that in the stock population as a whole.

Polled skulls have been found at three other Iron Age sites in Wessex; All Cannings Cross,[1] Swallowcliffe Down,[2] and Longbridge Deverill.[3] This feature in cattle is hereditary and almost certainly arose as a mutation. It is due to a dominant gene and, in Europe, occurs only in Scandinavia and Britain[4] and thus cannot have been introduced in the cattle of Iron Age immigrants.

The earliest evidence of polled cattle in Britain is from the Neolithic site of Skara Brae,[5] but south of that it has not been recorded, as far as the writer is aware, outside Wessex or before the Iron Age. Such a phenomenon is unlikely to have happened at more than one place in such a restricted area and its occurrence at several different sites all of approximately comparable date points to interchange of cattle. For the young men of cattle-owning tribes, stock theft was a favourite occupation and this, it is suggested, was the way such interchange may have occurred. The diffusion of the gene could also have been brought about by cattle trading, a more legitimate but duller activity.

Pathology

There were three specimens showing pathological alterations; they were from two animals, both cattle. From the Beaker levels there came a second and third lower left molar, both heavily worn and thus from an old animal, which showed coral-like bony outgrowths around the tips of the roots. A single tooth of Iron Age date showed an identical change. The cause in both cases was probably a chronic alveolar infection, possibly but not necessarily associated with *Actinomyces bovis*, the organism of the so-called 'Lumpy-jaw'.

Observations on some Comparative Aspects of Durrington Walls, Mount Pleasant and Marden

The Neolithic levels of these three sites produced nearly 9500 identified bones of which 8500 (*c.* 90%) came from Durrington Walls. The relatively small size of the sample from the other two sites, especially that from Marden, only 320 specimens (*c.* 3%), inevitably means that comparisons and conclusions must be made and treated with caution. It should

TABLE XXXI

*Percentage domestic species**

	Pig	Cattle	Sheep	Goat
Durrington Walls	68	29	2	1
Mount Pleasant	57	27	13	3
Marden	44	44	12	—

* Calculated from the minimum number of individuals.

[1] Jackson, 1923.
[2] Jackson, 1925.
[3] Harcourt, in preparation.
[4] Mason, 1963.
[5] Watson, 1931.

also be remembered that at each site only a small part of the total area has been excavated and in the event of further excavation, the picture might be markedly altered.

In Table XXXI is shown the relative numbers of individuals of each species of the domestic animals present at each site.

It will be noted that at Durrington Walls and Mount Pleasant the pig is paramount but that at Marden it is equalled by cattle and, at the two latter sites, there is a greater number of sheep.

When, however, a comparison of the meat yield is made (Table XXXII) these differences almost disappear.

TABLE XXXII

Percentage meat contribution of wild and domestic species

	Cattle	Pig	Sheep/goat	Wild species
Durrington Walls	69.5	20.5	0.5	9.5
Mount Pleasant	60	16	2	21
Marden	62	9	2	27
	(73)	(11)	(2)	(14)

The evidence for aurochs at Marden is not certain and consisted only of a single astragalus.[1] The second set of values for this site was therefore calculated to allow for the possibility that the specimen was that of a large domestic bovid. The study of bones from an excavation may well give more emphasis to the place of meat in the diet than it deserves. Accounts of pastoral peoples in various parts of the world in recent times are nearly all agreed that meat forms only a small part of the regular diet[2] and there seems little reason to doubt that this could also have been the case in prehistoric times except in hunter–fisher economies. Furthermore, meat is a terminal product whereas one that provides a sustained yield is more beneficial in a subsistence economy.

It has been argued on the basis of the great numbers of pigs at Durrington Walls, that because this animal is so difficult to drive, the people who frequented the site must have lived in settled farmsteads and not led a 'predominantly nomadic existence'.[3] This qualification is important because within the same group a settled existence may be combined with partial nomadism. The older people, women and children live permanently or for a large part of the year in a village tending crops and gardens while the men, or some of them, lead a nomadic life with the stock.[4] It is perfectly possible that some such system was followed in Neolithic times; the sheep being grazed on the more open country and the cattle either being herded there as well or taken to distant woodland to browse and the pigs kept close to the settlement and near the wooded areas. Browse may well have formed a substantial contribution to the diet of cattle during the summer months which would have the effect of conserving pasture for the winter.

At Durrington Walls very few pigs and cattle skulls were found from which it was deduced

[1] Harcourt, 1971b.
[2] Allan, 1967; Cranstone, 1969.
[3] Wainwright, 1971, 191.
[4] Cranstone, 1969.

that animals were slaughtered elsewhere and either complete or jointed carcases brought on to the site. It is of interest that at Mount Pleasant the same finding was made as indeed it was at Marden, but as has already been pointed out the collection from there was so small that such observations must of necessity carry little weight.

From the Iron Age levels of Durrington Walls and Mount Pleasant a total of 700 specimens was identified and for the most part these conformed to the general pattern of Wessex sites of the period in terms both of species and their sizes. At both, however, cattle bones were found which were well within the Neolithic size range and bigger than any previously recorded, to the writer's knowledge, from the Iron Age. The Mount Pleasant radius (318 tl) is of particular note. The presence of these larger animals would seem to indicate that the variation in size of Iron Age cattle is greater than had previously been thought. The excavation of more settlements of this period may provide useful evidence on this point.

PART IV

XVI. DISCUSSION

THE PRE-ENCLOSURE SETTLEMENT

THE fossil soil beneath the enclosure bank normally consisted of a dark brown humic loam 2.5 cm. thick overlain by 10–15 cm. of paler but still humic material. The molluscan fauna from this soil at the time of its burial reflects an environment of dry grassland and charcoal fragments from it have been identified as oak. Artifacts from the buried soil include sherds of plain Neolithic bowls, a flake from a polished flint axe and two transverse arrowheads. Bones of cattle and sheep were found and hazel-nut shells occurred. A radiocarbon date of 2122 ± 73 bc (BM-644) was also obtained. No structural remains were recorded and the settlement, as far as can be seen from the limited excavations undertaken was of a transitory nature in the later part of the third millennium bc. Contemporary settlements represented by the causewayed camp and bank barrow on Maiden Castle hill indicate a substantial concern for the latter which extended over several centuries.

SITE IV: THE TIMBER BUILDING

In brief, the evidence from Site IV in its early phase was for a circular timber structure represented by five concentric rings of post-holes with a maximum diameter of 38.00 m. and a diameter of 12.50 m. for the inner ring. The very regular layout was designed around four corridors which divide the rings into arcs. This structure was surrounded by a ditch 3.00–4.00 m. wide and 2.00 m. deep enclosing a circular area 43.00 m. in diameter. The bank appears to have been external and a single causeway 7.50 m. wide was provided in the north. Three radiocarbon dates from the bottom of the ditch (BM-663, 666 and 667) assign the construction of the latter to around 2000 bc. Pottery of the Grooved Ware ceramic style was associated with this ditched structure as were flint scrapers, a chalk ball, 11 antler picks, the tip of a bone pin and bones of pig, *bos*, sheep, dog, red deer, fox and bird. The relevant ditch deposits comprise a primary chalk rubble sealed by a lower buried soil, the molluscan fauna from which indicates woodland conditions. Charcoals of hazel, yew and field maple were found in the rubble and buried soil.

A detailed discussion of similar structures, which are interpreted as roofed buildings, can be found in the Durrington Walls monograph,[1] to which should now be added the small structure from Marden, Wilts.[2] Comparative plans, radiocarbon dates and dimensions for these structures have been assembled in figs. 90–3. The first such structure to be excavated was Woodhenge[3] — a timber structure sited within an oval enclosure which had an external bank and a single entrance facing north-east. The timber structure enclosed by the ditch comprised six egg-shaped rings of post-holes with a maximum diameter of 44.00 m. In 1940 Professor Piggott interpreted Woodhenge as a roofed building of one period.[4] More recently, Mr. Musson[5] has made an alternative suggestion that Woodhenge represents two separate

---

[1] Wainwright and Longworth, 1971, 204f.
[2] Wainwright, 1971.
[3] Cunnington, 1929.

[4] Piggott, 1940.
[5] Musson, 1971.

buildings, each with an outward sloping roof and a central court. The predominant ceramic association is with Grooved Ware and a single cutting across the bank and ditch in 1970 (described in this volume) produced material for radiocarbon determinations of between 1900 and 1800 bc.

The Sanctuary was also excavated by Mr. Cunnington[1] and was sited on Overton Hill in north Wiltshire. The complex history of the monument was initially elucidated by Professor Piggott[2] and has since been discussed in some detail by Mr. Musson. The initial building was a circular hut 4.50 m. in diameter which was succeeded by successive buildings 11.50 and 20.00 m. in diameter respectively. The final timber building was eventually replaced by two concentric stone circles which were linked with the West Kennet Avenue and Avebury. Grooved Ware formed part of the ceramic series from the site but no radiocarbon dates are available.

The interior of Durrington Walls was excavated in 1967 and the remains of two circular timber structures were recorded of which the larger is the Southern Circle.[3] Like neighbouring Woodhenge this was a six-ring structure in its final form, 38.00 m. in diameter, with a single entrance. It produced a great quantity of Grooved Ware and three radiocarbon dates which group between 2000 and 1900 bc. The structure was reconstructed by Mr. Musson as having a central open court with a free-standing ring of timber uprights.

The second timber structure at Durrington is the Northern Circle which has been interpreted as a roofed building about 14.50 m. in diameter, the four central posts perhaps supporting a raised lantern. This building was approached up an incline from the south by means of an irregular avenue of timber uprights through a façade of closely set posts. This building was also associated with Grooved Ware and a radiocarbon date of 1955 $\pm$ 140 bc (NPL-240) was obtained for it.

Finally, a simple structure was excavated at Marden in the Vale of Pewsey in 1969.[4] It consisted of a single ring of post-holes, 10.50 m. in diameter, which was associated with Grooved Ware. A radiocarbon date of around 2000 bc was obtained from the base of the ditch of the large enclosure within which the structure was sited.

The excavation of the Mount Pleasant timber structure has confirmed the occurrence of such buildings within large earthwork enclosures of Durrington type and has also confirmed the basic structural plans of such buildings as well as their date and ceramic associations. However, as the structure had been heavily eroded by ploughing to the point where the bases of the post-holes had begun to disappear, it has no information to add to the architectural reconstructions of such buildings.[5] It will be recalled that the large structure at Durrington Walls required over 260 tons of oak timber for its construction. Furthermore, over 1000 m. of timbers of varying diameters would have been required for the upright posts in the structure and lengths totalling 1500 m. for purlins, ring-beams and rafters. This information was obtained under conditions where the remains had been preserved by a thick layer of hill-wash and in default of evidence of comparable quality from Mount Pleasant the same general logistic conclusions may be made for Site IV. It has been estimated for example that the Southern Circle at Durrington had a maximum height of 10.50 m. A

---

[1] Cunnington, 1931.

[2] Piggott, 1940.

[3] Wainwright and Longworth, 1971.

[4] Wainwright, 1971.

[5] The author is indebted to Mr. C. Musson for discussions on this point.

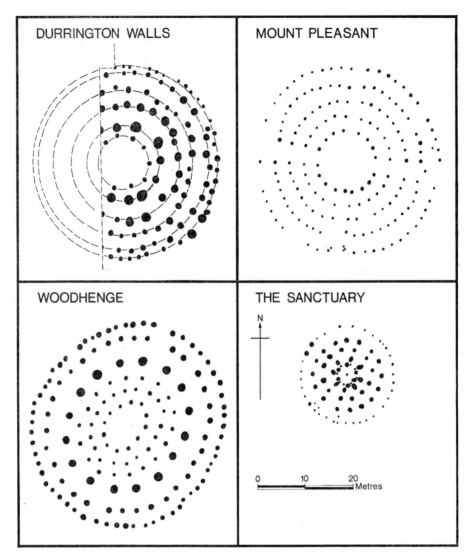

F<small>IG</small>. 90.   Comparative plans of the large buildings at Durrington Walls,
Mount Pleasant, Woodhenge and the Sanctuary

building of comparable size at Mount Pleasant standing near the crest of a prominent hill-
top would have been visible for miles around and provided a natural focal point for the
region. Discussions based around the survival value of oak timbers from the Southern Circle
concluded that the building would probably have survived for the best part of 200 years.
The building at Mount Pleasant was replaced around 1700 bc by a setting of sarsen stones,
the inner arrangement of which is based on the layout of the timber building. If these
foundations were still visible in 1700 bc a long life is implied for the timber structure.

By specific reference to fig. 90 it may be seen that the ground plans of the Durrington
(Southern Circle), Woodhenge and Mount Pleasant structures are closely comparable,

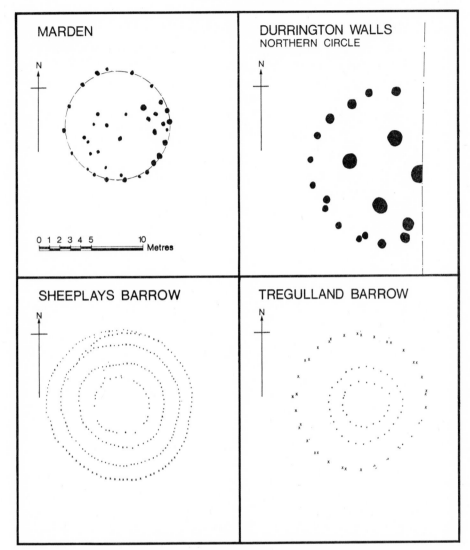

FIG. 91. Comparative plans of buildings at Marden and Durrington Walls and of structures beneath the Sheeplays and Tregulland Barrows

whilst the Sanctuary, although of similar design is on a much smaller scale. The dimensions of the rings and numbers of posts in each ring is shown in fig. 92. There is clearly a close agreement in the post sequences in successive rings between Durrington (Southern Circle) and Woodhenge. The reason behind such agreement is likely to be that such buildings were constructed to a predetermined plan and that the number of posts in each ring depended on the structural needs of this plan. The radiocarbon chronology of the structures is fairly consistent and is summarized in fig. 93. The chronological range represented at Durrington, Marden and Mount Pleasant indicates a potential genesis for these structures around or slightly before 2000 bc. Woodhenge was apparently built a century or so later, if the earthwork is indeed contemporary with the timber structure in this case. Each structure is associated with pottery of the Grooved Ware ceramic tradition in some quantity, along with flint artifacts, antler picks and animal bones. Not only is this distinctive pottery associated with the structures themselves, it also occurs with the earthworks which surround them. The buildings on occasion occur within large externally embanked enclosures (Durrington Walls, Marden and Mount Pleasant) which form a restricted group in southern England.

To summarize, therefore, a series of large circular buildings was constructed in Wessex to the same plan, at about the same time and associated with the same very distinctive

	Durrington S. Circle	Mount Pleasant	Woodhenge	The Sanctuary
Ring Diam.	38·9m.	38·0m.	44·1 x 39·6m.	20·1m.
Posts	50	51	60	34
Ring Diam.	35·7m.	31·0m.	38·1 x 34·1m.	13·7m.
Posts	36	48	32	16
Ring Diam.	29·3m.	25·0m.	29·4 x 25·2m.	11·5m.
Posts	34	37	16	12
Ring Diam.	22·9m.	15·0m.	22·5 x 18·8m.	6·4m.
Posts	24	24	18	8
Ring Diam.	15·2m.	12·0m.	17·3 x 14·0m.	4·5m.
Posts	12	17	18	8
Ring Diam.	10·7m.	——	11·8 x 8·5m.	3·9m.
Posts	10	——	12	6

FIG. 92.   Comparative dimensions of timber buildings from Durrington
Walls, Mount Pleasant, Woodhenge and the Sanctuary

ceramic style. It is clear from the distribution of contemporary earthworks that these buildings and the enclosures which are sometimes associated with them were focal points in the settlement patterns of the time.

The architectural reconstructions of several of the timber buildings seem to preclude a purely domestic purpose for them. In the case of the Southern Circle at Durrington and Woodhenge, the most tenable interpretations involve an open court in the centre of the building and in the case of the Southern Circle this unroofed area was occupied by a free-standing ring of timber uprights. One would not expect these features to occur in a purely domestic structure. Similarly, the smaller timber building at Durrington, though totally roofed, was approached by an avenue of timber uprights through a protective façade of closely set posts which one would not expect to occur in a domestic context. In the case of the Sanctuary on Overton Hill, the initial three phases were progressively larger timber buildings and there is no independent evidence to suggest that they were not domestic structures. However, like the timber structures at Mount Pleasant, the final building was replaced in Phase 4 by stone settings of a presumably ritualistic nature, linked to the Avebury enclosure by the West Kennet Avenue. This suggests that the earlier timber structures were also of a special character.

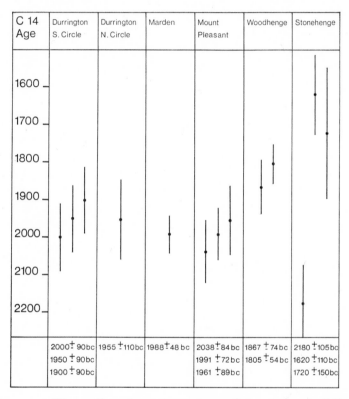

C 14 Age	Durrington S. Circle	Durrington N. Circle	Marden	Mount Pleasant	Woodhenge	Stonehenge
	2000± 90bc	1955 ±110bc	1988±48 bc	2038±84 bc	1867 ±74 bc	2180 ±105 bc
	1950 ±90bc			1991 ±72 bc	1805 ±54 bc	1620 ±110 bc
	1900 ±90bc			1961 ±89bc		1720 ±150 bc

FIG. 93. The radiocarbon chronology of the timber buildings

From this factual base one can develop a little of the abundant ethnographic evidence which is available. The limitations of this avenue of enquiry have received much emphasis in the past. It is a truism that human relations are complex and that totally different structures can often serve the same function. Conversely, similar buildings can often serve totally different functions, so that in one community an especially large house may be the private residence of an important individual, and in another a building used for public gatherings. In an earlier publication,[1] the author recalled documented accounts of early travellers such as Hodgson, Hitchcock and Bartram in Georgia and Florida in the eighteenth and nineteenth centuries.[2] These accounts describe the council houses of settlements belonging to the Creek Confederacy prior to the enforced removal of the Creeks to Oklahoma in 1836.

[1] Wainwright and Longworth, 1971, 232-3.　　　　[2] Bartram, 1791.

Certain of these structures have been excavated and the structural remains found to be in accord with the accounts of these early travellers. The graphic similarities of these buildings to the British structures under discussion are such that the descriptions are worth repeating.[1] Bartram wrote that 'the great council house or rotunda . . . is a vast conical building capable of accommodating many hundred people. There is but one large door, which serves at the same time to admit light from without and the smoke to escape when the fire is kindled.' In describing their construction Bartram says 'they first fix in the ground a circular range of posts or trunks of trees, about 6 ft. high, at equal distances, which are notched at top to receive into them, from one to another a range of rafter beams. Within this is another circular range of very large and strong pillars, about 12 ft. high, notched in like manner at top, to receive another range of rafter beams.' The excavation between 1937 and 1940 of the Irene Mound site on a western bluff of the Savannah River in Georgia (USA) revealed the plan of such a structure.[2] The remains were those of a circular building 40.00 m. in diameter with a conical roof supported on six concentric rings of timber uprights.

These buildings are very similar in size and plan to those of Wessex in the early second millennium B.C. and the contemporary descriptions of the Creek structures could be applied to those in Britain without putting too much strain on credibility. In Creek contexts the buildings were used for various councils and ceremonies and were important public meeting places. The totality of the evidence tends to the view that the Wessex structures also served a public or communal purpose and this in turn implies the emergence of a social hierarchy — a process which normally attends such developments.

SITE IV: THE STONE COVE

The timber structure was replaced around 1700 bc by a central setting of pits and sarsen monoliths which in plan resemble a 'cove'. The structure comprised four pits set on the corners of a 6.00 m. square and the sockets for four sarsen uprights along the west, north and east sides of this square, the base of a monolith being recorded in one socket. Outlying pits and monoliths were recorded to the west, north and east. This structure was built when the ditch was approximately one-third full of silt and a soil had formed over its contents. The positioning of the cove implies that the ground plan at least of the earlier timber building was still known, if only as rotting posts. The stone structure was destroyed when the monoliths were broken up *in situ*, probably to facilitate the cultivation of the hill-top in the first century B.C. The complete destruction of the monument some 2000 years ago so that no visible record remained is a salutary reminder of the incomplete nature of our megalithic settings as evidenced by surface remains.

The partially filled ditch surrounding the structure at this time was sealed by a weathered horizon, the molluscan fauna in which indicates a woodland environment. There is, however, evidence for a sudden and total clearance phase at the top of the soil and a change to an environment of short-turfed grassland. Charcoals from the relevant deposits are of hazel, yew, oak and poplar. Pottery from ditch deposits contemporary with the construction of the cove includes Grooved Ware and Beaker sherds whilst fragments of Food Vessels and Collared Vessels came from the later silts. Other artifacts include about 3000 worked flints comprising

---

[1] Bartram, 1791, 367–9, 450–7.   [2] Caldwell and McCann, 1941.

both transverse and barbed and tanged arrowheads, antler picks and spatulae and 300 lb. of fresh sarsen flakes with a few stone mauls. The latter are presumed to have been derived from the preparation of the sarsen monoliths for the cove and outliers. The flakes are quite fresh and many have a percussion bulb preserved on them. The source of the sarsen is of some interest and in this connection one should recall the single lump of sarsen protruding from a solution hole in Cutting I and Dr. Anderson's comments on the site geology. The latter suggest that the sarsens could have been derived from an original capping of Eocene sediments on the hill, traces of which occur in solution pits in the chalk. Alternatively, they could have been derived from deposits of Bagshot Beds nearby.

The animal bones from the ditch deposits of this phase comprise *bos*, sheep, pig, dog, red deer and birds and a single radiocarbon date (BM-688) assigns the event to around 1700 bc.

Four 'coves' are known in addition to that at Mount Pleasant.[1] They are Stanton Drew in Somerset,[2] Avebury in Wiltshire,[3] Arbor Low in Derbyshire[4] and Cairnpapple in West Lothian.[5] They normally consist of three tall monoliths forming a box-like structure at the centre of a stone circle or pit-ring. The cove at Stanton Drew, for example, comprises two widely spaced monoliths and a recumbent stone (now broken in two) between them, whilst that at Cairnpapple comprised three stone sockets at the centre of a pit setting which contained cremations. Two sherds of plain Neolithic bowls and two stone axes, one of Graig Lwyd and one of Great Langdale rock, were found on the old ground surface at Cairnpapple and may be associated with the cove. The Avebury cove is of interest in that it occurs within an embanked enclosure of Mount Pleasant type which also has four entrances. It is sited at the centre of the inner northern circle which itself lies within the outer stone circle. Professor Piggott[6] has suggested that the stone coves might be derived from the false portals of stone-chambered tombs and the arrangements of blocking stones at tombs such as West Kennet.

It may be that the Mount Pleasant 'cove' has its best affinities with these megalithic examples. However, its layout is rather more formal than that recorded at Cairnpapple or Avebury, having four pits at the corners of an exact square and the monoliths neatly arranged along the sides of this square. Unfortunately, because of the first century B.C. destruction we cannot say how high the monoliths stood above ground level. If small kerb-like stones were involved one could refer to Dr. Graham Ritchie's excavations at Balbirnie in Fife and Stenness in Orkney. At Balbirnie, the initial phase of a three-period structure comprised a rectangular setting of low oblong stones 3.25 × 3.75 m. surrounded by a ring of standing stones some 15.00 m. in diameter. It was succeeded by a series of cists, one of which contained a complete food vessel.[7] At Stenness, Dr. Ritchie recorded a Balbirnie-type setting at the centre of a ditched stone circle.[8] In any event, the Mount Pleasant 'cove' is a dated and associated addition to what is at present a very limited number of such structures. There is, however, a broader issue raised by the replacement of the Site IV timber building by the stone cove as this lithicization of earlier structures appears to be a widespread phenomenon in Britain at this time. At the Sanctuary on Overton Hill, the multi-phase timber building

[1] The author is indebted to Aubrey Burl for correspondence and guidance on this question.

[2] Dymond, 1877.

[3] Smith, 1965, 201–2, 250.

[4] Gray, 1903.

[5] Piggott, 1947–8.

[6] Piggott, 1947–8, 112; 1962, 65.

[7] Ritchie, 1974.

[8] *Discovery and Excavation in Scotland*, 1973–4.

was replaced in Phase 4 by two concentric stone circles which were connected with the West Kennet Avenue. A crouched burial associated with a Beaker decorated with 'barbed wire' ornament is thought to be contemporary and dates of around 1600 bc for Beakers of this type have been obtained on the continent.

Furthermore, Phase II of Stonehenge involved the erection of a double circle of 82 bluestones from Preselli in the Q and R holes as well as the construction of the Avenue to the River Avon at Amesbury. It succeeded the earlier Aubrey holes and possible timber structure on the site. Beaker pottery was recorded from the ditch at a level corresponding to the introduction of the bluestones and a radiocarbon determination of 1620 ± 110 bc (I-2384) was obtained from the tine of an antler pick found on the bottom of an incomplete R hole.

There are indications of a period in Wessex between 1700 and 1600 bc when certain of the timber buildings at Mount Pleasant, the Sanctuary, and possibly Stonehenge were replaced by stone settings. In this connection one can also tentatively include Avebury where excavations may yet reveal timber structures pre-dating the stone settings. The transmutation of timber structures into stone is not a rare phenomenon in the third and second millennia bc. It has been invoked, for example, to explain relationships between megalithic tombs and earthen long barrows and has been demonstrated at several stone circles, as at Croft Moraig in Perthshire. Its relevance in the present context is that the process should indicate some special function for the multi-ring buildings discussed above, which made it necessary for their sitings to be permanently indicated by stone settings.

THE EARTHWORK ENCLOSURE

It has been described how the externally embanked enclosure crowns the top of a low hill and occupies an oval area which covers 370 m. from west to east and 340 m. from north to south. The bank is now best preserved in its southern sector where it is 16.00–20.00 m. wide and 1.50 m. high, but under the Conquer Barrow it still stands to a height of 4.00 m. In the north sector, the bank is missing from where it stood on a steep slope leading to the floodplain. Elsewhere, it is separated from the internal ditch by a berm which is 15.00 m. wide in the west. Of the four entrances, two in the south-east and east are visible on the ground, the causeways between the ditch terminals being 20.00 m. wide (south-east), 30.00 m. wide (east), 40.00 m. wide (north) and 5.00 m. wide (west). In possessing four entrance causeways the enclosure is paralleled only by Avebury in north Wiltshire (fig. 95). The ditch terminals at the west entrance are extremely irregular and between 13.50 and 8.00 m. wide. Near the causeway, a more regular profile developed, 7.00 m. wide and 3.20 m. deep with a flat base. The ditch terminals at the north entrance were also irregular and were between 2.20 and 2.70 m. deep. Irregular settings of stake-holes dug through the stabilized primary silts were indicative of sporadic occupation and two infant burials were dug from the base of layer (8). Radiocarbon dates indicate that the earthwork was constructed around 2000 bc but that the ditch terminals at the west entrance were extended at about 1800 bc, resulting in its unfinished state and reduction of the entrance causeway to 5.00 m.

Dr. Evans has undertaken a major analysis of the molluscan fauna from the ditch silts. The land mollusca from a buried soil horizon above the primary fill at the west entrance

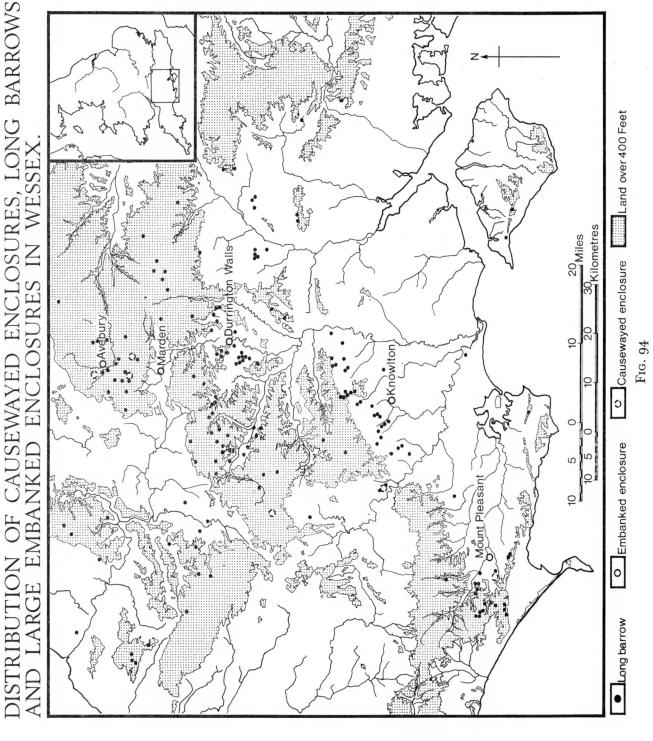

DISTRIBUTION OF CAUSEWAYED ENCLOSURES, LONG BARROWS
AND LARGE EMBANKED ENCLOSURES IN WESSEX.

Avebury

Marden

Durrington Walls

Knowlton

Mount Pleasant

N

20 Miles
30 Kilometres

● Long barrow
◉ Embanked enclosure
✇ Causewayed enclosure
▦ Land over 400 Feet

FIG. 94

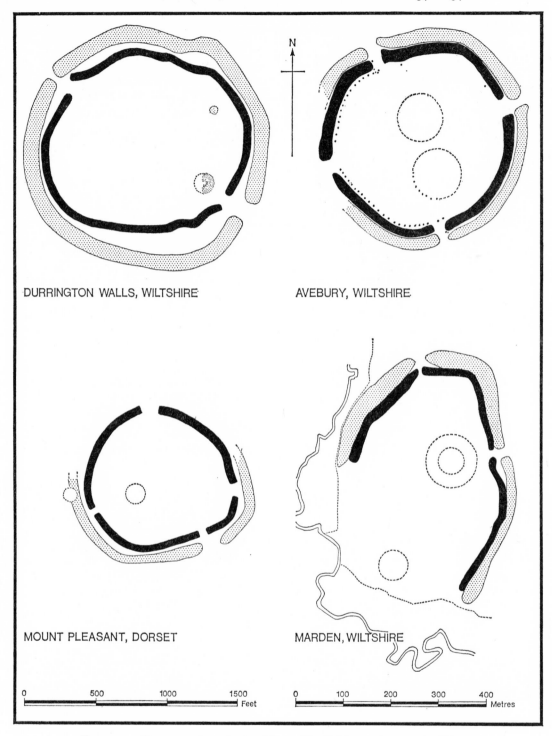

DURRINGTON WALLS, WILTSHIRE

AVEBURY, WILTSHIRE

MOUNT PLEASANT, DORSET

MARDEN, WILTSHIRE

FIG. 95.   Comparative plans of Late Neolithic enclosures in Wessex

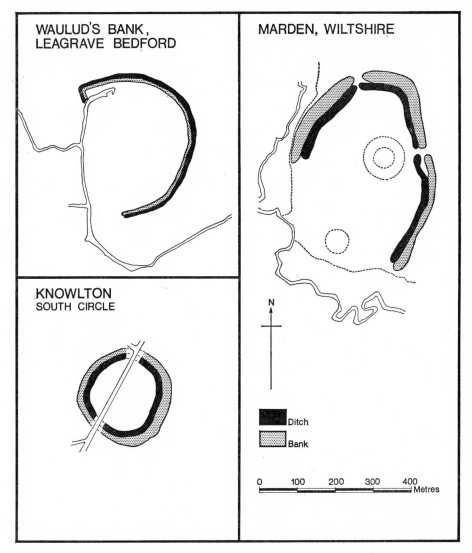

Fig. 96.   Comparative plans of Waulud's Bank, Marden and Knowlton

indicate a shaded environment with a high relative humidity, which Dr. Evans argues appertained over the whole site. Towards the top of this deposit the fauna indicates some clearance which can be related to deposits at the north entrance where it is dated by radio-carbon to 1509 ± 53 bc (BM-789) and 1669 ± 55 bc (BM-790), associated with Beaker sherds and Collared Vessels. A major clearance phase which follows this is represented by a deposit of chalk scree which sealed the buried soil and which is associated with a radiocarbon date of 1460 ± 131 bc (BM-664). This phase saw the total eclipse of woodland species and the domination of the molluscan fauna by a species which normally favours broken ground and a dry habitat and is interpreted as representing the onset of agriculture and ploughing.

9

It was followed by a thick aeolian deposit which contained an open country fauna divided by Dr Evans into three phases.

(i) A dry environment of short grasses.
(ii) A buried soil representing a possible change to taller grasses and locally higher relative humidity.
(iii) A possible relaxation of grazing pressure and the growth of tall grasses.

The sequence can then be followed through a succession of plough-wash deposits representing later prehistoric agricultural activities.

This framework was developed by Dr. Evans through the analyses of some 37 samples and represents a major achievement in mechanical preparation and interpretation.

A total of nine radiocarbon determinations was obtained from the ditch silts — three from the west and six from the north entrance. These indicate that the main enclosure ditch was dug around or rather before 2000 bc (2098 ± 54 bc, BM-793; 2108 ± 71 bc, BM-792), when it was associated with Grooved Ware, flint artifacts, antler picks, a broken chalk phallus, fragments of a human skull, hazel-nuts and the bones of pig, *bos* and red deer. During the period when a buried soil formed over these primary silts (1941 ± 66 bc, BM-791) Beaker sherds appear, along with transverse arrowheads, the blade of a flint axe and the bones of pig, sheep and *bos*. Sometime around 1800 bc the ditch terminals at the west entrance were extended (1784 ± 41 bc, BM-645; 1778 ± 59 bc, BM-646) and from the primary silts in these terminals were recorded a transverse arrowhead, antler picks, a ball and phallus of chalk and bones of pig, *bos*, sheep, horse, dog and red deer. The early silts in the north terminal of the west entrance also produced a bronze flanged axe which has been described and discussed by Dr. Britton. The later silts are distinguished at the north entrance by a sequence of deposits which are dated by radiocarbon (BM-788–90) and which produced Grooved Ware, Beaker sherds, fragments of Food Vessel and Collared Vessels. Later prehistoric and Romano-British pottery was recorded from the upper layers.

A full discussion of comparable enclosures and their origins was undertaken for the Durrington Walls monograph and there are few significant data to add to this. It will be recalled that, in the case of Durrington, Marden and Mount Pleasant (fig. 94), the remains of multi-ring timber buildings have been recorded within large externally embanked earthworks which form a restricted class in mid-southern England (fig. 95). Avebury has yet to produce evidence for such timber buildings. In Dorset, the largest Knowlton earthwork may yet yield similar structural evidence (fig. 96) and in Bedfordshire Mr. Dyer has recorded Grooved Ware from the bank and ditch of an enclosure of Marden type. The Durrington, Marden and Mount Pleasant enclosures are 30 acres, 35 acres and 12 acres respectively in area, are all associated with Grooved Ware, and were constructed around 2000 bc. In 1971 a case was made for deriving these large enclosures ultimately from the causewayed enclosures of the third millennium B.C.[1]

The evidence from the causewayed enclosures is unclear as to whether they were cult centres, rally points for the population of a fairly wide area, or whether there was any permanent occupation within their banks and ditches. Nevertheless, it is factually correct that each of the major territorial groups of long barrows in southern England has one or

[1] Wainwright and Longworth, 1971, 193–203.

more causewayed enclosure related to it (fig. 94) and it may be that they were focal points for territories. It is clear that these territories persisted into the second millennium bc, the focal points now being provided by the large earthwork enclosures of Durrington type, which relate closely to the earlier territories and to the causewayed enclosures which they superseded.

It has been apparent for some time that a new nomenclature is necessary to distinguish the large enclosures under discussion from the varied types of monument and earthwork included in the 'henge' monument category. Their size, association with timber buildings both large and small, and the quantities of pottery and other artifacts found with them allow for a more secular interpretation and distinguish them from those structures and earthworks with a more overtly ceremonial function. As with long barrows in the case of the causewayed enclosures, the earthworks of Durrington type occur in relation to areas of round barrow distributions and all the evidence points to their importance as focal centres for areas which may have had socio-political significance. The emergence of such centres in southern England implies the development of territorial units, each presumably with a centralized power base accompanied by stratification within the contemporary society and the emergence of a special class. Mount Pleasant and Maiden Castle nearby provide a particularly good opportunity to study the development of such a focus over some three millennia — an aspect which will be discussed later in this chapter.

THE PALISADE ENCLOSURE

The discovery of the palisade trench around the hill-top was unforeseen and has added a new dimension to our knowledge of the development of hill-top fortifications in the second millennium bc. It was recorded within and parallel to the main enclosure ditch, occupying the highest point of the spur between the 69.00 and 72.00 m. contours. The trench was of variable width and upwards of 3.00 m. deep and supported large timber uprights set close together. It enclosed an oval or egg-shaped area of some 11 acres (4.45 ha.), 270 m. from west to east and 245 m. from north to south. Two entrances were recorded in the north and east opposite entrance causeways across the ditch. These were extremely narrow and that in the east was flanked by massive oak posts nearly 1.50 m. in diameter. A reconstruction of that entrance has been attempted in fig. 98. The short length of the entrance posts is based on the shallow depth of the post-pits. Elsewhere in its circuit the trench had supported upright oak timbers between 30 and 50 cm. in diameter set close together. The height of the palisade is a matter for conjecture but if one assumes at a guess that one-third of the post-lengths was embedded in the ground, with a foundation trench 3.00 m. deep the stockade would have stood 6.00 m. high and on average 40 cm. thick. There were no traces for internal supports, although these may have been destroyed by plough erosion. Therefore, in order to obtain a view beyond the palisade from within, a parapet walk mortised on to the main structure and reached by a ladder has been assumed (fig. 97). The total length of the palisade trench is about 800 m. and for the uprights of the stockade approximately 1600 oak posts each some 9.00 m. long would have been employed. To obtain such a large quantity of good quality posts, no less than 900 acres of oak forest would have to be exploited. In addition to the raw materials required for this stockade, a large labour force would have been required

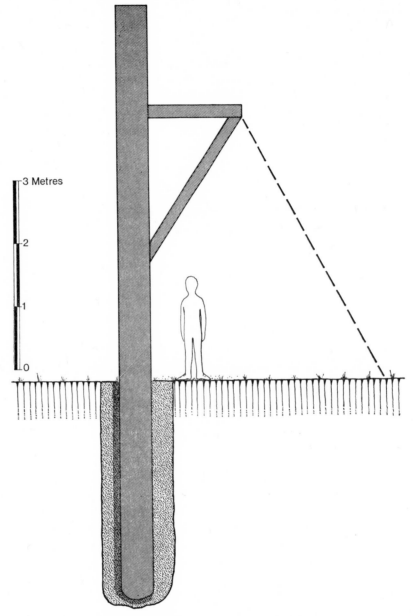

Fig. 97.   Reconstruction of the timber palisade

to select the trees, to fell them and to lop the branches, to drag them from the valley to the crest of the hill, and finally to erect them in the required positions, all this after a foundation trench 3.00 m. deep, 1.20 m. wide and 800 m. long had been excavated into the solid chalk with antler picks.

Two radiocarbon dates relate to the construction of the palisade trench and suggest that this occurred around 1700 bc (1687 ± 63 bc, BM-662; 1695 ± 43 bc, BM-665). Artifacts associated with it include transverse arrowheads, a polished stone axe and adzes of flint, one complete and one fragmentary greenstone axe, 38 antler picks and a large collection of carved chalk objects which include 30 balls, cylindrical objects, carved blocks and a bowl fragment. The animals represented include pig, *bos*, sheep, dog, red deer, roe deer, fox and birds. The ceramic range includes Early Neolithic, Peterborough, Grooved Ware, Beaker and Food Vessel sherds.

One may conclude that around 1700 bc, 11 acres (4.45 ha.) of the hill-top were enclosed by a timber wall 6.00 m. high which was set 3.00 m. into the ground, access through which was by two narrow entrances in the north and east. The structure was ultimately destroyed at an unknown date by fire and dismantling. Three processes were involved and these have been

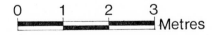

FIG. 98. Reconstruction of the east entrance through the palisade

MOUNT PLEASANT: PALISADE TRENCH

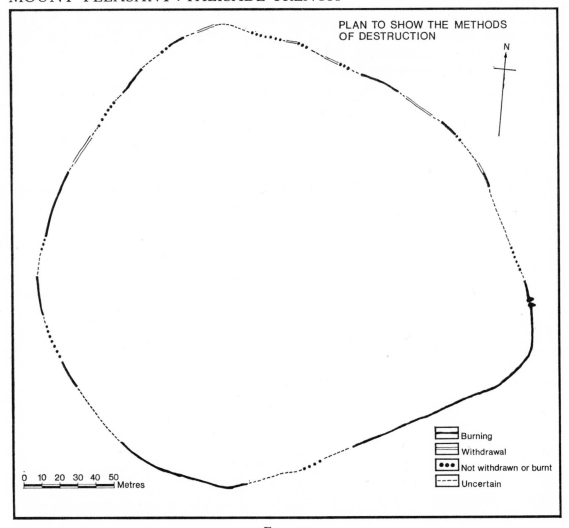

PLAN TO SHOW THE METHODS
OF DESTRUCTION

N

0 10 20 30 40 50 Metres

Burning
Withdrawal
Not withdrawn or burnt
Uncertain

FIG. 99

portrayed on plan (fig. 99). Some sections of the palisade were destroyed by fire — a conflagration so fierce that some posts had smouldered to their bases. Other posts had been deliberately dug out and presumably removed for reuse elsewhere — a seasoned oak timber must have been a valuable commodity.[1] Other timber uprights had been left to decay in position, although the question as to whether they had been severed at ground level can hardly be resolved. When collated from the various cuttings it is possible to reproduce in plan the pattern of destruction that prevailed. The date of this destruction is not known nor

---

[1] This process has implications for the radiocarbon dating of timber structures which may have involved the reuse of old timbers.

is the reason why it occurred. The act may have been voluntary or one of aggression and the probability is that it occurred within a century or two of its construction.

It is difficult to interpret this structure as anything other than defensive. The quantity of domestic refuse that accumulated in the partially silted ditch around the stone cove, around the base of the palisade as well as in the relevant deposits of the ditch of the earlier earthwork enclosure, suggests that other structures of a more purely domestic nature remain to be discovered on the hill-top and a timber wall 6.00 m. high is not capable of many other interpretations.

By the end of the third millennium bc, earthwork or stone-wall defences around settlements were not uncommon over large areas of eastern, central and northern Europe. In south Italy, ditch enclosed settlements may go back (as at Stentinello in Sicily) to the earliest agricultural colonists, whilst the rather later Apulian sites have multiple ditch systems that may enclose areas as large as 800 × 500 m.[1] In central Europe by the end of the fourth millennium bc some settlements of the Lengyel culture were enclosed by causewayed ditches as at Hlubokè, Mašvuvky in south Moravia where the area enclosed was 350 m. in diameter.[2] These fortifications have been fully discussed by Neustupný,[3] who suggests that by the end of the third millennium bc, the practice of constructing fortified settlements on hill-tops had become quite normal. For example, the settlement on Homolka Hill near Kladno in central Bohemia was defended by a palisade with two entrances, which protected a small hamlet, initially of six and later of ten houses. The multiple ditched enclosures of the Charente, such as Les Matignons, have continuous ditches. At Les Matignons, a radiocarbon date of 2620 ± 200 bc (Gay–32) was obtained from a burnt layer in the secondary ditch filling.[4]

In the Rhineland–North Hesse area of the Michelsberg culture enclosures were constructed from the early third millennium bc. One such enclosure at Mayen in the Eifel[5] has been selected for comparison with Mount Pleasant which it antedates by as much as a millennium (fig. 100). The outer defences at Mayen consist of a single interrupted ditch enclosing an oval area 360 × 220 m., one causeway in the west being defended by a massive timber gate. Within this ditch and concentric to it is a single palisade trench enclosing an area 300 × 160 m. The relationship of the palisade trench to the ditch is not clear, but they are not contemporary as the former runs across the causeways of the latter. The general situation is closely comparable with that at Mount Pleasant in terms of enclosure sizes and types of defence, although they cannot be related chronologically. An enclosure similar to that at Mayen has been excavated at Urmitz where two interrupted ditch systems enclose a semi-circular area 1250 × 620 m. on the south bank of the Rhine.[6] The frequently interrupted ditch systems were set close together, and immediately within them at a distance of some 5.00 m. was a single palisade trench which, although it ran straight across a number of ditch causeways (the latter, however, do not invariably coincide with each other), did possess at least five entrances related to causeways. The entrances across the latter were defended by massive timber structures, the entrances across the palisade trench being indicated by larger post-holes at the terminals as at Mount Pleasant. The defensive character of these camps is clear. Unlike the British causewayed enclosures they certainly enclosed settlements,

[1] Bradford, 1957, 95–103.
[2] Neustupný, 1951.
[3] Neustupný, 1950.

[4] Burnez et al., 1958.
[5] Lehner, 1910.
[6] Buttler, 1938.

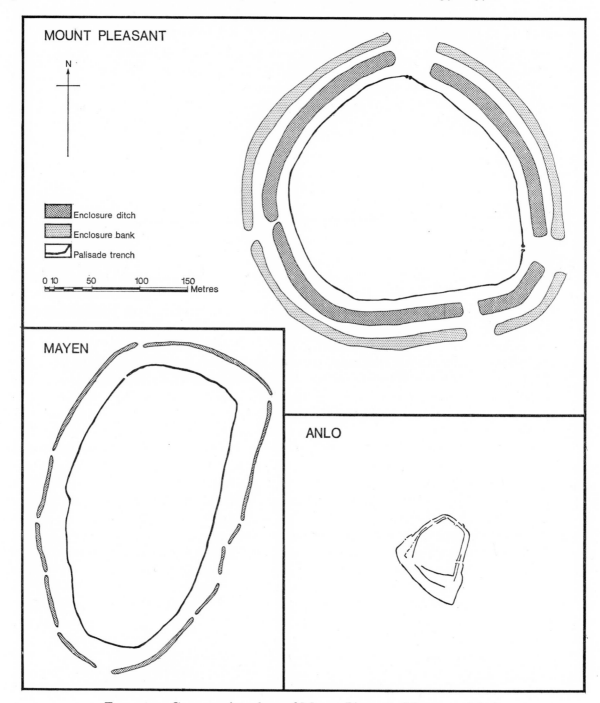

Fɪɢ. 100.   Comparative plans of Mount Pleasant, Mayen and Anlo

the houses being uniformly of simple rectangular type averaging about 3.00 × 5.00 m., with four corner posts for supporting a simple roof.

The palisade surrounding the hill-top at Mount Pleasant, which was constructed around 1700 bc, finds its best parallels in the similar but undated defences of the palisade enclosures at Mayen and Urmitz as well as in the sequence of palisaded enclosures at Anlo in the Netherlands. The excavations at Anlo in 1957 and 1958 revealed a sequence of three concentric palisade trenches, of which the inner appears to be the oldest, associated with Protruding-Foot Beakers. A radiocarbon date of 2470 ± 55 bc (Grn-1855) was obtained for a contemporary and adjacent grave.[1] The enclosures were small, the outer palisade enclosing a roughly trapezoid area 80.00 × 86.00 × 34.00 m. and were interpreted as cattle kraals on account of numerous narrow postern gates, which would give easy access to man when the main gates were blocked. No evidence for domestic occupation was found within the palisades, although the site had been heavily ploughed. As at Mount Pleasant, the main entrances through the palisades had widths of only 1.00–1.50 m.

Although the practice of enclosing large areas with strong fences in continuous palisade trenches for defensive or restrictive purposes was current in the third millennium bc in western Europe, contemporary parallels for the Mount Pleasant palisade enclosure in Britain are difficult to find. A timber palisade crowned the single bank associated with a third-millennium bc settlement at Broome Heath in Norfolk[2] and aerial photographs suggest the possibility of palisade trenches within the causewayed ditches of several camps in Britain and on the continent.[3] At Meldon Bridge, Lyne Hill in Peebles, Dr. Burgess has partially excavated what appears to be a 30-acre promontory enclosure defined by a monumental façade of posts 30 cm. in diameter behind which are scoops and pits which contained charcoal, burnt nuts, flints and pottery of Beaker type.[4] Radiocarbon dates from the bases of two post-pits are 2330 ± 80 bc (Har-796) and 2150 ± 140 bc (Har-797). However, at the time of writing the excavation is in progress and further comment must be deferred. At Hunstanton in Norfolk, Dr. Kinnes has excavated a subrectangular enclosure 45.00 × 38.00 m. protected by a fence of large posts. Contemporary finds include Grooved Ware.[5]

From these broadly contemporary but inexact parallels it is necessary to look to the end of the second millennium bc for palisade enclosures. A well-known example occurs at Rams Hill in Berkshire where three radiocarbon dates of 1070 ± 90 bc (Har-228), 1010 ± 80 bc (Har-229) and 1060 ± 70 bc (Har-232) are relevant.[6] From this time, earthwork enclosures were being built in southern England which are normally less than one acre in area. In plan they occur as roughly trapezoid, oval or rather shapeless enclosures, bounded by a bank and ditch and occasionally with a palisade.[7]

From these modest enclosures, defence works on a large scale became increasingly more common during the first half of the first millennium bc, either defending permanent settlements or providing refuge places in times of danger. The earliest defence at several sites was a

[1] Waterbolk, 1960.
[2] Wainwright, 1972.
[3] e.g. Mardant and Daniel, 1972.
[4] The author is indebted to Dr. Burgess for information in advance of his own publication.

[5] *DOE Archaeological Excavations 1971*, HMSO, 1972, 9–10.
[6] The author is indebted to Mr. Richard Bradley for information on this site in advance of his own publication.
[7] e.g. Burstow and Holleyman, 1957; Rahtz and Ap-Simon, 1962; Curwen, 1934.

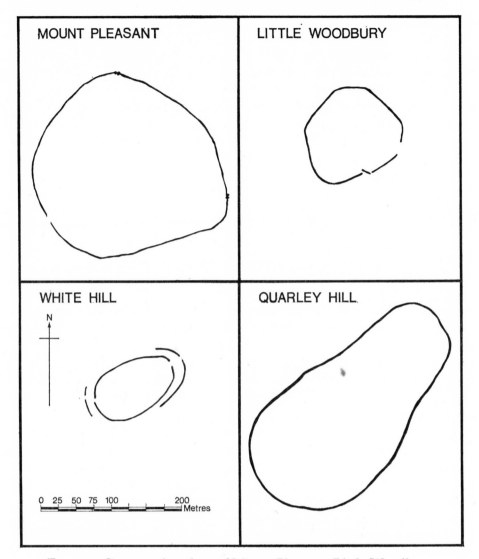

Fig. 101. Comparative plans of Mount Pleasant, Little Woodbury,
White Hill and Quarley Hill

palisade of similar though less massive form to that constructed in 1700 bc around the
Mount Pleasant hill-top (fig. 101). This was the case at Madmarston Camp, Oxon.,[1] Wilbury
Hill, Herts.,[2] and Quarley Hill, Hants,[3] to quote only three examples. In most cases the palisades are of unknown extent and undated. In northern Britain such palisaded enclosures
were first recognized from aerial photographs in 1946 and have since been grouped as a
specific class of defensive structure. Their distribution is centred on the Cheviot Hills of
south Scotland and north England and the largest known settlement at White Hill, Peebles-

[1] Fowler, 1960.   [3] Hawkes, 1939.
[2] Applebaum, 1949.

shire, encloses only 1.75 acres(0.75 ha.).[1] Radiocarbon dates indicate that such palisaded sites go back to the seventh century bc.

Dr. Ritchie would see the prototypes for the north British palisaded sites in the enclosed settlements of south Britain at the end of the second millennium bc and as representing the development of widespread permanent settlement. In Britain, the ancestry can be extended back to the beginning of the second millennium bc, although Mount Pleasant still stands alone in terms of size and scale of defence. However, a number of palisade-defended settlements must remain undiscovered, either beneath the later ramparts of hill-forts or because the decay of the timber wall left no trace on the ground surface. One may conclude, therefore, that any distribution map of palisaded sites reflects accidents of preservation or discovery and that this form of defence was certainly more widespread than the present state of our knowledge would have us suppose.

GENERAL CONSIDERATIONS

The excavations of 1970 and 1971 have provided evidence for settlement on Mount Pleasant Hill from the late third to the late first millennia bc. The evidence at certain periods is structural and at others is comprised of pottery sherds in plough-wash deposits. The sequence must be viewed in conjunction with that recorded by Sir Mortimer Wheeler from Maiden Castle, which is 2¼ miles south-west and visible across a broad valley.[2] Reference has already been made to foci of settlement patterns and the Maiden Castle–Mount Pleasant area provides a good example of the long-term character of these centres.

A review of the Mount Pleasant settlement begins with the pre-enclosure occupation, which is represented by ceramic evidence only. Around 2000 bc or perhaps a century before, the large earthwork enclosure was built around the hill-top at about the same time as the Site IV timber building was erected. The ceramic style in use at this period was Grooved Ware. The evidence from Mount Pleasant therefore confirms that obtained from Durrington Walls and Marden where similar building operations occurred at this time. The environment reflected by the molluscan fauna in the contemporary deposits is one of woodland when the hill-top was neither cultivated nor grazed. The animal bones show the pig as the most common animal (17 individuals) followed by cattle (8), sheep (4), dog (2), red deer (2), goat (1), horse (1), aurochs (1), wild boar (1), fox (1) and birds.

Around 1800 bc the west entrance to the main enclosure was made more narrow by the extension of the ditch terminals. It may have been at this time that the Conquer Barrow was built on the enclosure bank near the west entrance. Indeed, the chalk rubble from the ditch terminal extensions may have contributed to its fabric. The episode, although of limited duration, is of significance in demonstrating a continued interest in the site.

The next major structural phase occurred around 1700 bc when the hill-top was surrounded by the great timber palisade and the Site IV building replaced by the stone cove and its outliers. The contemporary molluscan fauna indicates that the woodland environment which had prevailed previously was removed by a sudden and total clearance and replaced by an environment of short-turfed grassland. To obtain the correct visual image it

[1] RCAHMS, Roxburghshire, 1956, 19–20; RCAHMS   [2] Wheeler, 1943.
Peeblesshire, 1967, 74–82; Ritchie, 1970.

should be remembered that the earlier earthwork although now three centuries old had not been subjected to ploughing and would therefore have been a prominent feature outside the palisade. It was for this reason presumably that the north and east entrances through the palisade were opposite causeways across the earlier ditch. The animal bones from the relevant deposits indicate that pig was still the most common animal (35 individuals), followed by cattle (18), sheep (12), dog (3), aurochs (2), red deer (2), wild boar (1), roe deer (1), fox (1) and birds. It has already been emphasized that the quantities of pottery, flint artifacts and other refuse from deposits around the cove and around the base of the palisade trench imply settlement on the hill-top at this time.

The palisade was eventually destroyed at some unknown date by fire and dismantling and the hill-top subsequently settled until the end of the second millennium bc and possibly beyond. The molluscan fauna indicates an intensification of tillage or massive overgrazing by sheep or cattle but the animal bones are poorly preserved and only indicate the presence of pig (5), cattle (3), sheep (3), goat (1) and dog (1). Continued ploughing in the first millennium bc is indicated by successive plough-wash deposits which contain pottery of Iron Age and Romano-British date. Various ditches and gullies cross the hill at this time and presumably have an agrarian purpose but the presence of a single round house within the confines of the old Site IV ditch suggests the possibility of some settlement in the first century B.C. in addition to tillage. It was at this time that the stone cove and its outliers were broken up, presumably because they were an impediment to ploughing.

When viewed in relation to the Maiden Castle sequence it is clear that in the third millennium bc the centre of emphasis is at that site with its causewayed enclosure and bank barrow. There was some settlement on Mount Pleasant Hill in the third millennium but from 2000 bc the focus of settlement moves to that site with the construction of the embanked enclosure and the large timber building which would have been visible for miles around. After two centuries, alterations were made to the enclosure earthworks but in 1700 bc the hill-top was enclosed by a massive timber palisade, whilst at the same time a stone cove was constructed on the site of the old timber building. The palisade stood for an unknown period but was eventually destroyed by fire and dismantling. There is evidence for settlement on the hill-top until 1000 bc or slightly beyond, but shortly after that the first earthwork defences were built on Maiden Castle to which the focus of settlement appears to have moved with only intermittent occupation on Mount Pleasant hill. In A.D. 43 the final Iron Age hill fort was sacked by Vespasian's legions and the inhabitants moved into the valley, finally creating the Roman town of Dorchester.

It is possible to deduce from this sequence the evolution of an embanked or otherwise fortified settlement focus which persisted on one hill or the other for 3000 years and which eventually descended into the valley. The impression is one of increasing centralization of power in the third and second millennia, culminating in the immensely strong timber fortifications in 1700 bc and the movement back to Maiden Castle early in the first millennium. This persistence of territorial and focal patterns can be paralleled elsewhere in Wessex but nowhere is it as clear or as prolonged as in Dorset. The rhythm or pattern of change at the centre having now been established in broad outline, it remains to develop an investigative policy which will elucidate the development of the landscape over a broader regional canvas and eventually to extend this in time to cover the whole range of human activity and its impact on the natural environment.

APPENDIX I. THE HUMAN REMAINS

by CHRIS STRINGER and PETER SANDIFORD[1]

THE NORTH ENTRANCE

A. *Human Cranial Remains from XXVII Layer (10)*

THESE remains consisted of 18 fragments of a human skull, which were reconstructed to form parts of the right and left parietal, occipital and frontal bones of a skull vault. As lambda was the only useful osteometric point preserved no other standard measurements were possible except for an estimate of the maximum cranial breadth (140 mm.). The general form and thickness of the reconstructed skull fragments suggest that this was an adult, but not elderly, male individual.

B. *Human Skeletal Remains from XXVIII*

The remains consisted of separate bones, some distorted *post mortem*, representing most of the vault and face of an infant skull and mandible, together with major parts of the post-cranial skeleton.

Skull

The bones of the skull were extremely thin and mostly unfused. The frontal bones were still separated by the metopic suture and the anterior fontanelle was open. The petromastoid and squamous parts of the temporal bone had fused, which usually occurs during the first year after birth, but no mastoid process had developed. The right maxilla contained the unerupted crowns of the incisors, canine and first molar of the deciduous dentition. The right central incisor was apparently about to erupt but none of the teeth had completely formed roots.

The various fragments of the skull were assembled to form a fairly complete but distorted cranium. The following measurements (in millimetres) were taken:

glab-occ length	nas-occ length	max. br.	max.fr. br.	bizyg. br.	biaur. br.	nas-pros. ht.	nas. ht.	orb. ht.	orb. br.
126	125	100	85	68	66	35	25	24	26

bijug. br.	nas. br.	palate br.	bifr. cd.	min. chk.ht.	front. cd.	pariet. cd.	front. arc	pariet. arc	min. fr. br.
68	15	38	65	8.2	75	90	90	102	70

[1] The human remains from the North Entrance have been described by Stringer and the Saxon remains by Sandiford.

Mandible

The mandible was broken into two fragments but it was possible to measure the total length of the mandible (54 mm.) and the chin height (13.5 mm.). The body contained the unerupted crowns of the first milk molars of each side.

Other Teeth

Also found were the fully formed crowns of four molars, four incisors and two canines from the upper and lower deciduous dentition.

Post-cranial Remains

These consisted of the following recognizable bones: 61 fragments of unfused vertebrae, 20 ribs, 27 phalanges, and the clavicles, scapulae, ilia, ischia and long bones of the right and left sides. All the long bones were incompletely ossified and without fused epiphyses. The following measurements of maximum size were taken using sliding calipers and are compared with measurements on infants of known age from cemeteries pre-dating the industrial revolution, taken by Miss R. Powers of the British Museum (Natural History). The measurements are in millimetres and have been averaged where applicable:

	femur	tibia	fibula	humerus	ulna	radius	clavicle	ilium br.	ilium ht.	mandible length
XXVIII Infant	88	77	73	74·5	67·5	60	46	41·5	37·5	54
Three new-born infants	71 74 79	59 64 62	58 61 60	62 67 64	59 60 56	52 53 51	46 44 41	34 37 30	34 35 30	50 52 50
Infant aged 1 year 2 months	118	100	97	94	76	71	55	53	49	62

Age

In every case the post-cranial and mandibular measurements of the Mount Pleasant infant fall between those of the new-born and the infant aged 1 year 2 months. This suggests an age of several months at the time of death. Further evidence for this is provided by the size and development of the skull and by the unerupted but well-developed deciduous dentition, which is comparable to that of a modern infant aged about six months.

Sex

It is difficult to sex the remains of infants although in this case the wide angle of the sciatic notch (80°) suggests that it may be a female individual.

Abnormalities

There were no obvious signs of disease or injury to provide evidence for the cause of death.

C. *Human Skeletal Remains from XXX*

These remains were extremely fragmentary.

Skull

There were approximately 130 small fragments of the skull, all of which were thin. Only the two petrous parts of the temporal bones were well preserved, and no reconstruction was attempted in this case due to the poor condition of the bone fragments.

Mandible

A portion of mandible about 20 mm. long was preserved, which contained the formed crowns of two unerupted milk molar teeth.

Teeth

In addition to the above mandibular fragment, the crowns of three molars, two incisors and two canines of the deciduous dentition were recovered.

Post-cranial Remains

A portion of femur shaft 70 mm. long was preserved together with part of the shaft of a tibia 68 mm. long with the fibula attached by a deposit of earth. Ten small fragments of the long bones were recognizable as well as three fragments of phalanges. Approximately 115 small fragments of ribs were preserved and a portion of the shaft of a clavicle 38 mm. long.

Age

The presence of the unerupted deciduous dentition with unformed roots indicates that the skeleton is that of an infant probably between the ages of 0 and 1 year old. This is confirmed by the nature of the post-cranial skeleton and the extremely thin fragments of the skull and ribs. The size of the fragments of femur, tibia and fibula suggests that the individual was not new-born.

D. *Additional Bone Fragment from XXX*

Amongst the remains from XXX was a piece of bone 25 mm. long which was thicker than the infant bones and displayed an angular cross-section. This would appear to be from an older individual and was probably part of the shaft of a long bone such as a fibula.

E. *Human Skull Fragment from XXIX Layer (6)*

This appears to be a small piece of an adult parietal bone. The thickness of the fragment and the presence of a groove for the middle meningeal vessels suggest that it was from the postero-inferior portion of the parietal near asterion.

Acknowledgements

I would like to thank Miss R. Powers of the British Museum (Natural History) for her permission to use the comparative measurements quoted above, and Dr. J. H. Musgrave, Department of Anatomy, University of Bristol, for his advice on the preparation of this report.

THE SAXON GRAVES

A. *Human Skeletal Remains from Grave 1*

The remains consist of extremely well broken up fragments of bone as follows:

39 skull fragments
mandible
13 lower limb fragments
27 upper limb fragments
4 pelvic fragments
2 scapular fragments
13 rib fragments
25 vertebral fragments
5 phalanges
6 metacarpal/tarsal fragments ·

The bones were so well broken up as to render meaningful osteometry impossible.

Skull

Sufficiently large cranial fragments were recovered to give the general impression of a fairly large, sharply contoured skull. There was complete obliteration of the sutures except in two small fragments, both from the temporal region, where the suture line was discernible on the outer table. Only the right-hand mastoid process was present and this was large and prominent. The skull showed very clear signs of the increase in thickness sometimes associated with the onset of senility. One piece of parietal, for example, was 8 mm. thick. There was no replacement of the denser cortical bone by spongy bone as occurs in Paget's disease.

Mandible

The mandible, virtually complete except for loss of teeth, exhibits well-defined muscle markings, especially in the region of the medial pterygoid muscle and the mylohyoid line is strongly defined. There is a prominent chin and pronounced eversion of the angle of the mandible. Characteristic of senility all the molar teeth were lost well before death with consequent alveolar absorption. At death only the third molar sockets remained and even these show some signs of absorption. In place of the others there is a relatively smooth alveolar ridge.

The teeth are all extremely worn with complete exposure of dentine, often hollowed out very near to the pulp cavity.

Lower Limbs

The two femora are extremely stout with well-defined muscle attachment points, especially the linea aspera. These bones give an over-all impression of a well-built, fairly tall individual. The articular surfaces are all well preserved and show no signs of osteo-arthritic deterioration.

Upper Limbs

Observations on these bones are similar to those for the lower limbs.

Pelvis

Very little has been recovered but fortunately a fragment from the right ilium containing a deep and narrow sciatic notch (angle 40°) was preserved.

Sex

The observations on the pelvis would suggest that the individual was male. This is confirmed by the general robust 'angular' nature of the remains, the size of the mastoid process and eversion of the angle of the mandible.

Age

In this case it is impossible to estimate the age of the individual in years, but evidence from the mandible — excessive, irregular tooth wear, loss of molars and alveolar absorption — all indicate the onset of senility, rare in early populations where average life expectancy was about 33 years.

Abnormalities

Some of the teeth show signs of decay: there is interproximal neck and occlusal caries present in both the upper first premolars and the lower left first premolar.

The first left metacarpal shows slight osteo-arthritic lipping of the proximal articular surface.

B. *Human Skeletal Remains from Grave 185*

These remains are even more fragmented than those from Grave 1 except for the skull and mandible. Burial in chalk has resulted in very considerable pitting of the surface of the bones, so severe in some lower limb fragments as to resemble periosteitis.

The following fragments were recovered:

23 skull fragments
mandible
1 scapular fragment
2 clavicle fragments
20 vertebral fragments
1 sacral fragment
4 pelvic fragments
28 rib fragments
4 phalangeal fragments
3 metacarpal/metatarsal fragments
22 upper limb fragments
9 lower limb fragments

Skull

Only the frontal region is well preserved but it is evident that this was a well-rounded skull. The forehead is swept back with little supraorbital ridge development and the mastoid processes are very small. The orbits are elongated laterally and are wide compared to their height. The nasal bone is quite narrow and consequently the orbits appear close together. There is a substantial degree of alveolar prognathism not reflected in the lower dentition.

Mandible

This has been preserved virtually intact. It has a complete set of healthy adult teeth, symmetrical, well distributed and with even occlusal wear. There is a prominent but well-rounded chin, and a shallow mandibular notch with little evidence of the muscle attachment points. The mylohyoid line is not clearly defined and there is only slight surface roughening at the point of attachment of the medial pterygoid muscle. Overall, although the mandible gives an impression of strength there are none of the features normally associated with the well-developed male mandible.

Sacrum

Only a small part of the promontory and right lateral mass upper surface has been preserved but nevertheless sufficient is present to give an impression of the large size of the bone in this individual.

Pelvis

The fragments include one large piece containing the acetabulum and sciatic notch. The notch is fairly deep but also wide with an angle of 60°. Like the sacrum the pelvis is physically quite large.

Lower Limbs

The best preserved bone, the left femur, has a poorly developed linea aspera. It is slightly bowed outwardly and is platymeric, with a femur shaft index of 79. The femur seems quite a small bone in comparison with the pelvis. None of the fragments shows any sign of an epiphyseal line.

Sex

The small size of the mastoid processes and the mandibular features suggest that the individual was female. This is confirmed by the nature of the sciatic notch of the pelvis and the development of the femur.

Age

The lack of epiphyseal lines on the long bones and the state of skull sutural closure indicate that the individual was adult. The degree of occlusal molar wear points to an age of between 17 and 25 years.

Abnormalities

Upper dentition. Right upper third molar. During the development of this tooth there was root obstruction such that instead of the three roots being virtually fused together as is normally the case, one of them, the lingual, exhibits a deflection of almost 90°.

The lingual surfaces of the crowns of the upper incisors are shovel shaped to varying degrees.

APPENDIX II. THE CHARCOALS

by G. C. Morgan
Archaeology Department, Leicester University

THERE are a few possibly structural timbers, i.e. + 100 mm. in diameter,[1] all of which are oak and occur in the palisade trench. The rest seem to represent brush or scrub, probably as firewood.

Old Land Surface
I (9). *Quercus* sp., oak + 50 mm.

Site IV
Segment V (9). *Coryllus avellana*, hazel 20 mm.
Segment IV (5). Hazel 50 mm.
Segment X alpha (6). *Taxus baccata*, yew + 40 mm.
Segment XI alpha (8). Yew 6 mm., *Acer campestre*, field maple 15 mm.
Segment XIII (5). Oak + 50 mm., hazel 20 mm., *Populus* sp., poplar 40 mm., yew fragments.

Enclosure Ditch
I primary. Yew + 40 mm., poplar 40 mm.
II secondary. Yew + 40 mm.
XXVII (10). Hazel 30 mm., oak + 50 mm.
XXVII (9). *Fagus sylvatica*, beech 6 mm., hazel 40 mm.
XXVIII (7). Field maple 4 mm., poplar 20 mm., hazel 20 mm.

Palisade Trench

XI. Hazel 40 mm., field maple 50 mm.
XII. Oak + 100 mm.
XIII. Oak + 50 mm.
XVI, Post No. 1. Oak + 100 mm.
XVI, Post No. 2. Oak + 100 mm.
XVII. Oak + 100 mm.
XVIII. Yew 30 mm.
XX. Oak + 50 mm., beech 20 mm., poplar 20 mm.
XXII. Oak + 100 mm.

XXIV. Oak + 50 mm.
XXV. Oak fragments of mature wood.
XXXVI, S side E entrance. Oak + 100 mm.
XXXVI, N side E entrance. Oak + 100 mm.
XXXVII. Oak fragments of mature wood.
XXXVIII. Oak fragments of mature wood.
XXXIX. Oak + 100 mm.
XL. Oak fragments.
XLI. Oak fragments of mature wood.
XLIV. Oak + 50 mm.

[1] All dimensions are estimated diameters in millimetres, + indicates 'greater than'.

APPENDIX III. THE DETAILS OF THE POST-HOLES: SITE IV

Post-hole No.	Diam. (cm.)	Depth (cm.)	Post-hole No.	Diam. (cm.)	Depth (cm.)
1	48	32	49	43	35
2	57	28	50	48	35
3	66	33	51	48	30
4	48	26	52	55	25
5	50	30	53	34	11
6	58	19	54	40	20
7	47	25	55	40	30
8	48	24	56	43	28
9	49	25	57	44	30
10	48	25	58	48	30
11	47	23	59	80	32
12	57	30	59A	36	29
14	40	27	60	66	36
15	50	39	62	?	30
16	43	34	63	45	20
17	40	38	64	35	30
18	44	29	65	48	28
19	40	26	66	48	37
20	34	24	67	43	28
21	42	20	68	37	24
22	47	37	69	34	26
23	48	35	70	37	20
24	53	32	71	53	30
25	43	28	72	48	35
26	43	32	72A	48	29
27	25	15	73	36	39
28	45	22	74	40	28
29	39	6	75	33	20
30	38	33	76	44	38
31	35	24	77	50	38
32	30	29	78	33	35
33	38	11	79	37	35
34	38	14	80	43	33
35	28	13	81	47	40
36	27	20	82	47	30
37	33	22	83	58	34
38	47	35	84	70	40
40	32	24	85	40	35
41	33	18	86	43	32
42	48	20	87	53	33
43	42	25	88	48	35
44	51	34	89	50	35
45	?	32	90	43	38
46	47	35	91	46	39
47	50	28	92	49	28
48	45	35	93	37	27

Post-hole No.	Diam. (cm.)	Depth (cm.)	Post-Hole No.	Diam. (cm.)	Depth (cm.)
94	42	30	134	50	33
95	46	24	135	47	33
96	44	24	136	55	30
97	47	24	137	66	38
98	39	19	138	57	48
99	38	30	139	50	40
100	38	30	140	50	30
101	40	24	141	54	33
102	49	27	142	51	40
103	50	35	143	41	20
104	53	30	144	40	40
105	?	32	145	45	37
106	49	32	146	40	35
107	49	36	147	44	36
108	51	27	148	52	37
109	37	26	149	42	27
110	44	28	150	47	36
111	48	37	151	44	31
112	50	33	152	46	30
113	55	31	153	45	35
114	51	40	154	50	30
115	57	34	155	50	37
116	?	10	156	44	37
117	?	37	157	48	30
118	63	40	158	50	30
119	46	50	159	55	39
120	22	5	160	55	24
121	42	32	161	72	40
122	43	45	162	58	44
123	53	38	163	65	48
124	45	32	164	72	38
125	37	24	165	55	39
126	53	29	165A	25	18
126A	25	15	166	55	40
127	40	38	167	49	37
128	54	36	168	41	31
129	30	23	169	57	40
130	40	25	170	51	37
131	35	11	171	50	45
132	43	40	172	48	38
133	46	30			

APPENDIX IV. THE GEOPHYSICAL SURVEYS

by A. J. CLARK

Geophysics Section, Ancient Monuments Laboratory

THE first survey was made in October 1969. Before this, the only known remains of the monument were the visible lengths of a substantial but badly eroded perimeter bank on the south and east sides. Additionally, aerial photographs faintly revealed a relatively small circular ditch within the monument. Initial tests on the south side, where the perimeter bank is best preserved, showed that the ditch within it was detectable by resistivity but not reliably by proton magnetometer; also there appeared to be a small inner ditch. The magnetometer did, however, respond to the internal circular ditch. The 0.75-m. square array resistivity system[1] was therefore used to trace the main ditch, measurements being made at 1-m. intervals along 26 cross-sectional traverses based on the Land Survey grid. The ditch gave substantial readings, typically rising from 180 ohm-metres on undisturbed chalk bedrock to 286 ohm-metres over the filling. Its width was up to about 15 m. including weathering. Three entrances were discovered; all of these, as well as the extant one on the south side, being confirmed by core augering. This was particularly useful at the east entrance where some confusion was caused by high resistivity natural pockets of remarkably clean sand, often white, apparently of Eocene origin. A proton magnetometer area survey (1.5 m. reading interval; plotted in dot density form by computer) across the interior of the monument, arranged to overlap the east and west entrances as well as the inner circle, was successful in defining the latter (maximum anomaly about 8 gamma), and also showed faint indications of a linear feature set back from the main ditch and apparently parallel with it and continuous past the entrances: it was also picked up in a 30-m. square area surveyed within the southern entrance, and clearly equated with the small inner ditch-like feature detected in the first tests. At the entrances, the uphill terminals of the main ditch were also revealed, presumably because an accumulation of humic material had washed into them. Several irregular features detected proved on sampling by excavation to be natural solution hollows.

Immediately before the second excavation season in 1971, a survey was undertaken to plan the northern sector of the linear feature, which excavation had shown to be a palisade trench. Improved magnetic equipment was used: a fluxgate gradiometer with automatic plotting of continuous traces 1 m. apart. Anomalies ranged from 1 to 5 gamma/m., presumably depending on the proportions of topsoil and burnt material to non-magnetic chalk rubble filling. Subsequently, the remainder of the circuit of this feature was defined where not previously excavated, using the gradiometer alone. The entrances of the palisade could hardly be detected because of their extreme narrowness, made worse by weathering of the great terminal post-holes.

[1] Clark, 1968.

BIBLIOGRAPHY

AKERMAN, J. Y. 1853. 'An account of excavations in an Anglo-Saxon burial ground at Harnham Hill, near Salisbury'. *Archaeologia* **35,** 259–78.

ALLAN, W. 1967. *The African Husbandman.*

ANNABLE, F. K. and SIMPSON, D. D. A. 1964. *Guide Catalogue of the Neolithic and Bronze Age Collections in Devizes Museum.*

APPLEBAUM, E. S. 1949. 'Excavations at Wilbury Hill, an Iron Age hill-fort near Letchworth, Hertfordshire, 1933'. *Archaeol. J.* **106,** 12–45.

ATKINSON, R. J. C., PIGGOTT, C. M. and SANDARS, N. K. 1951. *Excavations at Dorchester, Oxon. First Report.*

ATKINSON, R. J. C., 1957. 'Worms and weathering'. *Antiquity* **31,** 219–33.

ATKINSON, R. J. C. 1967. 'Further radiocarbon dates for Stonehenge'. *Antiquity* **41,** 63–4.

BAKKER, J. A., VOGEL, J. C. and WISLANSKI, T. 1969. 'TRB and other C14 dates from Poland. Part A'. *Helinium* **9,** 3–27.

BARTRAM, W. 1791. *Travels through North and South Carolina, Georgia, East and West Florida, the Cherokee country, the extensive territories of the Muscogulges or Creek Confederacy and the country of the Choctaws.*

BOESSNECK, J. 1969. *In* Brothwell, D. R. and Higgs, E. S. (eds.), *Science in Archaeology*, 331.

BRADFORD, J. 1957. *Ancient Landscapes. Studies in Field Archaeology.*

BRADLEY, R., 1970. 'The excavation of a Beaker settlement at Belle Tout, East Sussex'. *Proc. Prehist. Soc.* **36,** 312–79.

BRITTON, D. 1963. 'Traditions of metal-working in the later Neolithic and early Bronze Age of Britain. Part 1'. *Proc. Prehist. Soc.* **29,** 258–325.

BROTHWELL, D. 1972. 'Forensic aspects of the so-called Neolithic Skeleton Q1 from Maiden Castle, Dorset'. *World Archaeol.* **3,** 233–41.

BURLEIGH, R. 1971a. 'Radiocarbon dates for the enclosure ditch and phase 2 of the Southern Circle'. *in* Wainwright and Longworth, 1971, *Durrington Walls, Excavations 1966–1968*, Appendix X, 411.

BURLEIGH, R., 1971b. 'Radiocarbon dates for Marden', *in* Wainwright, 1971, Appendix I, 226–7.

BURLEIGH, R. 1972. 'Liquid scintillation counting of low levels of C14 for radiocarbon dating'. *Liquid Scintillation Counting* **2,** 139–46.

BURLEIGH, R., LONGWORTH, I. H. and WAINWRIGHT, G. J. 1972. 'Relative and absolute dating of four late Neolithic enclosures: an exercise in the interpretation of radiocarbon determinations'. *Proc. Prehist. Soc.* **38,** 389–407.

BURLEIGH, R., EVANS, J. G. and SIMPSON, D. D. A. 1973. 'Radiocarbon dates for Northton, Outer Hebrides'. *Antiquity* **47,** 61–4.

BURNEZ, C. *et al.* 1958. 'Sondages dans le campe néolithique des "Matignons", Juillac-le-Coq, Charente'. *Bull. et Mem. Soc. Arch. et Hist. Charente*, 2–28.

BURSTOW, G. P. and HOLLEYMEN, G. A. 1957. 'Late Bronze Age settlement at Itford Hill, Sussex'. *Proc. Prehist. Soc.* **23,** 167–212.

BUTLER, J. 1955. 'Irske bronzeøkser fra ulstrup'. *Kuml* 1955, 36–45.

BUTLER, J. J. 1963. *Bronze Age Connections across the North Sea.* Palaeohistoria **9** (Groningen).

BUTTLER, W. 1938. *Der Donauländische und der Westische Kulturkreis der Jüngeren Steinzeit.*

CALDWELL, J. and McCANN, C. 1941. *Irene Mound Site, Chatham County, Georgia.* (University of Georgia).

CAMERON, R. A. D. 1969. 'The distribution and variation of three species of land-snail near Rickmansworth, Hertfordshire'. *J. Linn. Soc. (Zool.)*, **48,** 83–111.

CHAPPELL, H. G., AINSWORTH, J. F., CAMERON, R. A. D. and REDFERN, M. 1971. 'The effect of trampling on a chalk grassland ecosystem'. *J. Appl. Ecol.* **8**, 869–82.

CHILDE, V. G. 1939. 'A Stone Age settlement at the Braes of Rinyo, Rousay, Orkney (First Report)'. *Proc. Soc. Antiq. Scot.* **73**, 6–31.

CLARK, A. J. 1968. 'A square array for resistivity surveying'. *Prospezioni Archeologiche* **3**, 111–14.

CLARK, J. G. D. 1934. 'Derivative forms of the *petit tranchet* in Britain'. *Archaeol. J.* **91**, 32–58.

CLARKE, D. L. 1970. *Beaker Pottery of Great Britain and Ireland.*

CLASON, A. T. 1967. *Animal and Man in Holland's Past* (Rijksuniversiteit Groningen).

COLES, J. M. 1968–9. 'Scottish early Bronze Age metalwork'. *Proc. Soc. Antiq. Scot.* **101**, 1–110.

CORNWALL, I. W. 1953 'Soil science and archaeology with illustrations from some British Bronze Age monuments'. *Proc. Prehist. Soc.* **19**, 129–47.

CRANSTONE, B. A. L. 1969. *In* Ucko, P. J. and Dimbleby, G. W. (eds.), *The Domestication and Exploitation of Plants and Animals*, pp. 247ff.

CUNNINGTON, M. E. 1929. *Woodhenge.*

CUNNINGTON, M. E. 1931. 'The "Sanctuary" at Overton Hill, near Avebury'. *Wilts. Archaeol. Nat. Hist. Soc.* **45**, 300–35.

CURWEN, E. C. 1934. 'A late Bronze Age farm and a Neolithic pit dwelling'. *Sussex Archaeol. Collect.* **75**, 137–70.

DEPT. OF THE ENVIRONMENT 1972. *Archaeological Excavations 1971* (HMSO).

DREW, C. D. and PIGGOTT, S. 1936. 'The excavation of Long Barrow 163a at Thickthorn Down, Dorset'. *Proc. Prehist. Soc.* **2**, 77–96.

DYMOND, C. W. 1877. 'The megalithic antiquities at Stanton Drew'. *J. Brit. Archaeol. Assoc.* **33**, 297–307.

EVANS, J. 1881. *The Ancient Bronze Implements, Weapons and Ornaments of Great Britain and Ireland.*

EVANS, J. G. 1968. 'Periglacial deposits on the chalk of Wiltshire'. *Wilts. Archaeol. Nat. Hist. Soc.* **63**, 12–26.

EVANS, J. G. and BURLEIGH, R., 1969. 'Radiocarbon dates for the South Street Long Barrow, Wiltshire'. *Antiquity* **43**, 144–5.

EVANS, J. G. 1972. *Land Snails in Archaeology.*

EVISON, V. I. 1968. 'The Anglo-Saxon finds from Hardown Hill'. *Proc. Dorset Nat. Hist. Soc.* **90**, 232–40.

FOCK, J. 1966. *Metrische Untersuchungen an Metapodien einiger europäischer Rinderrassen.*

FOWLER, P. J. 1960. 'Excavations at Madmarston Camp, Swalcliffe, 1957–8'. *Oxoniensia* **25**, 3–48.

OERINGER, J. 1967. *Tierknochenfunde von der Heuneburg einem frühkeltischen Herrensitz bei Hundersingen an der Donau*, **5.**

GIMBUTAS, M. 1965. *Bronze Age Cultures in Eastern and Central Europe.*

GODDARD, E. H. 1913. 'A list of Prehistoric, Roman and Pagan Saxon antiquities in the County of Wiltshire arranged under parishes'. *Wilts. Archaeol. Nat. Hist. Mag.* **38**, 153–378.

GODWIN, H. and TANSLEY, A. G. 1941. 'Prehistoric charcoals as evidence of former vegetation, soil and climate'. *J. Ecol.* **29**, 117–26.

GODWIN, H. 1966. 'Introductory address'. *In* Sawyer, J. S. (ed.), *World Climate from 8000 to 0 BC* (London: Royal Meteorological Society).

GRAY, H. ST. G. 1903. 'On the excavations at Arbor Low, 1901–2'. *Archaeologia* **58**, 461–98.

GRIGSON, C. 1965. *In* Smith, I., *Windmill Hill and Avebury.*

GRIGSON, C. 1969. *In* Ucko, P. J. and Dimbleby, G. W. (eds.), *The Domestication of Plants and Animals.*

HARBISON, P. 1969. *The Axes of the Early Bronze Age in Ireland.* Prähistorische Bronzefunde IX.1.

HARCOURT, R. A. 1971a. *In* Wainwright, G. J. and Longworth, I. H. *Durrington Walls: Excavations 1966–1968.* Rep. Res. Comm. Soc. Antiq. London **29**, 338–50.

HARCOURT, R. A. 1971b. *In* Wainwright, G. J. 'The excavation of a Late Neolithic enclosure at Marden, Wiltshire'. *Antiq. J.* **51**, 177–239.

HAWKES, C. F. C. 1939. 'The excavations at Quarley Hill, 1938'. *Proc. Hants Field. Club Archaeol. Soc.* **14,** 136–94.

HAWKES, C. F. C. and HULL, M. R. 1947. *Camulodunum.*

HAWKES, S. C. and MEANEY, A. 1970. *Two Anglo-Saxon Cemeteries at Winnall, Winchester, Hampshire.* Soc. Med. Arch. Monograph Series **4.**

HOWARD, M. M. 1963. *In* Mourant A. C. and Zeuner, F. E. (eds.), *Man and Cattle: A Symposium on Domestication*, pp. 91–100.

HYSLOP, M. 1963., 'Two Anglo-Saxon cemeteries at Chamberlins Barn, Leighton Buzzard, Beds.' *Arch. J.* **120,** 161–200.

JACKSON, J. W. 1923. *In* Cunnington, M. E. *The Early Iron Age Inhabited Site at All Cannings Cross Farm, Wiltshire.*

JACKSON, J. W. 1925. *In* Clay, R. C. C. 'An inhabited site of La Tène I date on Swallowcliffe Down'. *Wilts. Archaeol. Nat. Hist. Soc.* **43,** 90.

JACKSON, J. W. 1934. *In* Curwen, E. C. 'Excavations in Whitehawk Neolithic Camp. Brighton, 1932–33'. *Antiq. J.* **14,** 127–9.

JACKSON, J. W. 1948. 'The animal remains from Little Woodbury'. *Proc. Prehist. Soc.* **14,** 19.

JEWELL, P. A. 1963. *In* Mourant, A. C. and Zeuner, F. E. (eds.), *Man and Cattle, A Symposium on Domestication*, 80–91.

JEWELL, P. A. and DIMBLEBY, G. W. 1966. 'The experimental earthwork on Overton Down, Wiltshire, England: the first four years'. *Proc. Prehist. Soc.* **32,** 313–42.

KOHL, G. and QUITTA, H. 1966. 'Berlin radiocarbon measurements'. *Radiocarbon* **8,** 27–45.

LANTING, J. N. and VAN DER WAALS, J. D. 1972. 'British Beakers as seen from the continent'. *Helinium* **12,** pt. 1, 20–46.

LANTING, J. N., MOOK, W. G. and VAN DER WAALS, J. D. 1973. 'C14 chronology and the Beaker problem'. *Helinium* **13,** pt. 1, 38–58.

LEEDS, E. T. and RILEY, M. 1942. 'Two early Anglo-Saxon cemeteries at Cassington, Oxon.' *Oxoniensia* **7,** 62–70.

LEEDS, E. T. and SHORTT, H. de S. 1953. *An Anglo-Saxon Cemetery at Petersfinger, near Salisbury, Wilts.*

LEHNER, H. 1910. 'Die Festungbau der jüngeren Steinzeit'. *Prähist. Zeitschrift* **2,** 1–23.

LETHBRIDGE, T. C. 1931. 'Recent excavations in Anglo-Saxon cemeteries in Cambridgeshire and Suffolk'. *Cambs. Ant. Soc. Quarto Pubs.* **3.**

LIDDLE, D. M. 1931. 'Report on the excavations at Hembury Fort, Devon. Second season, 1931'. *Proc. Devon Archaeol. Expl. Soc.* **1,** 90–120.

LIDDLE, D. M. 1932. 'Report on the excavations at Hembury Fort. Third season'. *Proc. Devon Archaeol. Expl. Soc.* **1,** 162–90.

LOMAS, J. 1962. 'A Bronze Age site at Parwich, Derbyshire'. *Derbyshire Archaeol. J.* **82,** 91–9.

LONGWORTH, I. H. 1960. *In* Pacitto, A. L. 'The excavation of two Bronze Age burial mounds at Ferry Fryston in the West Riding of Yorkshire'. *Yorkshire Archaeol. J.* **42,** 295–305.

MANBY, T. G. 1969. 'Bronze Age pottery from Pule Hill, Marsden, W. R. Yorkshire, and footed vessels of the Early Bronze Age from England'. *Yorkshire Archaeol. J.* **42,** 273–82.

MANBY, T. G. 1974. *Grooved Ware Sites in the North of England.* British Archaeol. Reps. **9.**

MASON, J. L. 1963. *In* Mourant, A. C. and Zeuner, F. E. (eds.), *Man and Cattle: A Symposium on Domestication*, 100.

MEANEY, A. 1964. *A Gazetteer of Early Anglo-Saxon Burials.*

MEGAW, B. R. S. and HARDY, E. M. 1938. 'British decorated axes and their diffusion during the earlier part of the Bronze Age'. *Proc. Prehist. Soc.* **4,** 272–307.

MORDANT, C. and DANIEL, R. 1972. 'L'enceinte néolithique de Noyen-sur-Seine'. *Bull. Soc. Préhist. Francaise* **69,** 554–69.

MORGAN, F. de M. 1959. 'The excavation of a long barrow at Nutbane, Hants'. *Proc. Prehist. Soc.* **25,** 15–51.

MORTIMER, J. R. 1905. *Forty Years' Researches in Burial Mounds in Eastern Yorkshire.*

MUSSON, C. 1971. 'A study of possible building forms at Durrington Walls, Woodhenge and the Sanctuary', *in* Wainwright, G. J. and Longworth, I. H. *Durrington Walls: Excavations 1966–68,* 368–77.

NEUSTUPNÝ, J. 1950. 'Fortifications appartenant à la civilisation danubienne Néolithique'. *Archiv orientálni* **18,** 131–58.

NEUSTUPNÝ, J. 1951. 'Neolitiká opevnená osoda v hlubokcých mašůvkàch u znojma'. *Casopis Narodniko Musea* 117–19, 11–50.

OLSSON, I. U. (ed.) 1970. 'Radiocarbon variations and absolute chronology'. *Proc. 12th Nobel Symposium,* Uppsala, 1969.

PERKINS, D. and DALY, P. 1968. 'A hunter's village in Neolithic Turkey'. *Scient. Amer.* **219,** 96.

PERRIN, R. M. S. 1956. 'Nature of "Chalk Heath" soils'. *Nature* **178,** 31.

PIGGOTT, S. and PIGGOTT, C. M. 1939. 'Stone and earth circles in Dorset'. *Antiquity* **13,** 138–58.

PIGGOTT, S. 1940. 'Timber circles: a re-examination'. *Archaeol. J.* **96,** 193–222.

PIGGOTT, S. 1947-8. 'The excavation at Cairnpapple Hill, West Lothian'. *Proc. Soc. Antiq. Scot.* **82,** 68–123.

PIGGOTT, S. 1962. *The West Kennet Long Barrow. Excavations 1953–6.*

PIGGOTT, S. 1972., 'A note on climate deterioration in the first millennium B.C. in Britain'. *Scot. Archaeol. Forum* **4,** 109–13.

PITT-RIVERS, A. H. 1887. *Excavations in Cranbourne Chase,* Vol. II, 209ff.

POWELL, T. G. E. and DANIEL, G. E. 1956. *Barclodiad-y-Gawres.*

RADLEY, J. and SIMMS, C. 1967. 'Wind erosion in east Yorkshire'. *Nature* **216,** 20–2.

RAHTZ, P. and APSIMON, A. M. 1962., 'Excavations at Shearplace Hill, Sydling St. Nicholas, Dorset, England'. *Proc. Prehist. Soc.* **28,** 289–328.

RALPH, E. K., MICHAEL, H. N. and HAN, M. C. 1973. 'Radiocarbon dates and reality'. *MASCA Newsletter* **9** (1), 1–20 (University Museum, Philadelphia, August 1973).

RCAHMS 1956. *The Royal Commission on the Ancient Monuments of Scotland. An Inventory of the Ancient and Historical Monuments of Roxburghshire,* Vol. 1.

RCAHMS 1967. *The Royal Commission on the Ancient and Historical Monuments of Scotland. Peebleshire,* Vol. 1.

RCHM 1970. *An Inventory of Historical Monuments in the County of Dorset,* Vol. 2. *South-East, pts 1 and 3.*

RITCHIE, A. 1970. 'Palisaded sites in north Britain: their context and affinities'. *Scot. Archaeol. Forum.* 47–67.

RITCHIE, J. N. G. 1974. 'Excavation of the Stone Circle and cairn at Balbirnie, Fife'. *Archaeol. J.* **131,** 1–32.

SEAGRIEF, K. 1959. 'Pollen diagrams from southern England; Wareham, Dorset and Nursling, Hampshire'. *New Phytol.* **58,** 316–25.

SILVER, I. A. 1969. *In* Brothwell, D. R. and Higgs, E. S. (eds.), *Science in Archaeology,* 283.

SIDAWAY, R. 1963. 'A buried peat deposit at Litton Cheney'. *Proc. Dorset Nat. Hist. Archaeol. Soc.* **85,** 78–86.

SMITH, A. G. 1970. 'The influence of Mesolithic and Neolithic man on British vegetation: a discussion', *in* Walker, D. and West, R. G. (eds.), *Studies in the Vegetational History of the British Isles,* 81–96.

SMITH, I. F. 1965. *Windmill Hill and Avebury.*

SMITH, I. F. and SIMPSON, D. D. A. 1966. 'Excavation of a round barrow on Overton Hill, north Wiltshire, England'. *Proc. Prehist. Soc.* **32,** 122–55.

SMITH, I. F. 1967. 'Windmill Hill and its implications'. *Palaeohistoria* **12,** 469–81.

THOMPSON, M. W. and ASHBEE, P. 1958. 'Excavation of a barrow near the Hardy Monument, Black Down, Portesham, Dorset'. *Proc. Prehist. Soc.* **23,** 124–36.

TURNER, J. 1970. 'Post-Neolithic disturbance of British vegetation', *in* Walker, D. and West, R. G. (eds.), *Studies in the Vegetational History of the British Isles*, pp. 97–116.

VON BRUNN, W. A. 1959. *Die Hartefunde der frühen Bronzezeit aus Sachsen-Anhalt, Sachsen und Thüringen.*

WAINWRIGHT, G. J. and LONGWORTH, I. H. 1971. *Durrington Walls: Excavations 1966–1968.* Rep. Res. Comm., Soc. Antiq. London, **29.**

WAINWRIGHT, G. J. 1971. 'The excavation of a Late Neolithic enclosure at Marden, Wiltshire'. *Antiq. J.* **51,** 177–239.

WAINWRIGHT, G. J. 1972. 'The excavation of a Neolithic settlement on Broome Heath, Ditchingham, Norfolk'. *Proc. Prehist. Soc.* **38,** 1–97.

WARNE, C. 1872. *Ancient Dorset.*

WATERBOLK, H. T. 1960. 'Preliminary report on the excavations at Anlo in 1957 and 1958'. *Palaeohistoria* **8,** 59–90.

WATERBOLK, H. T. and BUTLER, J. J. 1965. 'Comments on the use of metallurgical analysis in prehistoric studies'. *Helinium* **5,** 227–51.

WATSON, D. M. S. 1931. *In* Childe, V. G., *Skara Brae, a Pictish Village in Orkney.*

WHEAT, J. B. 1967. 'A Palaeo-Indian Bison kill'. *Scient. Amer.* **216,** 1.44.

WHEELER, R. E. M. 1943. *Maiden Castle, Dorset.* Rep. Res. Comm., Soc. Antiq. London. **12.**

ZEUNER, F. E. 1963. *A History of Domesticated Animals.*

INDEX

PLATE I

a. Mount Pleasant, Dorset. Air view obtained 30.6.51. (J. K. St Joseph, Cambridge University Collection)

b. Mount Pleasant hill from the east
(*photo: S. J. Wainwright*)

10

PLATE II

a. Section of bank in Cutting I

b. Detail of *a*
(*photos: P. Sandiford*)

PLATE III

a. Air view from the south of Site IV and the palisade trench

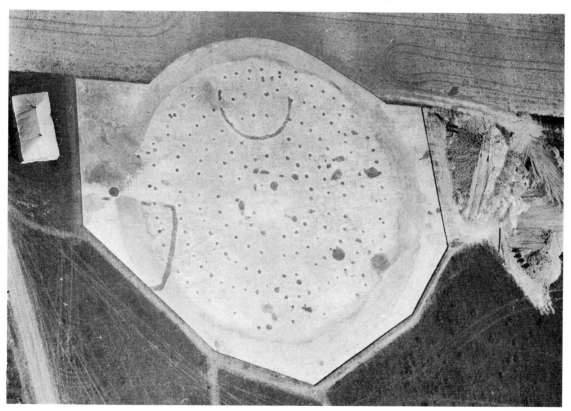

b. View of Site IV after clearance with the machine
(*photos: P. Sandiford*)

PLATE IV

a. Site IV at a late stage in its excavation

b. Site IV viewed at a low level from the south following the machine stripping
(*photos: P. Sandiford*)

PLATE V

a. Site IV: the inner post-ring and stone-holes

b. Site IV: the Iron Age house viewed from the south
(*photos: P. Sandiford*)

PLATE VI

a. Site IV: the angular enclosure viewed from the south

b. Site IV: west ditch terminal Segment XIII
(*photos: P. Sandiford*)

PLATE VII

Site IV ditch: sarsen fragments in burnt deposit, Segment X

(*photo: P. Sandiford*)

PLATE VIII

b. Site IV ditch: base of Segment VII

(photos: P. Sandiford)

a. Site IV ditch: south-east sector

PLATE IX

a. Site IV ditch: Segment X, south face

b. Site IV ditch: Segment X, north face
(*photos: P. Sandiford*)

PLATE X

a. Site IV ditch: Segment IX, section IXA

b. Site IV ditch: Segment IX, section IXB
(*photos: P. Sandiford*)

PLATE XI

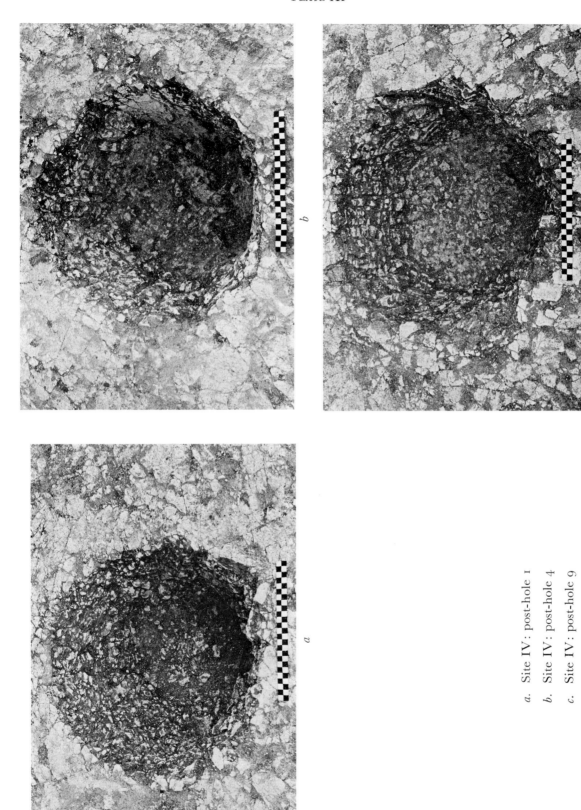

a. Site IV: post-hole 1
b. Site IV: post-hole 4
c. Site IV: post-hole 9
(*photos: P. Sandiford*)

PLATE XII

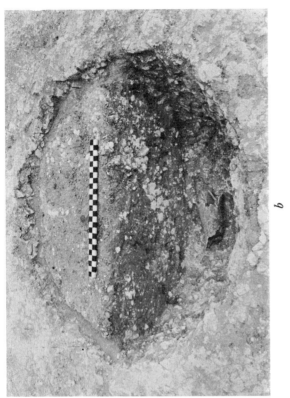

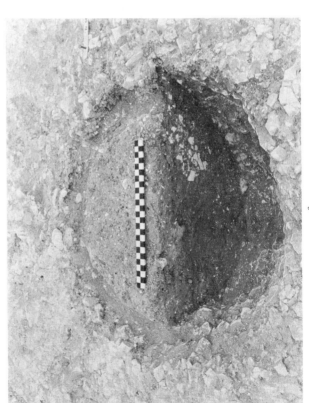

a. Site IV: post-hole 46

b. Site IV: post-hole 52

c. Site IV: post-hole 58

(photos: P. Sandiford)

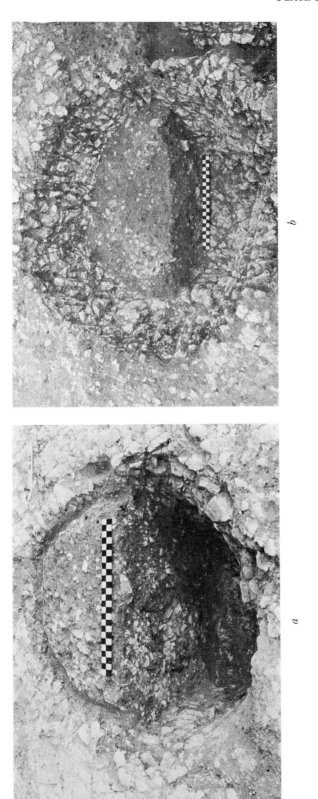

a. Site IV: post-hole 55

b. Site IV: post-hole 60

c. Site IV: post-hole 136 cut by 188

(*photos: P. Sandiford*)

PLATE XIV

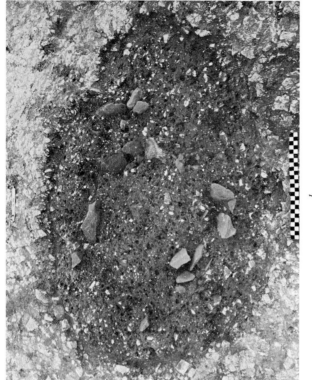

a. Site IV: post-hole 137 cut by 138

b. Site IV: pit 173

(*photos: P. Sandiford*)

PLATE XV

a. Site IV: pit 174 before excavation

b. Site IV: pit 174 with sarsen chips in place
(*photos: P. Sandiford*)

PLATE XVI

a. Site IV: pit 175

b. Site IV: pit 175 in section
(*photos: P. Sandiford*)

PLATE XVII

a. Site IV: pit 176

b. Site IV: stone-hole 177

(*photos: P. Sandiford*)

Plate XVIII

a. Site IV: stone-hole 178 before removal of the sarsen chips

b. Site IV: stone-hole 178 with sarsen chips removed and the stump of the monolith in position

(photos: P. Sandiford)

PLATE XIX

a. Main enclosure: the west entrance viewed from the north

b. Main enclosure: the west entrance viewed from the south
(*photos: S. J. Wainwright*)

PLATE XX

a. Main enclosure: west entrance. Section of the southern ditch terminal

b. Main enclosure, west entrance. Antler picks on the floor of the southern ditch terminal
(*photos: S. J. Wainwright*)

PLATE XXI

a. Main enclosure: west entrance. The oval pit north of the entrance causeway

b. Main enclosure: west entrance. Section of the oval pit north of the entrance causeway
(*photos: S. J. Wainwright*)

PLATE XXII

a. Main enclosure north entrance. Air view of the excavations from the north

b. Main enclosure: north entrance. Trenches XXVIII, XXIX and XXX
(*photos: S. J. Wainwright*)

PLATE XXIII

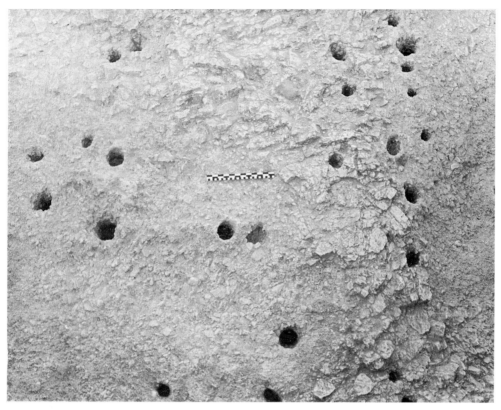

a. Main enclosure: north entrance. Stake-holes in trench **XXIX**

b. Main enclosure: north entrance. The north face of Cutting **XXIX**
(*photos: S. J. Wainwright*)

PLATE XXIV

a. Main enclosure: north entrance. Crouched infant burial in Cutting XXVIII

b. Main enclosure: north entrance. Crouched infant burial in Cutting XXX
(*photos: S. J. Wainwright*)

PLATE XXV

a. The excavation of the palisade trench in 1971
(*photo: S. J. Wainwright*)

b. Palisade trench: trench III before excavation
(*photo: P. Sandiford*)

PLATE XXVI

a. Palisade trench: trench III. Antler picks used as packing material
(*photo*: *P. Sandiford*)

b. Palisade trench: trench XII—north face
(*photo*: *S. J. Wainwright*)

PLATE XXVII

a. Palisade trench: trench XVI—north face

b. Palisade trench: trench XVI. Detail of the burnt post in the north face

(photos: S. J. Wainwright)

PLATE XXVIII

a

b

c

a. Palisade trench: trench **XVII** —
south face

b. Palisade trench: trench **XVIII** —
west face

c. Palisade trench: trench **XXI** —
east face
(*photos: S. J. Wainwright*)

PLATE XXIX

a

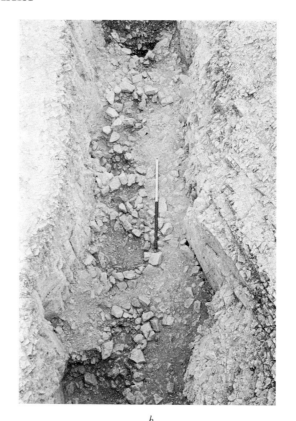

b

a. Palisade trench: trench III —
post-footings
(*photo: P. Sandiford*)

b. Palisade trench: trench XII —
post-packing
(*photo: S. J. Wainwright*)

c. Palisade trench: trench XVII —
post-footings
(*photo: S. J. Wainwright*)

c

Plate XXX

a.   Palisade trench: the north entrance from the south

b.   Palisade trench: the east entrance from the east
(photos: S. J. Wainwright)

PLATE XXXI

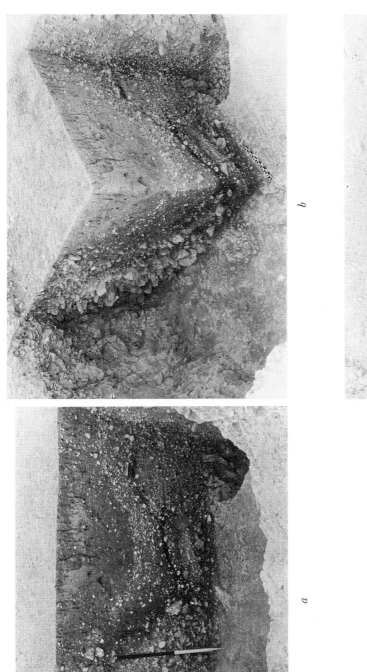

a. Palisade trench: east entrance. Section of the north terminal viewed from the east

b. Palisade trench: east entrance. Sections of the north terminal viewed from the east

c. Palisade trench: east entrance. Section of the south terminal viewed from the south

(photos: S. J. Wainwright)

PLATE XXXII

a. Palisade trench: east entrance viewed from the east

b. Palisade trench: east entrance viewed from the west

c. Palisade trench: east entrance completely excavated viewed
from the north

(*photos: S. J. Wainwright*)

PLATE XXXIIII

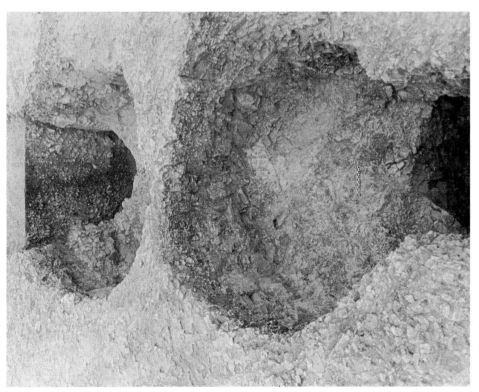

a. Palisade trench: the east entrance completely excavated viewed from the south

b. The Conquer Barrow ditch in trench XLVI viewed from the north

(*photos: S. J. Wainwright*)

PLATE XXXIV

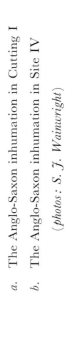

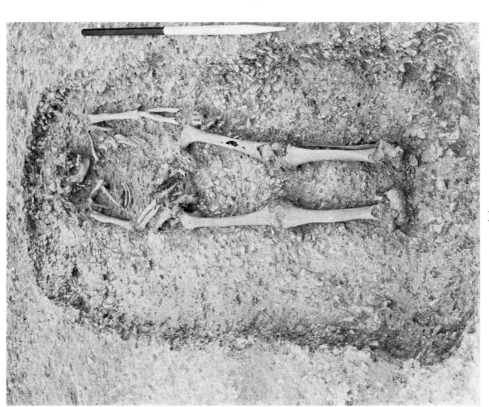

a. The Anglo-Saxon inhumation in Cutting I

b. The Anglo-Saxon inhumation in Site IV

(*photos: S. J. Wainwright*)

PLATE XXXV

b.   Woodhenge 1970. Antler picks on the floor of the ditch

a.   Woodhenge 1970. The cutting viewed from the west

(photos : P. Sandiford)

PLATE XXXVI

a. Woodhenge 1970. The north face of the cutting

b. Woodhenge 1970. Section of the bank and buried soil
(*photos: P. Sandiford*)

PLATE XXXVII

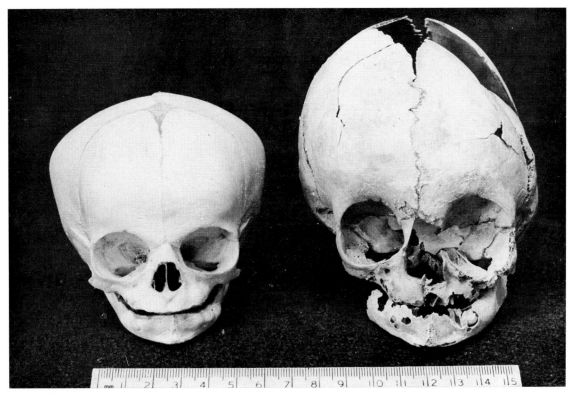

a. The reconstructed infant skull from **XXVIII** (right) compared with a modern new-born infant skull

b. The reconstructed skull from **XXVIII** (right) compared with a modern male skull (superior view)
(*photos: C. Stringer*)